AN IMMIGRANT CLASS

ORAL HISTORIES FROM CHICAGO'S NEWEST IMMIGRANTS

BY JEFF LIBMAN

photography by **STEVE KAGAN** *foreword by* **PHIL PONCE**

PUBLISHED IN THE UNITED STATES OF AMERICA
BY FLYING KITE, INC.

CHICAGO, ILLINOIS

© 2004 JEFF LIBMAN

DESIGNED BY DEPKE DESIGN, CHICAGO

PRINTED IN CHINA BY C&C OFFSET PRINTING CO., LTD.

LIBRARY OF CONGRESS CONTROL NUMBER 2003094954

ISBN 0-9741429-0-5

FOR MORE INFORMATION, PLEASE VISIT WWW.ANIMMIGRANTCLASS.COM

TO THOSE WHO DARE TO CHANGE

CONTENTS

MAP OF THE WORLD

AMADOU TANDINA *Burkina Faso*

ELI RAMÍREZ *Guatemala*

OVIDIU IUHAS *Romania*

PILAR LANDA *and* **CARLOS DOMÍNGUEZ** *Cuba*

MUHAMMAD DUR *Afghanistan*

FELIPE CHING *Peru*

ELENA RASKIN *Belarus*

TENZIN JAMYANG *India (Tibet)*

RUBÉN MONTOYA *Colombia*

EMIR HUSKIC *Bosnia and Herzegovina*

DENG DENG AGOT *Sudan*

SERGIO SOARES *Brazil*

LUISA CARDENAS *Chile*

ZAYA KHANANU *Iraq*

OSWALDO MEDINA *Mexico*

HARALLAMB TERBA *Albania*

CARLOS GANDOLFO *Argentina*

JAVAD KIANI *Iran*

MARDOCHÉE JEAN CHARLES *Haiti*

MEXICO

CUBA

HAITI

GUATEMALA

COLOMBIA

PERU

BRAZIL

CHILE

ARGENTINA

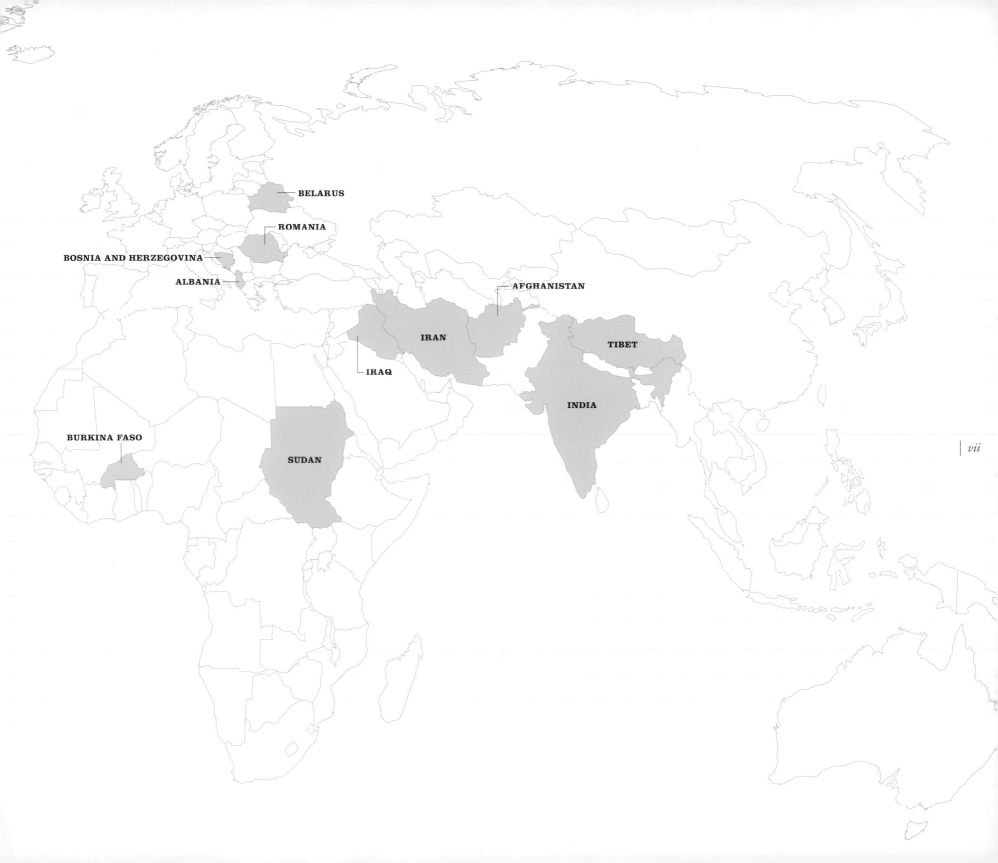

ACKNOWLEDGMENTS

This book could not have been completed without the support and effort of so many people, some of whom I would like to thank publicly.

I am grateful to photographer Steve Kagan for his patience, flexibility and commitment. His beautiful work is a gift to this project. I thank Phil Ponce for his eloquent foreword. Rob Koon's copyediting was an invaluable service to this project.

I would like to thank everyone associated with the Tibetan Resettlement Project-Chicago for giving me the opportunity to begin my work with immigrants and refugees. I am also grateful to Harry S Truman College for giving me the opportunity to work with and learn from such inspiring students.

I thank my friend and designer, Meighan Depke, who put up with my litany of design and printing questions and provided her elegant design to this book in exchange for a small fee and lots of chocolate.

I owe special thanks to my family and friends for their unconditional support through the highs and lows of this project. They continued to be interested in and listen to my stories about "the book" even when I, myself, wondered at times if it would be published.

Lastly, I am grateful to the many people who trusted me with their stories and made this book what it is. I tried my best to respect and take care of their words. I hope they are proud of how I presented their lives.

The book that follows is a collection of stories and photographs of 20 recent immigrants and former English as a Second Language (ESL) students of mine at Harry S Truman College, one of the City Colleges of Chicago. These stories were compiled from interviews conducted in English over a period of four years from 1998–2001. In each case, English was the second, third or even sixth language spoken by each immigrant. As a result, some of the grammar, syntax, or expressions that appear on the page may seem awkward at times to the formal English reader. I have been as meticulous as possible to maintain the integrity of the language that each individual used in describing his/her own experience. Each interview was recorded and transcribed word for word from the audio tape recordings. The language you are reading is the language I was listening to during the interviews, though not always in the exact order. While these stories have been edited for cohesiveness, the words are those of each immigrant. In a few cases, I have had to edit sentences for clarity, but I have tried to maintain the original intent and meaning of the speaker. Some words have been inserted in brackets to assist the reader in this process as well. Overall, my primary goal in this process was to preserve the authenticity of language, intention, and self-expression of each person to the best of my ability.

FOREWORD *by Phil Ponce*

Who is coming to this country to live? Why do they come? What do they go through to get here? And what happens to them once they arrive? These questions form the basis of the stories that follow—individual stories (told in the words of the protagonists themselves) which in turn tell a larger collective tale: a tale of this country's renewal and reinvention, one immigrant at a time.

These first-person accounts give freshness and vitality to the immigration saga. They emerge from a range of points around the globe. Each tale of immigration is not just a tale of a beginning but an exit interview of sorts from the country of origin, a gauge on the forces to which the United States is vulnerable, now perhaps more than ever. The distance between this country and Afghanistan, Bosnia, or Sudan has never seemed shorter and our sensitivity to the social and political tremors in far-off lands, never more acute. The connection between "us and them" has never seemed as immediate and profound.

In the past, that connection was no less pressing, but the perceptions may have been different. And the tale of past immigrants typically had a discernible—and comforting—beginning, middle, and end: struggle or persecution in the old country, the saga of the passage, and triumph over initial hardships once the protagonists reached the United States.

My own family's story has some of those classic elements to it, complete with its own mythology and comfort in the telling. There was a patriarch in Mexico whose death at a fairly young age in the early 1940's caused the collapse of a family business and threw his widow and children into economic hardship. There was a son, who inherited the patriarch's intelligence and verve, who made forays into the United States under early "bracero" programs. (A government program under which Mexican workers were brought to this country to fill labor

shortages, primarily in agriculture.)

That son (my uncle) eventually made his way to northwest Indiana where jobs in the steel mills were plentiful. He was the family's alpha male and he provided the leadership and structure for his siblings to follow—some directly from Mexico, others after a period of transition in Texas. For years, he and his siblings and their families lived hard by the steel mills, railroad tracks, and refineries of East Chicago, Indiana. Their homes were apartment buildings, from which they could see the glow of the blast furnaces, hear the pounding of foundries, and smell the biting fumes of industry. In time, with solid working-class mill jobs as their foundation, they moved into sturdy homes with lawns.

A new generation of American-born family members then started a cycle of education, home ownership, and participation in the workforce. Many members of that new generation served in the armed forces or in government—proof, if needed—of their status as Americans who love and are loyal to the country to which their parents came.

It is a tale with familiar and reassuring rhythms for many Americans. It is a theme and variation played by millions of other American families. In fact, the tale has such a predictability to it that I, for one, am slightly taken aback when I hear one that ends with a family member moving "back to Russia" or "back to Greece." I wonder to myself, "What went wrong?"

Many of us look to each tale by a new immigrant to retell our own stories. The country of origin, language, and particulars may differ; but there is an expectation that the basic structure will be the same and with a similar conclusion: the creation of new Americans who love this country and see themselves as part of its fabric.

The timeliness of such a telling is clear. The specter of domestic terrorism has changed the debate over immigration away from social and economic concerns to matters of life and death. Stories in the news about investigations and arrests of Americans of Middle Eastern descent are troubling for several reasons: the potential implications for civil liberties, the possibility these suspects in fact pose a threat, and perhaps at a deeper level the prospect that people are betraying a basic tenet of immigration. That tenet holds that to move to America means to develop an allegiance to her. One who would betray that tenet is a viper to us.

Once upon a time a critic or foe of immigration might have asked, "Is this person going to take away my job?" Now that person might ask, "Is this person here to kill me or the ones I love?" And while that may be an unsettling commentary on both our times and the current climate for immigration, it is a new reality.

Once upon a time immigrants were seen by many as this country's lifeblood—rich and renewing. Now some see the immigrant community as a potentially lethal virus to the body politic. Is this person a threat? Does he or she come from a background about which suspicions seem warranted?

No reasonable person can disagree that the United States government owes its citizens rational vigilance to potential threats. Such a threat is clearly not theoretical. If there were another act of terrorism, and it was traced to government sloppiness or inattentiveness to the people allowed in the country, the outcry would be monumental and warranted.

And no reasonable person can disagree that immigrants—and this country's openness to their intellect, labor, skills and spirit—continue to be essential to this country's human, cultural, and physical prosperity.

The challenge lies in balancing the legitimate need for security with the legitimate need for self-serving openness, "self-serving" in the best sense of the term: a direct acknowledgment that the United States needs immigrants to remain viable as a nation; and more importantly, to remain authentic to the remarkable historic impulses that resulted in this country's creation in the first place—impulses grounded in the need for human renewal and ascendancy.

As Jeff Libman so vividly illustrates in *An Immigrant Class,* the renewal, the reinvention continues. New storytellers are coming forward. To paraphrase Walt Whitman, I hear the new tale. And it is mine. It is yours. It is ours.

INTRODUCTION *by Jeff Libman*

In August of 1991 in Tanjung Pinang, Indonesia, near a United Nations camp for Vietnamese refugees on the island of Galang, I was witness to the reunification of a family separated by war and politics. It was an event that would change the direction of my professional life.

As a young man, Thuy had been among the Vietnamese who had made it to the United States after the fall of South Vietnam. As a former policeman, Thuy's father had been forced into a reeducation camp and his family had been left with severely limited opportunities when the North Vietnamese seized power. In 1980, Thuy left his home in Danang, found his way by boat to a refugee camp in Hong Kong, and was resettled in San Jose, California. His brother, Tuan, was 10 years old at that time and had remained in Vietnam. Crowded aboard a fishing ship with others fleeing Vietnam in 1989, Tuan landed in the refugee camp in Galang after a harrowing journey, which included attacks by pirates in the South China Sea. Learning of his brother's arrival and his emotional difficulties in the camp, Thuy traveled from San Jose with the hope of seeing his brother for the first time in nearly 12 years.

Thuy and I met near the dock in Tanjung Pinang as he told me his story. As we watched young boys playing badminton in the street, Thuy drifted off into a private stare. "Tuan was about that age the last time I saw him," he said in an empty voice as he tossed stones in front of his feet. The silence that followed screamed of the tragedy.

A visit to Galang turned out to be impossible, but with money and arrangements with the Indonesian military, Tuan was permitted a 24-hour leave from the camp. Perhaps because I had a video camera that could document the moment, Thuy invited me to accompany him as he walked into a hotel room in Tanjung Pinang to see the face of his 10-year-old brother, now 21 years old. As we walked into the room, Tuan stood in the corner shaking. Never had I seen hope and fear, joy and sorrow so raw and exposed as when I saw their eyes meet. I was

able to stay only a few minutes before my feeling as an intruder overwhelmed me and forced me to leave. Ten minutes later, Thuy invited me back in. Tuan was still shaking and now crying as he sat on the bed next to his brother. Thuy was too happy for words and, though he would have to say goodbye in less than a day, he was flooded with gratitude for the time he would have together with Tuan. Another year would pass before Tuan was given refugee status and began his new life in North America.

This was the beginning of my work with immigrants and refugees, work that has lasted more than a decade. Since that time, I have worked with thousands of immigrants and refugees in Chicago. Beginning in 1992 as executive director of the Tibetan Resettlement Project-Chicago, I coordinated the resettlement of 100 Tibetan refugees and their families from India and Nepal. Since 1994, I have been teaching English as a Second Language (ESL) to adults at Harry S Truman College, one of the City Colleges of Chicago and the largest ESL program in the state, where nearly 20,000 students attend free ESL classes every year.

Walk through the halls of Truman College on any day and you will immediately experience the cultural smorgasbord that is the emerging face of the United States of America. The three-story glass and steel building which hosts the majority of the classes at Truman College is home to probably the most diverse population in Chicago, and perhaps the entire United States. More than 110 languages are spoken by students from 144 countries. Indian women in fashionable saris chatting with West African men in colorful dashikis do not stand out as being unusual, as they may in many other places. A middle-aged Korean businessman may be in conversation with a newly arrived young man from Guatemala over lunch in the cafeteria. A Ph.D. holder from the former Soviet Union is likely to be sitting alongside a newly arrived refugee from Sudan, learning the same basic language skills and conversing with each other in English, a language foreign to both.

Truman College is the second home for many new immigrants in Chicago, who are taking their first steps towards membership in their adopted country.

During my years at Truman College, I have experienced daily how the highest values of our American melting pot play themselves out in such an inspiring and successful dance. From cafeteria tables to small group discussions in classrooms, students from around the world honor, respect, and wrestle with their diversity and what they can learn from one another. Here in the humble halls of this community college, the diversity of ethnicity, nationality, gender, religion, social customs, political ideas, and sexual orientation are not ignored, but celebrated for how they can so greatly enrich our lives.

While the students I have worked with come from vastly different cultures, all of these immigrants share the same human concerns. They are filled with hope and fear. They are torn between the past and the future. They have experienced hardship and success. They cherish family and friends. They want stability and opportunity to pursue their dreams. Their stories may seem different from those who were born here in the United States, but they share with all humanity these basic human qualities.

An Immigrant Class is an attempt to document the human experience of recent immigration to Chicago through 20 first-person stories and photographs of students who have attended English as a Second Language classes at Truman College. These students come from varied nations and cultures. Each reveals the unique elements of his/her life

before immigration, the circumstances that motivated the move, the experience of immigrating, and the impressions of life and identity that continue to unfold and change for each one in the United States. Some share their expectations and encounters with success, freedom, and opportunity. Others tell of their disappointments, frustrations, and regrets. You will meet those who have come legally and illegally, for opportunity or love, for education or tourism, for themselves or their children, fleeing war or economic hardship, alone or with loved ones.

An Immigrant Class is an attempt to break through the various stereotypes of immigrants to introduce the humanity behind the myth; and to share the hopes, fears, tragedies, and triumphs that make up the complexity of the immigrant experience. It is an exercise in listening and understanding. I believe that only when we stop to listen to each other can we recognize, respect, and celebrate our similarities and our differences. By doing this, we can reduce fear and mistrust and embrace the diversity that immigration brings as one of our nation's greatest strengths. In some ways, we are all strangers. Seeing the stranger in ourselves can hopefully give us greater compassion and understanding for the stranger in someone else. I hope that *An Immigrant Class* provides a sense of how making the time to listen to one another can eliminate that stranger in all of us.

While immigrants have always been viewed with some degree of mistrust and disdain, the period following the tragedy of September 11, 2001 has been a time of heightened suspicion. The passage of the USA Patriot Act and creation of the Department of Homeland Security has left many immigrants fearful. It is in the wake of these events that I believe *An Immigrant Class* has even more relevance.

I hope that by reading the individual stories of these recent immigrants, we will recognize part of ourselves in them and see that the struggles and hopes of immigrants are the struggles and hopes of all of us.

MY NAME IS AMADOU TANDINA *I'm 27.* I WAS BORN IN BURKINA FASO *on September 12, 1971. I got here on* SUNDAY, MARCH 9, 1997. *Two o'clock.*

[MY TOWN IS] KOUDOUGOU. It's about 60,000 people. My parents moved to Koudougou when I was about four years old. My father lived in the capital city [Ouagadougou] and then he moved to this small city because of his work. He told me that once he went to Koudougou for just some business trip and he realized that there were few tailors in this city and it was a city growing, so he decided maybe he should move his business to Koudougou. He had his own shop with six sewing machines.

My father, he was nice and he was always trying to guide us, to let us know that we should think about our future. And what I like now, thinking about him, is that he never forced me to do what I didn't want to do about my future in terms of choosing a school, what to study, what to do in the future. He always tried to make me feel responsible and make the decision by myself.

My mother was a housewife. What's amazing is that most of people think that African women, they don't work, meaning they don't make money. But the truth is that they are really the backbones of the families. They don't go to tailor shop, they don't work in the offices, but they do make money. They sell! They sell like peanuts, like fruits, like vegetables, like clothing, all these kinds of things. They have their own economic activities and they earn money. I remember when I was in elementary school, before going to school I had to help my mom sell her yogurt. I help her sell it because I was the one to carry it and follow her. And then between 1:00 and 3:00 [in the afternoon], I do the same thing. And right after school in the afternoon between 5:00 and 8:00, the same thing. We used to walk around, go by stores, tailor shops, or offices and sell it to people on our way to downtown. I carried it on my head and [served it] with small cups.

My mother is a very tolerant woman. Now I am the one who is taking care of her. [My father died] in '92. I send her money once in a while. And I'm taking care of the whole family, my two sisters and her. She is very maternal and what I like is that sometimes I know she dis-agreed with my father but she never let us childrens know that. When we were all out for school, then she and my father discussed. I've never seen them arguing.

It's a very simple area, very simple life. Sometimes we had the minimums and sometimes it was very hard. And the most important part in this simplicity is that we were not attached to material things. We were more attached to values like respect, solidarity, and modesty. In comparison to life here, for example, here in Chicago we were robbed in our house and Maria [his U.S.-born wife] was crying. They took our TV, VCR, even the pizza in the refrigerator. She was upset. And I told her, "They took things. They didn't hurt us physically. We could buy a TV. We could buy a VCR. And these things, they come and go." She couldn't believe it that I told her, "We can live without all these materials. They are coming and they are going. We don't care." She talked to her father and he was also upset and her father asked how I am feeling because he was worried about us. She said that I'm taking it philosophically, which is true! I said, "I don't care as long as we're not hurt physically. We're here. We can catch up with all what we lost." People here are very attached to materials. I don't know if this happened to an American, lost your TV, [Laughs.] I don't know how they would react. I can't even imagine American family without a TV.

I first saw TV in 1990. It was fascinating. The first time I saw was like a rebroadcast. It was not in live. I started to think that this is a

In his father's tailor shop, Burkina Faso, 1989

also very, very poor—poorer than we were. They had meals once a day. They don't have anything in their house. They don't even have a bed. They sleep on a mat. They don't even have washroom. Because we had washroom outside. There were some people who couldn't even have that. In my family we had three meals a day. That was something granted every day, but lots of my friends didn't have that. They only eat once a day, in the night. They were really poor. Usually we eat what we call *to*. It's a kind of millet cake and it goes with sauce, either okra or hibiscus or tomato or baobab and sometimes rice. My family, every day we had a piece of meat, very small, like this size. [Points to his watch.] Usually it's lamb.

Soccer was one of our hobbies, playing soccer every day. My father even used to make some balls. When we were between five and ten years old, we used to go for hunting. We made a [slingshot] for birds and lizards, just to kill them. [Laughs.] It's like a competition, and you kind of sleep with your [slingshot], you wake up with it, it's on your neck, it's everywhere. Also I used to look after some domestic animals, sheeps and goats.

Our city has a *jumelage*, like friendship between two cities abroad, overseas with Dreux in France, a small city at the southwest of Paris. Every year there were French coming from this town, and my father was the member of the *jumelage* committee. So every year when they came we connected, and I had lots of friends with them. And what was really amazing is that I've never put in my mind that I could go to Europe, or even the United States. When I was about 12 to teenager, they come and some of them even stayed at our home. Their parents came and learned how to cook African foods with my mom, and my father was tailoring some clothes for them. And I was also learning how to tailor and that's how I connected with them a lot. And lately, when I got here, I started thinking I have all these relationships, all these friends, and I've never thought that I could go, I could leave Burkina Faso to go to Europe or even the United States, never. They even never asked me, "Would you like to live in France?" The questions also never came in my mind. I realized later on that in my country, lots of people, they dream of going to Europe or going to the United States. I didn't have that feeling. It didn't come in my mind.

When I was in school, I really got involved in studying and I really loved it because, I remember my first year of school when I come home, the one who really helped me to love school is my mom because she knew how to read and write French already. And every night she

good, a wonderful way to communicate with people and to know other countries and to learn other cultures. This guy bought it. It has a very small screen, like less than 15 inches, and it was black and white and everybody in the neighborhood was meeting there. Fortunately for us, he has a big courtyard where he turned the TV on, and everybody went there. It was so loud and noisy. It was like in the market. It was a broadcast of World Cup soccer.

My home was bricks. We had three bedrooms with a living room. My father had one bedroom with a bed and a table, a small closet. My mother had a bed, two mattresses for my sisters, and I had a bed in the living room for myself. In the living room we had four chairs and a small table. My father had a stereo. The other room was a kind of warehouse where he had the foods, the dishes, and all that things. That's it. No washing machine, no fridge, no telephone, no TV, [no electricity]. Don't even think about microwave! [Laughs.] I would say typical. We had a well, and I was the one who was in charge of water for the family. We had three barrels and I had to fill them every day. It was in our courtyard. We had some community wells in the neighborhood, a big one. When everybody else wells is dry, we go there.

For example, for some rich people like businessmans, obviously their families were rich, but there were few. But there were some people helped me reading, doing my homeworks and reading stories for me, and that really attracted me to love school.

Burkina Faso—it's about only 20 percent of kids can go to school. The state doesn't have enough classes for everybody. Why I'm saying we were lucky, it's because of my father's relationship with his friends. He knew lots of teachers and right before the opening of classes he let them know that, "I will send my kids to your class." That's how I got a place at the age of six, which is unusual because usually it's eight. My father told him that I would only attend, I'm not registered. When we started, the teacher realized I was following and my attendance was good, and he registered me and I pursued it.

[I spoke English] a little bit, only some words from high school. We learned the greetings, most of the time the grammar, the uses of some words, and we even learned some songs, some poetries. There was one I lectured. For the new year, '85, our teacher gave me a poem to learn by heart and speak it. It was "1985." "Here is 1985 coming from the door. Welcome 1985. Your sun is bright, full of light. The birds are singing. The bells are ringing. Welcome 1985. Come and enjoy." Something like that. That was the poem. He wrote it. He chose me because I was the only one who could recite it with less accent. [Laughs.]

[There is] only one university [in Burkina Faso]. After high school, if you meet the requirement, you apply and a month before the university opens, they call the names on the state radio.

When my father died, I knew if I didn't have a very good GPA, my education was finished because I could never think of going to the university by my own and have that money, and it would be more expensive to live in the capital city. So I said, "I'll do my best." I had a GPA of A, but we were thinking you would get the scholarship according to who you know. So I was a little bit disappointed. I did not even think of it. I said, "OK, I do not care. If they decided that I will be granted the scholarship, OK, fine. If not, I don't care." Because there was really nothing I could do. I would say I'm the kind of person who always try to let things go their way. I never wanted something to be like I wanted, because I feel very anxious and it make me sick. And I don't want that, so I let things go their way. If it happens, fine.

The day they made the announcement, I was listening. Everybody was like in a suspense. They called my name and I was like, "Unbelievable!" And my mom, she started to cry because I told her what was happening, and I knew she was anxious and nervous more than I was. And she was really happy. I felt happy and proud because

she felt the same way. Right after she heard my name, she went straight to let her friends know that her son got the scholarship and was going to the university. And that make me proud of myself, proud of her. I felt very good. I said myself that if there is somcone who really taught me these things, it was really my father. And I'm really grateful for that.

In my high school I had a group of four friends who were studying together before the exam and I was the only one who passed. We were very close friends and I was a little bit unhappy for them.

I didn't find [university] difficult at all. The first year was like learning the rules and secrets of the university. The second year I wasn't even going to school! I only waited for the exams and I show up and I always succeed. [Laughs.] It's me. New subjects. I didn't go to school, but I just come see my friends. They give me their notes and I make copies and I read them before the exams. They were literature [classes]. Of course I read the books, but I didn't go to class. The teacher will give you some tips, but the rest is you. You have to think and use your brain. I was in the mood of understanding literature. And I'm really grateful for that. It's very easy for me to get through literature. I read the book and I can make the critique.

When I was going to university I was working two different jobs. I was teaching French and working as a tailor because it helped me to make some extra money. I got a part-time position in an American language center where I was a French conversationalist with American missionaries, volunteers. I started to meet Americans with this language center. During our conversation I asked them questions about life in the United States and they asked me the same. I started to have an idea of what the United States is. They have a baseball playground where they meet, so it was kind of American life that they have. They asked me [if I wanted to visit the United States], and I said no. Honestly, no.

My student friends [from the language center], I used to go out with them because the other part of my conversationalist [job] is to show them the culture. So I go out with them in movie theaters or performance or in market or whatever. So Maria told them that she just got here and she didn't know the town, and she wanted to get around with someone who knows the city. She was working as a volunteer with Save the Children. We organized something one weekend to go out together with seven or eight Americans, Canadians. And that's how we first met.

The first night we met, my friends introduced us and that was it, because I make myself my own idea that through my conversations with these different Americans, that Western people who come in Africa, they don't want to be bothered by the Africans. Because when I ask the questions, I try to make my idea of what they expect. They said that usually when they come, people hassle them, ask for money, and the women say that people try to date them, not being nice and thinking about money. Because during the French time, there were some French ladies who came in Africa just to have an African date and pay the money and to have sex. The same thing with women and men, both ways. So people still have this idea. They made me understand that. I was trying to notice, to take a look of how African will behave in front of the Westerners and I made my idea. It still exists. Lots of white women who got there are always harassed, always. Like people trying to date them by force. Here [in the United States], the thing is that if a lady say no, it's no, and American womens, they mean it, but in Africa it's different. A lady can say no, meaning yes. This kind of behavior sometimes hurt American womens. So I was distant [when I met Maria]. I told myself that I will never let a Western people to feel that way with me, to think that I am coming toward him or her to get something, to get money or to get some favors. And I was always distant. I always let them make the first move, make sure that they feel safe and comfortable with me, and then I accept. If they don't feel comfortable and safe with me, I don't pursue the relationship. Even today. I said, "Even if I try to be nice with her or nice with anybody else, there is no way that she couldn't have this small idea that I'm coming for these intentions." I remember we didn't even talk that much that night. After the introduction, I was talking with my other friends, which I knew. They were comfortable with me. They know I will never ask them money and I was comfortable with them. I don't talk to Western people I meet the first time unless they are comfortable with me.

We kept going out and going out and I had a very good German friend and we all started to go together. She felt comfortable because the other Americans were trusting me. She asked me some questions about how to handle the situation of some guys who are hassling her, and that's how we started to get closer.

I introduced her to my comrades and they were like, "Where did you meet her? What happened? Are you dating her?" Because during that time, we were not dating and in my mind we were not like girlfriend-boyfriend. Just a friend just like the other people. My friends always had this idea that I am dating American woman, that my mind will change. And people have this idea that Western women are con-

trolling, they control their men. They start teasing you, "Did she ask you to wash the dishes?" [Laughs.]

I said, "No." It was like I'm living in a world where no one understands you. You can hardly see a boy going out with a girl in Burkina Faso. Actually, there is not really dating in American sense in Burkina Faso. If you are going out together: girlfriend-boyfriend. Students are doing most like Western style, trying to find their own girlfriend, or their own boyfriend. But for the other people, they try to get through someone like a friend, cousin, or an uncle. The general population, it's kind of arranged marriage.

My mother had the same idea. She thought [Maria] was my girlfriend. I told her, "No, we are only friends." And I told her, "Do you remember my father? He had French friends who comes at home. They weren't his girlfriends. They were just his friends. The same applies to me." I don't think [that she understood]. [Laughs.] She didn't believe. Honestly, I would say [it was a problem for her] because she wasn't expecting that. And the thing is that it's an unknown relationship. I understand her, because she didn't know how to handle this situation.

When we were discussing about the future of the relationship, I told her that I'd like her to stay in Africa and she said that she would love to, but she have to finish her school. And then she is working in journalism. It's not sure that she could find a job in journalism in Burkina Faso. The closest country she could find a job in Africa is Egypt or South Africa. I said, "OK, I understand these reasons. I don't want you to drop your education and your job to stay with me. Since I am the one who is more flexible, I just finished university, and if there are possibility for me to get a job in the United States while you're finishing your school, we can try that. First of all, before getting a job we have to try and see if I could live in the United States, if I could feel comfortable living here." I was happy to be with her and let her finish her education. In this way I was happy for her and for both of us being together. But on the other hand, I was apprehensive of myself, how I will be integrated.

I first applied for a tourist visa, a nonimmigrant visa, a 90-day visa, because I didn't know there were a possibility of getting a fiancé visa. [The immigration official] denied me right away. I think he is thinking I'm trying to get advantage of the situation. I asked him, "Why?" He didn't give me any specific answer. He just told me that he would talk to Maria. I felt offended. If there is any reason why I am denied the visa, I think he should tell me directly. I know he can't do that in the

United States. If an American applies for something, you tell him that it's yes or no and you give him the reasons why, and I know that. Even if I'm African, I know the rights. I know I have some rights. Honestly, I thought he is thinking that he will talk to Maria and let her know, warn her about these foreigners who wants to come to the United States and try to date American girls to get the visa, and let her know to be careful not to be involved in such relationship. That's what I thought and it made me really angry. I became defensive. I told myself, "I'm not a refugee. I have a country. My citizenship is not denied. I can work in my country. I'm living decently, even if I wasn't rich. Why would I want to try to immigrate to the United States if they have this kind of stereotype for foreigners?"

The sad part of that is we don't really know the requirement. Honestly, I think it's stupid. It's treating people in Burkina Faso like less intelligent, less human. They [think we] don't deserve to know how to get to the United States. When you are United States representative in a country, your job is to grant or deny visas. Of course you have to let people know what the requirements are. That's obvious. There's nothing secret in that. First, Burkina Faso is a poor country; and second, more people are uneducated. That's what I'm trying to guess. People in Burkina Faso are likely to stay as are people from Romania or Poland. They're all likely to stay forever. I can't judge, but the facts are that Eastern Europeans are likely to get visas easier than Africans. These are facts.

The officer said that we should follow the American spouse's visa, which is a K-1 fiancé visa. When the guy denied the visa, that's when I said, "We can't just decide to get a fiancé visa for me if we are not really engaged. It doesn't make any sense for me and I don't want to be in such situation just because I need visa." I said, "If we have to make another step before getting here, the next step was we get engaged, and then we still can broke it because we're not married."

She said, "Yes." Both of us were excited, but we were scared because we didn't know what would happen next. Then, I went back and got the fiancé visa. I had another interview with the same guy. I was still angry with him. I did not want to meet him again. I told Maria, and she was afraid. She said, "Please don't insult him." Because she knew that I was very angry and I could have insulted him.

I get there. He asked me questions, yes or no. I said yes or no. He was trying to joke in English. [My English] was at the basics. He knew that the best way for me for this kind of interview is in French, and he speaks French, but he did it in English. That make me more angry.

I even heard him saying that, "If you're going to the United States, you should be able to speak English," which is stupid. I knew that in the United States there are lots of people who don't speak English. I knew that, even though I am living in Burkina Faso, because I asked my friends. They told me that.

Then he said, "OK, you will get the visa for 90 days." The fiancé visa, the condition is you get married within the 90 days. If not, you go back. This was in January 1997.

Those weeks were very tense because I was trying to get everything in order before leaving. I went to see my mom for three days. She wasn't really happy, or at least she was in mix of feeling because knowing that if I go to America, she knew that I would have opportunities to take care of her, take care of my sisters. And on the other hand, she felt that she would miss me, or we would miss each other. I remember we spent almost one night, lots of silence. Nobody says anything. We were sitting, couldn't go to sleep, couldn't say anything.

My family felt that I was going forever. [My mother's] only concern was, "Are you coming back?"

I said, "Yes, of course. Even if I stay in the United States for 100

Hiking with his wife, Maria, and friends, Maryland, 1999

years, I can't forget where I grew up. That is still part of me. I can't erase that from my life."

[When I left] my mother didn't go with me to the car. She was crying at home, and it was very emotional when I said goodbye to her at the door. I felt a little bit guilty. My sisters saw it first as more like a game. They wanted me to take them with me. Just as the bus was leaving, I think my sisters really understood that I was leaving for real and they were very sad and started to cry, and I began to feel terrible that I was causing all these people who I love so much hurt and pain. For 36 hours on the bus to the capital making all local stops, bad roads, police stops, I had time to think about this.

I realized I had no one who could tell me about the U.S. through African eyes. I knew no one in Burkina Faso who went to the U.S. before. My only perspective was through American eyes, and this was very scary. I bought a book, but this was a tourist book, not a realist book. It said all the people were friendly and the place was clean. I still have the book, actually.

Saturday, [the day I left], I went to took a shower and during the shower my heart started beating in my throat and my throat got tight. I felt that I was leaving a part of myself here. There was something here that I am really attached to, and I'm leaving this thing. That was very, very, very, very sad. I just tried not to cry because people would joke at me and say, "Oh, you're going to America and you're crying? What is that supposed to mean?" [Laughs.] I didn't speak much after that.

[My friends and I] went to the airport about 7:00 P.M. and I was quiet. I wasn't even thinking the United States. My mind was full of Burkina Faso. My friends and family were all that was in my mind. I didn't even think once about the airplane or the United States. I think they didn't understand my feelings. I think they were very happy for me. They were proud that they have a friend with this opportunity. I just brought my suitcase and that's it. No money. I had never seen a dollar. Never.

I wanted to be there right now. I was looking at my watch every 10 minutes for 15 hours. When I got to Belgium, I heard that O'Hare was the biggest airport, and I wondered how am I going to find Maria among all these thousands of people.

They have this screen in the plane to show the miles that remain and I was looking and counting. I was also cold the entire trip. I wore a light pair of shoes. I still have those. I said I would keep those. They put me right next to an emergency door and the air was kind of going

After a presentation about Burkina Faso to a middle school, Chicago, 1998

under the window and my feet were getting cold, very cold.

When I got here—the customs, the police dogs, and some electronic metal detector and drug detector. It took so long. You know there are two doors at O'Hare. I exited by the other door. I was out and no Maria. [Laughs.] "What's going on?" Just waiting five or ten minutes. Then she checked my door and saw me and told me her mom and sister were there.

It was raining and it was a little bit cold. It was March. Her mom brought me a jacket and we got in the car. We took Lake Shore Drive. [The city] was crazy. [Laughs.] I was actually looking at Maria and thinking of what would happen. I made a big move, it's like going to the unknown, and hopefully everything will go well. Her mom and sister, they were looking at me and asking questions.

Maria took a few days off to show me the basic things, the post office, the market, and take me to Truman College for English class, but she had to go back to work and I was alone and very lonely. We filled some papers for the work authorization. I was waiting for this and I was reading all the advertisements in all the papers, and I was even looking in the Internet. I was also asking people. Still waiting. I realized it's very hard to tell people that I want the job, but I don't have the authorization to work.

My first job was an internship at Facets Multimedia. I had some experience in my country for film festivals, since in Burkina Faso they have the African Film Festival, and I read some articles about Facets Multimedia. In my country nobody knows about job interviews. This is a new thing for me. It was about an hour. Yes, it was [strange]. I read some books about job interview and I said, "This is hard for me to do this—go and sell myself, present myself as the best." In my culture you have to be humble and have humility and let other people decide if you go for the job or no. Instead, here—sell yourself.

They're like, "Tell me about you."

"What can I tell about myself?" [Laughs.] Nobody ever asked me this question! I introduced myself, what I know, what I did in my country. The manager, she speaks French. So we made the interview, the first part was in English and the second part in French. I felt good that I was going to have something to do now. I wouldn't be bored anymore.

[I worked there] about three months. [I was] an office clerk: taking care of the files, making calls, and selling the company to donators. Then, I got my employment authorization.

The first movie I went to here, I didn't really pay attention to the film. I was so amazed at the quality. I thought, "Where was the sound coming from?" And the picture seemed in such good quality, I was amazed. In Burkina Faso, it is totally different. First of all, the theater in my country, the seats were bricks and outdoor and no roof and the quality of the sounds or picture is very, very poor, very, very low. Sometimes you could be watching and it just stops because the projector broke down and people are screaming and insulting the operator and insulting his mother, his family. [Laughs.] We had three kinds of seats. There is the second-class seat with chairs, and first, which is very expensive section. And what we call Indian seats. It's very cheap, right in front of the screen. When the movie stops, the Indians they scream. [We call them Indian seats because] when movies came first with western movies, Indians always when they want to attack something, they always scream. That's how people say these people are always like American Indians.

The first weeks were very, very hard, because I remember we had to decide if we were getting married or not. If not, I had to leave. So this was kind of an unstable situation. I was still asking myself if this marriage is really a true marriage, if we are doing something right. That was my every day's concern. I tried to gather, to think and think and think and think. I say, "I don't want to get married and one or two years or three years, divorce." I know in the United States it's easy to get married and divorce next year or next day, and I don't want to do that. I don't want my life to be that. I had to be sure that if we're getting married, it's going to be forever, or at least a long time. And if we're getting married, that I will not have to forget my own culture, or where I grew up, and that she would try to be part of this culture as I'm trying to be integrated in the United States, in American culture. I was always thinking of, "You have to get married within the 90 days." That idea couldn't leave my mind, and the idea that I'm getting married with someone I know I really love, and someone I know I met by myself. There wasn't any arrangement between us. She never gave me money. I never asked her any favor. I knew all these facts, but I still had the idea of that deadline. She felt like we having pressure. We both felt that it wasn't fair that you have to decide to get married within 90 days. While you love each other, you could decide, because of this situation, this pressure, not to get married and think back later, or you decided to get married and feel unhappy later. So it was like life was unfair for us. It was very short time, very quickly for both of us to decide.

The second thing was, I didn't have someone else to talk to. I didn't have a friend. I really felt alone. You felt alone in a crowd, this feeling. All my mind going back to Burkina, and I was trying to read all the papers to find where are some people coming from Africa here. And everything I see or hear, I had to ask Maria, "What does that mean? How do Americans usually behave in front of this situation?" And I didn't like that, asking her every single thing. It was too much. I wish I had someone I could ask about these kinds of things. And I didn't have this person, and I didn't want Maria to feel that I was asking her too much. I knew she had difficulties trying to adjust herself with me, and if I was asking, asking, asking, it was a little bit hard. She wanted me to discover things on my own, but it was very, very hard. Maria was my whole world here. It was difficult because I know I have to learn by myself, but I can't learn by myself if there is nobody in front of me. And Maria knew that and that was the hardest part.

Her parents also were nervous and anxious because they didn't know what to expect, how to treat me, and what to do. I understand it's very hard. And I know how American thinks: "Something which is not American, be careful." Lots of people here know that. I know there are arranged marriages or people who try to get here with marriage visa or get citizenship with American woman. I know there are a lot, there are a lot. And that was very hard also to deal with.

When we decided to do it, she talked to her parents and they asked, "Are you sure? Are you sure?" I remember one day we had a big discussion and it was very hard because you were trying to tell the truth, trying to put everything together so that it would work, and her parents told her, "If you're not sure, don't do it."

I said, "It's true. If you're not sure, don't do it." We have this 90 days. I don't want to be in the Immigration's file like someone who broke the law. If we're not doing it, I would like to leave before the 90-day deadline.

We decided just eight days before the deadline. When we decided to do it, we called city hall to make appointment with the judges. We went to city hall. It wasn't like what I used to see in the movies, on TV. We allowed to have 10 people, but it was about 15. The judge, he was nice. First of all, it was a Monday and the guy said, "OK, today is very relaxed. There is no stress. You can bring whatever people you want."

Most of the people were all Maria's friends and relatives. I had no family here, and I felt very homesick and very mixed of feelings. Nobody from my family was here and such events are very big in Africa. You're getting married like in secret. You don't have your family. Nobody's here, even a friend! I didn't have even a friend to tell him, "Come to my wedding." That was very, very, very, very difficult. It was like I was doing something in secret.

We did the civil ceremony. We went to a restaurant and then one month later we had a party in Madison [Wisconsin], where her parents live. Then she invited her friends from high school, university, colleagues, family members, and everybody. It make me think that her friends are my friends, and that I can connect with them and maybe they also have other friends who will help me.

The next job I said, "OK, I know for sure at Dominick's or Jewel-Osco [supermarkets], they are always hiring, so in the process of looking a better job, I'll go there." I went to there [Dominick's] and the next morning I started. [Laughs.]

There wasn't even an interview. "Fill an application and you will start tomorrow."

I was [surprised]. [Laughs.] "What kind of job is that in America? You just fill out an application…"

I was bagging, helping customers to find products in the different aisles. I did that about two months. There was no possibility to move up because I knew people there who were working for eight, ten years and doing the same thing. And the difference between our hourly rate is $2. I can't do that.

Next, I was downtown walking and I saw an advertisement that Banana Republic is hiring. I asked Maria, "What's Banana Republic?" She said it's a clothing company. I didn't know nothing about Banana Republic, so I went there straight. I filled up the application. There was this group interview.

They asked me, "How much do you want to be paid?" [Laughs.] I said, "I don't know."

They said, "You have to write something."

I said, "Can you give me five minutes to decide?" [Laughs.] I put $7 [per hour]. I said, "Is that too high? Is that too low?" I didn't know. I didn't have any idea. I didn't talk to anybody. I wish I knew someone who was already working retail who could tell me the standard. Then we went to the group interview. That was very hard. It was about 12 people sitting around the table and they were asking questions, introduce yourself and why you choose Banana Republic. [Laughs.] [The interview] was in a hotel. I had never seen a Banana Republic. They asked the questions and they always let whoever is ready first to start. I was always the last one [Laughs.] to answer.

When I told them I am a tailor, they asked me, "What is the best achievement you ever do as a tailor?" That was hard. I was kind of like caught. [Laughs.]

I said, "During all these 10 years, the best achievement for me was that I've never had a customer who came to me to complain that he or her clothes were not well done or I did something they couldn't wear. They were always satisfied."

And they said, "OK." They asked me, "What do you like about Banana Republic?"

I couldn't say, "I've never been there." [Laughs.] They had a video where they were playing some Banana collection of the summer and I watched this video and I watched it and I watched it with the music. I said, "What I like about Banana Republic is the clothes are very casual for everybody, the style is simple, and the ambience is very good."

They said, "Good." [Laughs.]

And then I told Maria that I'm going to try Manpower Employment Agency. I decided to do that because they were cutting my hours at Banana. I went to Manpower. I called them first. The next morning I made an appointment for an interview. I came for the interview and they had me pass some test. It was great. I had the highest score. That surprised me. [Laughs.] By 2:00 the interview was finished. I went home. I got home by 3:00. About 3:15, they called me and said, "We have a job for you at Xerox and it's starting tomorrow. Would you like to go?" [Laughs.]

I said, "OK." I like the Xerox job very well. I'm doing copies or what's related to papers, like desktop publishing, making copies, creating forms, and all what's around making documents, binding, folding. [The pay] is much better. When I have papers, I like to put them on my head and people, "What are you doing?" [Laughs.]

I don't feel like an American because lots of times many peoples have told me, "Where are you from?"

For example, I changed all my wardrobe because what I used to wear, I've noticed that it attracts attention, so I said, "OK, I will change all my wardrobe. Try to dress like American." That didn't even change anything. I told Maria that, "I'll start to read the *Wall Street Journal* in the train." [Laughs.] She laughed.

Even in the train people said, "Where are you from?" Just having a seat and look at me and say, "Excuse me, where are you from?"

I said, "Why? How do you know that I'm not American?"

"It's the way you have the seat. It's the way you walk." That's interesting.

One night I went to a bar in downtown, it's a sport bar, to watch the Bulls. I had the seat at the bar and the guy next to me looked at me and looked at me and looked at me and said, "Where are you from?"

I said, "What do you mean where are you from?" Even in this darkness in the bar people see you and can recognize where I'm from.

He laughed and said, "It's true." He thought I was angry.

I said, "No, I'm not angry. It's just that it's not funny. I'm trying to understand, to be integrated, but people always noticed it." He said it's the way I pull the chair to sit. I said, "What is the difference? How would an American do that?"

He said, "I don't know. [Laughs.] It's different."

Lately I started to tell myself that, "You don't need to be an American because you will not be an American 100 percent." I ask myself, "What is an American?" Honestly, I think it's very hard to tell what is an American because from one neighborhood to another neighborhood, it's different. I don't really still understand why people still think that I'm from a different country. It's not written on my head. I haven't think introducing myself like I am an American, because I am still adjusting. I am still in the process of getting integrated, meaning understanding fluently English, for example, and understanding the workplace behaves, the workplace rules.

One of the most important things I love here is this opportunity to learn and to be educated, this possibility to choose what you want, because I didn't really choose during my whole life in Burkina Faso. I didn't really choose what to study or what to do. But here you have this opportunity to choose and to do whatever you want with your life. It's still a little bit difficult for me. I don't have a long-term American dream, because I'm still adjusting. Meaning that, coming from a place where you didn't have no choice to a place where you have multiple choices, you always think that all the choices are good, so it's hard to make one definitely. That's why I'm in the process of appreciating all the choices and thinking of them, balancing all the choices, and then I think I will be able to project a long-term image.

It is possible [that I will be here in five years]. I'll put it in this perspective. If I have the preference, I would rather be in the place where I have lots of friends and where I have lots of interconnections with people. I couldn't say, "No," to the United States [just] because I don't really have lots of friends here. Maybe if I get lots of friends, it could change. It's not obvious that going back to Burkina Faso, my same friends will still be at the same place even though it's very easy to get new friends in Burkina. It's like within 24 hours you have people in your life. But I think if I get in a situation here where I can meet lots of people and build relationships, I can stay here. That's not a big deal. The hardest part is that I'm missing my family. That's the only thing, because you can't change family.

It's very difficult [to make friends here]. Usually I say, "Americans, they open their arms to welcome you, but they don't close." You meet someone, "Hi, nice to meet you. How are you? Nice to meet you." And then it's finished. The relationship stopped. It's an open and closed case. There is no follow-up unless you take their phone number and you call, try to make an appointment.

And he will say, "No, I don't have time. Next time." And next time will be next time and then it's finished.

I've met tons of people, "Hi, how are you?" And then… [Snaps his fingers.]

One case is that I met this guy. A friend of a colleague of Maria asked me to go out with him. We went to a barbecue party to a friend of his. We spent the afternoon there. And then I met the guy in the grocery store. I said, "Hi, Len. How are you?" He didn't even respond.

He looked at me like, "Do you know me?"

I felt so bad, so bad! It was terrible. I said, "I'm sorry. I'm sorry."

I told my friend. I called him right away and tell him that I just met Len and I greeted him and he looked at me like he didn't know me.

He said, "Really?"

I said, "Yes, in the grocery." I gave him the time and the location. He was embarrassed.

I came to the point that I've learned to live by myself and I don't really expect people to call me or invite me to do something or visit me. I came to that point. I can be at home and have all these peoples I know, or I have their telephone numbers, but they don't have time. I don't blame them. I go my work, I go back home and read or watch TV or go to a movie, and now I don't think of who am I going to see or who am I going to talk to. Yes, it is [OK]. It's not that I have changed all my feelings, but I think I have adapted to the situation.

I feel like there is a stereotype here of all strangers. I don't mean foreigners. For strangers I mean anybody you don't know, is bad. Offering to help, for example. You can see this old lady or anybody in the street who is carrying heavy luggage and you want to help, but this person will think you want to rob him, or you will pick pocket or you want to kill him. I experienced that. They say, "No, no, no. I don't want your help." That was unbelievable. This is very strange for me.

In one to two months I've never met someone who is living in our building. "Is there someone really living here? Are we alone?" Never. I said, "That's impossible." Most of the time I try for the first time to say, "Hello," but they don't answer. That's so hard to believe. People in my country in the neighborhood where I live, every morning you will say, "Hi," to more than hundreds of people. You will meet everybody first in the street, just raise your hand or say, "Hi," and keep going and everybody knows everybody or at least they try. You don't feel alone. There is no loneliness [in Burkina Faso]. None at all. You are always surrounded by people you know.

Children, I'd rather have them between the two, to experience both, because I think both countries has lots of values for children. For example, Burkina Faso has the moral values for children, for discipline, for respect; and the United States has the materials, like the medicines, like the schools, like all this education. And letting them be in both, they will be more open-minded than American children.

I think American idea of freedom is a very good idea in that it helps human beings not being always abused or not being under other people's rule, which is very noble for human beings in terms of having something granted for life; although I think it's a little bit unrealistic

Learning how to ice skate, Maryland, 2000

because the way people try to put it, everybody try to talk about *his* freedom. And it becomes not the idea of one freedom, like a unique freedom, but the idea of everybody's freedom, like a plural noun, "freedoms." You do something. You think it's right and you want it to be your freedom and you don't want anybody else to tell you are wrong. It's a freedom mixed with selfish. And then it becomes something you can't control. Like what's happening now with the gun control, abortion, the Internet, like this Jerry Springer show! It becomes freedom for everybody. In one side or the other side, everybody's talking about freedom. It's like you're talking different language now.

This idea of in French we say *chacun pour soi et Dieu pour tous,* which means, everybody for or by themselves and God for everybody. You think of yourself and God will take care of everybody else. In Burkina Faso, it's exactly the opposite. You don't think of yourself. God will pay you.

I don't really see the necessity of voting. But the way I see it, [the benefit of becoming a citizen] is maybe having a United States passport. I think that living here is already trying to be part of American life; and even if I don't realize it or I don't know it, I'm getting some American cultures and I'm becoming an American representative for my country. I talk about America lots of time to my friends. It's like I'm selling America. I'm doing something for America. The only thing in the citizenship is that if I would ever do that, it's for my childrens and for my wife. Because for me, it doesn't really change anything. I'm already who I am. It's only a paper.

I would say the most important thing that I've learned here is to help me see myself in a community, meaning helping me define who I am and thinking of myself. Putting it another way, being selfish. That's the most important thing I've learned here. Even though I don't like it, it helped me to know who I am, how I see things. It helped me to appreciate my culture. I know my culture had good things and bad things, and it helps me to see these things. And come and say finally that American or Burkinabe or Malian or Romanian or Argentinean, they are all human beings. They are all the same.

They simply live in different environment. Here, people are stereotyping each other. Most of these stereotypes, I learned them here. That's here [Laughs.] that I learned all these things. Blacks say this to white. Whites say this to black. I think this is lack of comprehension of other people. You're always having a wall between you and other people and don't try to understand them, how they behave. They don't have to be like you. They don't have to be as you expect them to be. And that's what's contradiction in American freedom. Everybody wants to be different and they don't want others to be different. If you want to understand people, you go to them, you understand how they live and you will know who they are. And maybe it will help you know who you are. And if you know who you are, then you can decide where you're going or what you're doing. That's the most important thing.

AMADOU NOW LIVES in a suburb of Washington, D.C., and is a computer programmer for an on-line academic support services company.

MY NAME IS ELI RAMÍREZ *and* **I AM FROM GUATEMALA.** *I came here about two years and a couple months [ago] in* **SEPTEMBER '98, EXACTLY SEPTEMBER 3RD** *I think, yeah.*

I WAS BORN IN A LITTLE TOWN IN THE MIDDLE OF RAIN FOREST AND WILD RIVERS in the Department of Retalhuleu, Guatemala. Actually, I just born where I have already told you, but afterwards my dad moved from this town to Quetzaltenango, the second city in Guatemala. He got a job with the government and I was eight months old when we moved to Quetzaltenango and I grew up over there. Quetzaltenango is in the highlands of Guatemala so the weather is cold, especially in summer. And it's rainy in the winter.

I didn't live in the city of Quetzaltenango, but about five kilometers away in the countryside pretty near to the city. So [our home] was in the middle of cornfields. There were two bedrooms and I used to sleep in the bedroom with my sisters, and my mom and my dad slept in the other one. At the very beginning, we didn't have electricity, so we used to light candles at night. And we didn't have water at home, so we used to go to a *pila;* it's kind of the big container of water where all the people went to get water. There was a pipe, but this pipe filled up all this container and people went over there and take water in containers. Public water. We didn't have a bathroom. Well, actually, kind of bathroom. All the people in that town used to dig a big hole and make a kind of little house on top of it and that was the kind of latrine that we used to have.

I grew up actually with very little commodities. My memories are that we didn't have refrigerator. My mom used to cook with firewood. We didn't have stove. We didn't have TV. Wow. Only a few persons in the town. The most we had is a radio, which worked with batteries. But if I think in relation with my neighbors, I think that at least we had food every day and clothes and we lived sort of better than other people in my town, which was a town of peasants and really poor people who used to live from corn and beans and things that they produced from the earth.

[We had] a little piece of land, but it wasn't big enough. We used to harvest corn, but it wasn't enough, so my dad always bought corn from other people and beans and all that stuff. My memories of my meals

when I was a child till I was about 12 maybe: beans in the morning, corn tortillas and kind of sauce maybe with tomato, cilantro kind of fried in a little bit of oil. When I think with relation with what I eat now—oh, it's big difference! We didn't have really good alimentation.

My dad used to be a mechanic. He worked for *Caminos,* which is a department of the transportation and roads maintainment. He didn't start as mechanic. He started working on the roads, cleaning up the sides of the road and all that stuff. And he ascended, climbed up until he became a mechanic. My dad was a silent guy. He didn't use to speak too much with us. But he was the kind of guy who we used to respect and all our neighbors respected also 'cause he always gave an image of a straight man, and fair, and very careful of his family. Yeah, that was him. From my father, honesty, and hard work, and to be fair with my fellows and responsible toward my family, I think I learned all that about him. We had small conversations sometimes, but mostly watching him. When sometimes he used to rub my head or beat softly my ears, those were the times when I really felt that love that he used to have toward me, but he never expressed it speaking. My dad passed away about four years ago.

My mom is still alive. She is the kind of person that always gave her life for her childrens and she always obeyed my father in everything. She never had a job, never. She was the kind of home woman. She always washed our clothes, made my father's and our food, and kind of submissive woman 'cause that is the culture in my country. They

Selling handicrafts, Honduras, 1997

never had more than the primary school. I think my father studied six years and my mother four or five.

My mom had five children, four women and I in the middle. So I am the only man and I was kind of the guy who my mother and my father loved the most I think 'cause I am the only man, so I was kind of something special in the family. I think my sisters were kind of jealous toward me 'cause they felt like my mom and my dad take more care of me than of them, but they were cool girls. At certain times they took care of me, of course.

My father was a really Catholic to death, and my mom also. So we grew up kind of Catholics, too. I used to say that I was Catholic, but really few times I went to church and I went to hear the *misa* [mass]. Almost never. I didn't really like to go to church. Usually they didn't either, just when there were weddings or *bautismos* [baptisms] and first communions and that kind of stuff, I think, because the weekends we have to go to a mountain to look for firewood. Well, because my mom cooked with firewood so on the weekends we had to go to a mountain, which is about four miles from my home, and we looked for dry firewood in order of saving money and not buy the firewood from other people. So Saturdays and Sundays early in the morning, my dad and me and sometimes my sisters, too, went to these mountains to look for firewood. Sometimes we cut trees 'cause sometimes it was hard to find

enough firewood already cut, because all the people used to cook with firewood, so it was kind of not very common to find dry firewood.

We called this thing *mecapal*. It's a kind of piece of leather that we put around our forehead and it was tied to a bunch of firewood and we used to carry that way. And sometimes we used a *carreta* [wheelbarrow] to bring the firewood. For me it was [hard work] and I think for my father too 'cause after we came from that mountain, we used to have some lunch and my dad rested to get ready for next day to go to work. And I think because that, we never really had time to go to church. [Laughs.]

People and my parents said that I was an imp. You know what is that? Very hyperactive, always making *travesuras* [mischief] and all that kind of stuff. It means doing something always, and without thinking too much if I broke a glass or a plate or I kicked somebody.

I really liked school. Actually, I went to school after my sisters and I finished school before them. I went a couple of years [to high school], but I didn't do well. I think it was because I never really had the books, I never really had the uniform, and when I saw another people with all that kind of stuff, I felt kind of mad at myself or disappointed and kind of rebelliousness caught me. [Laughs.] I just dropped out of school. I think sometimes I answered my teachers in a wrong way and they kicked me off the class. So I got in a lot of problems. That was by the time I was about 15 or 16. So I was a rebel.

Besides of girls, [Laughs.] I think I liked language a lot. In fact, I have a lot of diplomas in my house 'cause I won a lot of speech contests. And how you say when you know a poem by heart and you say it in front of public? Recite. So I won a lot of that kind of contests. And actually, my teachers liked me because of that. I went to another [high school] and I say, "Well, I come from Werner Valle Lopez," which was my [high school]. And I recited saying I came from there. So my [high school] was kind of getting famous because they had a good reciter over there. I like poetry. There is one. It's called "Cornman." [Laughs.] Let me think a little bit about it. I can't remember one of these phrases right now. I'm going to, I'm sure. I won several contests with this poem. Yeah, it's a beautiful poem.

Maybe from 1965 to 1989, 25 years, more than that, many things were forbidden in my country. Those were very hard times in my country. Those were times when army had the power in my country, and on the other hand there was the guerrilla. So we were in a civil war and it was pretty unsafe. If the army caught you with a book of Che Guevara, for example, or listening protesting music, you could get in a real bad problems with the army.

When I was a teenager, once I was wearing a shirt of camouflage, a shirt with colors of the army, with camouflage colors, green and you know. And I found some people from the army and they asked me what was I doing wearing that shirt. And they told me to take it off and give it to them. And I was kind of unsafe and fearing and I gave them the shirt. It was in a public place and I had to go home with my underwear. And that was the way, army.

In Quetzaltenango, a lot of fights there. There were groups of guerrillas in the mountains. How can I explain this to you? If you wanted to stay alive, you [couldn't] talk against the government, and there were also a lot of people, we call them *orejas* [ears], which is the kind of people spying you and looking what you do, ready to tell the army. And so you have to be very careful 'cause army used to kidnap people, kill them, and disappear them. A couple of uncles of mine were disappeared by the army. One of them used to have a rifle and he used to live in the countryside. Somebody told the army that he had a rifle, and army went to caught him 'cause they thought he was guerrilla or he has something to do with guerrilla. And my uncle never, never appeared again. Never. A lot of people from my town disappeared and we didn't know whether they went to the guerrillas or the army killed them either. So those were really hard times in my country.

I think because the environment that surrounded me as I was growing up, I became a very troublemaker in my country. There were about three years when I used to go out with my friends at night and drink, smoke. We never did drugs, but we used to drink and smoke. And I was always fighting and beating down other guys. Luckily, I never got beated. [Laughs.] I think it was because the environment that surrounded me. You know, newspapers and radio news, sometimes television news, always speak about kidnappings, disappearances, people killing people, and poverty. I think because of that. And my daddy was very busy trying to bring home what we needed, then he never sat and talked to me about these kind of things or how should I behave in front of this situation.

When I left school, my daddy said, "Well, you didn't want to study, so go to work 'cause I'm not going to sponsor you. You are almost a man and you gotta see what to do." [I was] 16 or 17. So I start working everywhere in any kind of job. I used to fix crashed cars, painting and that kind of stuff. After that I worked in a bus getting money from the people, the tickets and all that kind of stuff. And I worked in the countryside also for less than a dollar daily, working eight hours in the corn plantations picking. A dollar a day. With a dollar, [you couldn't buy] much. So maybe I could buy a lunch with a dollar. I had to work maybe one week to be able to buy a pants or a shirt and about 15 days to buy a pair of shoes. At the beginning, I didn't give my money to my mom or my dad. I just used it for me. There was some money left to go out with my friends. Not much. By that time I didn't care what kind of job I did. I just wanted to get some money. I learned a lot about a countryside job, harvesting and all that kind of stuff. I think I liked it.

Actually when I was 18, I was in the Boy Scouts movement in my country and they gave me the opportunity of coming to United States in 1988. I was in Washington, D.C., then I came to Chicago for a while, then I went to California. I was here about two months. Well, I liked the country.

To be a Boy Scout is an adventure and this was kind of, wow, exciting. I was going to United States to meet another Boy Scouts and to stay there for a while and go camping. And I got really excited 'cause some friends of mine who were in the Scout movement had came here before and they went back telling stories. "Oh, United States. Big buildings. Nice people. Nice places." So I was excited at that time.

The first day when I came, [Laughs.] we came to Florida airport and we stayed in that airport for about two hours and then we got in another plane to Washington. And in Washington we stayed in a hotel and, wow! I left the hotel a couple of times without permission, just to go out and walk on the streets and look everywhere. It was exciting for me. Everything [was amazing]. The city, the beautiful city. The streets, neat streets all with pavement and the houses. How the people wear nice clothes. I don't have memories of watching somebody begging or kind of that, which in my country is very common. That was quite amazing for me. All the environment. And the next day we went to the Washington Capitol and visit some monuments: Jefferson's, the Washington, and Potomac River, and all those places. It was exciting. And that's it. After Washington we came to Chicago, just to the airport. I think it was O'Hare, and we took another plane to San Francisco. And we were there a couple of days. I traveled in these kind of trains in San Francisco, the trolleys. And we crossed this Golden [Gate] Bridge and we took several pictures. We went to the Chinatown in San Francisco. I really enjoyed that trip. Two months. [Mostly we were] in a Scout reservation in Santa Clara, California, in the mountains with another Scouts making scouting stuff—camping, going to the mountains, making my own bed out of leaves, and making a kind of camping house with a piece of plastic, and making fire and cooking my food in the mountains, listening to the birds, watching the sunrise, and all that kind of stuff. Being in the mountains was the thing that I most liked about being a Boy Scout.

I didn't [speak any English]. I came with a group of about 30 people from my country. And a couple of the guys who was taking care of us, they spoke a little bit of Spanish 'cause they were gringos, and we have translators also.

Actually when I was going back, when I was in the Los Angeles airport, a cousin of mine came 'cause he knew I was going back to Guatemala. And he said, "Eli, make a decision. Outside is my truck. Leave the things you have in the plane, leave your luggage, your baggage. Leave your luggage over there. Anyway I don't think you have too much to lose and go with me and stay here in United States."

But I was a Boy Scout. And I had made a promise. And I told him, "No, I don't think I really need to stay here. Maybe someday I'll be back, but I think this is not a time." And believe me, I really regret to not go out with him and to stay here. It was in 1988. I think by this time, I should be a citizen at least. But I didn't. [Laughs.] So I went back Guatemala.

I think that was a really important thing for me when I was a Boy Scout. They taught us the value of the word and the promise we made and all that kind of stuff. It's kind of the Scout philosophy. So I went home.

After I dropped school, I started working everywhere and anything and this day a friend of mine came and said, "Eli, you want to go with me to Honduras?"

"To do what?"

"To sell the handicraft at a fair, in an open market."
And I said, "OK, I'll try." And I went with him, and that was the way I get this kind of business. And I worked not only with him but with other people selling handicraft in fairs around Central America. And I worked about two or three years for these guys, and after that I realized that I could have my own business. And I started making my own things, creating my own styles of handicrafts and selling them. I just learned it watching another people and trying to make things at home, and I think the time was important to perfection in this kind of job.

But I never really had a teacher, so everything born from me.

What did I do? It's kind of epoxymil. Well, this kind of paste came from Mexico. It has two parts, one is white, one is green. And you gotta mix them equal parts and [it] became kind of soft paste. And you have about half an hour to work it out 'cause after that time, it start getting hard and hard and hard till it's completely hard. [I made] several things: lighter cases, knives, and machete sheaths and necklaces, bracelets, earrings. But not everything from epoxymil. I used to work with bamboo also, with little canes of bamboo. I cut them in little equal pieces and I make also necklaces and beautiful earrings. I used to have a shoemaker knife and I used to cut piece by piece by piece of these little canes.

Sometimes my family said, "Eli, you don't have to be so perfect when you do these things. What you need is to make lots of them! What you need is to sell!" But I never pay attention to them. And I liked to be perfect with my things, and I used to work long times doing one thing till it was perfect for me. And people pay me more money for my job than for other people's job, who used to produce things in a row, lots of things. I used to have three or four knife sheaths, not a lot of them, three or four, but I got well paid for them. This job could maintain me for hours sitting and working out till it was perfect. It became kind of religion for me. I really liked it. I really, really liked it.

And I met some people from other countries who used to work with this kind of paste also and they said, "Oh, this is beautiful. This, too. You work very well." I invest a lot of time to perfect this kind of job. I think that when I was performing this job, nothing else was important for me. I didn't care about what was going on around me. It just gave me kind of an escape from all the stuff and obligations that I had in my head and it gave me kind of peace. [I did this] about four years till I came here.

When I was working in fairs in Guatemala, it was a word of mouth to hear people talking about another country's fairs. "Oh, there is gonna be a fair in San Pedro Sula, Honduras." Or "San Jose, Costa Rica, has a very big festival."

And I started thinking, "If I sell this here, why I can't sell it over there?" So I started traveling around Central America. What was interesting, I met a lot of peoples and I learned a lot about other countries' cultures, food. And by that time, I met a lot of girls [Laughs.] from other countries. I told them, "Where are you from? I'm from Guatemala." And it was kind of nice 'cause you are from another country, and people from other countries like people from other countries, and it wasn't hard for me to have a girlfriend in another place. I never traveled by plane. I used to travel in buses from town to town till I get the place where I was going to work. You know the landscape when go in a bus. You go and you go, watching everything around you. You stop to eat somewhere and that was cool for me. Sometimes I had to travel two or three days. When I went to Panama once, I had to travel three days in a row passing a lot of places and cities. I used to read a lot when I was a teenager, so I started knowing things and cities and places where I just had read about it. And I liked to talk with people and ask them how is their lives in their countries and what people eat here and all that kind of stuff. And I learned a lot.

My mom, especially, my mom [loved to hear the stories]. 'Cause I was already an adult and I had my own bed, but when I came, so I slept with my mother. And we used to speak almost the whole night, she telling me all the things that had happened while I wasn't at home, and I telling her about the things I had known, how much money I had made and people that I'd met and people to say, "Hello," to my mom even when they didn't know her. And of course, my friends also. I was special when I came back to my country. Sometimes I didn't

With his wife, Dunia, and daughter, Bethel, Guatemala, 1994

make that much money, but it was cool. It was cool.

Getting married was a really nice adventure in my life. [Laughs.] I was working in this festival in Honduras, a big festival, which is called La Ceiba Carnival. It's a port city in the Atlantic of Honduras. And I had this girl. She was my girlfriend and she used to live in Tegucigalpa, the capital of Honduras, and she knew that I was going to be in La Ceiba at this festival. And she came to visit me. She was supposed to be back at home the next day. And, well, we went to dance. I got drunk 'cause I drank some beers. And in the heat of the moment, I asked her for marry me. And she said, "Are you going to hold your word?"

"Of course, you aren't talking with the liar." And then I asked her, "Are you going to hold your word also?"

"Oh, yes. I'll take the risk." And next day, she didn't go back home, and her mother was waiting for her. [Laughs.] And we slept together that day. So next day, she said, "OK, let's get married." And my pride didn't let me to go back and I got married.

And we signed up and we were wife and husband. [Laughs.] It was incredible. When I came back home, [Laughs.] I came with wife and I wasn't really ready for this 'cause my bed was a little bed, and I didn't have too many things that I needed, and I went to my dad's house. So that was the story of my getting married.

She [his daughter, Bethel] born in 1994. I think it was the time when the World Cup was being played here in the United States, the football soccer World Cup. I remember that was the day when Brazil was in the final against Italy and my wife was about giving birth and I was in the hospital waiting, but I was thinking of the football game also. I was in a hurry to see my daughter born, and I remember I couldn't resist. I left the hospital and I went home to see this football game. [Laughs.] And I thought, if it's a man, I'm going to call him Bebeto or Romario, one of those famous players' name, but it was a girl. She was born in the time I was watching the football game. [Laughs.] She born in Tegucigalpa, Honduras. And we came to Guatemala a little time after she was born on July 13th, '94. I brought them to Guatemala and I went to the *municipalidad* [city hall] of my town and I told them, "OK. Here is my daughter. She was born here." And they made an act and then she is Guatemalan [Laughs.] and she is Honduran also. [Laughs.] I don't know if this is going to get her in trouble. [Laughs.]

When I wasn't at home, my mother-in-law took care of my little girl. But when I was at home, I usually spend the whole day with my daughter—taking care of her, bathing her, changing clothes, giving her the meals, feeding her. I miss those times a lot. My daughter and me were pretty close, pretty close of course.

We started renting a house in Honduras and [my wife] started working, and we got in troubles 'cause sometimes I went out to some festivals and when I came back she wasn't at home. And she came from her job tired to sleep, and the other morning early go out. So we really started not having enough time together and we started having problems. And then we agreed that we needed a house and not to keep paying rent when we could invest that money in our house. And I think that was the time when this idea born. I was working hard. We had food. My daughter had what she needed. My wife had what she needed also, but I never had money enough to build a house. And in my country, we always hear of people who came back from United States with money, with car, with things and stories that this country you can make much more money than you do over there. Well, one day I decided to come here to try to make some things real—like my house, like a better level of life, to give my daughter better college.

My wife kind of pushed me. I remember that sometimes when we got in conversation she said, "If you don't go, I'll go."

Well, I said, "If she go, I can lose her. What about my daughter? I'm going to have to take care of her." But she didn't really mean that. What she wanted was me to come, so that impelled me to come over here.

By the time we decided that I was going to come here, then the problem was the money 'cause I needed to give the *coyote* [smuggler] about $1,000 over there and pay the rest here. So I started looking for money. I remember that I had a very good festival over there selling handicrafts. I made about $500 and a brother-in-law of mine who is working in a boat around the world, he lent me $800. So in total I had about $1,300 and from the morning to night I had the money.

I remember the day when I left from Tegucigalpa. It wasn't hard 'cause I think I didn't really believe that I was going to make the trip, I was going to get here. Maybe the bottom of my heart I didn't really want to. So, that last night, I just kissed my daughter, and early in the morning I kissed my wife and I took the bus to Guatemala, stayed a couple of days with my mother, told her about it and left home just with a bag, backpack with couple of pants and shirts. And let's go.

The next step was to gather with another lot of people who were going to make the same trip. We reunited in a hotel in Quetzaltenango and from there we came to the frontier line, to the border with Mexico in a little town lost in the mountains. And in the night, we crossed one mountain and in the morning next day we were already in Mexico, hidden of course.

The *coyote* was with us but not all the time. There are people who are called *guias* [guides]. They are kind of lower than the *coyotes,* so they are in charge of taking us through these paths and taking us to a certain place. And I saw the *coyote* in Guatemala. I saw the *coyote* in *México Distrito Federal* [Mexico City]. And I saw the *coyote* in Matamoros, *frontera* [border] between Mexico and United States. And I saw the *coyote* in Houston again, just short periods of time. I think he was flying from city to city.

When we crossed the frontier line between Guatemala and Mexico, we gathered with another lot of people. So, in total we were about 100. About 6:00 in the afternoon, we got in a gas truck, in the tank without gas. So this tank was locked. So supposedly this truck was transporting gasoline. I remember that we really had very, very less oxygen and we didn't have food, just bottles of water. Each one had two bottles of water and we were really close. We couldn't even move. And we had to make that trip 24 hours. A couple of people older, the older guys, were about dying in that truck 'cause no oxygen. Sometimes I think when the driver found police, immigration Mexican police, he had to lock the tank and police used to knock. "Somebody in there?" And we had to say nothing, remain completely silent. And those moments were when the tank was completely closed. So it was when the oxygen became less and less and less. And it was a tremendous heat inside of it. It was terrible. I think it was one of the hardest parts of that travel. On the top there is a kind of window and it was always open and the air was running inside. But when police showed up, so it's gotta be closed. Dark, completely dark.

There was a moment when the truck was caught by police and we didn't know what was going on outside. So we felt like this truck were deviated from its real way. And there was a moment when we didn't hear any more noise outside. And so we start to wondering what was going on. And it happened that the driver wasn't anymore in the truck and the truck was parked in somewhere. And that thing was locked. So it was when the panic caught us and oxygen started being less and less. And I don't know how, but thanks God, we made a hole on top of this tank and we tore, I don't know how, but we did, and we came out. No driver. It was a solitary place. Sometimes I think we could die over there and nobody had realized till it was too late.

From where this truck left us, was in Puebla. From Puebla to *Distrito*

Federal [Mexico City] we took a bus, five in each bus. And we went to a hotel in Mexico City. It was beautiful 'cause that hotel we had a bed, we had food, we had carpet and nice place to take a shower. We went to the central *camionera* [central bus station] in *México Distrito Federal* and we took a bus to Matamoros at the frontier. In Matamoros, we stayed about four days in a room, kind of this big [a small room], and a big patio. And this house was surrounded by a brick wall. The weather was hot. We didn't have almost food. And a lot of flies everywhere. Garbage. Just one pipe of water. One bathroom that it was broken. There were about 400 people crowded in that small place. Every day we expected our *coyote* to come and say, "OK, my people. Come on." The only thing I wanted was get out of there.

Some people thought they were going to die. They spoke about it. "Oh, this trip is getting so hard." I never talk of that. I had kind of security inside me that I was going to do well in this trip. We became close with so many people, of course, especially women. You know, women is kind of the weak sex. So we had to take care more of them. They were more sensitive, more fragile. Of course, we became very close one another.

Sometimes I thought of coming back. But what I thought of that was I already owed $1,300 and if I came back to home, how was I going to pay this? So, sometimes I doubt about it. Of course when I was in that house expecting for the *coyote* to come and say, "OK, let's go," and he never appeared, so I thought, "What the hell am I doing here? I would be better eating beans and corn in my country in my home with my mom." Yeah, sometimes that kind of thoughts came to my mind.

Since I was in this small town in the borderline between Mexico and Guatemala, I realized I was in the middle of a lot of people who needed to grab their faith of something, so I became kind of a leader. I started talking with a couple of these people saying, "We should pray. We should make a prayer for all of us. We should ask God for help." And I started like this with a couple of friends. And among these people came some people who were Protestants in Guatemala. These people is kind of people who pray all the day, believe in God, and all that kind of stuff. So since that point on, we used to pray every night, anywhere, even when we were in the desert, in the mountains, or in that big house.

And people gathered around and they said, "OK, Eli. Please, make a prayer for us." And I used to pray loud and they hear me and we asked God for help. And sometimes this was very helpful for a lot of us, especially the people who had already lost all kinds of hopes, or who saw

this trip was turning very hard. So we used to pray all the nights. And sometimes the *coyotes* got involved in these kind of things.

It wasn't a kind of a prayer that I already knew by heart. It's just spontaneous relating with the moment we were living and what we wanted. If we didn't have enough food, just asked God for support us.

Let me tell you that I have always believed in God, always, even when I didn't go to church, or when I don't believe very much in things that Bible says. But I think this is one of things that my father taught me: There is a God somewhere watching at you and he's gonna help you whenever you ask him for help. I believe in God, and if I had the opportunity to be a kind of guide for these people, I just did it. I think I had the courage to do this.

After that, they took us to the edge of the river and we crossed the river with kind of *neumático* [inner tube]. And we crossed the river at night, about 12:00 [midnight]. Actually, we found the Mexican army at the side of the river and they said, "Oh, where are you from?"

"Mexico."

"OK, where are you going?"

"Well, you know."

"We are not supposed to let you go."

"Well, what are you going to do with us?"

"You have some money?"

"Sure." So everybody gave them some money.

"OK, go." And they left us.

After we crossed the river we had a big, big walk, a long walk, about 12 hours. We landed in a kind of desert and we stay the whole day over there. It was the place when I told you we started getting these little leeches who sucks you. It was hard. I remember that we ran out of water and there was rainwater, but it was very dirty and it has little leeches, little bugs, and I said to myself, "I would first drink my own urine instead of drinking this water." And I did. I drank my urine. I urinated in a bottle and I drank it.

And all the guys, "What the hell are you doing?" But I was really thirsty. I didn't like the taste of my urine, [Laughs.] so next time we went to this water and we take a cloth and put it in the hole of the bottle and water went down kind of filter. And we drank this water and it's amazing that, at least not me, I didn't get any kind of infection in my stomach. The hot was very high, no food, and the leeches, a lot of them.

We had to lie, to sleep on the earth. So we slept there and next day they say, "OK, let's go to the edge of the road. A couple of trucks are going to stop and you have to jump in the truck and lie like this. Fifteen people each truck." These trucks were kind of high trucks with thick tires. You can see the truck, but you can't see the people 'cause all the people is lying inside the rear part of it. Not covered. Lying down the truck, the rear part of the truck. Some people had their elbows or their feet stuck with somebody else over. It was very uncomfortable. And we start coming to Houston. [Laughs.]

There were four trucks. Three of them made the trip up to Houston without problem, but the truck where I was going was caught by police. So I remember that we were praying silently inside of us to make this trip. And I remember I started looking at blue light which passes and I knew it was the police, and I get ready to jump out. And I had the feeling that these guys had dogs. [Laughs.] And I didn't know what I would do if a dog came towards me. Well, *coyotes* had already told us, "If you hear a siren and you see lights moving red, the driver is going to pull over and stop and you gotta jump out and run, wherever! Run, 'cause it's the police." And we actually did, we actually did. It was in a countryside road and we jumped out the truck and we run in a big field of, I don't know, maybe pineapples or something. None of us was caught by police, none of us. I'm a runner you know, I didn't have problems. [Laughs.] But there was this woman who was from El Salvador and she was making this trip with her husband. And this woman had her legs kind of, when you have your legs in one position for a long time it gets kind of asleep, cramps. She couldn't really run, but for some reason the police didn't caught her. And her husband was pulling her. We walked for about two hours and we gathered in some place.

After the police stopped the truck, I started thinking that we were lucky. They didn't catch us. I was the guy who the *guias,* one of them especially, trusted. "Eli, about two miles from here there is a gas station. Take this 50 bucks and go over there and buy some water and some

With his daughter, Bethel, Guatemala, 1998

stuff to eat. Be very careful." And I used to walk this distance from the kind of mountain where we were hidden. I went to the gas station and get some stuff and I came back. Whenever he wanted to make a decision, he said, "Hey, Eli. What do you think we should do?" I always helped him. Actually, they took about $400 out of the really price for my trip because this *guia* told the *coyote* that I was helping him.

We stayed there for about three or four days till another truck came for us. The *guias* went to a gas station and they talked by phone and they came. And we went to Houston. First we were in one hotel. They started asking, "Where are you going? Where are you going?" Some people were going to Nebraska, other people to California, others to New York. And I was the only guy who was coming to Chicago because my friend was waiting for me here to pay them. [Laughs.]

There was 15 people who were coming this road and we started the trip in the North American territory. And we left Houston about 7:00 at night and after 12 hours, about 7:00 or 8:00 the next day, the van where I was coming was stopped by immigration police. They saw the license plates. The license plates said Texas. And they thought, "Well, this van. Where is it going or what people go inside of it?" And they stop the truck and they started asking, "Papers. IDs." [Laughs.] None of us, of course. "OK, where are you from?"

"Mexico."

"Who is the President of Mexico? What is this? What is that?" Things that *coyotes* had already talked to us about it and we already knew what were the answers.

Since we start traveling in Guatemala they start talking about this kind of things. "Listen, guys, this is the most common question a *migra* [immigration officer] can ask you. And this is what you have to say. Please learn by heart an address somewhere from Mexico and tell them this is my address. This is my address. Where are you from?

20

Mexico, Mexico, Mexico! You gotta talk like Mexicans."

And also we were finding out how Mexicans say this, how Mexicans say that. Some people didn't do it. Let me tell you, some people didn't do it. But the weapon of these people was that they remain silent. They said, "We are Mexican." Nothing else. Then they can't say anything. Silence. "We are Mexican, Mexican." That's it. [Laughs.] I didn't remain silent. I answered. Most of these people who came this trip was peasant, some farmers, some not very cultured people. So I felt like I was kind of little bit upper.

They sent me to jail. I felt secure because I knew that I wasn't really making anything wrong. I was just trying to come here and work. And I knew my rights and I knew these people couldn't take advantage of me nor I wasn't supposed to answer strange questions or things like that. I knew that. And I was with the police. I took it easy. I said, "Well, it's OK. I'll go back to Mexico and try again." [Laughs.]

We had been already warned about this. This might happen and this is what you might do. So, I knew that if I was on the other side of the frontier line, what I had to do is just try again as many times as I needed. So after that, I never thought about going back to Guatemala. In jail was about 15 more guys, really convicts. They were waiting for complete 60 guys to put them in a plane and fly to Mexico. They gave us food—no bed, but food. I stayed there one day and next day, people was complete and they put handcuffs, the feet also, around our waist with a big chain as if we were criminals. They led us out to the plane. We flew about an hour and a half.

We flew to Laredo and they brought us to the bridge and they take off our handcuffs and said, "OK, go back to Mexico."

We crossed the bridge. Then, I called my coyote and I said, "Hey, they caught me. What should I do now?"

"OK, go back to Matamoros. In certain hotel, ask for this guy and he's gonna take care of you."

And actually, he did. I went back to Matamoros. I remet with this guy over there and I made the trip again. I stayed in the same house with another people of course, none of the guys who came with me, and crossed the river again. When I crossed the river, we started walking again. I got lost, me and other guy. We lost the rest of people. And I was alone in United States without money, without knowing what to do. And we said, "OK. You see that light over there? OK, this is Brownsville, the frontier line. That's Brownsville. Let's go over there." And we start walking. We came to this place. The other guy had some

money. We rent a room in one hotel and then he start calling some people he knew. And people came and pick us up. But this was really new people. I didn't know them at all. Nothing to do with the coyote who brought me from Guatemala.

But anyway, they were coyotes and they said, "Where you going?"
"Houston."
"You have money?"
"No, but I have a friend who can give you money."
"OK, give me your number."
"How much are you going to charge me?"
"$1,000."
"$1,000 from here to Houston?"
"Yes, $1,000. You want it or you can just leave?"
"No, I want it." I didn't know the city, didn't know anything. I was kind of scared. "OK, $1,000."
"You know what, $800 for you."
"OK, $800."

And again, crossing the desert, the truck, Houston again. When I was in Houston one more time, I talked with my friend and he said, "What happened?"
"Well, immigration caught the van."
"OK, take a bus. Take a bus."

The van was charging me $350 and the bus $100. But these coyotes said, "If you go in bus, police is stopping buses every city and asking for papers."

"Well, the guy who's paying my trip told me take a bus. I'm going to take a bus." And they took me to the bus station and I made more than 24 hours from Houston to here. Nobody asked me for papers. And I came here in September [1998].

I was pretty scared when I left Houston. I was sitting in my seat and whenever I saw lights outside the bus, blue lights or red lights, I was kind of, what can I say? It's this kind of feeling when you are very insecure, when you feel like if the bus jerks, [Laughs.] it's because somebody is gonna get in the bus and ask for papers. But as the traveling was going on, I started feeling more secure. Nobody asked me for papers. In the bus there were traveling another Mexican people and kind of shy I started talking to them, and getting confident. After five hours I didn't feel insecure anymore. We were stopping and people get in the bus, people get out and nothing. I got here in the morning, about 5:00 in the morning.

I didn't talk English at all. I remember some people tried to talk to me in the bus and, "I don't know what are you saying. *No sé lo que ustedes dicen. No entiendo nada inglés.*"

Well, in my country I heard of Chicago. Oh, Chicago—big buildings, big city, one of the biggest cities in the world. Wow, I felt very cool. And when I came to the bus station, I called my friend. He was to leave to work, but there was another guy who slept in this room and he said, "OK, I'm going to go for you and I'm going to have a blue handkerchief in my head and I'm going to have a black jacket. If you see me, talk to me." I didn't know him.

Some people had told me that here in Chicago there were immigration police always. I knew that they wear green coats, and when I was in the station I didn't see nobody in green. I behaved natural. I bought some food and I sat and I start eating. And I was eating when this guy came. He was of course very friendly. We are very good friends now. And he said, "OK, let's go." And he brought me here. And when we were coming from the station to here, he said, "You know what, Eli? I already have job for you."

"Where?"

"Where I work."

"Oh, beautiful. I already have job." [Laughs.]

"So, you wanna go today?"

"No, no. Today I gotta rest a little bit and eat." And I stayed the whole day alone here. And next day, I went to Charlie Trotter's restaurant and that was my first job. [Laughs.]

They said, "Oh, this is the best restaurant in Chicago." Actually, it wasn't a bad experience at all. I learned a lot over there. Wash dishes. That was my first job. And after three months, they take me to the polishing room where you have to wipe wine glasses and silverware. And after that, they started thinking of me as a busboy or running food. But always they kept me close to the dish machine. About one in the morning, I had to change my clothes and wear cook clothes, put a funny hat and go to the dish machine and help the guys to close the machine.

When this friend of mine took me over there, he warned me that I needed to go to 26th [Street], to Little Village, and get papers over there. Well, I said, "OK," and we went. He told me to take a couple of pictures and we went over there. When the car get in the parking lot, there were people signaling like this. And so I realized that these were the guys. They came close and, "Do you need an ID?"

"Yeah, how much?"

"$100."

And my friend said, "Last time I paid you $80."

"OK, $80. Give me the money, give me the pictures, come back in half an hour." And we stayed little bit over there walking around and then we came back. We had the papers. I always used my name. I haven't changed my name. I haven't changed my birthday. I don't know if it's good or it's wrong or I don't know. I think I'm not doing anything wrong, so I'm using my name. Since then, those have been the papers that I have showed to anywhere I had wanted to ask for a job.

I had been going to school about one year and I already knew some English, and I asked my manager, "I know some English. I don't wanna work anymore on the dish machine. I wanna do something else."

And he said, "OK." But these people were very exigent. The first time you take a plate to a table, they want you to do everything perfectly. And of course I was nervous and I did some things wrong 'cause I was a beginner. Because I served maybe in the wrong side. I have to be on the left, with the left hand, not put the elbow in the face of the customer. So they said, "Oh, no. You're not ready. You gotta wait more." I felt since that day, he got some kind of angry toward me and he started treating me bad for anything that I made in the restaurant. He laughed at me. One day he said, "No more Spanish in this restaurant. None of you guys." There were about five Mexicans. "None of you. I don't wanna hear Spanish in this restaurant."

And I said, "You know what? I know my rights. You are not supposed to forbid me to talk in our language 'cause sometimes when I have to communicate with these guys, I understand better in Spanish."

"Yeah, but this is the best restaurant in United States and I don't want customers to hear you speaking Spanish here."

I retort him kind of, "Fuck you!" 'cause I was angry. And things start going bad. And after that, I said, "Well, Chicago is a fuckin' big city. Why should I stay here all my time? There is a lot of restaurants in the downtown. Chicago is not only Charlie Trotter's." [My English teacher] helped me to write a resignation letter and I gave it to Charlie and to my manager, the guy who hired me, and said, "Thank you." They asked me for stay a couple more months. I didn't want and I left Charlie Trotter's and I start looking for another jobs and I realized that nowhere people have treated me like those guys treated me there, even when I was always trying to make things good, trying to achieve more knowledge and trying to perform better every day. It wasn't matter for them.

I have always liked education. As I have told you, I used to read a lot. And when I came here, when I start working as dishwasher over there, I got mad 'cause people talked to me in a slang language and I didn't know how to answer. And I didn't even know what they were saying to me. Maybe sometimes just looking at their faces I knew they were angry or saying something bad to me and I didn't know what was that. So, my friend told me, "I'm going to school. You wanna go to school?"

"Sure, I want to go to school." And I also heard that if you speak English, you will have better opportunities, you will be a busboy or this or that, earn more money working less hard. But when I went to Truman, there were no inscriptions [registrations]. So I was one month since I came from September to October, and then I start going to school in October. And I made the test. They send me to level 2 and I never left school since then. Those days when I was working at Charlie Trotter's, I worked from 5:00 [in the afternoon] to 3:00 or 4:00 in the morning, and Truman is far away from here. And I had to take the train. And several times I fell asleep on my desk in my English class. Those were really hard times. And all the money I got from my check, it was to pay my ticket. I wasn't making that lot of money at Charlie Trotter's. Several times I thought of getting two jobs and leave school, but I didn't. And I did not regret that 'cause at this time, I can choose what I want to work and what I wanna do.

I have always asked my friends, "Why do you think this government gives you the opportunity of studying for free? They are not stupid. They know that you don't have papers. What is the real reason? What is behind this opportunity? You think they are giving something without wanting anything else in change?" Yeah, it's surprising for me. Of course it is. I don't know. I have thought of maybe government do this because they want people well prepared to perform jobs 'cause they need workers maybe, or because it's a way of trying to discover smart people who can import something to North American society in the field of science or something else, art. I don't know. That's the kind of feelings that I have. But it's good for me 'cause it's for free. And I wonder why even when it's for free, many people don't go to school. 'Cause I know a lot of people who I work with, and they don't care about going to school. They don't care about culture maybe or...I don't know.

Since I am in Chicago, I haven't had a set schedule to talk with [my wife]. Lately, I have been talking to her every 15 days, couple of hours. She thinks I have changed a lot. She says, "Oh, I think you are more smart now. I think you are more mature. You see things different and I

With two friends from Truman College, Chicago, 2000

think I love you more." I love her, too.

In fact, two days ago I was talking with her by phone, and suddenly I made this question to her, "Dunia, how is the house going on?" And she said, "You know what? It already has the roof on it." Wow! And I got so happy. It's almost done. And it's a big house and it's a good house! And we start this house in May, about six months and it's already done. And then we started talking about what we had three years ago, how was our life and it's kind of incredible. It's almost done. This is the house that we are planning to rent. And we hope it's gonna be finished in January and then she will move to Guatemala if she don't get the visa. She's going to move to Guatemala and build another house over there and wait for me over there. This house is for rent, but it's a good house, though. I'm really happy. She's going to send me a video. She promised.

The last months I've been able to send $1,000 every 15 days, which is a good amount. I have talked with gringos and they say, "Whew, man! That's a lot of money!" [Laughs.] Sometimes I think it's not enough, but it's kind of a bless from God. I think sometimes life pay us back when we have to face certain things and came over them and make right the things, being fair, trying to be straight in everything. And I think this is the time to harvest 'cause I think my life haven't been easy, but now it's better.

When you are here, people over there thinks that here you find money so easy, maybe on the streets. You came here to make money easy, but that is not the true. You have to face several things and obstacles to make money. So I tell them the reality of things. It's not easy. You gotta be very focused. And you gotta know what you want. And of course, be fair, be honest, things I think I try to be sometimes.

You know what? I have friends who have been longer time than me. For any reason, they don't have too much. They haven't built houses or learned English, at least how to write. And in such a short time I have made things that most people don't do in this period of time. And I think I have some potential inside of me that I need to exploit more and more and more. And I have discovered this here in United States.

But what I would like the most is that my wife and my daughter could come here. She has been trying to, but they have denied the visa to her. So the only thing I say to her is, "Keep trying, keep trying." If you really want something, I have learned that here, if you want something you have to draw it in your mind. You have to think frequent. You have to tell the people. You gotta write it down and someday it's going to be real, you are going to reach that. So she's going to try this day again and I hope this time they do give her the visa.

I feel like my daughter haven't seen me in two years and I think the image of father for her is maybe her uncle or her grandpa. I don't really know what is going to happen when I go back and I will ask her for some respect or to do something this way or that way. I don't know how she is going to react. Maybe she has an idea of her daddy, but I don't know. We talk about how is the school, what have she learned. She used to read some things to me. She is learning English. She knows that I am studying English, too. And she says, "Papi, I'm going to read something in English." And then she starts [Sings.], "I have a headache.

His daughter, Bethel, Guatemala, 2000

I have a headache right now." Small things like that. And sometimes she says, "Big hat."

And I say, "What is that in Spanish?" And then I try to teach her some things.

And then she always said, "Papi, send me a doll."

"What kind of doll?"

"A Barbie, papi. I want a Barbie." [Laughs.] You know, things like that. I think my wife is playing a big role in this thing 'cause she is always talking to her about her daddy. And they are waiting for me, and that her daddy loves her and that stuff.

If I think of my daughter, try to understand this. I would like her to study here but to live over there because I love my culture, I love my country, I love how parents grow up their children over there. When you are here and you see that parents are always working or somewhere else, and several times you have to take your children to other people to take care of them. I think that sense of family and parenthood and all that, it's kind of secondary. But in our country, whew, since a child is born and starts breast-feeding and is always with their parents and everything. I think the education of childrens is better in my country 'cause that sense of family and respect and all that stuff.

If I think of my plans when I came here, if I think of the things that I want to do, then time gets shorter. And when I think that I want to be back with them, then time gets longer. So there are not really special days. Moments, moments. Maybe at night when I go to bed and I start wishing my wife to be beside me, and my daughter, read her a tale, those are the hardest times.

This is America. America is for Americans and for anybody else, why not? As I came to this country, you are always waving the flag of liberty and democracy and human rights and all that stuff [Laughs.] and sometimes it's kind of contradictory because they are kind of discriminating us in certain way. 'Cause if you live in Europe, you don't have a problem to get your visa, do you? I don't think so. But why us? I went to the embassy in my country and my wife's been trying and no. You have to be rich, wealthy to come here.

I feel like arrogant when U.S.A. people say, "I'm American." So if they are American, where I am from? I'm American, too, even if I don't have white skin or golden hair. So it's not my country. Definitely it's not my country, but it's my continent and I'm American. And I feel like I should have an opportunity to be legal here. Why not?

I know the truth is besides of me. The truth is with me. The truth is I'm an honest guy. My only sin is that I don't have papers or that I don't have permission to work here, but people in places where I have worked have a very good impression of me. And I'm sure they would like me to be a real citizen to keep working over there in those places. People like how I work. I haven't had problems with police. I'm paying my taxes. My only sin is that I don't have papers. And sometimes I think that if United States hadn't played part in this kind of broken democracy in Guatemala— because the CIA was involved in this—life would be better and a lot different in my country, if they hadn't. They kicked out our president, Jacobo Arbenz, and they put somebody else to work in order to keep U.S.A. interests over there. And I think sometimes they are guilty in part of this lot of people coming here and me staying here, too. They had the power and they got their nose over there and that is part of the subdevelopment of my country. Things would be better maybe.

Well, if we talk in being a citizen in the sense of having the same opportunities of people who was born here have, yes I do [want to be a citizen], but Guatemala is my country. I love it and I'm proud of born over there and I wouldn't change my nationality. That's for sure.

I actually don't have too many friends here. Actually, my circle of friends is really small, mostly guys from Guatemala and maybe a couple of Mexicans. But I think that people here is kind of not willing to make a relationship, to make friends with. Well, they say they are friends, but they truly aren't. People is, and sometimes I do to, people is focused on reaching his goals—who has more money, who has better job, who has better cars, who has the world in their hands. Really honest people, a few. I don't feel like having a lot of friends here.

Sometimes I behave as people do, too, but I'm always open to new friendships. I think this society have taught me to be very careful and kind of doubting when somebody wants to be my friend, like somebody always wants to get something from you. It's a kind of feeling you know. It's really different than in my country.

My friends always ask me when I am going to go back. I always tell them, "Three years. I came to stay here three years and then I'll go back, whether I build my house or I do not." But [Laughs.] wow, these two years here have changed me in such a way that sometimes I get scared 'cause I don't think I want to go back anymore. Several things like how much I'm going to earn over there, what am I going to live from there. I don't think I'm going to fit in that society again. I have my plans also. I think if I go back, I'm going to keep studying, go to university, get a better job. And sometimes I think if I save some money, I'm going to have a good capital to invest in this kind of stuff, and maybe have two or three stalls in two or three different places at the same time.

This is really the country of opportunities. I think everything is possible here. You can do whatever you want here. I mean in the right ways. If you wanna study, you can study. Even if you don't have papers, you can study. Who doesn't work here is because he doesn't want 'cause there is job for everybody. Sources of information and everything is easy to find here, so it's easy to grow up here intellectually and culturally.

I am happy. I'm very happy because I'm reaching my goals. I feel like I can't wait to go back home. And I'm going to go back with my mind broadened and knowing a little bit of another language, which would help me over there. And that's it. I hope [I won't come back here]. I hope no. But if I need to, I will. I will. I will know how are things here and I will have many doors open. I will have job. Sure, if I need to, I will.

| 25

ELI STILL LIVES IN CHICAGO and works two jobs as a bartender and food runner. He has built a house for his family in Guatemala and plans to return in 2004.

MY NAME IS # OVIDIU IUHAS *I remember exactly [I came]* **24TH MARCH, 1993.** *I'm 49 years old. I was born in 18 February, 1951.* **I'M EXACTLY FROM ROMANIA,** *my country.*

THIS IS MY COMPLETE NAME. The intellectuals from Transylvania, they give to their childrens these original Latin names, like Ovidiu Trian. Ovid was Latin poet and he was exiled in Romania. He has his books and everything in Constanza. Trajan was the Roman king from Italy. King Trajan. So, that's why. I feel not like poet. I feel little bit different than others. [Laughs.] Not smarter, but always I used to have other ideas. Like if you got this idea to get over there, maybe I got something strange. [Laughs.]

I was born in one small village in Satu Mare County that's located in northwest of Romania. We are border with Hungary. In that village I lived only till three or four age old. After that, because my parents, they were teachers, they was [moved] in other village. They put my father like director of that school and my mother was teacher. Because in that time, our communist country, you should go over there where they put you, not where you want to. My mother, she teach math and physics. My father teach Romanian language and history. But with the time, after 1960s, they teach just in the primary school.

I'm proud of them. They keep us close, very close. We were one really close family. That's usually not just in Romania I would say, because I was in Hungary, I was in Poland, I was in Czechoslovakia, and in Europe usually the family are very close. And I think this is very good.

He [my father] was very straight. He wasn't that strong to say he's very strong, but you feel he is strong. How I can tell you? In Romania is one saying: *Mina de fier in manusa de catifea.* I'm gonna try to translate this. This is "Iron hand in fine gloves." Very thin, very fine, very smooth. He was like this, you know. He never give you the impression he is dominate you or something like that, but you feel that. He was very good man.

They gave us good education and I learned a lot. Little bit I was my own teacher. *Autodidact,* in Romanian we say [self-taught]. I'm a little bit self-taught, but I take lot from my mom and from my father, like how to organize your life. I take from them to don't be lazy. This is

very important thing, and always, always to respect people. They teach us, "No matter color, no matter religion, everybody same in face of the God." This is very important for the life when you start.

After that, we moved in other village little bit closer to Satu Mare [town] because my father and my mother wants to give us one better education. And over there where they teached in those villages was only from [grades] one to seven. No higher in those villages. So, they tried to be closer or if it's possible exactly in Satu Mare town. And we moved in 1960 in Botiz village. It's like seven kilometers of Satu Mare. From over there, I went with the train. I made my school, every day. I wake up at 5:00 in the morning and I came back at home afternoon at 5:00 because the schedule for the train was made for the people who work in factory. So, I have to stay that long. I stayed in the class like two, three hours [after school]. So, from that time I went in the train station. Over there we were lot a kids who did this trip. And over there we sit, we read, or we play something.

Never I missed the train. This is interesting, never, believe me. So, this was like from 5th class [grade] till I was senior in high school. I'm not lying. But in springtime, so like from second part of April, I went with a bicycle. It was more healthy. Just my mom and my father, they were scared because in our country it's not that wide the street. They made everywhere economy over there. [Laughs.]

It's very interesting. I had one very good friend. He was very, very good in math. He's very smart guy. He wrote book. His father always,

I don't know why, when I went over there he didn't call me, "Come in Ovi," or something like that or, "Your friend." His father just he told me always, "It's coming, the American guy." I don't know why. I think because always I was, I told you, I was different in thinking and everything. I think I emanate little bit like freedom, independence. I was like a leader.

In that time we look here like here is the paradise. This idea because the freedom. It's lot of things to tell you. If you can imagine they didn't let us to listen Beatles music. That was the years when Beatles they just came, '60s. But we did this, too. Believe me! We did this, too. Sure! Kind of secret, because you cannot. We just make like some parties and we were over there and we listened Beatles. Was this *Radio Europa Libera, Vocea Americii* [Radio Free Europe, Voice of America]. This was in Romanian and they don't want us to listen to this post because this was against communism. But I'm gonna explain to you, this was like teenagers years. In our country to buy one blue jeans, was something amazing! Was around 400 lei, and in that time $1 was just 12 lei. So, it was very expensive. Was like around $30, one blue jeans. Oh, and even you cannot find everywhere. After that was the dollar shops. So, you can buy only for dollars. We looked in the windows like it was impossible. Because if you get in, they asking if you got dollars. If you got dollars, [they ask you], "From where you got?"

I remember when we were kids, when we were in the high school, first May was the labor day. So, we have to go in parade. We stay over there even though if it's raining or something like that and just in pants, T-shirt in white to make that parade. For five minutes you was in front of the tribune and after that, you have to stay over there one day long. This was amazing.

So after high school, I have to leave my town. I went in Timisoara for mechanical engineer. Over there I study, in one word, trains. Locomotives and wagons.

With friends from university, Romania, 1974

I like the way how we did the school in Romania. I cannot say I have something bad to tell about this, because I hope they teach us very good. We got courses, we got laboratories, and when you finish the school, after you take the exams, every year final exams, one month you have to go and work in one factory for what you are prepared. But you're not going to go by yourself. You go with all your class and with your teacher. Was one teacher who's responsible from our class, like here, counselor. We made practice here in Turnu Severin.

After I finished my college, I'm licensed in nonconventional vehicles, like trains, but with magnetic systemtation, like monorail. Not to drive it, to concept, to build it. In our country, there used to be regime. Everybody have to work. For everybody they find work, so everything was drive from Bucharest. Only if you were in first five in the college, you have the chance to choose where you wanna go. After that, everybody [go] where they put you. If you got good relations, if you have somebody close to the God, you got choice. [Laughs.] My situation was like in middle. Everybody choose, but you choose what they put in your face. So, from what I got in my face, I choose this place [Satu Mare].

They didn't put me in the locomotive part. So, they put me in where they made the mining transportation with the coal. Here, this factory was enough big, was around 10,000 people. I organized all the lines, everything. I feel like it's part of me when I'm thinking over there. I was proud. Not now, because everything fall down over there.

Never I'm gonna forget from my salary, when I start with my salary, was like 1,700 and something lei [per month]. It was enough good salary, in that time, in 1975, 1976. Over there [in dollar shops] you can see radio with cassette-a-phone. For us was something amazing to have one cassette-a-phone in that time. I just looked. I bought one Romanian radio because that was one half of my salary, 750. That radio now keeps my mom because that's from my first salary.

It's lot of things like this. TV, like color TV, I bought just couple years [before] I came in the United States. I just bought after revolution. During that years, you cannot buy one TV. In Satu Mare is one person who is the boss. Just that person make list and when is coming yours, stay in the line five years, six years to get one color TV. This was in 1985! With refrigerator, the same way, or with wash machines, not dishwasher. Here I saw first of all dishwasher in '93 when I came here.

We have to say the good things and the bad things, too. They gave to everybody house. Was hard to get exactly what you like, but the rent was like, how I can tell you. If you come here and you want to rent my apartment and I'm gonna tell you with four bedrooms, I'm gonna tell you 50 bucks per month. It was just symbolic. That wasn't expensive.

From '75 till '80 I stay in Satu Mare. In '81 I moved. I used to work in this factory in different divisions and in that time they built in Kriova one big automobile factory, Olsit. That was the name, with Citroën, if you know Citroën from France, and I used to work over there. I built like seven kilometers of conveyors in that factory with 100 people. And I was one year over there. Over there was not just Citroën. Was Italian people, was from Sweden, was from Germany. So, from everywhere they brought the machineries.

There was the minister of industries from Romania, and he knew me because he knew everybody. And he was asking me how many days I'm gonna build that conveyor. And he told me, "Hey, if you're gonna do this in three days, I send you to Paris for one week."

"OK. Let's go. Let's start the work!" [Laughs.] I did and he sent me. 1980 in May.

Starting from the airport, with everything I was impressed. I cannot tell you something specifically. I saw Tower Eiffel. Because I like tennis, I was around Roland Garros [the French Open tennis championships]. And in that time in May, always in May, is Roland Garros. But I just go and watch like I told you, like a window in our shops where they sell only for dollars. You just went and looked on the window. I saw Champs Elysées. I feel like I'm in other world. But after, you have comparation. So, that was the point of the communist system: to close all borders, to don't let you go out, to don't have comparations.

But I was that stupid. I came back! [Laughs.] It's unbelievable. And my big mistake was from Citroën. They proposed me to stay over there, to don't come back.

After I came home, but never I told nobody, just I feeled like you can live better. After that, I changed little bit my mind. Step by step

I changed my mind. Never I thought I'm gonna come back [to Paris] because maybe I haven't even courage to say, "No, stop." This was one. The second one, because I was hard worker. I had good salary over there. Maybe not just the courage. Because I had good salary. I had little bit better life than others, not much better, just you know, and I was somebody. Because in that town, everybody knew me, everybody, you know. So, maybe that's why.

In one time, was that good the life in Romania. Until 1980s you can say almost your salary and the power of what you can buy with that salary was almost like here. The system worked. But from 1980s start the bad, bad, bad things in our country. Start from that time. So, that's why I'm telling you in those years maybe I believe what they told me. I was that stupid because everything works. And let me tell you something. After 1980s they start to control and screw more, more, more.

I was like scared sometimes because I got relatives in the United States. It's from Olimpia [my wife]. It's her first cousins. My mother-in-law's sister is here in United States with four childrens. They came here in 1970. Her husband was born here. [I never communicated with them] because I was scared. I'm telling you the truth. I never tried to because I was scared [the government] gonna kick me out [of my job]. OK, [the government] knew that, I'm sure. They knew because her aunt came home many times and she was in my house and we were out and this and that, but always we were by Black Sea with her aunt. We were camping. After one day, next day, came somebody from security and was camping right by us. If you went somewhere, one restaurant, next table was somebody. So, always you were scared it's gonna happen something. I haven't enough courage to do this one. I just think about this because always they catch lot of peoples on the borders, and they came with them and cops, and they show us this and that, and I just don't wanna be between them because my son, you know, my wife. I thought about these things, too.

I remember before the revolution [1989] was a lot of French tourists in our village. And I feel like something is gonna happen and everybody thought this was the last congress for Ceaucescu. And everybody said, "He's not gonna finish in couple years." But everybody thought his son is gonna take his place.

I don't know what to tell you about Ceaucescu and about his wife. I was very happy when they killed him. But after that, I start and I thought, "No, they shouldn't kill him. Why? Nobody kill his president." And we lose a lot.

[Bogdan, my son] came home after the revolution in one day. In every class, in every book, first page was with Ceaucescu's picture. Every morning you have to start and sing the hymnos, the national anthem. It's not bad thing, but you have to look at him. Not right, not left. After they killed Ceaucescu, he came home and start crying. "What you crying?" Olimpia asked him.

"Oh, now from tomorrow if they killed him, when we gonna start to sing the hymnos, where we gonna look?"

And when I see this, and I saw what kind government comes, what kind future, I said in my mind, never I told them, "Hey, let me go to see how is the world." I saw my son and I said, "OK, it's time to think about him. Time to leave." Never I thought they start that brainwash, because it was that brainwash in my country. I cannot say never I thought they start with these kids, but never I thought my son is gonna be like that.

And in that time, was over there [my wife's] cousin's wife [from the United States], in Romania and I ask her, "Hey, I want one invitation from you, if you wanna make for me." She made one for me. I didn't told them what I'm thinking. And I got like two months vacation, so I could leave the factory for two months. And I got the right to take another unpaid month. And I told them, "OK, I'm gonna go in United States for three months. And I'm gonna come back." I wasn't sure I'm gonna stay here [in the United States]. I'm telling you from start. In my mind was like this, "Let's go to see if I can become legal." Because this was my point. I didn't want all the time to hide, to don't be legal. I knew maybe I'm gonna be illegal one year, or something like that, but I want to become legal. I want to see what is the ways. And I thought maybe after one month or two months I have to go back, and after that I'm gonna come prepared. Everything what they asking me I told them and they gave me the visa. I came by myself. They gave me six months here.

Before I came here, I left the factory with contracts for these 800 people till October. I left them covered for 10 months. So they got work. From here I paid every month around $400 or $500 in telephone. I ask them, "Hey, how you stay with that? How you stay?" I call them over there. And after that, you know in one morning I told to my wife, "Hey, maybe I'm gonna stay six months."

She told me, "Hey, I don't wanna get you mad, but they was waiting exactly when is finished your legal vacation and they change you." I didn't knew exactly how to get this. They change me! Why? Because I gave them 10 months work? I gave them bread!

With coworkers, Romania, 1987

And I stay and I said, "OK." I called her after two days and I told her, "OK, you know what. I don't know if I'm gonna come home or not, but I'm gonna stay here six months, how many months they gave me." And in this time, I start to ask people how I can become legal.

And her cousin told me, "Hey, I have here in Wheaton one lawyer. If you wanna talk to him you have to pay him." He was very nice guy. And I went to the lawyer. I told him what's my situation, my wishes and he told me exactly what I have to do. I didn't know how important here is in United States the lawyer. [Laughs.] So, I take lawyer. And I was glad.

He told me, "If you find somebody to sponsor you, because you are educated people and I think United States needs educated people."

"OK."

When I came here, I borrowed $1,000 to pay my ticket from Romania here and I got in my pocket like $300. I lived in one basement on Drake Street. I got here lot of friends, lot of workers who used to work for me over there. Over there I went one day with one to work, another day with other one. He paid me 50 bucks per day. So, I worked sometimes for $3 per hour, $4. You know, I did different things. Garbage first. I broke walls and I take out all that garbage in containers. Like first three months only this I did. I prepared myself. This I told you, I was like self-teacher. And always I prepared myself. And I knew one thing: It's not shame to work, and I know what I can do.

And one day, I went to Lake Shore Drive. So, I was in my off day. [Laughs.] I saw this big building, nice building. They doing remodeling over there. Now, I knew to do plumbing. Electric I knew from my country and little bit plumbing. Over there I met a Romanian guy. I knew him from the church. I saw him outside. And when I saw him outside, he didn't saw me. He went in. I just run. I went in the lobby. I want to see him. I was like lost in lobby. And somebody asked me, "Could I help you?" Or something like that.

I just played like I don't know [Laughs.] and I went out. And I stay out. I said, "OK, he's gonna come back at lunch or something." So, I was decided to stay over there whole day. And then like 20 minutes, he came back to take something again from outside and I stop him. And I ask him [about a job].

[He said], "Let me ask my boss."

This was my chance and I felt like this is my chance in my life. I don't know why. Something told me, "This is gonna be your chance. Play your card." You know what, I get these feelings.

His boss said, "OK, come from tomorrow."

I start from tomorrow. He likes me. I was serious over there. I did, I think, good job. First of all I did remodeling, plaster, painting, this and that. And in one afternoon, it broke one pipe. Hot water in one apartment. I knew from where I have to turn off the waters. I went over there. I didn't wait. They page everybody. I stop the water. I told him, "Hey, I know to do." But my English was that bad, he didn't understood me. And I just bring his hand and I let him know. I went upstairs. I turn off the pipe. I cut the pipe until the engineer come, but was fixed.

And he told me, "Hey, you wanna work for me?" Because in that time I didn't work exactly for him. I worked for second hand, for somebody else.

I told him, "Yes." But I told him, "You wanna help me?"

And he said, "Let me know what you want."

With his son, Bogdan, Romania, 1987

I told him, "Look here, I'm this. I don't wanna tell you I was this in my country. Maybe you're not gonna like me. You're gonna say, 'If you were director, how you gonna work?' No." I told him, "I was top and down and I can do this." And I start the work. He start the papers with me. So, now I start to become legal. To sponsor me.

I start to feel good. Until that time I feeled I'm the last person in the world, but never I gave up. I'm telling you, I'm that kind guy. If I have one *eşec* [failure], that don't make me to stop. No, that encourage me more. And these months was very good for me and my life. That encourage me. And now I got that courage to tell you even though if my English is not that good, I can do more for me and for this country.

I didn't tell her [my wife]. Just always when I call her, "When you gonna come?"

"In Christmas time I'm gonna be home."

In Christmas time, "It's Christmas time. You're not home. You promised me. When you gonna come?"

"I'm gonna come by Easter."

So from Easter to Christmas, like three years, I had to make this joke.

"What's your plans?"

I don't wanna tell her in the phone because I knew over there they [the government] listened. So I just let the people from over there think I'm gonna come back, just I'm staying to make some money. In my mind, no, never was to go back. Now was fixed exactly all my steps.

In the phone sometimes was only fight. But I told her, "If you wanna trust me, it's OK. It's gonna be OK. Just patience, please patience." [My son] cried always. He couldn't talk with me on the phone because start crying always. He wants me back. And only to him, I told him because I couldn't keep this, "In one day, you're gonna be here with your father."

My wife told me, "He needs you. You have to come home. You have to decide what you gonna do."

Now I was very close with my papers and I told her, "Please don't tell him nothing because you know the kids, how they are. I don't want nobody knows I'm doing my papers." Because is lot of bad people, you know. Who knows what could happen? Maybe they can do for them something.

So, I told her because now was very more, more crying. Now she start crying. And I told her, "Hey, I sent to you guys enough money to can have one very decent life over there."

"Not the money! I don't need any more money! I need you!"

"OK," I told, "I need you guys, too. But in the life to do something," I told them, "you have to sacrifice. Now, this is our sacrifice. If this is gonna work, we gonna be very happy together." And we are. Believe me, trust me, we are very happy here.

I don't blame her, but I told her in meantime, "I can think about this, too. So, don't think about this. Let's think about other things. Read one book, do something, go out." Because, you know, if you start to think about this, it becomes the jealousy. And when this is come, this is like, everything is down.

Anyway, in 1994, December, I should have the paper. Because I start with visa H1-B, that's work visa they giving you for three years. And I thought, "OK, I'm gonna start with this visa." And when you got this visa, you can bring your family here. So, when they are here I can start to apply for green card. And before Christmas, I sent everything to be over there [in Romania] for 1st December. And exactly in 1st December, because it's Bogdan's birthday, exactly in 1st December they knock by the door and one big bag from United States. You think what that means over there.

Now, they got my package. Everybody was very happy. I was unhappy, but I didn't told her why. Because my lawyer called me and he told me, "I don't know for what reason they cancelled your papers."

"Who?"

"Your owner!"

In that day, I felt like everything, all this fell down. We going down with the building, with everything. Just now I realize I could make one heart attack or something like that, because never I was that desirous and I didn't get, [and I was] disappointed. Never I was in my life that. Never I felt that one. Eight [in the] evening till 4:00 in the morning. Was raining. I was on the street. I was in one bar. I drink one beer. I came out. I wasn't drunk, you know, because I couldn't drink. Just I wanted to stay somewhere. Till 4:00 in the morning. Four o'clock in the morning I came to building. I couldn't sleep.

Next day, the owner saw me. "Hey." I didn't work. Just I stay over

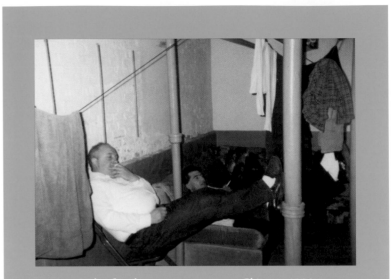

In his first basement apartment, Chicago, 1993

there. And he asked the other guy, "Ovi's not working."

"No, he has something."

"No, I'm not working." And he wants to talk with me. OK, I went over there. I just ask him, "What's the reasons? What I did?" Because I thought I did something wrong.

And he get mad at me. He just told me, "Don't ask me. Don't ask me. Ask my brother."

I talk with his son, because his son is the guy who responsible directly of us. And I told to his son my history little bit and I told him, "No, this is from outside. Somebody told you guys something. I know is lot of bad people, they don't want this and that."

And his son told me, "You know what they told us? If you gonna get your family here, you gonna ask us to support you this and this." Because if somebody sponsor you, they support everything. That's the law.

"No," I told them, "No. If you want I can work for you guys one year without money. Just bring my family here. You don't know how honest I can be."

And he talked with them and the next week, my lawyer called me, "Hey, they want to do again."

But now I waste time. I waste one year because you need to start again with immigration. So, we start again. And in '95, in May, the lawyer told me, "Hey, you have to go out of the country to put your H1-B visa by one embassy, don't matter where." He told me, "You can go home."

"No, I'm not gonna go home," I told him. "I'm gonna go here somewhere. I'm not sure if I'm going home and coming back."

So, I was in El Paso. It's El Paso in United States and the other side is Juárez [Mexico]. Over there is United States embassy. In the morning, I pass with one taxi the border, and I walk from over there. Over there I got one other interview. I get the visa only in afternoon, that big was the line. And when I got that in my passport, I came to El Paso. I came back around 5:00. I took hotel in United States part. I took a shower. I ordered dinner. I ordered two glass of beer, but never I drink those. Only one, maybe. That one I didn't finish. That tired I was. Almost I didn't touch the dinner, too. I was that happy, that tired. I was that happy, you know. Now, I was like opposite like that time when I was mad. Now like all this world was mine.

And after that, next day, when I came back in the airplane, now I made my future plans to get them here. Bogdan finished eight grades over there in this time. In my country, always when you finish the eight grades and you have to go in the high school, you have to take one test.

With his wife, Olimpia, and son, Bogdan, on the day of their arrival, Chicago, 1995

If you don't take that test, you cannot go in the high school. I came home. I called them. I told to my wife, "Look, here. I got my visa." And next day Bogdan had the test. And I told her, "Don't tell him nothing this evening. Please don't tell him nothing. Can you keep or not?" She kept. And next day in afternoon when he came out from the test, he was exhausted. Those tests are around four or five hours and you cannot come out. When he came out, he was like eleventh in the school. So, I was proud.

So, he did the test and she told him, "You know what, Bogdan? You're not gonna use this test, never from now. You don't need, but your father wants to see where you are, what you did. And we gonna go in United States to your father."

She told me, "I was scared he's gonna have something, because he couldn't say nothing. I saw his face is very happy, but he couldn't say nothing." He got white and she was scared. He was that excited.

They put the visa and they came in August. 8 August, '95. I'm again like emotion to tell you. Never, I can't imagine how I'm gonna meet them, how it's gonna be after three years. She told me, "Yeah, Bogdan is taller than you."

I never want to believe that. Yeah, he start to be taller because I let him. He played basketball over there. So, the sport helps.

And when land, because it shows the Bucharest plane is landed, I start to cry. Just I start. So, I went to the toilet. I washed my face because I don't want to be like this. And Bogdan, he doesn't have patience. Was the security guy, everybody, they didn't can [couldn't] keep him. Because I told him, I knew he's gonna do this, and I told him in the telephone, "Don't make me to go in the jail for you or something like that because it's border. You have to stay in the line to put your visa and everything. After you got that one, leave over there all your packages, you can come and see me. But until that time, you have to stay over there." So, he left all the packages with his mom. Everything. And he just came to me running! And you know, it's something weird when somebody runs in the airport. And he came by me. When they saw, they start laughing, everybody over there. [Laughs.] Was very, very emotional.

Was very hard with them in first three months. It's unbelievable. I knew that and I was prepared for this. I got lot of patience.

They teach us over there, "Hey, in America, it's not safe life. Over there they killing you on the street. And you cannot live like safe. Over there nobody talk with you." We had that bad image, not just from

America, from all capitalist countries. That kind image they make for us. And Olimpia told me, "Hey, here people are very friendly!"

[One day] I [asked] her, "What's your problem?"

"I miss my mom."

"So, you stayed with your mom until now, you don't miss me?"

"No, I'm with you."

I told her, "All the time you gonna miss something because in life it's that thing. You have to make one sacrifice if you wanna live better."

In the school, everybody teases him [Bogdan]. He is good kid. He was quiet. And when they see one is quiet, they start everybody to make joke. And he came home every day, "I don't understand nothing in this class. I don't understand. I can't conversate. The kids are laughing me. Give me back the ticket. I wanna go back. I wanna go back."

And then one day I gave him advice. I told him, "You're not gonna go back. Please wake up!" So, that was the last one. And I told him, "Look here, I'm gonna take out from the school and I'm gonna pay somebody to teach you English."

"No, I wanna go in school. I'm gonna learn over there."

"So decide, my man."

He graduated from St. Patrick High School. I like that education and how they care about the childrens. I like and I would recommend for more people that school.

He first of all wants to do lawyer. Little bit I disagreed this. I don't know why. Maybe because always I'm technical mind. Maybe that's why. I don't want to be strong with him to tell him, "No, you have to go over there, not here." Just I start to talk with him and to drive him a little bit in this way. And I know Bogdan. He's not the guy like me to stay in one factory and work, work, work. He likes little bit more freedom. I told him, "Just take computer science or computer information or something like this." One other reason why I told him this to take because I think in computer information or computer science, he's gonna have more opportunities for jobs.

Now, he miss, I'm sure, he miss his buddies in school. He miss lot. And I let him times and times to call his friends. And he was home two times, and Olimpia. I was just in '96, two weeks when I was home to see how is everything. I'm gonna tell you. It was something. When I landed with the plane, I start to cry again. I don't want it, but just I start to. I was very happy. I met my family, my friends. And everybody told me, "Hey, you didn't change in America."

"What you guys thinking about? What America have to change me?

With his wife, Olimpia, and son, Bogdam, Chicago, 2002

Why I have to change over there? Because it's life over there, too, like here. Just is better life." It's our mentality.

I was only two weeks, not more. When I came back, believe me, I felt like here I was born, not over there. And I want to come back. And I told to my mom before I came last night, I told her, "Look here, I don't wanna hurt you."

Because she was asking me, "You guys, you wanna stay over there all your life?"

I told her, "I don't wanna hurt you, but my feeling is, not just my feeling, I'm sure I'm gonna stay all the rest of my life." Maybe this, don't need to tell her, but I told her. Always I was open with my mom. I told her, "Look here. I feel like I belong from that world, not from this one. I'm sorry."

She just told me, "It's OK. Just don't forget your country."

I told her, "I'm not gonna forget." And I explain to her, "Look here. It's like one children have two moms."

"Cannot have two moms."

I told her, "Yes. Sometimes yes. Sometimes yes. I'm not gonna forget my mom or my country. But now I got one other mom over there. It's my country, United States, now."

And just this year she could understand what I told her because in

34

this year she was here three months, and she told me, "Now I can understand you." Now I feel like she's not hurt if she's understanding me.

Look here, I was in Detroit. I was in Cleveland. I wasn't in that many places because I work a lot. I was by Niagara Falls. All the time when I came back, when I entered, I feel like this is my life and I feel Chicago is [my home]. I cannot explain. I cannot.

If it's gonna be possible, I'm not gonna renounce my Romanian citizen because, you know what, how I told you, it's two moms. I'm not talking about what I hate. I hate what happens over there, believe me. I hate what happens because the people, they are so good people, Romanian people. I'm telling you. In 1992, I was in Bucharest. I got one meeting with some German company. And after the meeting, I invite them to restaurant. They were my guest. And one German guy he told, "You know, Ovi. You Romanians, you are very, very nice people. And when the God made Romanians, he was in very good mood. He gave you intelligence, everything, everything. But when he placed your country, he was in very bad mood." [Laughs.]

And here is very good, this saying like, "This is rich country with rich people." Not like in my country, "Rich country with poor people."

What I like here, the laws. The laws are made to work. In my country the laws are made to don't work. [Laughs.] This is very important. And from over there starts all this bullshit, all these things what happens over there. Yes, here maybe is some corruption, too, because hey, where people works, it's human thing, but I told you the law it works here.

Now, we bought this house. I rehabbed a lot and I improved a lot in this house. And I spend a lot of money here. So, I have to make this house to look like I want. This is one. So, for this, I have now to work. I don't have too much time for schools. Bogdan is doing like part-time in my company, but his friend found one other job for him downtown in some Internet company. And I like if he's gonna go over there because now he's gonna be in his field. So, now I want to see what is gonna happen with Olimpia because she is very talented in these things like drawing, but artistic, not technical. So, she's taking now in Wright College every Thursday like flower designers. She has her school from Romania like in clothes, dress designers. She's gonna take one other class in Christmas decoration after this. She bought from stores the little things and she made the wreaths and all that decoration and everything. And everybody says like it's professional hand. So, I want to see where she's gonna find one place. This I want. And after she's gonna be in her [path], I want to do computer class first. Yes, this. Maybe in parallel with Olimpia I'm gonna do computer class. So, I want to improve better my English. This is other thing.

When I'm talking with somebody and I'm making lot of mistakes, in that time I'm feeling like I'm that small. Like with you, I got more courage and maybe I'm not making that much mistakes like when I speak with somebody I don't know. In that time, always I concentrate to don't make mistake and I'm making more, I'm sure. And you know when I'm making more mistakes? When I'm very tired. I saw that. Sometimes I speak like in my first month English here when I'm very tired. But otherwise, I can feel like American. Why not? Hey, I'm working here. I'm doing all my things like one American. I respect all these laws and I follow the laws. Why I shouldn't feel like American? I have to work less so I'm gonna have more time to spend for my education. And for sure I don't want to stay in this level, if the God helps. I'm gonna help myself, but you need little lucky. Inspiration and perspiration. I got a lot of plans. And my dream is not just this. To go around the world. To see the world. To see people. To see their habits. Maybe in one day I'm gonna write one book. I got a lot of ideas about this.

OVIDIU LIVES IN CHICAGO and has bought another building. He continues to work as a building superintendent.

MY NAME IS PILAR LANDA
My husband is
CARLOS DOMÍNGUEZ I COME FROM CUBA
and I came three years and a half ago on **JUNE 27, 1995.** *I am 35 years old.*

WE OWNED A HOUSE. It was nice because we have our own backyard and in both sides and in the back of our house was a lot of trees, bananas. It was very quiet house. Then in front of our house was just land, empty, that the children used to play baseball or play with a kite. Next to our house and in the back, my father was the one that planted bananas, and many other fruits. In the back we had a backyard where my dad had pigs. He made a small house for pigs. We have goats, chicken, doves. I have a hamster. We have a dog, a cat. Then it was very, very nice because I saw how the animals are. When I was small, I drink goat milk. If I was bored, sometime I went and sit outside with bananas or avocados. It was very like child life.

At the beginning of the revolution and still continue, we have like booklet where we only can buy certain quantity of food, and then this is the reason we have animals and we have vegetable and fruit because they didn't give us everything that we need. The animals, too, we eat at home. That means we have plenty of meat beside the meat the government gives us.

My father, before revolution, he used to sell hams. He was private then. He sell ham to the store. He buy in a big quantity and he sell to small stores. Then he owned a car and he start working as a taxi driver with his own car. After the revolution, then of course not any private business was allowed. To be a taxi [driver], it was part of the government too. Then he start working in an office as a clerk taking care of the taxi drivers.

My father was a man that he didn't use to talk too much. Very, very hard worker. With 14 or 16 years old he came to Havana alone, only with just a little bit of clothes and that's it, and he started working in Havana. First of all, he said he worked like in a pharmacy delivering medicine. Then later in a restaurant he delivered the food to the people. Later he start working in restaurants and then he make his own business. Before the revolution he already had his car, his own house, money in the bank, and some business. He had a cafeteria near the beach with another friend. It was amazing.

I always was very close to my dad. I remember when I was child, when he came to home every day, I only listen the car is coming. The dog say me that he is coming. Then I run to his bed. I took the slippers. He came home. He sit down. I took off the shoes, the socks, and I put the slipper every day. And when the gray hair start here in eyebrow, I took out. [Laughs.] I sit in his lap and I took out. [Laughs.] I don't know why I always was very, very close to my dad. My mom, she never worked. She used to read a lot. She's life was read.
CARLOS: Reading for her is a disease! [Laughs.]
PILAR: All her bedroom, the books are from the floor to the ceiling. All four walls. She read about everything: politics, science, history, anything. She only finished 6th grade, the same as my dad, but she loved read. I remember after my parents' divorce, of course we were very, very poor. The money she earned was just a little to survive. But the only thing she bought for herself was every two weeks, she went to the store and she bought books. She didn't bought clothes nor shoes, nothing.

The only thing she liked to buy for herself was books.

CARLOS: This is very interesting because [her mother] is the only person I found in my life that did what I'm about to say. You know everybody in Cuba has to study Marxist philosophy, but everybody hate that philosophy. But you know, it's an obligation. And her mother, I remember she read a philosophy Marxist dictionary. Nobody in Cuba except her have done that! Only her, believe me! No philosophy teachers, no philosophers. Nobody have read the whole dictionary and she did.

PILAR: After seven years old when my parents, they divorced, then everything changed totally. We didn't have more animals. We didn't take care of any plants. My mom had to start working. [Before the divorce] we have everything. We have plenty of food, animals, fruit, everything. We had money in the bank. Then we didn't worry about the money. But when my father left, he gave us our monthly payment, but it is not enough. What the father have to pay, I'm sorry, this is not enough for living. Then my mother doesn't earn a lot. Then we didn't have animals. We didn't have fruit or vegetables and we have to survive with this money to clothes, to eat. Then what happened. Before, my mother was always at home and everybody in our neighbor respect my father. But just as my father left, near is another neighbor not so good, and they start during the day coming to our backyard and they steal all animals. They steal everything from the backyard. Then we couldn't take care. And they steal bananas, and they steal the animals, the doves. Everything they steal.

CARLOS: Bottom line is, there wasn't a man who could take care of the land, you know. So sometimes they take advantage.

PILAR: Just from seven years, I lost my naive as a child. Then I opened my eyes and I saw the reality. From there I learned that I have to be somebody because no matter how you get married, it doesn't mean it's forever. It can change, and then you as an individual have to be somebody and be able to survive for yourself. This is what I learn from there. [Laughs.]

And my mother, she instill us to study. She said, "You have to be somebody. The most important is to study."

And I remember I said, "OK." My philosophy all my life was: No matter how poor or no matter how I am dressing, the way people have to respect me is not what I am wearing. Is because my mind and my intelligence. And this is the way I was all the life. I have to prove that I am very good student, I am intelligent and they going to love me and receive me. Because when you are young, the people look only how you

Moscow, 1986

looking, how beautiful. I never was beautiful woman. I was just a normal person. And I didn't dress so fancy. Then I didn't look so nice. But the only way all my friends respect me, accept me in the group, is because I was smart and they need me because of my mind.

I think I was very mature for my age because with nine years old, I start washing my clothes, cleaning the house, taking responsibility, buying food. For example, with 15 years old I went to buy the food we should receive by the government and the meat. And I remember we had at home a balance [scale] and I went to the store and say, "You know, I know how many pounds by [per] person I should have right to have." Because they used to steal you some ounce. They sell in the black market. And I remember with 15 years old, they look at me. And I went up and I look in the balance, "This is not right. Give me all the ounces exactly what my family should have!" I was fighting. And when they gave me potato, "No, this potato is no good. Change it!" But I have to fight for my right and for my family. Since 15, 16, my mother and my family listen to me. I really fight what I thought. Yes, I was very, very, very strong.

What I really wanted to study, I remember I was in 10th grade, I wanted to be captain of the ship. And my mother went where she's supposed to ask about this question. And I remember she went there

and they said, "She have to wait until she finish high school." In Cuba is only one woman captain and she studied in Poland. I think because my character, I wanted to be a boss. And a boss of men! [Laughs.]
CARLOS: She wants to be my boss!
PILAR: [I didn't become a captain], because when I finished high school in Cuba, you can't say, "I want to study this. I will take." No. You have to choose from this that they gave you. I remember that time I was the number six, the sixth best student in the whole school.

The truth is the career I took, my sister-in-law was the one that took it. I wanted to be engineer. The same way my brother and my sister. Then I want anything that is engineer. Really, when I finish high school, I didn't know what the careers, many of them is about. I didn't have idea. I just wanted to be engineer, that's it. I doesn't want nothing about reading, history, nothing. Have to be engineer. Then we went there and we look at the list and my sister, "OK, this looks nice, interesting." And I took it. Train constructor or train maker, the one that designs the whole locomotive. This is my bachelor's [degree]. Then I study one year in Cuba, the Russian language, and then five years in Russia.

At the beginning it was hard because I only studied [Russian] one year in Cuba. Then of course when I get there [to Russia], I was as an Indian [Laughs.] talking with my hands and my face. They didn't know a word in Spanish. None of the teachers. I remember the first year they decide to put all foreign students in the same classroom, not with Russian students. I remember, I wrote what I listen. Later, don't ask me what I wrote. It was a nightmare. I said, "What they are talking about? Oh, my God, how I'm going to pass this test?" But I don't know. When nobody understand your language, you are forced to learn, and then I did. Then in the second year, I already went to the regular classroom with Russian students.

I was in Moscow. For me it was the first time I saw the snow in my life. Only, I wasn't prepared because all the clothes I brought from Cuba was for summer. Then I remember one night I was walking along looking at the store, just window shopping, and the snow start falling in November. And I said, "Oh, how wonderful." But it was so cold! [Laughs.] Because it took me several months until I got boots and a good coat. It was very nice experience, very, very nice because in my opinion, every culture, every country has something interesting, something bad, and something nice. But I learned many things good from them. And I really love, I really love. I enjoyed it. I was very, very young and I only have to study.

When I come back from Cuba to Russia after my third year by ship, Carlos was there on the ship to Russia, too. We never met. He was already a professor teacher at the university. He went there because at that time they use some teacher from Cuba for two years. They serve in the minister of education for Cuban interest. That means they take care of the students, to see what problem, to organize them. And I remember some of them, but I never saw him. [Laughs.] And then when we get to Odessa, we took a train to Moscow, I didn't saw him either in the train. When I get to my school, to my university, later I knew that two new Cuban teachers was in charge of all Cuban students. We were around 200 Cuban students in this university. Then we met because I was a leadership in the university for Cuban students. And I remember I met him and we were talking but actually I said, "Oh, he's so ugly!" At that time, he had a girlfriend, very beautiful girlfriend, nice and beautiful. I said, "How she's looking at him? She's so beautiful, so good shape." She really was.
CARLOS: The first time I saw her it was in a house, in a friend's house. There was many people in there, and she came. She was a real nice girl, real nice believe me. And I was with a friend. And I was single. Cubans are a little bit different like Americans. If we like a lady, we talk to her 10 times, 12 times, 20 times until she gave up, maybe one year, two years it doesn't matter. If I like her, every time I go to her, I talk to her. There is no sexual harassment. There is nothing about that. So when I saw her the first time, "Oh, my God. What a nice lady!" And I talked to my friend, "That lady is going to be mine."

And my friend say, "Oh, you always doing the same."

"Hey, what do you want to bet?"

He say, "OK, a pack of beer."
PILAR: This is my value? [Laughs.]
CARLOS: This is how everything started. It was a bet. It doesn't matter if a million dollars or a pack of beer, you made a bet.
PILAR: When I finished my bachelor's, I get Cuba June 19th, and I got married in July 31st, 1987. I continue living with my mother but there was my mother, my brother, my sister-in-law, these two nephews...
CARLOS: A lot of people, believe me. [Laughs.]
PILAR: ... my sister-in-law's parents, and her sister and Carlos. All in the same house.

In Cuba, you have to work where they put you. They put me in a workshop repair, where they repair trains. There I started working.

I didn't like it. Then for the first two years, I was in different departments working just as a regular mechanic, learning about everything, getting dirty. But I was working there for four years.

When I came from Russia it was already '87. In '87, '88, '89, was Mikhail Gorbachev in Russia. He started making change and I was totally agree with some change he did, except with the one that he separate some states. I think this is the only stupid thing he did. He should keep everything together the same way Lincoln did. Because at that time was 15 states or republics and he leave the independence to some republics and I think he shouldn't. But my mind start changing about the things in Cuba. I saw that Fidel Castro didn't want to change, and I thought it's time to make some change. I was thinking about the necessity to make change in the Cuban government and in the Cuban policy. And then I was of course talking with my coworkers the thing I am not agree, what things I think, why Fidel Castro is so stubborn and he doesn't make any change. And in 1990, Carlos and I decided that we have to leave the country, because I saw that Fidel doesn't want to make any change and everything is getting worse and worse. Because before Gorbachev our economical situation in Cuba was very dependent from Russian government. They supply us everything. After '89, the relation was just business. The same as any other country. They didn't gave us everything that they gave before for free. And then of course the economic situation started getting worse, and Fidel Castro wanted to continue dreaming with the same way before when we receive everything. And I say, "We have to make some change. OK, if you want to keep one party, do it. If you want to be communist, do it. But make some change in the economy to be able to survive." And he didn't want it and I say, "This is no way. We have to leave."

[Our money] wasn't valuable. Then the government didn't give you all the month all the product you need as before. Sometime

With her father at her wedding,
Cuba, July 31, 1987

they don't have soap. For example, they don't give this month. But you have to take shower. How you going to wash yourself? Then you have to go to the black market and buy. They don't give you meat, and you have to buy in the black market. Of course, very expensive. Then your salary is not enough. And everybody then start steal something. For example, the people that work in the factory where they make soap, they steal the soap. They sell it to buy meat or to buy shoes or to buy clothes. You understand? It's a circle. Everybody was stealing whatever they can from the job to sell, to buy another product that they need.

Before '90, Carlos wanted to leave. Several times before he said, "This country, I don't like this and this." But I was still trying to keep in. I didn't want to leave my country. But when everything was getting worse and I think that nothing change, then I started being agree with him.

CARLOS: My decision was based on the reality I saw in Russia. When I came to Russia the first time, I went there with a mind: This is perfect, everything works, and there is no problem in here. I am not ashamed to say that I was a communist. I believed in the communist. I hated Americans. I thought Americans were people that think that they have the right to go anywhere to do whatever they want. And I was disagree. So the problems we have in Cuba with the communists is because we are the problem, not because the system is the problem. When I came there, I saw people is not the problem, the system is the problem, so I woke up! After two years there, I knew that the system didn't work. And I started to talk to her, "Hey, we need to change because we only live one time. We need to change the life. We need to go to another place." Even in 1989 I went to Russia and I told her, "Hey, you know what? When I return, I will stay in Canada."

And she told me, "But if you stay in Canada we are not going to meet each other again because you know how it works."

PILAR: He said to me, "Pilar, this is our opportunity. When I come back from Russia, I have to stop in Canada and I want

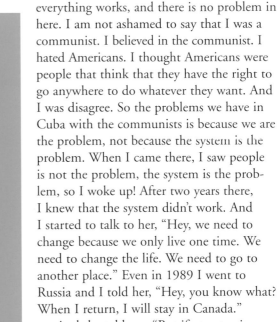

40

to stay there. Then later we can reunion together."

I say, "Carlos, I am afraid. I don't think because you know how hard it is. It's going to take you three or five years. After three or five years, our marriage is gone. Then if you live there, our relation won't continue to the end."

And he said me, "OK, then I will be back."

It was very difficult for me to leave from Cuba. First of all, I already was in a [foreign] country before. I know when you get there, you doesn't have nothing. You need time to find a job, to have money. And I know that the government sometime when they get angry because you leave your country, they keep your family and they don't allow you to go out. Then I say, "No, you know what? The day we leave, we leave together! All together or nothing." Then he come back. At that time I wasn't ready to really see that it doesn't work. I was hoping that it going to change, that it would be better, it would be OK.

In 1990 we start looking. At that time, as Cubans go illegally, we start crazy looking for people that going to go illegally because we need a boat. And we don't have thousands of Cuban pesos to buy a boat or to make a boat. Then we have to try to find somebody. Sometime they have a boat and you give some money, and it's a whole group that's going to travel. And we were for a year looking for somebody that want to leave illegally.

I don't know how to swim, let me say. But we decided that it's better to die than live in the way we were living as a vegetable, as a plant. And then we decided that it's better to risk. If you doesn't risk yourself, you doesn't get nothing. And I wasn't afraid. We talk about that, but I was so confident that I won't die. And Carlos helped me a lot. He said, "Don't worry."

I said, "I don't know how to swim. If something happen in the water, I'm going to drown."

He said, "Don't worry. I'm going to drown first than you. If I have to save your life, I will save."

CARLOS: Nobody knew about it. You cannot talk in Cuba to anybody about that. Her father and my father, they both knew about our ideas, but nobody else. Very important point. One thing that affected the decision we made was the way we were living. We were two professionals, two engineers. I was a teacher in the university, and we lived in a way that no American can imagine. We were living in two rooms without bathroom, without water, in a place where people used to smoke marijuana. It was so bad place that I remember I suffer a lot in that

place. No matter how hard you work, you cannot change your way of life. It was because I think the communists have two philosophical problems. No matter if you work or not, you live anyway. That was the moment Pilar woke up.

PILAR: I have a friend. I knew her from Russia and she have parents that live near the coast. We started visiting this family near the beach 'cause we think if they are in the beach, there are the people that have boat and we can find a contact, somebody that going to leave the country and we can join with them. And we started going there for months until we found another aunt from this family, [who] met a man that she know from another city years before, and he say that he have a contact with somebody that have a boat. And then we decided seven people going to leave the country.

And one night we went all together there in this beach and we were in the coast waiting for the boat, and we were making like we were having fun, eating there, conversation, and we supposed that this man, it was a trap. I think he work for the government. Because we were there, no boat at all, and the police came. The army came, took us.

That night we were in a small place near the coast where all the people that was trying this night to leave illegally were kept there. And the next day we were sent to Villa Marista. It's a place where they keep [people] during interrogation, when they want to interrogate some political or economic people with problems. And we were there 12 days.

It was a prison. It is worse than a prison in the way that, for example, you doesn't meet nobody in the hall. Only one prisoner can be at a time in the hall. You stay in a cell. I stay with three another women. They never turn off the light. You have the light 24 hours a day.

CARLOS: You need to sleep with the light in front of your eyes.

PILAR: Then, for example, the food, I remember, I think that sometimes they give us a fish that they ground it with everything inside because the taste and the smell was horrible.

CARLOS: Eyes, bones.

PILAR: I think it was everything. But I decide at that time, "OK, I think it's a good time to lose weight." [Laughs.] And there was very thin lady that she was always hungry. Then I give almost half of my food to her and I just eat a little bit. It was so hot. There inside you only use underwear because the clothes they were so thick. You don't have window. There was only a small space that you only can see a little bit of the sky. You don't know nothing else, and it was so hot, and then I said, "OK, this is good time." Then I was running all day in the cell.

Running, making exercise, and taking showers. We could take showers. I took showers, like five a day. But for men, Carlos told me it was totally different.

The food was horrible and the last food, the dinner was at 5:00. Of course at night, we were hungry, thirsty, hot. They give us every night at 9:00 P.M. a glass of grapefruit juice. It was sweet and cool. The only cool thing we drink all day. One night I was looking [and there was] a lot of white stuff there. I took with my fingers. This was pills! They smash pills and put there, so we didn't sleep during the night. And I knew, but I drink because I was so thirsty and this was sweet. I drank. But of course all night, I stay awake. I couldn't sleep. The pill made me not to sleep.

They wanted us to sign on a paper where they said that we were planning to leave the country. And I said, "No, I wasn't." And they were keeping us until we signed this paper.

This afternoon, they called to me and they said, "You know what? You should sign that you was trying to leave the country."

I said, "I'm not going to sign because I wasn't leaving the country. I was there just for fun."

And he said, "But, look. Your husband signed already."

I looked at the sign [signature]. I said, "This is not my husband's sign. I don't believe."

And he asked me, "If your husband signed the paper, you will sign?"

I said, "Yes."

"If your husband threw [jumped] in the water, you are going to throw?"

I said, "Yes. What he do, I will follow him."

They said, "OK."

CARLOS: It was real hard. The conditions for men are a little bit different for women. We were four men in a room. This is maybe two by three meters wide with a little space with some water, and every time they were making noise for you not to sleep. When I come there the first time, they took me apart. And I remember they told me, "Carlos, you are a smart guy. You are the teacher of the university. So let us make this easy. Tell us what you was about to do and that's it. Everybody goes home."

"We wasn't about to do anything. We was having fun."

"OK, that's your opinion?"

"Yeah. This is my opinion now and this will be my opinion at the end."

"OK, so go to the cell."

They keep me there for I don't know how many days. They didn't ask me any questions. They didn't call me for anything. But they are observing everything and they noted that I didn't eat food because it was even not for—cats and dogs in this country eat better than prisoners in Cuba. And I remember I was sleeping one night and they called me only to ask how I was eating food because they was so cynic people. I tried to be more cynic than them. And I told them, "You know what? It's wonderful! This is great! This is the better place I have found in my whole life!"

So the guy looked at me. He was real angry and told the other guy, "Take him to the cell!"

"OK, thank you."

The only time they called me for an interview when I came, Pedro Chávez, I remember that name. He was the officer that interviewed me, Pedro Chávez. He started to ask me questions and I gave the same answers I gave the first day and he told me, "I don't want to waste time with you. Let me say you, we know the whole history about this. This is like this, like this, like this because we got a guy [spy] in your group. And when he told me about that, I ask for my wife. And he told me, "You know what? Your wife is in the same situation you are now." So believe me, for a man, it was a real, real, real hard situation.

So if somebody told them the whole story because he is an agent, so I thought, "What do I have to hide from them? I don't have anything to hide if they know everything. So, OK. Give me the paper." And I signed the paper.

PILAR: Then they do something that they don't used to do. They call him and they bring him to the office to say me that he signed the paper. Then Carlos said, "Yes, Pilar. I signed the paper. You can sign it, too." Then I signed the paper. And the next day we were released, but my father have to pay 1,000 Cuban pesos for each, 2,000 Cuban pesos until we waiting for our trial.

CARLOS: After that we went to a trial with a judge, everything. And I remember we had a lawyer and I had to assist the lawyer because if I don't assist the lawyer, we were in jail. [Laughs.] We were freed because we didn't kill anybody.

PILAR: We only have to pay. There were thousands of people every day. I say you it was something like going to the party. Everybody was trying leaving, they caught you. They was making money because the only way they make was to take money from you. But you was just

With their coworkers at a locomotive repair shop, Cuba, 1989

leaving and you didn't steal nothing from the government.

What happened? When we came out of the jail we lost our job right away, immediately. We didn't have any money. Some money we have saved, but it's just a little. And then I remember I knew through a neighbor that they are going to have some classes, give some classes for the people that wanted to train to be a waitress. And she have a good relation there and then I sign all the papers.

It was a training from September I think to November. During the day, we study in the morning, and in the afternoon from 4:00 to 10:00 was like training in the cafeteria where they sell ice cream and cake. And it was wonderful because they didn't pay us for this training, but because the way I treat the customer, I receive tip. And this was the only money came to our house. And because I was there, I could buy ice cream and cake very, very cheap, because in the black market, it's really expensive. But it was exhausting because I came at home at 10:00 P.M.

On December, I get a job as a waitress. But unfortunately, they put me in a small, it's like half of a bathroom [kiosk], where you sell coffee. You don't receive tip. It's only just Cuban coffee. And the people stand there in line and it's something very fast. But the people that came

there was homeless, drunks. I remember sometime the words they answer you back, they say you bad words. And sometimes I have to work during the morning, sometime the afternoon, sometime during midnight. It was awful. It was awful because in the money they gave me for a month, it wasn't enough to eat, to buy one liter of oil to cook. This was my salary, one liter of oil for a whole month.

CARLOS: When we lost our jobs, we didn't have any possibilities to work as a professionals. And we didn't have any possibilities to work as anything else because we were bad people for the government. One day our thought was what can we do in the future to get ourselves alive and we didn't found the answer. One day I was desperate. And I went out of the place I was living in and I saw a guy walking with some chickens, baby chickens in the hand. And I came in and said, "Pilar, you know what? I found the answer. We are going to grow up chickens in two rooms."

And Pilar told me, "You are crazy. You are completely crazy."

And I told her, "OK, I am crazy but I am keep my family alive, so let me do what I want to do." And I talk to her father and I told him, "Hey, Pop. I need at least 20 baby chickens." In that time, government was selling chicks for people to grow at home. One peso. And her father bought 20 chicks. When they came home, I didn't have any place where to put them.

PILAR: We didn't have a cage for these animals. [Laughs.]

CARLOS: We grew up 75 chickens and I keep alive my family that way. I sold some chickens. I have food for my grandmother, for my wife, for her father, for me that way. But I had to keep the chickens in my room.

PILAR: Next to the bed.

CARLOS: Because otherwise, somebody could steal the chickens. It was terrible. I get sick because there is a sickness associated with the chickens. So some people that used to live with the chickens get sick. When I realized that. When I knew about that, it was too late. I was already sick. But I had to keep the chickens; otherwise OK, I will be OK for that disease, but I could die from hunger.

I went to a friend and I told her, "You know what? I need to move to another place."

And she told me, "You and your wife can learn how to make shoes. My husband and I can teach you how to make shoes." They were not professionals. They only were people that were trying to live in a country that there is nothing. And they started to show us how to make shoes.

43

The first shoes we made, it was funny. [Pilar laughs.] Some friends ask me, "Are you making shoes for clowns on the circus?" Because they were so big! They were so strange! And we started to learn. But it's important when you study, when you have an education, when you have a preparation, after a few months, the situation reversed. We started to show them how to make good shoes.

PILAR: We made shoes, but just a little to people that we really know really well, and just to get the minimum money we need to survive, but not to have more money than that. And actually, the last two or three months, we almost stopped making them because we thought it's better to be hungry now, but don't lose the opportunity to go. If the Cuban government catch us making illegal shoes, we go to the prison, to the jail, and we're going to lose everything. The goal to go to the United States was more important. I think we make sometimes one pair of shoes a month, something like that, or two.

Then, after that, '91, '92 we went to the Canadian embassy asking to leave to Canada and they said that we had a lot of probability because I was engineer in the transportation and he, too. And they said that they need engineers, especially in transportation. But they were trying to make agreement with government to take people from Cuba, but at the end it doesn't work. They sent a letter if we wanted to go to

At the Copa Room del Havana Riviera, Cuba, 1990

Canada, we need to have $25,000. With $25,000 we would be rich, millionaire in Cuba! Then where I'm going to get that?

Then we wrote a letter to the American office saying we lost our job; we can't work as an engineer again in Cuba. We doesn't have any future there.

CARLOS: I have to be honest. We never wanted to come to U.S.A. because we knew through the movies about the mafia. We knew about the corruption. We knew about the racism. We knew so many bad things about Americans that I didn't want to come to America. I preferred to go to Australia before to come to America. Canada or whatever place, but no America, no U.S.A. But our last resolve was to send a letter because I was about to die. I am not lying. Inside and outside. I was like a cover. My body weight was 124 pounds, no more, and I didn't have resources to keep my family, so I was about to die inside and outside. And I wrote a letter to the American office and they answered me, "You classify as political refugee." It was 28th January, 1994.

PILAR: And they say, "OK. Then the next appointment will be for October 12th." And then Carlos went alone because the first interview is only for the one with the name on the [application].

CARLOS: You know what happened that day? The first interview I went alone. And I remember an American guy interviewed me. Even he introduced me to his wife when he knew about my story, because I present to him the documents from her [Pilar's] job telling that she was like a prostitute. That's the opinion of the union.

PILAR: Because I went to several trials with the union because I wasn't agree.

CARLOS: But I gave him this paper. It's a trick. This is my wife. I gave him the papers. When he read the papers, he look at me.

"Did you finish?" [I said].

"Yes."

"OK, now I want you to read this. This is my wife, too, but from other point of view. This is from technical point of view." From a technical point of view, she was a real good woman.

And the guy after that, he told me, "You know what? I have seen many, many, many cases in my life, but the things I see in this country are crazy, are crazy! Let us finish this and let me introduce you to my wife."

PILAR: Then we have another interview on November 12th. We had to wait there whole day after interview for hours. It was a nightmare waiting if they say yes or no, if you are approved or no. Carlos was really nervous.

CARLOS: I was about to die.

PILAR: I was nervous, but he was shaking.

CARLOS: The guy that was interviewing us told me, "Do you want a candy? Do you want a water? Do you want something? Let me know what you want!"

The second interview it was a problem, because there was a lady that Pilar knew and Pilar keep a place for her in the line. The lady was called before us by the same guy that call us later. And the guy didn't give them the possibility to come here and the lady come out of the office crying and was crazy. And at the same moment, the guy called us. So I don't know how to say in English, but that situation made me, I don't know. My psychological stabilization, I lost my mind when I saw that lady crying and the husband, and the same guy called me. It was terrible for me.

PILAR: I was nervous, too. For me it was hard because let me say. I said at that time to Carlos that if we don't leave the country, if they don't accept us, this was our last hope, I will kill myself. The situation in Cuba was so…I couldn't stand the situation.

CARLOS: And I believe, too.

PILAR: And I said, "If they don't approve us, I kill myself. I don't going to continue living this way." In this moment, my life was in his hand. If he approve or no, it depend I'm going to live or no.

We had to wait about three or four hours. We were there at 7:00 in the morning and we leave at 4:00 [in the afternoon]. This time he call us again and he said, "OK, you have been accepted as political refugee." It was incredible. [Carlos laughs hard.] It was so incredible.

But in this moment you are so nervous that you almost doesn't do nothing. You stay still. And because you think everybody is looking you, how you behave, you think if you do something crazy, they going to say you, "I'm sorry, we changed our mind." [Laughs.]

Because we knew the story before a woman that she was asking to come here as a visitor and she was approved. Then she went to the washroom, the people say, I don't know, she went to the washroom and she steal the soap. Then when she came out of the washroom they say, "You know what? You steal. You never come to the United States."

CARLOS: It's real, it's real.

PILAR: I don't know.

CARLOS: But I believe it. You know what? It's so easy in an American place, soap for you or for any American. You Americans are born, and you take for granted that whatever you have, you have to have. That's a point of view. You are free because you have to have free. You can go anywhere because it's your right. For other countries, it's different.

PILAR: After he said yes, we have to wait for a paper in another office. We were there just talking and so happy. Before, we didn't talk almost. And then we were talking and then we left walking and walked to our house. We remember we leave the American office, and we couldn't take a bus. We couldn't. We needed to walk. And we were walking and walking and walking. We walked a lot because we were so emotional energy, so happy, that we have to walk. We need to relieve this energy, this oppression that we had been for the whole day. We were hungry. We didn't drink, nothing. We just were sitting there for seven hours. And I remember we have to walk, and we walk and walk and walk.

CARLOS: That day when we were approved, I remember when we came home we were so tired that we had to go to sleep. It was 5:00 or 6:00.

PILAR: Nobody knew nothing.

CARLOS: Nobody knew. Only her father. When her father came home at 6:30, more or less, I woke up and I told him, "Hey, Pop. You know what? We were approved. So we are so tired. I don't know how to explain, but we need to get a rest. So take a seat, watch TV, and let us to sleep."

Her father told me, "I am real happy. Go to sleep and forget about me."

We sleep a lot. After that, she woke up and make some dinner, poor dinner for her father and me and her, and we started the process with the papers. It's a lot. It's a huge process. But thanks God, we got it all done and we could get out of the country.

PILAR: It was hard because in December we have already our passports and our American check-up, but the problem start with the United States and Cuba. It was already January, February, March, April, and nothing changed and we were, "Oh, my God. We're going to stay here." And because we were making before illegal shoes, we stopped making. We didn't have any money.

Then, we knew that the United States started taking the people out through Cancún. "Oh, that's nice. Soon we going to leave the country." I think it was April or May [1995]. April they begin, but it was so long line. Only at the end of the May or beginning of the June we receive a letter telling Carlos to go to the office. Then Carlos went to the office and they give the plane ticket. And they say him that we're going to go

45

to Houston, Texas.

Then they told us that we going to fly, but we going to fly through Costa Rica. They say, "OK, you going to leave the country on 26th June at 5:00 A.M. in the morning."

[Leaving was] horrible, because my parents are old. We knew that my father had cancer in his prostate. And then I was the one that take care of him. He always came to our house for a lunch, for a dinner. I was the one that take him to the hospital. I was as his mother. I say what to do. I order him.

Every six months I took him for a check, for examine, and the cancer was back again. I knew that probably this is the last time, but I have to leave. It is hard. He didn't say nothing. I never told him that he had cancer. Of course, he was smart and he knew, but he never said a word that he's sick. Never. He make it that nothing happened, that everything is OK. He never wanted to show what really happened. He knew that probably he wasn't see me and I knew the same, but he knew that this is the only way, this was my best. He said, "You have to leave. You can't stay here." I remember how much I cried at the airport. It was hard. [Cries.] I was crying, crying. Carlos was trying to help me because I cry so much because I knew this is the last time. You never know when you going to come back.

I knew if I stay, I will take my life. I will. I knew that. But on the other side, if I leave, I am leaving my family, especially my father. Because my mother is old, but she was healthy. I know that my brother take care of her and my sister, but my father, the one that take care was me, only me, I know. I thought, "I am leaving him alone. Who going to help him?" Because the closest relation with my father was mine. My brother didn't have almost any relation. Some kind, but nothing. It was hard. But it wasn't any option. It was, my feeling, his life and my life and you have to choose. This was the only opportunity. And I thought, "I will come to the United States. I will make money. I will send him money." Because in Cuba I couldn't give him nothing! Then I said, "If I go to the United States, at least I going to send money. And I'm going to buy him a TV, anything that he will need to the last year he going to live, I give him." Then we took this airplane to Costa Rica.

When I came to Costa Rica, actually, we were tired. This is the reason I was there sleeping in the seat [in the airport]. I was exhausted. I wanted to get to the United States and that's it. I was hungry, tired, sad. I didn't know what will expect me in the future. I don't know my future. It's like you are floating in a cloud and you don't know where you go, where you live, where is your future.

Suddenly Carlos came. I was sleeping there sitting, and Carlos, "Pilar, there are a store!"

And nobody wanted to move. Then I was sleeping and I thought, "If I go out, probably the police don't let me go out, or if I go out, I won't come in, and I'm going to be lost in this country." And I don't move. I sit there sleeping. They give us some snack, but just a soda and something very light. We were hungry! It was already 24 hours almost.

I was sleeping and I don't know how, but Carlos say, "Oh, you know what? The people is starting to go out." But it is our mentality, how we came. We used not to be free and we are unable to move from the place that we are!

CARLOS: Only few people started to move. Among them, I was. And I remember the first step I took was go into a store. I went out the store. When I went out the store, I saw nobody was watching me. I went a little further. I spent some time. I waited some time and I saw nobody was watching me.

PILAR: Because he was expecting some police to say, "Hey, you can't go there. You have to go back." This is how we think.

CARLOS: I went a little more and a little more to the end of the airport. When I went to the end of the airport, I come back. For the first time in my life I felt myself free! And I come back with so energy with so happiness. When I met Pilar, Pilar told me, "What are you doing? You are crazy!"

I said, "Hey, hey, hey, hey, hey. Hold it. Hold it. We are free! We are free! We can go wherever we want. Come with me!" And I took her to the end directly.

But it was for me, it was interesting. When I came to Russia, the first time, I didn't feel that feeling about liberty. I knew that I came Russia to study, to work, to do the best I can, but it wasn't nothing about liberty. But when I came to Costa Rica I felt myself free. I felt like a human being. I can do whatever I want. I saw the police like nothing, you know, side by side. I don't have to hide myself because I am walking by here. It was totally different.

It is interesting. When I came to America, I used to see the police, I remember. I used to put my hand in my left pocket, because in Cuba you have to have the identification. And when I saw the police here, it's a custom, it's a reaction. I see the police and I, "Oh, my God, I got the identification." Because in Cuba you can go to the jail because you don't have the identification. But here nobody ask you for identification.

Celebrating her birthday, Chicago, August 24, 1995

Can you please come to my coat and take my wallet, from the coat? I want to show you how many identification I have. It is because a custom. OK. [Shows ID cards.] So, I have here my driver's license, ID card, resident card, every card I have. Even credit cards I have with me all the time. It is a custom. Americans doesn't have that custom because no police ask you. If you commit mistake driving, they ask you for your driver's license and for your insurance, but nobody ask you for anything else. But in Cuba you have to have all these cards and many others.

PILAR: Actually, we took 63 pounds of books. [Laughs.] I only came with the shoes I was wearing, two blouses. That means we didn't bring clothes. Nothing, no clothes, no money. Only 63 pounds books. Carlos, he loved books. And because we knew that here in the United States the books are very, very expensive. We don't have money. And we say, "Maybe for our job, we're going to need this book to study." Then I bring actually Russian books, Russian dictionary. I brought the English dictionary. It's still the one we have.

Carlos say me, "What to take dictionary? There should be better dictionary."

"Yes, but how long it going to take you to buy a dictionary? You don't have money and we have to get right away there and speak

English. We need the dictionary with us." Then we took the dictionary. We took books, mechanic books, 63 pounds in a box, in a carton box with a rope. It was ugly how it looked.

For Americans, "Where are these people coming from?" A box. A regular box with a rope. That's it. And then we came here.

CARLOS: Before landing, when the plane was about to landing, I saw Miami and I remember I stand up and say everybody, "If Fidel Castro see Miami from this plane as I can see now, he won't talk any bullshit like he used to say all the time, because this is beautiful. This is great."

It's a very nice experience because it is like you born second time. And nobody has experienced that thing. You was born one time, but you don't know how you experience at that moment. So at this time, in my case when I saw Miami, when I saw that I was in the United States, I feel myself like I was born again. I don't have words in English, but that's not the problem. The problem is I don't have words in Spanish to describe the feeling when you come to the liberty. This is the most important thing people can have in their life. The liberty.

PILAR: But this is a moment really very strange. All feelings are together. All feelings because you are leaving your country where you born, you grew up. You leave your family. Some of the people there leave maybe their children, the mothers, the brothers. Then it's a feeling of sad because you are leaving everything. It's a feeling of expectation, of insecurity because you doesn't know what expect to you in this new country, new language. You doesn't bring nothing, only you, your body. And it's a feeling of happiness, the great happiness because you think you are, at the end you are free. You have a lot of expectation. You think your dream will become reality. In Cuba we didn't have any dream. We knew we can expect nothing. Then we were dead, alive or dead. And then we say, "Oh, we going to make true our dreams." But at the same time you doesn't know really if you could or no. Then is all feeling are mixed.

We came to Miami at 9:00 P.M. All we going down to an office. In this office there was immigrants, people from immigration office making like some questions and filling out paper and putting in our passport a white card where they say that we can live here and work how long as we wanted. It took, because we were whole plane, it took until 1:00 A.M.

When we went to the Miami, they told us, "Your advisor didn't found the conditions needed in Houston. Then you go to Chicago."

I said, "No way I go to Chicago." [Laughs.] In Cuba I was reading a little bit about Houston to have an idea what is Houston about. "Where is Chicago? No, it's in the north." Carlos got so angry and mad. With us was another couple, elderly people. They were supposed to go to Houston, too. She had a sister in Houston. We both were sent to Chicago. And I said, "Carlos, what are you angry about? You always said that you wanted in the north where it's very, very cold. Then why you worried? Didn't you want cold? You going to have." But we didn't know where is Chicago. Only we ask, "How is the city? It's good, it's bad?"

And I remember the guy said, "Oh, it's OK. There are some gangs, but it's OK."

When I listen to this, I said, "Oh, my God! Where they are sending us? [Laughs.] Are we going to survive there?"

Then we took the airplane at 12:00 [noon]. The plane, I don't know why, have some problems and we have to sit in the plane for an hour or two until we leave. We came here on June 28th around 6:00 P.M. We have like a label on our chest with our name because our ticket was paid by OIM; this is an international organization of immigrants. Later, we have to pay them, but they pay first of all. And then we have this label. When we get to the airport there was this Ethiopian guy, because our sponsors were Ethiopian Community [Association]. And we were surprised, "Ethiopian, why are they taking care of us?" Usually it's the church.

And we get there and we were studying one year before, we had a private teacher and we were studying a little bit of English. But I only knew maybe 20 words: he, she, it, and that's it. Carlos was better than me, a little bit better. I was dumb for English, as I said before. [Laughs.] For he it was easier. Then with words, he was talking to this guy in English. Then he took us to our place.

When I saw Chicago for first time, I have to say, I don't know because it's the way he took, but I remember one street and I saw in the middle a lot of newspaper, and I said, "Oh, how dirty is this city. How awful." And everything was gray and this brick was too dark. And I said, "Oh, I don't like this city. It look awful and so sad city. I don't like."

He took us to the building there near Broadway [Avenue], and when he opened this studio it was horrible. It was a regular building, but they pay the first month of the rent and later the welfare give us money to pay. But there was only two individual mattresses in the floor. Two small mattresses.

CARLOS: Nothing else.

Her first job as a housekeeper, Chicago, 1995

PILAR: No tables, no chairs, a lot of cockroaches. Thousands! And the refrigerator, one big bottle of apple juice, a lot of packages of bread for hot dogs, hot dog buns, hot dogs, some spaghetti and that's it. Nothing else. I started crying and Carlos get angry and he said, "But didn't you say you going to take us to eat something."

"Oh, OK, OK, OK!" Then he took us.

CARLOS: They gave us $15 a week for each. And I was begging them for my social security [card] to start to work. Because I know if I can work, I can do whatever I want.

PILAR: We started, as I say, receiving this welfare. The next day we came here, Carlos went out. I didn't move from the studio. I was afraid to [get lost]. He went out and he started walking and walking and whenever he see some Hispanic face he start asking, "Do you know any Cuban people?"

This way he found a Mexican who say, "Oh, yes. I know a small store where are Cuban people there."

Then he met the first Cuban, very nice old man. And then from there, he start meeting with a lot of different Cuban people. Then the people, they bring us clothes or food, or somebody gave us $10 or $20. Some started inviting us to go out to some place, to see some places. It was nice, but we were asking everybody, "We are looking for a job. We don't care what it is." Because we knew from Cuba, we were sure that we won't work as a professional, but we have to start cleaning, washing dishes, whatever! And we were looking and looking for a job.

Then, it's interesting, we met a lady, too. She's very, very religious. In her free time, she's in Santa Ita, the church there in Broadway. Because we went there to the church for help, asking somebody that can help and the priest say, "Oh, we going to send you a Cuban lady." And then she came. She really help us a lot. She bring a lot of clothes. She knew many people and she used to do, still does for Mexicans, too. She used to bring a lot of food. She go to buy or take us to the store, buy food.

Then Carlos needed glasses because the glasses he bring, he couldn't see well. And then, she was very nice. She said, "OK, I will take you." And she was ready to pay for this. Then she took us to the Cuban optic there on Ashland [Avenue]. And then she was there talking, "A new Cuban arrived and he need glasses."

And then when she was ready to pay, this Dr. Torres say, "You know what? You don't have to pay. I pay. I give to him." Then it was a gift. Everything was free.

And some people didn't help. For example, we went to the Cuban commerce chamber just next to this optic where we went for the glasses. And we get there just to talk. They called us to go there and speak about Cuba. And the first thing I remember they say is, "Oh, I'm sorry but we don't have any job to give you."

And Carlos say, "I'm sorry, we are not here asking you any job." And they didn't give us a penny. We didn't went for money, but I mean, you know people that have been living here 30 years, and you see that somebody is coming, and you see and you know that this Ethiopian Community [Association] only gave them $15 a week. And some week they didn't give us any money. We live from the money gave us, the Cubans. I'm sorry, knowing that and you don't have nothing to help these people.

Because at the beginning, can you imagine $15, $30 a week for two people. We have to walk again to the Aldi [supermarket] every week, and carrying these heavy bags walking because we can't afford to pay $1.80 for a bus. I remember I wrote a letter to my family because I wasn't working. I wrote extensive, large, huge letter to my family explaining everything, but I say, "You know what, I am buying at the Aldi. There is very, very cheap place. I don't know why people doesn't like to buy there. It's the same food that's in the Jewel [supermarket]. It is excellent. It is good. I will buy there forever." And I say, "The Family

Dollar. Oh, this is fantastic. For one dollar you can buy very good things there."

Now, I don't know how long I have been in this Aldi or this Family Dollar. Now I hate these place [Laughs.] because the quality is not the same. I have learned that the things that are cheap are no good. And because when I came from Cuba, I was so, so poor that for me anything was good. Now I know to distinguish what is a good thing, the quality of the thing. At the beginning I wasn't able. I didn't care it cost $1 or $5 or $10 or $20, for me it was the same thing. Now I have changed. Now I know what is good, what is a good clothes, what is a bad clothes, what is a good shoes, what is not. At the beginning I have to buy my shoes at the Payless Shoes. Now, I don't buy any shoes at Payless Shoes. Now my shoes have to be no less than $40 or $60. Because I am looking for a good shoes, a good condition, comfortable. Many requirements.

We didn't work for three months. Then, in this place where Carlos was making the glasses, this doctor said, "Oh, you know what? I have a friend of mine that a few days ago was talking to me by the telephone and telling me that they need some engineer, mechanic engineer."

And gave the telephone to Carlos. Carlos went for interview. And this is where Carlos is working there now.

CARLOS: [I started working] on September 25th, 1995. I started as an operator, machine operator, $5 per hour. And after three days or four days, I ask to the plant manager to let me know about how to program machines. And he told me, "You know what, I don't need anybody here to know how to program machines. I got the guys."

"OK, that's no problem for me."

I told Pilar, "You know what? I need to change the job because in that place I am not going to be anybody."

But after eight days, exactly eight days of being there, the plant manager ask me, "Do you want to go back there and become an inspector?"

I said, "OK, it is more money and more comfortable place to work. OK. No problem for me." And I started to work as an inspector.

I remember I standed many, many, many bad things from Hispanic people. They rejected me because I am Cuban. But I think the smart guy is not the one that is all the time fighting for his position. It's the one that knows when is the moment to fight for his position. I remember they used to tell me, "Could you please go out to check the parts in other place, no in here." And I knew they didn't know how to multiply,

Dancing at home, Chicago, 1997

CARLOS: That's why you got problems now.

PILAR: I hated. I said, "Why do I need the English class? Every book here is in Spanish. I don't need English." I go to sleep. The day before the test, then I start learning. What is the meaning of "what"? What is the meaning of "where"? I never learned a word.

And in the Truman College, I knew in our class Clara, from Ecuador. I knew her there. And she was the one that told us she was working as a housekeeping, and she going to talk for me at the Belden-Stratford. Then she took me there. I went there for interview. I filled out application and I got the job in October as a housekeeping. And I remember it was hard because we have to use uniform and the uniform is $40. But I say, "I don't have any money."

And they say, "Oh, no. Don't worry. We going to take from your paycheck." After a month of working, I received my first check and they discount from there the $40 of my uniform.

I was, "Oh, my God." And I only earn $5 for hour. It was $320 every two weeks. This was my salary cleaning rooms. I feel rich. We bring from Cuba $40. Then for me, $320 was, "Oh, I am rich."

CARLOS: How come people can live in here and they are not rich earning $300 every 15 days? [Laughs.] That was our thought.

PILAR: You know, it wasn't my job. I have to work with people no educated. It's another way of thinking. Then I couldn't have a conversation with them. Then I feel strange, totally strange. I am unable to have a long conversation with any Americans. Besides, I can't because I was working only with Afro-Americans and Hispanics. And my close friend was Clara, it was the one that I was talking almost all the time. Then, I feel alone. In my job, only Clara. That's it. This is the one I can really talk and share my feelings. It was like when you are alone in a boat in the middle of the ocean. This is what I feel, and you have to survive. That's it.

We were so isolated. We didn't have relation with Americans. Then we didn't know how Americans are. We live our own world, and my world was my house and where I work, and I work alone usually because cleaning you are alone cleaning rooms, [but] we were real happy.

CARLOS: No happy. Real, real, real happy.

PILAR: Yes, because I always thought that this going to be transitional, that this is necessary because it's my beginning, that this have to be because I don't know the language, I don't know English, and I have to do the job I am doing. But it won't be forever. What I have to do, I have to continue my English and sometime I will get where I should be.

how to divide one number by other.

But I told him, "It's OK for me. No problem. That's what you want? OK. I go out." And I used to go out. But when I went out I learn from the people out on the [floor] how to check this, how to do this, how to do that. In five or six months, I learn so much that the two guys that were making me the life impossible were laid off. In three years, I became the chief of the department, quality control department. It's a real, very important department. Now by this time, I know every corner of the company. I know every trick of the operators. I know everything. [Laughs.] Nobody can make me fool. Because at the beginning, I didn't thought, "I am an engineer. I don't have to…" No, no. "What do you want? You want I go out? OK, I go out. No problem." Everybody have to know his moment. And there is a moment for everything in this life.

PILAR: Tila, this lady that I say you is very religious, Tila took us to the Truman College. She helped us there in the line, filled out all the applications to take free classes. Then we start in August. But because we didn't have any money, we have to walk around 20 blocks back and forth to the classes at night. It took us one hour one way, one hour another way.

In high school, they taught us English, but I never learned. When my teacher came to the classroom, I went to sleep. When she left, I wake up. This is the only class I hated.

I wake up at 6:00 in the morning. I went to my job. I finished at 4:00. I went to Truman College and then I studied at Truman College later twice a week from 5:00 to 9:00 and then another two nights at Loyola University another two hours, from 6:00 to 8:00, something like that. I was really busy. When I went home it was just to lie down, take a shower, sleep, and next day wake up again.

CARLOS: I used to make a brief of everything that happens during the week. And in the weekend, I talk to her everything. I make the whole history, or story, about everything that happened to me in the last week because we don't have time. We don't have time. Anyway, we are real happy here.

PILAR: For us, many things was new, like for example the telephone, I never saw before a answering machine. It was a little bit nightmare, too, because anywhere that you call you have a answering machine, and you get nervous and you don't know how to talk to this answering machine. I never had before a video. And the TV, many, many things. Especially the technology, everything was new for us. And that everything is from bottle, or the machines, like the pop machine, where you can buy the drink. I was afraid to go there and buy any drink. I said, "No, I can't handle this machine. I don't know how they work." The technology is the one that shocked us. Everything. Oh, my God.

CARLOS: It was too much.

PILAR: When I was a housekeeping, I was there six months. I thought, "I can't continue with $5 [per hour]. I need another job." Then I was looking in the newspaper about jobs, but I didn't know the country usually, real way.

Tamara and Steve [two American friends] say me, "On Thursday, buy the newspaper and there are all the jobs." And I was reading and reading.

Then one night Steve say me, I was looking at the newspaper and he said, "You know what? I have a friend of mine that is looking for people [for his restaurant]." And then he gave me the telephone number of Jeff.

I called him. I made an appointment. And then I went there for an appointment. He and his girlfriend at that time made me an interview and he said, "OK, when can you start?"

I used to rest on Friday and Saturday at that time. I say, "On Friday." Then I worked until Thursday, I quit my job, and I start on Friday.

[I was a] waitress. To waitress where I have to heat the food, pizza, or strudel, take the order and take the money, too. And then it really was hard. I didn't know the English. And the worst, all the food was there "Oh, my God. What is the name?" For first time in my life I see many of these food, or the name. I didn't know this Italian food. Then I was with the menu trying to remember the name, and it was funny. If somebody ask me something else that it is not in the menu, that is not food, I didn't understand. They sometime ask me for matches. I say, "What are you saying?" I have to call another waitress. "Oh, please, can you…"

"Matches!"

"Oh, OK." Or to speak. It was a nightmare.

The worst of all was one guy get there asking me something, and I couldn't understand what he was talking about. And then he said me, "Can you find somebody that speak English!?" But in a way like you were [dirt].

I didn't answer because it was Jeff's restaurant and I know I was very glad he took me no matter he knew my deficit in English. It was his business and I don't create any problem. But the way I look to him, I was showing how much I hate him. And in myself I was thinking, "Yes, I don't speak English, this is true, but how many language do you speak? What is your degree? Who are you? I don't speak language, but I am not stupid." But I didn't say nothing. I only look at him all the time until he sit down. And when he left, I still keep my eyes on him and I look to let him know what my feeling was about him.

At the meantime, in Truman College when we start, we met there a lady. She said she was a doctor in Colombia, Marta. And she said me, "You know what? I am making all the papers to become a teacher because here is very easy. You have to take your Cuban diploma, your translation and you send to the board of education and you become a teacher."

"Oh, how great." Then, it was as I say you, in September '95. Then on December, I start making the translation of my paper. For me it was expensive. I pay $120. And I remember Tamara helped me to fill out application and I sent it. And then it took a lot of time, but since December 1995, my goal was to make all possible to become a teacher.

I really have to say, I have said before, I didn't want to become a teacher because I didn't like it. I was afraid. Because in Cuba, Carlos say to me many times, "Why you don't become a teacher if you don't like the job where you working?"

I say, "No way. I am afraid. I can't stand in classroom and talk for six hours. I don't used to talk." But because of my father was sick and I knew that I need to do money to send to him and to help my family,

| 51

I say, "I'm going to do. What the hell! [Laughs.] What the hell! Let's see what happens."

And then, I make all the papers. I receive my translation maybe in February or March and then I sent it to Springfield [Illinois] to board of education. To get my transitional bilingual teacher's certificate I need to do an English test at the Northeastern University. "Wow, my God. I am not ready."

Then I saw Marta. I talked with her where I am and she said, "Oh, you know what? I know that the Department of Culture and Language, they going to have for the second year a new program, where they help you to study English to take the test."

"Oh, yes." I went there. I see the lady. I say, "You know what? I am interested because I would like to become a teacher."

And she said, "But you are a teacher now?"

I said, "No."

She said, "OK, fill out application, but I don't give you any hope because many people have signed up. It's only around 50, and I have more than 100 applications, and you are not a teacher. The priority is for those that are in a classroom teaching."

I said, "OK." But I wait. Then on June I received a letter that I was accepted. I only have to pay $200. I was accepted for 20 days to take intensive class at the U.I.C. [University of Illinois-Chicago] for preparing me for this test. And then I talked with Jeff and I said, "You know what, Jeff? I have to study these 20 days. I can't work for these 20 days. I would like to see if it's possible to keep my job after."

He said, "OK."

It's a risk. I had to pay $200 for my classes and I didn't earn money. And maybe when I come I don't find a job. But I say, "The risk is the risk." Sometimes, I really never think very, very deep the things I do. I just jump. And I don't look. If I jump, well, it's OK if I go down. But this is the way.

And then we [Carlos and I] start arguing because I wanted to work, to go to the school, get home, take a shower, sleep, and that's it. And he wanted a wife. He wanted somebody that take care of the house. Then he said, "Quit your job and we live with the money I am doing, and just study." But it's something I can't change and I will never, because I knew I suffer from my parents' divorce. Maybe it's a wrong idea, but I'm sorry, it's something that happened when I was child, and I can't change. And I say that when you get married, it doesn't mean have to be forever. It going to be until somebody, he or I, want it. Then

I can't live thinking that somebody going to give me everything forever. No. We are two persons. We have our dreams. And we live together because we want it, but it is no problem if someday he doesn't want to continue with me. It is not any problem. He doesn't have to think that he going to leave me alone, or no job, or miserable life. No, take your way. Of course, I going to suffer and everything, but I can survive.

I say, "No, I have to work." I need to know I have my money. No matter the money we use together, but I think when I bring money, too, I have the right. If I don't bring the money, I going to start losing my right because I have to expect what somebody's bringing. I am very feminist. [Laughs.] And I think my character, I am so, so strong in this way. When I decide something, I don't look nothing else. I decide I have to study and I have to work, I don't care anything else is more important. That's my point.

I think the big point was principally because here I had my point that I wanted to work and to study, and then we have a confrontation about tradition. It is a tradition in Cuba that you cook every day, three times a day. And you have to cook and have a fresh food. Of course, when we came home at night, I was so tired I didn't want to cook. Actually, I was only worried about to work and to study. I didn't want to do nothing at home. That is the truth. I started changing my mind. In Cuba, the most important is that the women, besides the work, the house is very, very important place. Everything have to be very clean, very organized. To be a good wife you have to cook every day fresh food. When I came here I say, "No. This is not the most important point. The most important point for me is to learn English and to be somebody." And he is a person that he like the food at home. He is very traditional. And I wanted to change. I wanted to make a change very quick, very fast, and he don't accept that 'cause for many years we have been living another way. And I was ready to change and of course, he couldn't.

CARLOS: We did not understand each other.

PILAR: Then we separate in November 1995. That means we were only here for four months or five. We separate this time. We didn't get along. Everything was fighting. He said me, "OK, we going to separate. I'm going to leave the apartment." I was afraid because in this building is only African and a lot of men from Africa.

I said, "What I going to do here when I have to leave at 6:00 in the morning. Oh, my God." I was afraid. Then I moved.

Carlos always was take care of me. I didn't give at the beginning the

At a Christmas party, Chicago, 1999

address or nothing. I didn't say him where I was. I didn't have medicare [medical insurance] for my job, but he paid my medicare. Then we start seeing again, talking, sometimes going out. But we still have disagreement. We still have disagreement because I still keeping my way that I have to study and work, and the house is not the most important at that time. And we reunited on August [1996].

I start teaching on September 24, 1996. On September 27, 1996, my father died. I was so happy with my job, thinking, "I'm going to have a lot of money now. I'm going to send a TV, a video," because he stay at home, "and money to have a good food." And this same day, we had an interview for our citizen. And this day he died. Then I never could give him what I wanted for him. This is really the worst pain you can have in your life, because I still don't really realize that he's dead because I didn't see. For me he's still alive and, I don't know, I think when you see this person is died, OK, you suffer but you realize. But this is an [eternity]. The feeling when you lose somebody that you wanted and you don't see, and you are not near him, and you couldn't talk to him how much do you love, you couldn't listen from him the last word. This is a nightmare, forever.

I start teaching bilingual 2nd grade. I didn't know how to teach! I didn't know how to treat the kids because I don't have kids. And my

nephews, I was far from them. I say, "Oh, my God, with 28 kids, what I'm going to teaching? I don't know the methodology. I don't know what they are learning. I don't know how was the school in Chicago." They used to give information every day in the morning by a loud speaker. I couldn't understand a word what they were talking about. I always have to say, "What they say?" Because I was lost. I came home every day [and spent] until 11:00 [P.M.] preparing class, "What I am teaching?" Desperate, nervous.

Now, it's the same. [Laughs uncontrollably.] No. I enjoy. The six hours I spend in the class is so fast. For me the six hours, it is not enough for everything I want to teach to my kids, but still, I am in the same horror because this is my first year in the 3rd grade. This is my first year where I have to teach everything in English. And I understand there are many things that I still need to improve in the way you teach here, language arts or history or social studies. Then I have to study to really become a good teacher.

Now, I really enjoy my job, and I feel great because I think I can do and I can help a little bit to my community, in this case Hispanic community, to grow up. And I do my best. When I teach, I think I am the only person going to take care of the child. I think the next teacher going just come into the classroom, teach and that's it, in a cold way. Then, I teach them giving all my love, the same way I would teach my own son or children. This is the way I teach.

I am learning a lot and I am trying to change the way they are. Because these Hispanic children, I see there are many problems in the culture or in the family, the way you know the fathers are the most important. They drink. The mother is nothing. I am trying to change this every day. I have a big fight in my classroom every day because I teach them that girls and boys are equal. They have the same rights. And they both have to try to be somebody else in the future, and see that they don't have to follow the same like their parents. Their parents doesn't know how to read, doesn't know how to write because they couldn't. They lived in a country where they couldn't, and they have to start working when they were child. But they [my students] don't! They are child. Their parents work very hard to make sure that the children doesn't have any problem. Then, your only problem, your only job is to study and become somebody in the future. Because I say, "You don't have to be part of that, that work in the factory for $5. You don't have. You have brain. You have to prove that we are Hispanic. We are smart and intelligent and we are good people." That means my goal is not only to teach them how to read, is to make them good people and to show them that the gangs is not the best way. The gangs, yes, they gave you a lot of money, but for short time or your end is dead or you finish in the prison. Then, you have to find an honest way to [earn] money.

For example, I have a kid. They are 13 kids in the family. He maybe is the number nine from up to down. This family, the older kids have a lot of discipline problems in the school and he was really rough. Actually, in the second year at the beginning of the 2nd grade, when I have him, I have very crowded classroom. Then the facilitator took some of my kids, some from monolingual classroom, some from bilingual and made a classroom for her. And she took him. After two months she talked to me, "Pilar, give me any student you want, but please take him back. I can't stand him. I can't."

I taught this boy. It was hard last year. It was hard because when you say him something, he laugh at you. And when he doesn't want to walk in the hall, I have to hold him sometimes by the hand and push him to go to the washroom. Or he's hitting everybody, the girls, the boys, and running. It was a nightmare.

But I say, "This year, I have to change." This boy, he needs love. His mother can't take care of him. Then, this year I started taking care of him. It is a little risk because I used to hug him, to kiss him. I risk, because maybe someday somebody going to say it's sexual harassment or something. But I was treating him as a mother, as I think a mother should kiss, hug. And he started changing. And then when he did something bad, I say, "You know what? I love you and I care."

Sometimes I am teaching and when he is very active, I have to take him, hug him next to me, stand in the middle of the class. I am giving the class and I am with him, rubbing his head to control him. But when he was out of control I say, "You know what, I love you and I want the best for you, but if you become so silly and you doesn't control yourself, I'm going to ignore you." And this make him change.

I remember on October of this year I was talking with the social worker, because I said last year he used to say that he would be happy to die or to drink some pills. And she talk with him. She was talking and at the end he said it was just to [have someone] pay attention. But when she ask him, "Somebody take care of you or something at home?"

He say, "No." He say, "The only person take care of me is Miss Landa."

And now I found a way. He's doing all jobs. He do everything I say. He's very, very smart. He do all the jobs. He do all his work. Now he

In her classroom, Chicago, 2000

doesn't hit so much as he used to the kids. He control himself a lot. Now I can leave him in the hall walking with the whole classroom.

I feel so, so good because I think I am saving this child. I am worried what will happen in the future, but I hope that this time with me will help him. 'Cause I hope and I think, "Oh, I am saving somebody from the street. I am taking somebody. I am risking somebody." This is my feeling. Unfortunately, next year I don't know who will be the teacher because everybody know that this is a family troublemaker. They label. Then, I don't know.

The future. Now for this next three or four years, my goal is to finish my master's in education. I would like to have family, to buy a house, and then, I still think I would like to continue taking classes relating to English, something that help me writing, reading, speaking. I think we never going to end. We never end. Carlos and me are persons that need some stress I think, some pressure.

CARLOS: We used to take a seat, talk about our life before, our expectations before, and our expectations we have now and the life we have now. For example, it's a very simple example. In Cuba, I never ever can hope to have a car. Here we have had three cars. She never thought before to drive a car. Now she drives a car every day.

The balance is positive. We are much, much, much, much better in here than in Cuba or in any other place. I'm going to tell you something that maybe will be funny for you. We pay taxes happy. When they say us, "Hey, you have to pay $1,500 taxes." We pay happy. You know why? Because we have the money. We have the possibility to pay. It means we are improving. I remember the first year we were here, they return us $800. The second year, we had to pay $500 to IRS. Third year, we had to pay $1,500 to IRS. This year I don't know how much, but anyway, I will be happy because it means that we are improving, we are having a better life. We like to work hard. This year I don't know how much we are gonna pay, but what I know is we make $70,000 this year. We are people that like to work hard and to get better every day.

PILAR: I feel it's strange for us. I don't feel where I belong to. I want to say you why. One side, many Hispanics doesn't have our system or the way to look [at] the life. They only take care about drinks, and play, and gamble, and don't study, and this kind of life. We don't identificate with these people. Another, the Cubans that came 30 years ago, they think that they are better than us because we grew up with the revolution. The Americans, I think we think in many ways as American but I think [the Americans], because we are immigrants, because it's hard to understand us, because we are from different countries, they don't accept us in their groups. Then, we are in the middle. We are rejected from one group. We are rejected from another group. We are just alone in the middle. We have some friends but...

CARLOS: Few ones.

PILAR: Few ones, just few ones. For example, we in three and a half year have improved and we are proud of ourselves. It doesn't mean we think it's the maximum. We want to continue improving, but it's just the beginning [Laughs.] or in the middle. But unfortunately, some Cubans didn't have the same luck. They are working. They don't make a lot of money. They are working in the place there where they don't like. And actually, let me tell you. We have friends of us. I know that they doesn't want to see us very frequently because when they see us, they are professionals, too, but they are not working as a professional. When they saw us, they feel bad. Because we all four are professionals. They feel, "These two guys they did, they are improving, they are earning money, they are studying, and they get everything and we can't." And I think that made them to feel so bad about themselves that they doesn't want to see us very frequently. It is really a strange position.

Of course, we were in some ways lucky or fortunate, however you want it, that we don't have children. Then, I could spend 18 hours a day at the street, working and studying. And I didn't have to take care.

If I don't cook, if I don't clean, nothing happen because nobody was depending on me. But these families, many of them come with children. Then, it's harder because they need to spend time at home. Another I think make a mistake. When I came here, I say I will work eight hours, just a few money, because my goal is not to make now $5 for hour. My goal is it's possible to make $50 per hour. I am not worried about now for money. I won't become rich with this salary. My goal now is I have to work because I have to survive. I need money to pay the rent. I need money to eat. But the most important is to take my English. Then, I work only eight hours. The rest of the time I spend studying English. Of course the people, some because they have family, they need money and they work 12 hours a day. When they going to study English? And another is because they think that making overtime, overtime, overtime they going to make money and money and money and they going to live better. No! This is a mistake in my personal opinion. Because when I get a good job, I going to earn all this money I didn't earn before in overtime, I going to earn later and in an easy way. This was my point. I did my overtime and sometime when they needed me, in the two days [when] I rest of the week, they needed me, I work. But it wasn't my obsession as some in where Carlos working. They work 12 hours a day, and then some of them have another job in another place during the weekend. They don't study.

What I think is to be immigrant—what an immigrant feel, only an immigrant can really understand. But really, when you know that you are closing the door you have behind, it is closed, and you are opening a door that you doesn't know what is in front of you, you doesn't know your destiny, it is really, really hard. You have to change the way you think sometimes. You have to change some of your culture. You're obligated to change. Not everything. I don't mean you have to Americanize, but I mean you have to make a lot of change. And it is really hard. Everybody are not so lucky as us. Then, I really feel sorry for those immigrants that doesn't come here with any education. What will be about them? If we with education have been discriminated, have been a long way to get to the place where we are, what do we think is for these common people that come here? How is their life? They keep forever in a factory for $5 an hour. It was a nightmare only for a year for me. But what about people that is a nightmare for 15 years or 20 years? This is what I think some people have to think about. And besides that, I think that the only really Americans are the Indians. Why there are people they are looking at us, if they are immigrants?

The only Americans, I'm sorry, is the Indians. The rest are immigrants because here wasn't any white people. Then the white people are immigrant as me, only they were lucky that their family came many, many years ago.

I think we sometimes work harder than the Americans because we have to jump many barriers. The barrier of language, the barrier of culture. We didn't, for example, never before knew about taxes or credit card, or nothing like that. We have to learn. When you are a boy, you have five years to learn the basic language. When you are immigrant, you don't have any years. You have to come here and you have to start speak if you want to survive. All Americans here have 20 years when they are studying in the school. They study the life, the technology, how does the system work, how the city is. The immigrant doesn't have time. They don't give you 20 years. Then you have to learn so, so many things in so short time that not everybody is able to do. I think many people can get so stressed and so depressed. And to be immigrant, they can't change totally their life and their way of think. Maybe the people that was before very fun, or happy, or very nice, they can get angry, sad, until they suicide. We have to think that an immigrant usually, I think, 95 percent are depressed. And I'm very conservative because we sometimes are depressed, too. They feel that they are not human, that somebody's better than you and you are nothing.

Yes, I felt that, especially at the beginning. Still, when I go to a place where many Americans are meeting or something, I stay sometimes very quiet because I think they don't want me. And still in the university, they don't interesting in me because I am an Indian. I am not part of their group, the high group, the good group. I am nothing. And sometimes I am sitting there and they are unable to say, "Hi, how are you?" Because for them, I am nothing. They don't have to spend their time to talk to me, to waste their time. What I going to give them? I don't going to give nothing. This is their opinion.

CARLOS: In reality, as a human being, I feel myself much better in this country than I could feel in any other place. I think everybody in this world should know America. Because besides the problems we find here, as the ones we have talked to you about many stupid things, it doesn't mean that all Americans are like that. I am sure most of the Americans are trying to get a better world and they are trying to do the best they can. And this is the only country in the world that accept people like us that have problems in their own country, and they accept them. Oh, OK. It's hard when you come here and you are engineer,

you have been teacher, and you come as we came to Truman College as a lady said you, "Oh, you know what? All these papers you have is nothing here. You are nobody in this country." It's hard because I have spent most of my life studying. And that is hard. But you need to let the time goes and you get your position.

I think this is the country of opportunities. I think you can become somebody in this country. Besides the thoughts about racism or everything else, if you study, if you work hard, you can become somebody.

I have found American guys that in a funny way, they have asked, "How come this Indian guy is making $40,000 a year after being here three years, and I cannot do that? How come? I am American." Because this country is plenty, plenty of opportunity. The guy that don't earn money in this country is because he's stupid. Because if you make an effort, if you work hard, you can earn whatever you want in this country. You don't have limitations like in Cuba. I think the ones that have the opportunity to come to this country have to thanks God for come here and we have to do the best we can for improve what we see is not good in this country.

I remember sometimes at the time I used to go to bed in Cuba, I was so, so, so hungry that I got a pain in my stomach and I couldn't sleep. And I told Pilar, "Pilar, you know what? I am so hungry that the pain is killing me."

And Pilar told me, "You know what? There is nothing to eat, so go and drink a little water with sugar and there is nothing more." And in this country, a homeless has $5 to go to McDonald's or Denny's or whatever. Even I don't understand now, I couldn't understand before, and I won't understand in the future how come in this country there are people homeless. Because here if you got a job, even the worst job, $5 an hour, you can live, because we did it. Without English, without anything. So how come American people can be homeless?

PILAR: I feel very happy, very, very happy. We used to talk a lot [about] everything we have gained here. This is the reason we sit sometime and make history about our past, how different our life is now from the past. But, sometimes we lost, too. Because here, we feel that we only have each other. That means, because of the way the people live here, because everybody is so, so busy and everybody is studying, working, doing, so, so busy, you are alone. Not lonely, because I have Carlos, but besides Carlos, yes. I think in this country the only person really going to take care about me or going to worry about me is Carlos. I work with people. I have a nice relationship, but this is just relation of work. Later, everybody go to their homes and that's it. This is hard. Especially because in our country as I said before, everybody know everything, but when you are sick, your neighbor bring you soup or a pills or a medicine. Whatever they have, they come to your house. They bring something to you. And they say, "Do you need something? How are you feeling? How are you?"

And I say, "Thanks God I have Carlos." If I would be here alone, I can die here and the people [are only] going to know when they smell.

PILAR STILL TEACHES in a bilingual elementary school classroom. **CARLOS IS NOW TEACHING** math at St. Augustine College. They recently bought a home in Chicago.

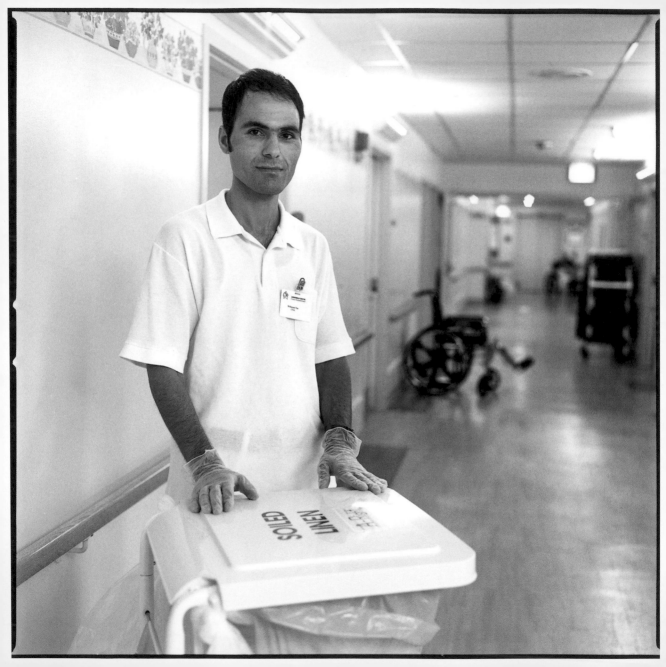

MY NAME IS MUHAMMAD DUR *and* I AM FROM AFGHANISTAN. *I was born on September 13, 1975 and I came to the United States as an immigrant* MARCH 16TH, 2001. *It is exactly the date.*

YOU KNOW, WE ARE MUSLIMS, and all Muslims love their prophet. My father was a kind of religious person and he loved to put the name Muhammad on the beginning of all his sons' names. And that's why my all brothers have Muhammad, and then their first names. Actually, my name is Muhammad Yousif Taheri. And I'm going to change it when I receive my green card and my citizenship. Muhammad Dur, it's my father's name. It was in my passport and immigration office in United Nations High Commission for Refugees. They wrote this one in my document and it was my original document. They thought that my last name is Muhammad Dur. They asked me, "If we write Muhammad Dur, is it OK?"

I told them, "It's not OK, but if you write it, it doesn't matter." It means, I agreed.

At first, I am an Afghan. Afghan contains a lot of tribes, and there are many, many tribes that live together, and they are called Afghan. And I am proud of being an Afghan. When someone call me Afghan, I love this word, but specifically, I'm a Pashtun Persian. My mother is Persian, Tajik actually. And my father is Pashtun.

I am born in a big family. My father, actually, he was migrated from his province to the province of northeast side of Afghanistan which is called Takhar province. It's on the border of Tajikistan, former Soviet Union. I don't know actually the dates when he migrated. You know, the dates in our country are not counted. I don't know why. A lot of Afghan people don't know their date of birth, and it is not important. Most of them are illiterate and they don't celebrate. Literacy is very low in our country. My father wasn't a peasant. My father was not an illiterate person and that's why he understood many things. Even in that culture, sending a girl to school was crime, but my father dared and sent his daughters and his sons to school. And when he earned money, he spent all his money to his sons and daughters in order to keep them going to school.

And my father, when he came to Takhar province, I think he thought how should he survive here. Then he started selling tea. He came as a tea merchant to our province, and he married my mother here, and then he married another wife. It means he had two wives at the same time. You know, Islam permits a person to marry with four wives at once, not more than four, if a person has the ability of keeping satisfaction of all wives. I have two sisters and I have seven brothers. We are 10. We are nine [from my mother]. Let me count it, [Laughs.] because I should not be confused.

My mother is alive now fortunately and I'm thankful of God. She's happy [even though] she has a lot of sadness. And she is a poor family's girl. She is a strong mother. She even was losing her brother and her two sons, but she did a lot of struggle and effort and she never cried, never upon these happenings. And also, she was supportive of my father a lot. Once she was telling a story of her life to the family, and I was hearing her. She told us that once from kingdom regime, police came to take him [my father] to the district and deal with some investigation. He wasn't guilty, but they have doubt about him being guilty. And my mother resisted and didn't let the police. At first, she took the sword, and she told them at the main gate, "If you come to our house, I will kill you at first. If I couldn't, I will kill myself. But I will never let my husband [go] because I have no support here. If he is not in this fort

With his medical school class, Azerbaijan, 1999

for one night, I will die. It's better to die before something happens." Then they tried. My father was in the field. And then he came and they took him and sit him in their car. My mother says it was American jeep. Then my mother took her son, elder than me, and put near the tire of the jeep, and on the one [other] tire, she sat and told them that, "You will kill my son and me, then you can take my husband."

At that time, my father was telling her, "Don't do this. It doesn't matter. I will go and back."

But she didn't listen to her husband, too. She told us that, "I was very crazy in that time. I don't know why." And at last, they left my father.

They married and they started to make a house, but they couldn't make a house in the early times. They lived in a rented house for about two or three years. After that, my father made a fort. It was a very big fort. We were very far from villages. Maybe one hour far from one village and half an hour far from the other village in our both sides, right and left. We were in a valley in the foot of a very high mountain. It was a very beautiful place. Greenery all the time except winter, of course. Winter is very cold. And then he made this fort because in that time, he was an immigrant and he was Pashtun, and people who lived there were all Uzbeks and Tajiks. But maybe in that time, was a little discrimination, but not as much as today. My father was curious about his

security. Why he made this fort, it was only because of security and his children and his wives' security, to protect himself from every kind of danger which may be threatened by people or may be threatened by animals, because our house was in the valley in the foot of a mountain. And this mountain had a lot of dangerous animals, like lions, and many, many wolves, and other kinds of animals.

This fort was very famous. Even today, all our province knows about this fort. It was about 300 meters to 300 meters. It was square. Very big, very big. Maybe it takes a lot of time, and he collect many engineers to do this. You should remember that in our country, the forts are not made from concrete, from cement. It was made of stones and some kind of soil, mud, and also in the foundation it had concrete. And inside was good. We slept on the carpet and we had a special kind of mattress. We had beds made of cotton. We slept on that. No electricity. Not at all. We had gas lamps. We had well for how to get water, to keep the inside of the fort green and beautiful.

Half of the fort was built for human and half for animals. We had a lot of horses and a lot of cows as well. I will tell you about the cows, too. We had 50 cows for two purposes. Ten or twelve of them were plowing and 20 of them were milking for us. There was no day without milk or yogurt to eat the meal. We always drank milk and we always had yogurt with our food.

And it was very interesting when Russians invaded our country. When they passed from the side of our fort, they thought that this may be a military fort, but it wasn't. And after maybe a month of invasion, they came to see inside. My father didn't let them. No Russian could enter. My father told them, "No. There is my children. They are afraid of Russians. I don't let. I will kill myself, but I don't let Russians to enter in my house." I remember I was crying. Very, very scared because it was like a specific attack on a house which was targeted by the invaders, and it was our idea that maybe they harm us, maybe they do something which is against our conscience, against our religion. Yes, the fort still exists but ruined, like ruin. We cannot see now.

My father sent us to school after six years old, being six-year-old children, and the first days we went to school on the horses. For example, I was six years old, my brother was maybe, the elder, 10 years old. He took us to school in two horses. Even three in a horse, in one horse. We were little boys, we could sit. It was fun, too, for us. Then, our school area had a meadow, and it was very big school, very beautiful school. We tied the horse to the post, and then the horse was there. And after we finished the school, again we took our horse and came back to the fort. It was very far. It was about two hours by foot every day, but it was maybe one hour by horse. And after coming to the fort, then we had a religious teacher. He was a scholar. He was also from very far away. My father hired him in order to come once a day from after evening prayers, which is after 5:00 or 6:00, till 9:00 at night. And it was reciting the holy Koran and reading many, many books, all Arabic. My father didn't like to memorize. My father liked to see his sons being doctors, engineers, teachers, and scholars. But the Islamic part of teaching was religious teaching and ethical part of our life. He wanted to develop our ethical point of perspective of personality. And I think he did very appropriate for that time. And we learned a lot of things from him. It was very enjoyable and I think we were progressing.

When communists came and took the power, I was three years [old] until nine, ten years. I cried a lot that I cannot continue my education here, because everything is changing.

When I was nine, I went to graze the cow. Me alone, outside on the mountain, very far. Maybe four or five hours far away. Inside there was danger where there are caves, there are flood river, and many dangerous animals. And I was very little boy. But I found one little girl was with her brother, and they also brought their goats, and sheeps. We were grazing and suddenly, helicopters came and bombard the village, and I thought about our fort. And it was very dangerous kind of helicopters. We were in a very high mountain. We went up the mountain. We left everything. The cows, the sheeps, we leave them, but they know. They have this idea. They were good animals. They were very good animals. They knew that, "We should not go far because a little boy is with us and we should not disturb him." [Laughs.] They knew, really! They were walking and grazing around, and we went up and we saw these helicopters. And this girl cried and made us a little to cry. But we couldn't do anything. And we saw the helicopters come, fire and go back, and then again two of them came directly from Russia. We thought that maybe fighting lasts for one day, two days, and what should we do? If we stay there night, the wolves will come and eat all our sheeps and cows, and maybe lion come to eat us. Then, I choose the way how to go to a different village which is far away from us, one hour. Even there is also that bombing. Bombing is all over [everywhere]. But we went there, and even I had the little girl on my shoulder. She was maybe eight years old and I was maybe one year older, but

I was strong. And we helped each other, and we went. We were three. With all animals. We went to the village, and village dogs jumped on us, and we were trying to defend ourselves. Suddenly, a man appeared and he helped us and he took us to his house. He knew us, who were we. Even they knew from our cows, too. [Laughs.] This villager went to my father and told him, "Your son is here. Don't worry about him and about your cows." She [my mother] tried to find us and was crying [when I got home].

Let me tell you what makes the actual idea of our family and our brothers. My brother makes all ideology of our family. He made, this elder brother, and one of my other brother, too. They have a kind of revolutionary ideas, which was hated by mujahideen as well as communists. And it was a different kind of idea. They see Islam not like mujahideens. For example, there is no freedom in mujahideen's and Taliban's Islam, in a word. In my brothers' friends, a lot of friends, a lot of scholars, and a lot of good people of Afghanistan, they gathered together and they are also trying, they are continuing their struggle to reach their ideas, to reach their goals. And it was an Islam with freedom, an Islam which respects the values of humanity. Modern Islam. It was based on reformism of Islam. Not reform that Muhammad did the mistake. No! The followers of Muhammad who are living now in the 21st century are committing the mistakes. This is not Muhammad's Islam. They were trying to show Islam's view, the real view to the people. And it was including of all human rights, freedom of speech, freedom of action and women's emancipation. All things like other developed nations.

My father told him, "Keep your struggle in the path of God. This is an invasion."

But my brother told my father that, "I'm going to do something else. I'm going to struggle in the field of education as well as in the field of fighting against them, but mostly in the field of education. At first I take my brothers to Pakistan. There is peace, and the educational situation is good, and our neighbor, they support us. We should take them there."

My father agreed, but not me because I was child and he afraid that maybe I die on the way. The way is very difficult, very difficult. They couldn't go by roads! All by mountains because the roads were all controlled by communists and they couldn't go. All by mountains. Then I cried at that time they were deciding to leave me there. But I didn't agree. I told them, "I will go, even I die on the way." Because I wanted to go to school. I wanted to go to school. Nothing else. Because I wanted to be something in the future.

And I came. It is a very long story. I will tell you shortly that after 45 days of walking and waiting for two days in a village, three days maybe in some places, that maybe the way is blocked by Russians, we reached Pakistan. But the people were helpful when they saw us, that a small boy is going to learn. It was strange for people. They were helpful. I crossed the border and also we climbed the Hindu Kush Mountains, one of its part. It was snowing and I cried a lot because of coldness, and I was on the horse. With a lot of harsh and difficulties, I reached Pakistan and I started school again in a religious school of mujahideen. I was maybe 10 years old. It was not like *madrasah* of Taliban. It is entirely different *madrasah*. *Madrasah* in our language means school. It had mathematics, not English, Persian, Pashtu, and nothing else. But mostly we learned logic and grammar of Arabic language and religious books. There are many books, illustration of Koran, and illustration of the speech of Muhammad, peace be upon him, and these things.

This is a very special part of my life in *madrasah*. What happened there? I was a prominent student there. It was the biggest *madrasah* of mujahideen, and it was counted very well. It had a lot of guards and 3,500 students were there. It was very big. In 7th class [grade], 14, 15 years old, there was a gathering of all mujahideen leaders, and I was selected as a person who should give the speech of this *madrasah* in Arabic language. And I gave this speech very well, but I had something from my own ideas. I mixed, and it reflects bad on the school masters. I can say as compared to them, it was very and very liberal, and in a very appropriate way of dealing with the matters in 20th century. The main idea was reformation. It's more human. My talking was based on the reformation of religious thought. A very big and essential part of the reform was changing the religious rote system of education into modern ways. This illustration brings the Muslim world out of the dogmatic way of thinking, out of the sleep. And this was the big conflict between us and them.

And they sent four to six very strong boys, 16 years old, 20 years old, 15 years old, with rods and they beat me one day. This *madrasah's* masters sent them. And they hit me on the head, not anywhere else. It was a very specific way of beating. It was planned. At first they came to me like brothers. They told me, "Yousif, we have a very special conversation with you. Will you please? Let's walk along this small river."

I told them, "I'd be happy. Let's go." And we talked to each other

because I have no idea of this horror, of this beating or hatred that much to beat a person. I didn't create hatred. I was always preaching love, but they were who didn't like love. I don't know why they don't like love. Maybe my love, maybe. Then, they closed the door, the big gate. And I saw there four or five sticks for beating. And they jumped on the sticks and they took the sticks and they started, without talking anything. And I told them, "Why?" Three times. "Why and why?" And I made ready myself then and say nothing.

Then [other] students came to the door, but they couldn't open the door. And they hit the door and they told, "Don't do this, don't do that." Maybe they asked why something is happening. Then they finished their mission and they went away. They didn't want to kill me. I think they wanted to punish me seriously, and I should not be able to talk more about my ideas, and also to not have the dare afterwards to give speeches, to talk, to activate, to continue my activities.

They hit on my head and I nearly felt unconsciousness, but I wasn't in unconsciousness. Then, they left and I was sick. After that, I have bandage here on the head. I didn't say anything. And this went to the administration and they complained about me that I was telling something against Islam and that's why I was hit, beaten. And they called me, and they took a very big written interview. "What's your ideas? What are you doing right now?" These things. I answered them. And they told me, "We are going to put you in exile from this hostel [dormitory] to the dormitory which is very small and very far." It's only for elder students, the dormitory of 11th and 12th class [grade]. These were bearded students, big students. Twenty-five-years-old, thirty-years-old students. They were far away and it was small and closed because they were studying, they were researching. And I was exiled there and they gave me a little room there. There was some little rooms for one person without bed, without anything. And they told me that, "We put you here in order to watch you, what you do, what is your activities." And I was there. After that, they expelled me, dropped me from the school, and I went to Afghanistan. This is the time when two of my brothers were in prison in Afghanistan and one of my brothers was in prison in Pakistan.

I went to Bamiyan. This is a province where the two huge Buddhist sculptures were there. The only foundation and the only base for this [reformation] thought was in Bamiyan, and they had power. They had guns and weapons and a lot of soldiers, and I went to them. I went there for six months. I had refuge, actually, there. I trained to use guns

In Baku, Azerbaijan, 2000

there. And they showed me a lot. They helped me a lot, a lot. And they gave me again, they put on me a soul of peace. They sent me back to Pakistan, not to go to religious school, [but] to go to a very modern school in Pakistan. And one of my brother's friends paid all the tuition fees for me, and I started learning in English medium school in Pakistan. It was high school.

I finished school in Pakistan in 1994. And then I went to the northern province [of Afghanistan] after Pakistan. One of my brothers was in Mazar-i-Sharif. This is a province in north, very big province. And there, he married and he needed a brother to be with him. And I went there, and I told him that I want to come there because of going to university. There is a very good university. When I graduated, I had no good score to get admission in medical university. My brother had some kind of friends there in education ministry. He told them that, "My brother will come, and please enroll him in his absence. This is his picture." And he enrolled me. I took the examination when I went there and I passed. It was in 1995.

I studied medicine for one year. There I had a lot of good friends. I had a lot of friends with whom I had contact and talk about the future of Afghanistan and the future of this generation in university.

Then, I realized that one day Taliban will capture Mazar-i-Sharif,

and this happiness which is here, and all the girls and boys go to school and go to university and they're happy, and this will one day come here, we will see blood instead of water here in the streams of this city. And I was not able to see a way to rid of blood.

At the beginning, they [Taliban] emerged as a mysterious group in southern area of Kandahar, which is the border with Pakistan. The Taliban emerged from Pakistan. Whatever the reason was, I don't know. Maybe there is a lot of political reasons behind Taliban and beyond my knowledge, but they did something because they are religious students. And I don't support their ideas, but they did that when they came. They took Kandahar very soon, very soon. It's very big city, but they took very soon because the people help them. The people are religious.

When they came at first from one place to another place and they were going forward, they were preaching humanity and they were preaching peace. And really it was peace at the beginning and they really were doing well. For example, during the mujahideen factions, there was anarchy ruling. There was killing each other. There was raping, a lot of stealing. There was a lot of social problems. And it happened. There were a lot of misery. The people don't want to see these sins by the name of Islam and mujahideen. They [the Taliban] finished this world of anarchy and they provide stability, a stability which is based upon very fundamentalist Islamic thought.

When I was in Mazar-i-Sharif, we were evaluating the level of literature, the level of studying, and the level of knowledge in Afghanistan and many other countries, as we had access to Internet. And we had information, a lot of information, newspapers, the news, American, we received this one. A lot of newspapers. *Guardian* from London. And also we saw in dish antenna, in satellite TV. There were some scholars and some specialists and they discuss about matters. CNN, and also The Discovery Channel and these things. These all were helping us to rely upon the fact [learn] what is existing in this world. And also we were discussing as a human that, "Why we are in misery? What should we do? If I'm here, I cannot receive good knowledge here. I cannot attend high schools here. Ultimately, I will be a school master or a very primary doctor or something like this. Let's move because migration brings civilizations." My friends were mostly boys, but girls were also included in our rounds of discussions. But the girls, you know, were not able to go far away from their family. If they go to foreign country, they should go with their father and mother. And unfortunately for girls, I am very sorry for them, although there are a lot of talented girls among them.

I fled Mazar-i-Sharif towards Russia in 1996. I wanted to go forward, forward, forward until the West, to reach the West. I had two destinations, whether in European countries, specifically I should say England because of Oxford, or in America because I love English as well. I am fond of knowledge. I'm not ambitious, but really I see myself in the climax of my thoughts, proud when I will be graduated from a high level school. That's why I had these two destinations to accomplish my goal, which was graduation from a high level medical school. Right now, this is my field. Even I told all my friends, "Please go to search and go far away from this country. Learn, but don't live there. Come back to serve for your people." And me, also this idea, still.

I received the visa of Turkmenistan. And I went to Turkmenistan, and I was there for a month, and I crossed the border of Azerbaijan illegally to Caucasus countries. It's beautiful country. This is a lake which is Caspian Sea. I crossed the Caspian Sea by ship. It was very long journey, about 18 hours. I had my passport. Of course I had. When I was in Turkmenistan, I had my passport, my visa. I was legal. But when I crossed this border of this Caspian Sea, no one asked me, "Where do you want to go?" because this is commonwealth countries of the former Soviet Union, and within commonwealth countries, the people can go. But me is not from commonwealth country. And I went

On the beach, Chicago, 2001

to there. The police officers of Azerbaijan were very helpful to Afghans. Our north neighbors are good with us. They feel sorrow about Afghans because we are suffering and they know.

I went there in Baku, Azerbaijan. In Baku city I was alone, but there I had a lot of friends. And I had a letter from one of my friends to another friend who had there power in Azerbaijan in education ministry. He was from Shiite party. But you know, I am Pashtu, Sunni party. I don't think about, but they think about this a lot, they count about this. This was the problem and I faced with the challenge of this problem, and I couldn't solve this one. And I couldn't go to school for two years because of this. I wanted to attend the medical university. For one year, I learned Russian language in Baku. I stayed in Baku waiting, waiting, waiting all the day, thinking and losing hairs alone. In my suffering, I was alone. No one paid attention to me. I was attacked by malnutrition. Do you believe? In Baku, everything is cheap, but I was attacked by malnutrition because I had no money. I tried to work there, but I couldn't find any job. There is no job. Employment is very, very bad for the people themselves. Not only in Baku, all over the Russia. I couldn't find a job. Nothing. I had some grains of rice, put it in water—nothing else. No oil, no onion, nothing, no meat. And I ate this for about 15 days. And suddenly one of my friends, he was from Jordan, Arab, he was my best friend, he came and he understood, realized from my face. My face was yellow, white. And he told me, "You are weak. Why?"

I said, "I don't know why I am like this." I didn't say many things.

But he realized and he told me, "I will be with you in this room for some days." And he wanted to know about me, what is the problem. He was a real friend and he helped me. And then my brother sent money.

When I went to Russia, I realized how people are good people, educated, and how they love human. And I never forget, even I was in Azerbaijan. In that time, we were against the policy of Soviet Union, but we are never against the people of Russia, as well in America. I am critic towards the policy of America. If you ask me, I will tell you. I'm critic. But the people of Russia, or the people of America, are very good people. They are human and they are helpful. So, let me answer this for today. So, I should leave America? Should I? No, today is also fighting in my country, and it's air invasion. It's real. Sure, the policies are different. The people, culture, and knowledge, these are the links in humanity which will never be cut by any policy.

I found some kind of warmth there, and some kind of attraction that maybe I will study until my bachelor's degree there, and then I will go to farther investigation and further studies in western countries. I planned to go to Moscow and attend there because I wanted to know about the medicine in Russia, which is a very developed country. It has a lot of things there and medicine was also very advanced in former Soviet Union. In December '98 [I started medical college] for one and half years, but I realized that the level of study in Azerbaijan and all over Russia is collapsed. It's not like former Soviet Union. It's not like that level that I thought before. And all these brought me in one conclusion that, "Let's leave." It became a sudden conclusion, and I did it.

And one day, one of my friends also told me there is United Nations. Even I haven't seen this United Nations office. In Azerbaijan, Baku the capital, there is an UNHCR [United Nations High Commission for Refugees] office and I went there. He took me there and I went. They showed some kind of tendencies to help me and I was also interested. Then, in this time, I 100 percent decided that I will leave Azerbaijan towards any country which accepts immigrants, European or Canada or America. I wanted to release myself from that situation and it was a very critical situation for me. And I couldn't go back to Afghanistan as well, because the Taliban would kill me or would send me as a soldier and ultimately I would be killed. And I don't want to serve for my people by killing them, by having gun in my hand. I wanted to serve my people by having pen in my hand and having good plans, economical and social plans for them, and that's why I told the United Nations that, "I'm such kind of person and I need your help."

Then, it occurred. I had an interview with a girl from Italy and we had an interview in English and she told me that, "I hope that you will be saved by us, because as we see, your case is strong enough."

Then, I had interview with Dawn Sparkle. Miss Dawn Sparkle. She was from Washington, D.C. and she was the special envoy of the Immigration and Naturalization Ministry [Service] of the United States. She was very nice and she told me, "You haven't solved a small question. When you solve this question, you will be accepted."

So I told her, "What's the question? Can I solve it now?"

She told me, "Sure, it is this question. You told me that Taliban took the power of Kabul in 1995, but my record and the world's record showed that they took power in 1996. This is a difference between our record and your claim."

So at first I started to tell her, "I told you the west of Kabul, is it OK?"

She told me, "Yes, you told me half of Kabul. Yeah, it is half of the Kabul city."

I was in that half of the Kabul at that time when they took the power. I saw by my eyes. I saw many people were killed by my eyes. I even helped some bodies. And I proved. I told her many details.

She told me, "OK." She gave me appointment for about two weeks.

Then, during these two weeks, one of the workers there, she was from Azerbaijan, she told me, "Yousif, you have been approved and we are going to send you to Chile." It was in April, 2000.

I [was] shocked in that time. I thought, "Oh, Chile. What country it is?" So, I found out in that time that it is Spanish, and I cannot speak Spanish. This is a barrier for me to my goal, which is going directly to school. So, I became a little sad and disappointed.

I called Dawn Sparkle. I called her and I found her with very difficulty in telephone. The other worker, the one who told me this message, she told me, "It's impossible to talk to her directly. You can leave us a message and we will give her."

So I told her that, "It is very special. It's a request and if it is possible, even not today, tomorrow, it would be very good to talk to her."

She told me, "No, tomorrow she is going to leave the country."

Oh, I became...my heart was...I was trembling in that time like a malaria attacked person. So, I succeeded to talk with her because I insisted that I will talk to her. And I started to talk. She was in an interview with someone. And she knew me when I told her my name.

So she told me, "No, why you don't want to go to Chile? Chile is a very good country."

I told her that, "No, there is no matter of good or bad. At first I am very thankful that United Nations gave me refuge in the world. It's a matter of thanking, and there is no question that I am very thankful. Even Chile, even Bangladesh, even Somalia. There is a matter that I speak English, and I have learned your language for many years, and I love this language, and I hope I have some careers in this language, and I hope I should serve for this language in some way and also for myself as a human being. So, if it is possible, would you please transfer me from Chile to the United States or Canada? It doesn't matter for me because both of them are English speaking countries."

So, she told me, "In Santiago, we have got a lot of English universities and if you want to continue your education, you can continue. Don't worry about it."

Then, I told her, "OK," with a little disappointing sound. And it was the end. She didn't accept, but my talking affected her after hanging up.

After a week, I went as a routine, so this girl again told me, "Congratulations, Yousif. You have been accepted to the United States." And I was very happy in that time. I was very excited. I thought that when I'm able to go to America, to the United States, so as we defined the United States, the land of opportunity, so maybe I have the opportunity of succeeding in my life, which is very related to my society, and go back to my country or being a citizen of America, as a useful citizen there, to continue my education to be able to do something in scientific field. So, many reasons were making me happy.

Then they told me, "Where do you want to go? Do you have any relatives in the United States?"

I told them, "No, I have no one. I don't know anyone in the United States." It is a fact that I didn't know, and right now I don't have any relatives. They were sending to different states of the United States. Sending me to Chicago, to Illinois, it was not my choice. It was accidental.

So, when I know that I'm going to Chicago, I went to Internet and I found about Springfield and about Chicago. Chicago was defined as a great city. Sears Tower was mentioned there. OK, this was about the buildings and the beauty. And also I was interested about education, so I found about University of Chicago. And the other universities, Northwestern was not permanent name for me because "north" and "west", this was not attractive to my mind. But when I came here, it is a very great university, I realized. And University of Illinois, these were listed but I didn't pay attention. But University of Chicago, I paid attention because this was the name of the city in which I was going to be and going to live. So, I read about it and this was my interest to read about the University of Chicago.

We had a meeting. It was sponsored by Immigration and Naturalization Service. So, they gave a speech before coming here. They told us that Immigration Service and settlement agencies provide you this and that and that, and they don't provide you this and this. Our expectation were not high, but before that illustration, it was high. This was my own expectation that I will be a student there. It was my own fantasy. And when I go and I write an application, it was a fantasy making for myself [Laughs.], that I will receive scholarship because I am from a war-torn country, and they will pay attention for me because it is a part of humanitarian help of an education institute to help me because I am deserved.

They sent me here and we came by German airplane, which is Lufthansa. It was a good journey. I was not happy, not sad—between them. I was remembering. I was reminding myself all the changes and loneliness in the world.

[At the airport in Chicago] came people who were in charge of taking care of us. Officially they were from Ethiopian Community [Association]. One Afghan was employed there and he was the assistant of case worker. He came with his car. So, with him was two other Afghans who are here, and they brought their cars and we could put our luggages and baggages and all things. We were 13. Nine of us were related to Ethiopian Community [Association] and four of us to Catholic Charities. We got separated from the airport. Four of us, we didn't even meet with each other till maybe one and half weeks. So, when we came, they brought us all together and put us in one apartment. Two bedrooms. Nine of us. And there was some [mattresses] and pillows that was the arrangements, all on the floor. Nine mattresses, like for dead bodies. They were like this. [Laughs.] Four were in the salon, two in one bedroom, three in another bedroom. So, we looked around and all Afghans were with us and we laughed, but we didn't show anything from ourselves because we lived much better than that in Russia when we were students.

Washing dishes, Chicago, 2001

Receiving his Certified Nursing Assistant certificate, Chicago, 2002

They cooked some Afghan foods, which is rice and these things, and we sat and we enjoyed eating. So, after that, they left and we all together sat. I didn't say anything. So, they started to talk that, "Is it America?" [Laughs.] One said, "What a country we came! What a name and what a fame and what a place we came in, and what a bedroom. It is made of 18th century and there is no arrangements." In former Soviet Union republics, when you rent an apartment, they will provide you everything. For example, the dishes, the bed, everything, the carpet, everything. You don't need to buy anything for yourself.

So, we thought like this that, "We are refugees and we have nothing." Even some of us didn't have clothes. Some of us were not students. They were very poor. Maybe $20 in pocket. Myself, I had $5 when I came to the United States. Do you believe me? Because in Germany, I had $20. I bought $15 phone card to call back to Baku to my friends that I have arrived.

One of our friends woke up at midnight [the first night]. We didn't see the watch. He came and told us that, "Get up, get up. I prepared you breakfast." We were hungry. But you know, when you come from east, there is day, here is night, so the change of the daily day and night, the time, make a big difference. You cannot properly sleep and you wake up in that time until you adapt yourself. So we ate breakfast.

We didn't see anything, because around us was snow and there was a light. We thought that it is day and because of cloud, there is no sun. Actually it was midnight [Laughs.] or maybe 2:00 [A.M.]. We had watches, all of us, but these watches were not according to the time of the United States. We didn't know. We didn't pay attention to these things. When one American or one European goes east or anywhere, first they will get a map and they will confirm themselves about the tradition, the time, everything. But for us it was a dream coming here. When we were accepted, we were happy and we were enjoy. We didn't think about those things.

We had breakfast. I saw far from the light there was darkness and I told my friend with a skeptical sentence, "Maybe it is not morning my friends!" [Laughs loudly.]

All of them said, "How do you know?" Actually all of them were doubtful about the time. So, after eating again, we slept.

In the morning 8:00, the person who was working with Ethiopian Community [Association] with our case worker, both of them came and woke us up. So, they told us, "How much do you sleep? It's 8:00. Get up."

I asked them, "What? 8:00? [Laughs.] We had breakfast at 8:00! [Laughs.] It's P.M. or A.M.?"

"No," they told me, "A.M." So we realized actually it was between one and two in the morning when we woke up!

In that day, we went to social security office and we did all our legal processes which should be done. We went to Public Health and Public Aid.

I came here and I faced with a big problem. So I thought that, "What should I do?" I have no good qualifications because these transitions, these changings were my enemies in some ways. So, the first job that I found was in a hotel as a steward. And you know, it's a very dangerous and difficult job. Dangerous to health. Always in wet and humid, which is dangerous to health. Always eight hours a day you stand and all your body is wet, because I work in kitchen. We lift, for example, many plates and dishes to help the cook. And also there is a washing machine which washes the dishes. We put from one side, get from the other side, take it from the other side. When we take it, it is full of water and we should do it quickly. So, it was my first physical job. I had never this job, such kind of job. And I adapt myself as well, and I have learned many things from there because my colleagues are all from the third world as me, and how they are treated by American fellows and also the differences between these levels as I see. No verbally discrimination. No officially discrimination. But being curious, you can see many things. For example, not respect, rudeness, not paying attention, which are ethically bad. And also a bad word when you hear from your boss or a little higher rank, it effects 10 times more than many other injuries. It has bad effect in mind. It shapes your attitude always to obey. I don't mean that obeying a law is not good. No, this is not law. This is something else. Always you are passive and your mind shapes in passive ways, so you cannot show yourself, you cannot do what you want, even you are free. You lose your identity. It's an experience. To maintain my pride, for me, I have a lot of problems there, [but] it is an opportunity in financial field for me here that I'm very appreciated.

The way of life is very liberal here, especially for women and also for those who have their own ideas, they can express. There is full freedom of speech, which is very good. One of the big surprises that I have is that I can say anything that I want, even in this time of war with Taliban, a person may say that Taliban brought peace in one stage of chaos in Afghanistan. Even he can claim this one. So this is also very big issue for me. And also, there is more access to everything to develop every aspect of personality. If you want to be a movie star, you can go. If you want to be a dancer, you can go dancing. If you want to be a teacher, you can. But in my country and in many eastern countries, there are no opportunities. The way of your life shapes you and frames you. You should go like the horse of a carriage. They have the [blinders] that you should not see. So, here you can see, you can move around your head. This is very good. This is big surprise for me.

And one more, making a lot of friends. People are honest here. Most of the people are honest here. From many ideologies, from many thoughts, from Jewish, from Christians, from Muslims religious thought, if we think about religion, from homosexual, from heterosexual, from atheism, many thinkers, scientists, artists, many other fields. You can make friends from different fields and people are always smiling here. And smile I think is window towards having a lot of friends, having to enter into a person. So there is a lot of differences.

All the time I was separate of home and family. That's why when someone asks me, "Do you have family?" I say, "No," just, "No." It comes suddenly. It's not intentional. I think I adapt myself because I

In Chicago, 2001

adapt many times and I have experience in adaptation. [Laughs.] You know, adaptation, to adapt self in a situation, it is I think common among human beings. It has all the negative sides that we think, for example, loneliness, not knowing, not able to go back to country, not have enough money, not have desirable lifestyle, not have ability to live in a family—to have wife, to have children—not able to live in peaceful and calm place, and not have an area where you have your own workroom or workshop room where you can do all your activities; but that atmosphere sometimes reveals and helps the person's ideas to come out.

The experiences and consequences of all these changings which occurred in my life shows that the evil of war has a great role in changing life of many and many innocent young people or teenagers, or children, more intense than me. It affected me 100 percent. If there wasn't war, I think I would be a simple doctor. But besides that, I have learned a lot about the fate, and how [it] plays a role in changing the personality and the thought of a person.

So today, I am not a doctor. I am much more than a doctor. I think I cannot cure a physical injury. If I go back to my country I can cure a lot of deficiencies and a lot of injuries which are impossible to cure by a physician. But now, I am going to be a physician if God is willing. If I succeed, I will be.

The biggest problem is my uncompleted education. And I am determined to complete that one and nothing else. My dream has "if" conditional. American dream. If I succeed to continue my education as I am determined, I will have a bright future and a brilliant one for myself. It looks like as a physician curing people, maybe psychological people, maybe physical injuries or physical illnesses.

There is hopes for forward and future and near future that I will come over these problems and barriers, and if I have good education, if I have abilities, I will be in a good position here or back in my home.

I'm gonna die if I will not, because I was attacked with misery that changed my progression. And now I came to opportunity I got where there is sunrise from the morning till the night come. It means it's my time that I've reached.

I haven't felt myself being an American yet. But if I have this feeling, I will be a different American, not a usual American because Americans are raised in a comfortable life, in a different situation, in a different environment. Now I am living here in this environment and I am a combination of two environments. I will be an American, but… I have confessed to the American embassy that I will be a citizen and I swear. I want to be and ultimately I will be. If I will be a citizen, of course at first I should obey all the laws. America is resolved to take this world and combine many nations, many religions, many ethnicities. And I think if I swear, then I swear to be an honest citizen of America. It doesn't affect my own beliefs. Being an American, I think I will create another big responsibility on myself. I will be an Afghan American, so I will have two responsibilities. And I hope and it is more than hope and I am determined, that I will be honest and pay attention fully to both status of being citizen of these two countries. Being a citizen of America and Afghanistan is not, for me,

enough. Actually, my thinking is I am a citizen of all the world. Being honest, I don't accept in my mind any geographical lines.

I will live in both places. But if I will be a doctor, a prominent one and a good one which is remarkable not passive one, so I will be in Afghanistan. My country needs me. That's why I should go there. [My heart] is back home. Being honest, back home. Maybe in future, my heart will be divided, here and there. But right now, my heart is in Afghanistan, and I hope so it should be there because I think that the United States doesn't need me as much as Afghanistan needs me. My humanitarian thought tells me and reveals me that I should go back.

I would tell them [Americans] if they asked me, for example, "Why you came here?" At first I will tell them that I'm thankful of their progress and they have succeeded to make a humanitarian society here. And that is the reason that attracts us toward here. I will tell them that in some regions in the world, a lot of regions in the world, there is a trend and tendency of people to be immigrants to come here or anywhere like here, developed countries. The war plays a great role coming here because war destroys their basic things, basic materials and doesn't let them to do their daily routines, to do whatever they want, to live properly and naturally. So from other side, the communication plays a great role. The communication means media, and it tells about the advances and the lifestyle of you to us and to our countries, that there is prosperity, there is hopes, opportunities. So it is an instinct in us that we run towards the opportunities, towards these all beauties. So, you have succeeded to do this one. This part of the world succeeded. This part of our earth is peace, is favorable to survive, to live. In that part, it's not favorable. It's natural they migrate, like birds.

MUHAMMAD LIVES IN CHICAGO and is working as a nursing assistant.
He still plans to pursue his medical degree in the future.

MY NAME IS FELIPE CHING *I am 38 and* **I CAME FROM PERU** *four years ago now. It was just* **BEFORE MOTHER'S DAY, SOME TIME IN MAY, 1997.** *It was a cool day.*

IT WASN'T COLD, BUT KIND OF CHILLY BECAUSE I ARRIVED WITH JUST A T-SHIRT, you know, because my country, it's still a little hot in that part of the year. I wasn't really aware of, how do you say, [the season] of the year. I was maybe oblivious how the country was, but I kind of get used to almost everything around me. I go to some place and just accustomed to the place like every other human being.

The people always make a mistake with me because I look like a Filipino or something. It's because my grandfather was Chinese and he went to Peru in maybe the 1900s looking for jobs because China was a very poor country, and it still kind of is. Well, he went to Peru and he got married with a Peruvian, my grandmother. And my father was with the last name Ching. And my other grandfather was Chinese as well. But they didn't come together. So my other grandfather got married with another Peruvian girl, and my mother has the first last name, Chinese, and the other Peruvian. So, in Latin America usually they take the first last name and they put it together, father and mother, to the kids. So actually, my full name is Felipe Ching Laos. So my both last names are Chinese. So when I say to somebody, "Well, my last name is Ching Laos," they think I'm Chinese. Well, I have Peruvian blood in my veins, so this is the reason people get mixed up with me.

Well, my mom, she lives with me now here in Chicago, but she has another compromise [partner]. It's not my father. He's my stepfather, but I love him like a father. I want to tell you something about that because it's part of the whole story why I'm here. Actually it's the base of the whole story. My mother, when she was young, she was engaged with a guy. And she broke up with him because I guess problems, and then went with another guy, passed a couple months or a year, I don't know, then got married with my father. And they moved to Lima, the capital, and they had four kids. I have three sisters, older than me, and I'm the last. They didn't really hit it off. It wasn't really paradise, you know. But the last years that I remember she was living with him, kind of the things didn't work as well. I was like, 18. I was working at the

time. I was in the university and I was working. And my father, he tried to keep my mom down because of money, because he was working and she doesn't. And when I began to work, so I always giving money to my mom and the thing got worse between he and me. And then one day, among all my sisters and me, we united some money and buy a ticket for my mom. And she left him at dawn, before it's day. Well, we make the luggage, everything in secret, and we take her to the airport in secret and my father never know what happened. He probably suspect something, but well anyway, she came to United States about 12 years ago. And by surprise for everybody, she again met with the first love she has in her life, the love she broke up before she got married with my father. They bumped into each other in a party. My cousin was throwing the party in her house. And she didn't know he was now here, and the other way [vice versa]. So that is destiny. He was a widower, two times widower. Well, he was alone. And she came alone. And it's like a story of TV. One thing led to another and they got married.

I don't want to brag, but when I was a student I was very good. I'm not that good now. [Laughs.] I recognize that, but when I was a kid my grades were always excellent. Actually, before I left high school, I began to work. I was studying in the morning and working all afternoon and part of the night. I went to my house at 8:00 [P.M.] and then do my homework for the next day. I haven't really, what can I say, spend a lot of time with my peers. I remember one Saturday in special. I had a party to go to and all my friends call me on the telephone, "What time are you going to go there?"

"I'm going to be there in an hour." But when I was getting dressed, I remember the test to get into the university was maybe two weeks ahead, and I thought to myself, "Maybe I shouldn't go." And I spent my Saturday night studying for the test. If I really want something, I have to go for it. I could go maybe three, four, ten times and when I realize I can do it, I can go for it one more time. I'm like a person who wants something ideal, something unattainable maybe sometimes, but this is the way I am.

School was a challenge. And I finish [high school] at 15, because I took classes in the summer, so I was advancing a little bit. When all my friends were in the beach, I was studying. I was like a twerp, that kind of guy I was. Well, this was the reason I got out of school early.

I took two times the exam [for the university]. The first time I didn't do it. They asked for minimum for example 33 points and I did 32.95, something like that. It was very near, very near. But you know what, I had to spend a lot of time trying to study to get into the university the first time, so I felt like everything was under me moving. I feel like my effort wasn't well paid. And I sacrificed a lot of time. And well after that, I tried again. It took six more months and then I did very well. It was 60 people possible to get in and I was the number three. So I did good. But anyway, I got in a program that I didn't like it, because my father. I wanted always to be a doctor. I really loved anatomy. But [he said], "No, a doctor is going to take eight years, six years. The career that really is important to you is something with food industries. This is the future." Practically, he got me. He push me, push me, push me. Well, OK. Food industries. Exactly it's engineering of food industries. What it is, is all relationated with the food, like conserving or processing or maybe creating. I know how to do beer. I know how to conserve grapes.

And after five years, I finished my career and I got the degree of bachelor. And then I had to do my thesis. And the thesis in this kind of engineering, you have to do work in the laboratory. It's not like economist. I have to do practical. And I did it in one year.

I began to work when I was in high school, and I was working all my career. So I really didn't need to be in the university to make more money, because I was in a good job and I was doing for example, here like 50 bucks a day. In Peru it's a lot of money, you know. I make a society [company] with a guy, because I had money saved, and we buy a couple of buses and we began to do transport between Lima and the cities around. It was well. We bought more buses. And well, until came a government, it was Alan Garcia, and they took all

With his nephew, aunt, and mother, Peru, 2001

away. It was terrible. There was a lot of things that he do by himself. He didn't consult with anybody. He took over the banks. He took over the big industries. And well, then all the money that was in the bank, they froze that and give change to Peruvian money, and all went down. They put a lot of taxes and well, we have to sell. We have to sell to pay all the stuff we got into. Actually, I was possibly 19 or 20, something like that. I was very young. Maybe I began at 13 and I was saving my money because I didn't have time to spend it. School in the morning, job in the afternoon, night homework and sleep. I don't have any time. Even Saturday, Sunday I have to work. But you know what? The life is that way. Sometimes you're up and sometimes you're down.

Well, I was hoping my career help me after that. And I got in front of a wall because there is a lot of professional people in the street and there are no job for them. So when I went to an interview for example to get a job, the boss can say me, "Well, how much do you expect for do that?" I can tell $300, something like that. "OK, I will call you."

Next I can bet you there are guy who is just beginning and he wants a job, "I can make it for $200." And then another for $100. I was working a couple of years in my country. I was in several jobs, but it didn't pay me much. I was exporting grapes. I was in a beer *fábrica* [factory], as well. And then I saw the reality in my country. I was working a couple of years in my career. So, when I was like 25, something like that, I decided to go to Japan.

It's because it was kind of a boom in Peru. Everybody wants to go to Japan. Everybody went to Japan because the people was earning like $2,000 for month, minimum. It was true. In Peru we do a lot of things fake. So, everybody wants to be Japanese in order to get Japan. Because you, like a Peruvian, can't go there because you don't get a visa. But if you are descendant of Japanese, you can go there. It's easy in Peru because the people is so smart to do that kind of thing. And even the government is kind of related with that, because they sell the IDs and they put only the photo on the top. It's like a real mafia in Peru.

When I got to Japan I didn't know anybody. I've always been the kind of spirit to see something new, get going and well, whatever happens. At least I knew a little English. In all the signs, there was Japanese on the top and English on the bottom.

My other name was Isao Irae [alias]. So, I was in Japan with that name. Everybody called me Isao. "Isao, come here! Isao, over there." [Laughs.] So, I was Isao in that time.

I was planning to stay. At the beginning, for starters, I could get there because I was legit Japanese in the paper. They gave me three months to stay like a tourist. After that three months, they asked for a lot more papers. And I wasn't able to get it, so I just stayed like illegal. But there is worse. Maybe being illegal here [in the United States] you can do something, get your own house maybe. But in Japan the people take advantage from you if they know you're illegal. The people who I was working with, these people they were Brazilians. I don't have anything with racism, but they were looking for money because they were from another place, too. They weren't Japanese people. For example, if I earned like $1,500 every half month, they took from me like $600 for apartment. It wasn't an apartment even. It was like a little room and we were living, like, three people. Apartment, alimentation and, well, always I have remaining like $400, $500 monthly. Anyway, it was something. And I stayed there like two years and a half.

I really hate it. I really hate it. First, the language is very difficult to learn. And the jobs you can get there, they are the dirtiest or the most dangerous. It has to be something that a Japanese don't want to do. Once somebody offered me a job. It was I have to cut the dead people. First I have to frozen them, and cut them and put them in a metal can, and then burn them. I didn't do it because I knew the people who have done that, they always kind of get crazy, you know, cutting people all the day.

Well anyway, at the beginning I was a garbage man. Kind of shocking, because in my country I was accustomed to give orders because my status. But in Japan, I have to take the garbage from the people. And even I was doing that, I was earning four times I was earning in Peru being an engineer. So I really don't care about what kind of job is. If I do [make] the money, I go for it.

You know what? You wouldn't believe the things the Japanese throw to the garbage. For example, when I began my journey every day, the truck was going to a place to another, and you always see in the garbage, radios or CD players new! The Japanese people, for example the professional people I mean, they earn a lot of money, a lot, a lot of money. So, for example, they have a radio or a CD player or even a big device and they know that another one, a new one is nicer, and it sounds a little better, they throw it away because nobody buys secondhand things. And they throw it away because they don't have space in the apartment. You wouldn't believe the things I have found there. Even the bottles or the cans of beers with the expiration date, they don't drink it. Even though I can assure that the beer's gonna be fine. The Japanese people is very intelligent because putting that for the customer, you are pushing them to buy another one, even though this is good. And they throw the beers, and throw the wines in the garbage. I always had my refrigerator full of this kind of stuff. And all the people

After a snowstorm, Chicago, 2000

from Peru, "Oh, let's go to the garbage man's house. He has everything!" I always had a lot of people in my house. It was fun sometimes.

The worst part was communication with the Japanese people. I think this is the bottom line why I left, because I couldn't be able to communicate very well. And I have to always be with my friends. And I couldn't have the possibility to go to school. I thought I always gonna be the same thing, an outsider and working with my hands and not the opportunity to get a little better.

This is the only place I feel really discriminated. I really got hurt because of that. When you go, for example, to a shopping place, if you're not Japanese, you just got in and the owner follow you for every place. Even they are behind you because they think you can steal something. There was places in Japan, for example, some karaokes you weren't allowed to get in because you're not Japanese. The Japanese people, I can't deny, they are very nice. But when it brings it to the relationship, really relationship, it doesn't work with a foreigner. Maybe between them they could be fine. This is the reason I always hate Japan.

I knew a lot of Japanese people, but I got kind of infatuated with a girl. It was a mutual sentiment between us. And this is the silly part. The thing is, the father was against the relationship between his

With the staff at Fiesta Mexicana restaurant, Chicago, 2000

daughter and me because they are very closed between them. They don't want anybody else. Even though you can be Japanese like me, no. I was Japanese for everybody. Everybody believes me, I was Japanese. But they don't want, they call them *gajin,* foreigner. They don't want a *gajin* in the family. He was opposed to the relationship. Actually, he was a former *yakuza.* Do you know something about the *yakuza* people? These people is with all the body with tattoos. And usually they have one finger less or two fingers, all depends the grade. And this is like mafia, the Japanese mafia. I didn't know that until he threat. He called me to my house and he told me, "We have to talk about my daughter."

This guy was, when I was a garbage man, he was the guy who drive the truck and I was always behind picking up the box and putting it in the compressor. He kind of liked me. This is why and how I met her, because he took me to the house. He kind of liked me, but he loved more his daughter and the family. Even if he accepted me, for everybody else, it's gonna be like, "What did you do with your family? You let an intruder get in. It's not right."

I thought it was gonna be OK. All right, so we got together in a karaoke. In that time nobody knows karaokes, but in Japan it's like a bar here. And we began to drink and talk about one thing or another. He knew a little English. I was mixing Japanese with English because he didn't know a word in Spanish. So, we kind of communicated each other.

He told me, "The thing is my son, you have to leave my daughter, but you got two choices. You can get away with money that I can give you, or you can get away to another life. So, you have to decide." Well, he didn't give me much of a choice! He going to send somebody to kill me. Because the mafia in Japan is something you can't see it, but it's there. They move all the drugs, prostitution. But you see the people in the street is well dressed with tie and everything. But when they take off all the clothes, all the tattoos and other things. And the *yakuza* is like a mafia.

I told him, "No, I love your daughter." That was my real feeling. "I really love your daughter," I said. I tried to convince him. But we were talking like hours! Hour after hour.

And he said, "You don't have any other choice. What do you want with your life?" He told me, "If I see you with my daughter again, well, you're gonna pay the consequence." But I can't do anything. I'm a stranger there. I don't have any right. Even if my lawyer saw, I'm not going to fight with a *yakuza.* It's nonsense. Well, I took the money! I took the money! It was like $10,000. It was 100,000 yens.

At that time, I had been there like two years almost, so I was a little homesick. Plus, I was threatened not to see her again. So it's kind of difficult being in the same city, even being in the same country without trying to get there. So, I slept that on my pillow. I thought about it night over night and over and over. Well, what can I do? I had like $16,000 in my account, $6,000 mine and $10,000 from the little bribe. [Laughs.] Well, I have to go back to Peru. And I went back to Peru.

At the beginning, I just wanted to relax a little because I had two years like hell there, but I began again to be in my profession. I began to work even though I really don't need the money, but to get in touch with the people I was working with. And the money disappeared because in Peru, it's really difficult for people to earn enough money to survive. You have to see it. That's the reason that most of people are trying to get another place. And I tried, I tried, I tried several times to do it by myself, but no. It didn't work. And I was working in several companies all the time like eight years or ten years, but the money got away always.

I accepted my possibilities. I tried to be happy. I was engaged two times, just a step to get married, but the circumstances of the life, thank God, doesn't work. My whole family there, they really bad wanted me to get married. Everyone in my family, everyone.

I got a son. He's 16 now. He was a product of an affair I had a long time ago, 16 years ago with a girl. We were friends, but I didn't love her. But I don't think I can say the same thing for the other part. She got pregnant and she went to another place like six, seven months and then she come back, "Well, this is yours. Surprise!" It is mine for sure 100 percent. I got a photo here. It's undeniable. He is mine.

I knew that she had gave birth, but I didn't see him because I didn't like the way she caught me, going away seven months and then come back. At the beginning, I didn't accept that because it's unfair. And I didn't want to see him or anything about her. But then, before I went to Japan, I have to see him. Maybe I'm not going to come back, but I have to see him before I leave. And he was very, very small at that time. And I saw something similar with me in the face, but I wasn't sure because all the kids when they're small, they're all Chinese, you know!

In all that time I was working in Japan, I got in touch with him. When I came back from Japan two years after, I saw him. I saw him running. I brought him to my house and my father see him and I accepted at all because it was undeniable. Well, I began to love him. I know right now I love him very much. Right now he's living with my sister [in Peru]. He's maybe the only reason I can keep fighting for the life. I don't expect anything for me now. What I'm doing is just for him because I got almost everything in my life. I got my son. I got my own life. And I don't really need a woman on my side to be happy. I have my friends.

I was working in Peru, but I was moving around Peru and doing other things. I didn't try to get another place. I was almost resigned to stay there. Maybe Australia, maybe not. Japan's not a good life. There was another possibility, Spain, but it wasn't too good to make money. And I don't have any possibility in another country because I don't know anybody. I was resigned to be there till the opportunity presented itself and my mother told me I can be here. And he, my stepfather, do all the papers. He's very nice guy, very nice guy. Anyway, he did all the papers and they sent me to the embassy in Peru and everything was OK.

I was preparing him [my son] like a month or two months before [I left Peru]. And I think that was a little worse because the whole month was an agony for him. You're expecting something very ugly. But anyway, he was 12 years [old], so he up front [understands] the things. He is like a man I can say. He took it very well. [He stayed in Peru.]

It's difficult but, for example, your boat is in the middle of the sea and it's stuck in the middle of the sea and you got your family there, what would you do? It's better everybody die together or you will say, "I'm gonna go to the shore. I'm gonna try because if I don't, for sure we are going to die." Well, I put the extreme case, but it is the same idea. I have to evaluate both parts and make sure. Somebody has to do something to change that stuff we are living in Peru, so I have to do it. Well, I got no option.

I was working in a place far from the capital a week before my trip [to the United States]. And I came to my house just to get my stuff together. And I did it. And two days before, I spent all the day with my friends, my family. Drinking here, bye-bye there. When I took the airplane, I was really hung over with a headache because it was supposed the last time I was seeing them. [Laughs.] It was a good way to say goodbye. Anyway, when I got to the airport, I took a cup of coffee, and then I was sleeping all the day because it was like six hours to Miami and then two hours to Chicago, something like that. When I got here, I was really awake. [Laughs.]

Well, emotions in me, of course. When you are in the airplane and the airplane is taking off and you see your land, you feel something. When you're going to a place possibly you're not gonna come back, you see with a nostalgia your place. It's kind of weird because when you're in your country you want to leave, but when you're in another place, you want to come back. [Laughs.] I don't know how to explain that, but I think everybody gets bored of something, or what you're doing or the place you are. At least, that's the way I am.

But when I was in Peru, I saw movies from United States. So, I had that kind of idea from United States. I thought everything was hookers on the corners and well, you know, drugs over there. Well, my parents live in a very nice neighborhood. And it's OK. No gangs around here. Well, now I know other places. I've seen them, but where I am, I'm OK. It wasn't expected really because I thought all United States was the same way that movies present. Sometimes the people who doesn't know Peru, they ask me, "Do the people from Peru know what is a car or television set?" Because the scenes they broadcast from the television is people very poor, people from the mountains, people with the face painted. Well, that might be, but all Peru is not that way. So you get the impression from what you see in TV. Well, that was my impression.

At the beginning I was feeling bad. For example, wherever I go, maybe it took me a couple weeks and I get used to be there. No problem for me. I can be here, there. And even I always think about my son, my family, I can get going, get going, get going because I have to do it. I have no other choice. So even if it's still painful, I have to keep going.

Of course, when you are going to a place you never know, so everything is new. Everything is so clean [Laughs.] because my country is not that way. There are no dogs walking in the street. The people wait to the light to be green. The people stop in the stop sign. I like that because when you drive, you go behind the other. You don't go that kind of stuff that I was accustomed to see in Peru. And I paid for that learning, because I got a lot of tickets. [Laughs.] But I really like it. I like the United States. The first thing is, if you really want a job you can get it. There is a possibility for everybody. This is the main thing. Other things I like it, the organization, the law. For example, the other day, we have in the restaurant [where I work] like a button when somebody want to stick you up, [rob you]. You push the button and the police come. And the manager, accidentally he pushed the button because he was doing something, and the police arrived like in two minutes, something like that. Quick, quick. And like that, the police is there.

The education is free. This is a good achievement here, for English classes of course. Well, other classes are very expensive. Anyway, with the English classes free, you are giving the opportunity to the people

With the girl he sponsors, Julissa, and her father, Peru, 2000

to get into the culture, not being just a worker. So you can be a person among the other people. You can talk. You don't feel like you are marginated. They embrace you and take you with them, no matter what country you are. And this is good. I can bet in Japan there are not kind of program they teach the language or something. I don't think so. I really admire the fact of the city of Chicago is paying infrastructure, paying teachers to teach people who is not from here, not native American, people who is coming from another place. I really admire that because I don't think in another place in the world that could happen. I can't imagine. I recognize it's the best thing the city of Chicago could do.

I studied English almost all my life, but you are not obligated to use it, so you do the English because you have to pass the course. You don't need it really. So, I have been studying, well, all my life. I always have a course of English in all my courses since I remember. But when I got out from the high school, I didn't use the English anymore. If you don't practice, you're gonna forget it for sure.

I have realized and I'm for sure that the knowledge of English have several steps. The first step, you don't understand anything. [Laughs.] You begin to find out or look it up something in the dictionary. At the beginning, you slightly can understand some words when somebody's talking. More you can understand when you're reading. Reading is one thing. This is the first step. You can understand reading. The second step is understand listening. The third step maybe is improving your vocabulary, but a lot. And the last step is talking, talking fluently with a full vocabulary. You can talk a lot of words different. I think I can understand more than I speak because I have to think. In between all those steps, there are a line when you have to begin thinking in English. Because all before, when you are expressing yourself, you are thinking in Spanish and then translating in English, so kind of you get a little stuck in the middle. But there is a time when you have to begin to think in English. And even when you are counting money, you don't have to [can't] count in your language. You have to count in the other language. Like the artists say, it's a crossover, but in your mind. I don't know if that happened yet. [Laughs loudly.] I'm some place in between in the transition of this, but I recognize I don't do it very well. I recognize I got a lot of faults in grammatic or even words, but I suppose I'm going to make it someday. No, I don't suppose. I'm very sure of it. [Laughs.]

My cousin has a restaurant and the next day [after I arrived] I began to work there. Next day! I began to work like a dishwasher and then I was doing some painting in the restaurant. And then I take a bartender book, and I took it with me and I learn a couple of drinks, the usual in a Mexican restaurant—margaritas, screwdrivers, something like that, rum and coke, you know—and I got into the bar. Then after that, I was a busboy and then after that I was a waiter. And now I'm a waiter, but I have another things to do in the restaurant when my cousin is not there. So practically I run the restaurant in the morning, but I have to take care of the tables, too. I have to do the orders from beers or meat, whatever we need.

I think for me, my goal is always to make money because with money, I can pay a lot of things for my son. Nobody else is gonna do it. I have to keep looking for money. I'm a waiter. I really hate it, but I make like $500 a week. It's not bad. I really hate serving people. Not all, but some customers they are so picky. When I, for example, go to a table and I come back to the bar, I tell the bartender, "I'm not for this job. I have to find something else." Well, I do it. But I have to go after the money, man. If I don't do it, we're lost. I'm not expecting to be a waiter all my life. [Laughs.]

Of course, I always thanks God because I have seen people going to a restaurant asking for jobs. "Look, I have been six months here, I don't have a job." I feel really lucky, really, really lucky because it just wasn't a simple job. I work with my family and the money is not bad. It's OK.

It's OK. Even though I really hate waitering the tables, but the money is there and that is what counts.

The people say always to me, "The money is not everything." And I'm agree. It's possibly not everything, but it could be the 80 percent. You cannot get love maybe, but you can focus on love when you have a big bank account because everything is coming at that time.

I can't understand why so many people I see in the streets, and they are American citizens, and they have a lot more opportunity. They have total control in the language, but they don't want to do anything. I don't want to talk about any ethnic, but they always fat waiting for the state to give money. Fat, very fat. You maybe can imagine who am I talking about. They're really fat. Maybe 300 pounds. And the state pay for everybody. I don't know. They have everything, but they don't want to take it. We don't have anything in my country, but we want to take it. [Laughs.] That's maybe the reason for the people who came from another place can be something here. They wanted to do it. They came here to do it and just the reason to do it.

I don't know where I'm gonna die, but I'm gonna stay here possibly till I die. I'm not gonna say the following because you are American, but I think really this is a great place to flourish your hope. Like I said, the possibility is out there and you have to go for it if you really want. And you don't have the doors closed. You can open it and go through them. Just you have to encourage yourself and go there. That's it. This is a big thing here. Like everybody said, the land of opportunity. The opportunity is there. You have to go for it.

He [my son] has now got the papers in the embassy, the immigration. And they gave me the answer that the process is going to proceed. So, I think it's a good sign. And when the visa comes, he's gonna come here. But he's 16, I don't know really. He's 16 and I want him to choose freely. I really want him to do what he really wants to do. Not like my father, "Ah, you have to be…" and you go for that.

And this is the reason for my next trip I'm gonna do in January. I always imagine that in my mind to sit him in a table just the two of us. "Well, I can talk with you about another things more important in the life. Let's talk about your future. Let's talk about womens. Let's talk about whatever you want to talk because I'm not just your father, I'm your friend." And I really am dreaming about that day to sit in front each other. And I know he's very mature. He has done everything very well. And I'm very proud of him. It's most for my sister. It's her credit. I know he is OK there, but it's not the same. I want him to be with me, but I can't do anything before the papers. I would like to go to Peru and stay with him, but it's nonsense. There is no future for both. So kind of I have my hands tied because I have to stay here and he cannot get here before the papers. So I feel frustrated. But I know that God has a time for everything and I have to wait and he has to wait also.

The people in immigration, they are processing papers of 1996 now. They are really behind. So, I don't know. It could be easier if I am a citizen and that is gonna be in a year, but anyway I presented the papers. So I am doing whatever is in my hands to get him here. When I be a citizen, I'm gonna present another papers and whichever it comes first, it is.

I know I missed already a big part, but I can't do anything to change that, but I can do a lot for change what is coming. What can I say? What's done is done. I think I'm gonna be there when the real important time comes. I'm gonna be there.

I always wanted for my son what I couldn't get. All my life in the university, I was self-sustaining. I always paid for everything. And that's the reason I couldn't maybe take more English, because I was working. Almost all my youth was in between the work and books. I want my son to live the life. And I want to make flat all the road that's coming in front of him. I'm gonna try to put a lid in the holes in all the road, but I'm gonna leave a couple of holes so he can get in and see, "Well, that could happen. OK." But I'm gonna try to make the things easier for him.

Well, I'm planning to be a citizen of the United States, but I have a strong roots and more than my roots, there are my fidelity to my friends, to my son, to my family, to my country, to my team in the football. Even my team is down, I'm gonna be for my team because it's principles. It's like a marriage. You have to be there in the up and down. I really love my country to visit, my family OK, too, but I don't want to be there to work. If I can get a job there that pays like here, I absolutely be there. I like this country [the United States]. I don't *love* this country, but I really like it. I don't love it to put an American flag in my T-shirt, but I really like it. Possibly, when talking about the teams, your team is OK, but you always have a second one. This is my team, but I like them, too. That is this country. I can't give my back to them, to my country. I can't. For example, if there are a war between United States and Peru, I have to kill you guys. Even though you gave me the opportunity, but it's kind of my principles. But I know there's no chance to be a confrontation between Peru and United States! Forget it.

I've always been preoccupied for saving money for everything. But

now, I have the possibility to save a little more because it's something, more money involved here. For my son always, my nieces, for example, my nephews and I can do a lot of things. When I go to Peru, I have a lot of friends there, a lot of people I have to take care of. I have two little childs in World Vision. Have you heard about that? World Vision is a movement that take care of the little kids. I have two.

This thing happened that way. I was seeing television and I see a commercial. There was a Latin guy, the guy from *Fantasy Island,* Ricardo Montalbán. He was saying in Spanish, "You can do it. You can take care of the kid. There are thousands of kids without a sponsor. You can do a lot of things with only $22 a month." Well, he washed my brain. And I wrote to them, to World Vision. I didn't care the age, but the only detail I wanted was being Peruvian. Without that condition, I won't take anybody else. At the beginning, they gave me a daughter. And I took her under my wings. I have had her three years.

All the months I have to pay $22 for her. I got a picture. I have a writing from her. That was the time I was a busboy. And then I got promoted to a waiter. And I said, "God has been good to me." And I took another one. A boy. $44. Well, let's not mention the money. The main thing that made me feel good was if I can't get money like I'm doing here, those guys would be abandoned by now. That made me feel a little useful because it's something, it's something. More than that, I'm the godfather for a little child, too. So I have my son, my godchild and other two kids. So I have four and then my nephews. I have to be careful because if I don't have that kind of job, or even I am not here, I couldn't do anything for them. I'm not supporting really, I'm just sharing. Let's say that, sharing.

One more thing. When I went back to Peru I saw them [the World Vision children]. I got picture in my house. It was very nice because the little girl, actually she is twin with another one. So when I saw her coming to the door, "Oh, well. That's OK." I was surprising her. And then another one, the same identical, the twin, came to the door and I got a little confused. Well, I was supposed to call on just one. [Laughs.] Well anyway, the other one has another sponsor. They live in like, the translation exactly would be Youngtown. It's like a little town on the skirt of the city. They don't have water or bathroom. They have only four wooden walls and a poor roof. They were very poor, in one word. But in a nutshell, the main thing is that when I saw her or when I saw him, too, because I saw them together, I took them to the Kentucky Fried Chicken. We have Kentucky Fried Chicken in Peru. I took them

His son, Christian, Christmas, Peru, 1997

there and a little party and I felt good. I felt great.

I'm doing things that I couldn't be able to do, because I have a little possibility to do. So, I feel useful to the humanity, useful to myself. When you do something, you get your payment right now when you're feeling good. Because before I got here, I wouldn't be able to be useful to support kids. So, my point of view is I have changed, of course, because I have the possibility to do. Like we were talking, the money is important so I can get something and I can help some people. And I feel good. I feel good. I'm like an idealist. I can change the little world around me.

I want to change something. When I was in Peru, sometimes I was in a project with people who have problem, little kid violated or raped, people with the problem with the family or alcoholism, drug addiction. I was like a consultant giving advice and I think this was the best part

of my life because I felt being useful. It has no price when you, for example, see coming a person and they're totally wretched, very unhappy and they come in that way and when they leave, they leave with a smile on the face. It's a great sense, a great feeling.

For example, the other day I was with a girlfriend in my car and a bum came over to the door. Because the bum was near to her door, I gave her the money to give to him. And she told me, "What are you doing? Why are you going to do that kind of thing to those people? And he's gonna probably go to buy a drink or buy a drug."

"It doesn't matter to me. You give it to him only." And we were arguing all the way down because she wasn't agree with me. But at the last, finally I convinced her because I told her, "Even though the money could be spent some other place, it really doesn't matter. Because even though the money could end in a drug dealer, but maybe it could end in a McDonald's. So, you're not gonna ever know. So, the main point is that you have done the right thing." Get into the problems of other people and try to do something to help. It's not enough, "Oh, I'm sorry for you, man. OK, see you later."

Let's not talk about immigrants. Let's talk about in general all the people. You can't judge anybody just for the appearance or the color of skin or the nationality. Or you can't judge anybody for the money they have. You have to go a little more behind the face, a little more behind the rags the banker can have on, or maybe a little more than the blond and the pretty eyes. You have to go to the person, not the body or the appearance. You have to go for the person because everybody has a lot of story behind, and you don't know why the person is here, what circumstances of his life brought him here. And maybe you have to think that maybe you can be in that position sometime because the life, you don't know where you are going to end. In my country there is an ancient saying that, "You don't spit to the sky because sometime it come back to you." *No escupas al cielo porque te puede caer a ti mismo.* So, you can't judge anybody, so you are not going to be judged. Well, I think this is it.

| 79

FELIPE LIVES IN CHICAGO and continues to work at his family's restaurant. His son is still waiting for his visa in Peru to come to the United States.

MY NAME IS ELENA RASKIN *[I'm] 35 years old. I came to United States at the end of the* **MARCH, 1995.** *I came to United States with my family: my husband, my son and I.* **I WAS BORN IN WESTERN PART OF RUSSIA, BYELORUSSIA [BELARUS].**

I GREW UP IN A SMALL TOWN. ACTUALLY, IT'S VILLAGE, SVETILOVICHI, and I spent there 17 years. It was beautiful nature around the village, great lake and good people. I spent my childhood in a big family. It was eight people in my family: my parents, my mother's sister, my mother's mother and four of us children —my three handsome brothers and me. It was big and small house. Big, because it was perfect relationship between people, always warm and comfortable. It makes feelings great because it's big. And small, because it was small house. It's a whole different feelings about houses, not because in my country it was house more beautiful than here, or here is more beautiful than there, it's because the place where I was born! Maybe it wasn't so perfect as it has to be, but it was place where I was born. It's just my first place from where I had my first steps in life. Unforgettable.

We didn't have enough room for everybody. We shared like three people in just one room, and no bathroom in the house, no washroom in the house, everything outside of the house. But as long as our relationship was perfect, everything was perfect also. No complainments. Of course we had problems because we are human beings. It's impossible not to have problems, but everybody intelligent and smart enough to make nice decisions and smart decisions. If I had bad feelings or somebody from my family, before go to bed, somebody or even me going to explain what is right, what is wrong, what I have to do and give it to me advice.

My father used to be a dentist for almost 47 years. He was a real leader because of his intelligence and smartness. I afraid I cannot find right now words to describe what kind of person is my father. He's kind, smart, intelligent, sometimes powerful. Everybody in my family, my brothers and me, never had a physical punishment, even if we did something horrible. It was punishment, but it was different punishment—soul punishment or moral punishment. If I did something wrong, my father looked at me like eye contact and I immediately understand I did something wrong. He said, "You want explanation? You need some help with that?"

If I said, "Yes," he's going to explain to me from up to down, everything in details. If I said, "No, I don't want explanation," he said, "OK, I'm going to leave you alone. If you don't need explanation today, it will come tomorrow, but it will come. I promise." He was happy man because he has beautiful wife whom he loves very much, and children of course; but he wasn't happy also because my mother, his wife, was very sick. This thing made him very unhappy. But all the time he laughs and he knows a lot of jokes and stories to tell us before we go to bed.

My mother was an example for many women. It's perfect example how mother has to be, how wife has to be because she has everything: kindness, understanding, love from heart, trustness. Probably she used to work before I was born, but I remember she didn't work. By the time I was born, she got sick already and she couldn't work. My mother died 10 years ago.

Don't ask about religion anything. We had about 10 Jewish families in the village. That's it. Maybe 1,000 people [in the village]. To be surprised, my father, as a Jewish person, had great respect from people because he was a dentist and people asked him for help, and even if we had problems with other children, for him it doesn't matter. He did everything possible to treat them, to cure them. But nobody likes Jewish people back in Russia. People said horrible words just because you are Jewish. For example, if I'm going to store and I want to buy a piece of sausage or piece of meat, a gentile person can ask, "I don't like this piece of meat, give me another one."

And the salesperson says, "Fine, take it, another one."

If I ask them to change, he said, "Jewish! You're not supposed to be change, you're Jewish. Take it." I know a lot of other people have different experiences, but I had like this.

It was impossible [to light candles on Friday night]. Everybody looked in your window and if they see you have candles for Passover, they saw challah on the table, which made by my grandmother in big secret, they will call KGB and pick up my father. It was for real. I'm not just making it up my mind. He spent a couple of days in jail trying to explain. I don't remember the details because I was maybe five years old, but then they let him go. It [religious education] was impossible. He wants to do it I know for sure, my mother, too. Immediately after Second [World] War it was possible for a couple of years to keep religion stuff in family for Jewish people, but about '48, '49, close to '50, forget about it. It was illegal. Everybody can hear us, can listen us and can see us, like secret agent. If you practice, go to jail. They [my parents] explained to us once, "You are Jewish and you have to be proud of that." We never asked. We were proud.

I didn't have any dreams about United States or another country, but one of my brothers was in medical school. I was in school, 7th or 8th grade. It was springtime and he came for vacation after final exams and he said, "What a horrible life."

My father said, "It's life. Today's horrible, tomorrow will be good and sunny."

And he said, "No, I don't think so in this country it will be someday sunny or good."

Now I can understand something from this day. It was a nightlong conversation between two people, my father and my brother. They spent whole night speaking about life, immigration, another country and something like that. My father already understand and my brother is going to understand what life is all about. [My father] explained to him everything possible and my brother just looked at him. I almost know nothing about that conversation, but it was something like, start to move, like pushness. Something happened in our family. My father told my brother, "So, I will move to United States. It will be possible if your mother will be healthy woman." But he had too many reasons not to move, because of my mother.

[I got married at] 20. I just finished [university]. I met him [my husband, Leonid] because I knew his brother [Boris]. [Boris] wasn't my boyfriend. He was great guy to spend time with, intelligent and smart enough and we spoke about different things in life. It was pleasant to spend time with him, but we never talk about marriage. I knew him like for eight or ten months. He was in university, too. On Sundays or Saturdays we spent time together. Once, he said, "My brother is going to come from different part of Russia for vacation for a couple of weeks and I have to be with him." Some day he called me and he said, "I have tickets to go to the movie, do you like to go with us? I'm going to introduce my brother to you."

I just finished university and I got a job and I worked second shift in a kindergarten and I came late home and they were in my house. They took me to a movie and after movie, [Leonid] said to his brother, "Would you mind if I take Elena home alone by myself?"

[Boris] said, "I don't mind, but it isn't polite."

[Leonid] said, "I know it isn't polite, but I will explain to you later. We're brothers." [Leonid] said to me, "Are you planning to get married someday?"

"Yes," and he proposed me marriage after two hours of conversation. I felt something inside my heart and I said, "Yes," right there. I felt it is person whom I need in my life. Before my husband I had a couple of boyfriends and I already had some experience how to choose. I still was young and I still know nothing about life, but I felt something. Before I said, "Yes," I started to remember conversation between my oldest brother and me, who explained to me what is real life look like. That's why I said, "Yes."

Next day he came to my house. He asked for permission from my parents. They were surprised. They could see a real person, perfect man, but who knows? First step doesn't tell you whole life, but they said, "Go ahead, guys. Take a risk."

My husband went home and explained to him and [Boris] said, "What? I just was ready to propose her marriage! I wasn't ready yet. You broke everything. I hate you."

They came both to me and asked me whom I love more. I said, "[Leonid] is my choice."

Boris said to me, "I hate you, too," but it was OK.

Now he lives in Chicago and he has own family, his wife and very handsome son.

It was very, very difficult to make our house because he used to be an officer in the army. After our wedding, which was in two weeks, we had to leave and move to different part of Russia far away from my house. It was Lake Baikal. Like 10, 12 hours I have to fly from my house. It's behind Siberia! It was military base, but it was built houses for officers and for their families. Ten to twelve hours by plane I have to fly from my house. It was just difficult because I didn't have experience in life to live by my own. Twenty years I spent with my family and my parents took care of me and they explained to me everything, and now here I am responsible for my family. I have to make my home

Her wedding, Byelorussia (Belarus), 1983

beautiful and comfortable.

[Life was] horrible: no friends, no water in house, no bathroom in house. It was some kind of food. In jail in the United States, people eat better than I ate there. Bread, milk, sometimes meat, frozen potatoes, and pasta, very dirty pasta.

My husband and I, we are responsible people and we wanted to build our family right away quietly and we didn't have enough time to think about United States, but I hope each of us, my husband and I, have now dreams to move to United States. I didn't express my feelings to my husband. He didn't, too. But I hope, I believe he did think about United States to move. I had not nice childhood, my husband either, because of Jewishness and I don't want the same thing to my children. It influence me to think about moving to another country. It's like small steps to get deep understanding what I want to do. Today I think and tomorrow I forgot about it. I knew it's different, it's great country because everybody said so. That's it, a couple of sentences. Nothing else. Maybe I seem to you like a small child. It was in my dreams when I was a child seven, ten years old. When I went to bed and I couldn't sleep, I think about United States, "It's night in my country. It's day in United States." I thought about that.

I never talked about this idea because I was afraid to talk about this idea. It was something like itch you. You feel something every day all the time, even if I smile, if it's sunny day outside, it's not going to be rain, but it's still very deep inside you. Even my family decided to come to United States for sure, nobody knows I'm here, even now, just except my close friends. I came in secret. Many people didn't come in secret, but I did come in secret because of my husband [in the military].

By year '90, many, many Jewish people immigrated to United States and Israel because of political situation and Gorbachev. My husband already worked for 22 years in military and he was going to be retired very soon and after that, no future. He had no choice. What he's going to do? What kind of job he's going to do? I had my job, but it wasn't enough to pay for everything. After he retired we thought nobody wants to take a retired person. So it's big problem, no job, no future. My son, who was born in '85, already was in school and some teachers hate him because he was Jewish.

A lot of people immigrate. It like was panic. Everybody moved. My coworkers said, "If you will be smart, you will move, too, first because you are Jewish. Go ahead. If I were Jewish, I will move. Go ahead. It's a horrible life here. Everybody understands that. Nobody's going to

With her son, Alex, and husband, Leonid, Russia, 1987

take me. Everybody can take you because Jewish people." I didn't listen to them, but it hurts my feelings.

By that time, my husband's brother came to United States in '91 or '92. We missed him very much because he is great guy and we always shared everything all together even if we live in different places. We call each other, we spend time together. There was no replacement. Once, I asked my husband, "Should we go to United States?"

"Don't think about it. We couldn't make it."

I said, "Why not? Why not? He is there. Maybe he can help us somehow."

He said, "I'm in military. It's almost impossible to get permission. So, it's bad luck."

He sent us each month a letter from United States. He said, "You have to be here! It's great life, great country. Don't stay there. I'm not going to leave you there." He didn't want to lose his brother and secondly he understood here there was no life, no future, especially for children. "I'm going to do everything possible to take you here." He said, "You can buy a suit and pants for men, but you still have money to buy food like natural life." And he sent a lot of applications to immigration office and Washington.

It wasn't words to explain. It's United States. It's America. I got a letter from United States, I smell it. I smell it and I opened it immediately. I read, I cried. My husband, too, and we never spoke about it because it was understood without any words. It's too much emotion jump out of our body. It seems to me handwriting was different and everything was changed.

Once at night we got a phone call. I picked up the phone and said, "Hello." I thought it was friends.

"It's United States. It's Boris on the line."

I said, "Who?" It was the first time he called us.

I started crying and he said, "I'm not going to pay for your tears, your crying. I have to pay. [Laughs.] Stop it. I have to tell you something, very important information. Your papers, your application, and documents are fine and you are going to go for interview in Moscow at the end of this year. December 16, '93 you have to be in Moscow in American immigration center."

I said, "What? It's impossible."

He said, "Helen, calm down yourself. I'm telling you the truth. Give the phone to your husband. I can't deal with you!"

My husband pick up the phone and they had big conversation about that and after my husband said, "Is it true? I'm dreaming or what? I'm alive? I'm dead? What happened?"

I said, "Are we going for interview?"

He said, "Of course we are going. It's big secret. Nobody's going to know about that."

Immediately my husband took a couple of days for vacation, and we came to my house. My mother was dead by that time. My mother died in 1989. My father and aunt were there and we spoke about that. My father said, "If you have permission, and everything is going to be fine at the end of this year, you have to go. It doesn't matter what's going on here." He said, "Don't worry. There is someone who is going to take care of me and I'm sure I believe in the future I'm going to come, too." He was happy for me. He said, "It's no life. You have to go. It's no speaking about."

It was like I changed my mood. I changed my opportunity about everything. I was different person at all and he saw me and became happier. He didn't tell me about his feelings anything, but I felt something is going on inside of him. He was afraid to let me go to United States. It's natural because I am his daughter and he was afraid to be alone.

I said, "I'm going to take you a couple years later when I find something in United States, some place to live, some job, some support. I'm going to take you 100 percent."

He said, "Don't worry about me. Make your life. Now it's your time."

[My brothers] cried because they afraid to lose me, to lose my family, and nobody knows what happens in the future.

It was secret and everybody asked me, "Suitcases and luggage. Where are you going, for vacation?"

I had to tell not truth. I had to lie. I said, "I have to go to Moscow because I have to see some doctors. I'm not feeling good." They felt something. Nobody asked me. I can't be sure.

My son was so excited. He asked me, "Why we have to go to Moscow? I hate the trains." A child, six years old.

[Whispers.] "Because we're leaving to United States. Don't tell anybody. It's secret."

He said, "United States. Oh, I have to go to school there?"

"Of course,"

"I don't know English,"

"You don't know English. It's no problem for you,"

"Really, you know this for sure?"

"Yeah, I know this for sure."

"OK, I trust you."

I was very nervous. I couldn't sleep the night before I go for interview. I couldn't eat. I couldn't breathe. I got up at 4:00 in the morning. I came to perfect building in Moscow, immigration center [United States embassy]. For first time I saw people from United States who spoke in English. I opened my mouth and I opened my eyes and I couldn't tell and I couldn't breathe. I was so excited. My husband and I was in line from 8:00 in the morning. It was big line. After that, they opened the doors and invited us inside very politely and they said to us, "This family this way, this way." Organized. Everything like in United States.

[I felt] I'm not in Moscow. I'm somewhere else. [In Russia] it would be big lines and open the doors, "OK, cows. Come on, sit down!" Nice chairs. The most important thing, when I came to the bathroom, because I have to spend whole day in there, of course I'm human I have to go to the bathroom, toilet paper, hot and cold water, soap. Oh, my God! Surprise! Oh, because I'm in Moscow? Because it's United States! It's here, small United States. It smells perfectly in the bathroom, air fresh, and they have vending machines and paper towels. Oh, my God. I never saw! We don't have. Just hand towels. That's it. Oh, my God! Maybe it's because I came from small village, because I change place

to place, because I'm officer's wife, because I used to live in the bases. I don't know. I was surprised.

I had to explain to someone from immigration office to believe me. Someone invite me, American man, in secret cabinet [office] and he said in Russian with accent, "OK, guys. Sit down and tell me about your life. Just feel comfortable." My husband did tell him everything he knows and [the man] said, "OK, I'm going to give you an answer by 4:00 tonight."

Then we went outside and sit in the park in Moscow. We didn't speak with each other. It was mixed up in our heads—thoughts, dreams, real life, something in the future like small pictures from the movies, episodes from whole real life. Sometimes we looked at each other, little bit smile.

Four o'clock came. We came to the building and they said, "Families this, this, this in this line. Families this, this in this line. You got permission, you don't have permission." Oh, my God. We were in this line. We got permission! "Take this paper. It explains everything step by step what you have to do next day. Go ahead. Congratulations." We looked, my husband at me, and I looked at him, cried, smiled, sit on the floor. It was impossible. No way! Everybody was crying.

I see now in my mind some woman. She was in our line [pulling her hair] and yelled. Ambulances came and took some [in the other line] to the hospital because of heart attack and everything. They don't have tears to cry. It was more than cry. It was big emotion. But I'm sure they got permission next year or little bit later on. I hope.

I came home to my husband's relative house and she said, "Should we open a bottle of wine?" [Laughs.] We ate supper and we called my family and he called United States also because his brother was worried.

[Boris] said, "No, no, it's impossible! Congratulations!"

We came at the end of the March, 1995. [I expected] very clean streets and perfect clothes on the people. Big and beautiful buildings. Something like that. A lot of stuff was in my mind. A lot of cars in the street. English and stores. I didn't think about school. I didn't think about education. I didn't think about job here because I was stupid. I was thinking about the place, about people. That's it.

My brothers came, picked up luggage. Neighbors, they brought cakes and chocolate. It's custom. My brothers took me in the car and brought me to Minsk to airport. You know, I was excited. I was happy. I'm not worried about leaving my country. I was worried about leaving my brothers, my friends, especially my father. Who knows can I see them again or not? I couldn't say goodbye. I just cried. Tears come to my eyes, and my brothers were crying, too. They said goodbye. I said, "No goodbye. See you."

From Minsk to Warsaw and then to Chicago. Five times, maybe seven, they fed us. Corn, I never saw corn in a small plate and small pieces of meat and mashed potatoes. "What is it?"

"Do you want wine? Do you want vodka? Do you want whiskey? Do you want liquor? Do you want 7-UP?"

I said, "What?"

"7-UP."

"What does it mean 7-UP?" They spoke in English. I didn't know English. I said, "Tell me in Polish. I will understand you."

"7-UP!"

"What is it, 7-UP?"

"OK, I'm going to give you now an orange! Do you know what is orange?"

I felt like a small piece in the big world. [Leonid] was thinking, thinking, thinking because he is responsible for the family to get job.

March 30th. We landed in O'Hare. It was already 5:00 at night, getting dark and all my husband's relatives were inside the building, and Boris, also. Oh, my goodness. It was hugness! I was almost dead. I thought that I was dreaming. Hugness, laughness, tears, smileness. They touched me and they touched my family like we we're not here, just the shape of us is here. Boris said, "Oh, my God. You're here, you're here!" 200 percent we knew it was for good.

First of all, I wanted to sleep because I couldn't sleep on plane I was so excited to come to United States and I couldn't eat. I fell asleep and for me it changed day and night and I had to accustomed to that. After that I became little bit a person, a human. [Laughs.] I looked at the window from the 18th

floor from my aunt's house outside at Sheridan [Road] and I said, "Oh, my goodness. It's United States. I never lived in big city as Chicago. It's light. It's sunny. It's big buildings. Everything is great."

Always in Russia I felt something in black color even if it was sunny outside. I mean black compared with problems. Here in United States I have problems, too, probably more than I had in Russia, but everything is sunny, still sunny, no blackness. Somewhere I realized I lost the feeling of blackness. It never comes back to me again. I was happy person. Even now I have too many problems. My car got hit by somebody else, and I had to go to new school with new teachers to make another friends to make myself to be a good person, and everything is good in life. Sun is shining. I know I will find the way to solve this problem. I know for sure. Back in my country, I wasn't sure. Here I know for sure. My father, he has nice proverb to say, "Don't wait for any luck. Don't wait for anything fall down from the God. Someday, somebody, luckness come and knock in your door. Here I am. Take it."

Behavior of people [was strange]. I never saw people carrying cups and plates to eat outside of the house. They walk and they eat at the same time! I saw a girl. She had pasta with sauce on the plate and she ate by hands, no fork or spoons. She walked and playing with music on her ears, and she ate and she walked at the same time. Boris was with us and he said, "Come on. It's OK. We are going to lake now."

"What is lake?" And he translate me.

Oh, my God. It was horrible. I didn't know English! Maybe five words I knew when I came to United States: mother, father, cat, dog and house—from my son. He taught me. That's it. No grammar at all, no vocabulary, nothing. I spent just one month to be adapted to this new life. My husband's relatives told us [Truman College] was a great place to learn English and they explained what we had to do step by step. I start to

Graduating from Truman College, Chicago, 2000

speak in English after two months living in United States. It was horrible English. It was small phrases, but I started. I feel much better but I still disappointed. I still have accent. My English, maybe I can speak faster than I did before, but I still have accent and grammar mistakes by one hand. By another hand, as long as I can explain my feelings, I'm happy.

My husband's uncle took us to fruit and vegetable store. He said, "What happened? [What's the matter?] Go ahead and take it." Huge piles of apples, pears, oranges, bananas, potatoes, tomatoes.

"How? Someone is going to watch me. I cannot take it."

"Take it by yourself. Choose! One piece, two pieces, whatever you want. Ten pieces."

I took one and I put it back. I took one and I put it back.

He said, "Helen, what's wrong with you? Take it!"

I never saw it before. In Russia if I want apples, I ordered apples in the store. I said, "I want one pound of apples," and they gave me what they want, not me. Everything was new.

For first six months I didn't know nothing. Nothing come to my mind. My husband he said, "I very difficult to pick up languages." You have to have natural talent to study English or any different language besides your native language, so he said, "It will be nice for me if I go for some courses or study something close to my profession in Russia, like engineer, to support family," because we are going to receive government money, public aid just for limited time. He went for some courses. He took two of them and he finished. He does some electronic stuff on computers inside machines.

I didn't think anything. I spent three years to decide what I wanna do. I liked my job because I used to be a teacher there, but because of English, I not decided to take this job. I can make it. I can explain. I saw many teachers, even at Truman, who is not native speakers, came from different countries and the English maybe not better than mine, but I want not take this opportunity because I would like to have my job like 100 percent to give to children, explain to them everything. So I changed my field and now I'm going to medical sciences. For first time [taking classes] was difficult. Maybe three years more, then maybe physical therapy or nursing. To be honest with you, I proud of myself because now too many people ask for my help [in English]. It's something. I made it. For other people, my opinion is important. I became useful for people.

I have [worked here] at Truman College. That's it. My job was com-

With her pre-school class, Chicago, 2001

puter assistant. I have to explain and teach people how to use basic computer and different programs to improve knowledge. So today, actually, is my last day working in the computer lab as computer assistant. It was enjoyable. It was pleasant time. Five hours every day, four days.

It's great [my son's English]. It was difficult for him and for me and for everybody in my family. I spent six months teaching my son how properly he has to study English. It was helpful for me. It was very useful for my son and after that, he picked up very quickly. I asked him 1,000 times, "You wanna go back to Russia?"

He said, "No way. Look in my eyes, look in my eyes and you will see it! No way. I'm going to stay here."

He is gonna finish 6th grade next month in a Jewish private school and he's gonna work as an assistant teacher for summer camp. It was difficult to afford it, but we decided we have to.

Now I know everything about Jewish history, about holidays and how to make a table for Passover or whatever holiday it is. I go to synagogue. I attend bar mitzvahs, bat mitzvahs, Jewish weddings. I feel proud. I feel like I am human being, real person, individual. There wasn't place for me there before. No way.

My father came to United States one year and a half ago. He doesn't practice his religion more, but he reads newspapers, magazines about Jewish people, about Jewish community, activities about Jews and what they do each month. He goes to synagogue also. He doesn't express his feelings. If I ask him, "What do you think or what do you feel about?" he says, "Me?"

I say, "Yes, you." Big tears in his eyes, big tears of happiness. To be honest and to tell the truth, he is 73 years old. At the end of his life he got everything he wanted to get before.

[I feel] United States is my home now. [It took] a couple of months. [I still feel like a foreigner] only because of language. If I can speak in English perfectly like you do, no problem. But it's no problem either. If I have accent, if I speak sometimes incorrectly, it's OK. I'm going forward. I feel comfortable now. I don't feel I'm a stranger. I want to be a citizen and I will do it in five years. It's important to me. I became accustomed with American life. I never will be an American because I wasn't born here. That's my problem, but I will try my best to understand more deeply life of United States and American people to become more adapted and accustomed to this life, to give my life experience to my children.

From the history about Jewish people, they have to have place to live, their own place, nice place, nobody's going to touch them, nowhere except United States and Israel. Even in Israel it's still war, blood, and pressure. I hope in United States it won't be like in Israel. Just one country, United States, in the whole world make Jewish people comfortable. And I want to be United States my home, my place. That's why I wanna become a citizen.

Money hurts my feelings somehow because in United States the most important thing is money. But what is it? Money is nothing. It's material things. What's the most important thing? Relationship between us, love, justice, moral, ethics, education. It's the most important. Money is behind us. We have to pay for everything. I'm not saying it's supposed to be everything for free because in comparison two countries United States and Russia, there everything is free, it's horrible. Here we have to pay for everything, it's good. If you have money here, you can buy whatever you want. In there it was impossible.

[Freedom] is big opportunity for people. Freedom, it's the base of the life, to live perfect life. Another proverb, "What is prohibited, it's always sweet." That's why if you say all the time, "No", you wanna do it. So in United States, people smarter than in Russia in comparison

With her husband, Leonid, Chicago, 2001

because they prohibit something, but they allow most of the things. Freedom and prohibition like in the scale, balance each other. That's why it makes people more unlimited. In Russia, all the time it's, "No" for everything. For example, if you compare a country to me as a mother, I say to my children all the time, "No, no, no, no," without explanation and they do it because they don't know why it's, "No," why they not supposed to do it. It's the same situation to transfer from the family to country. I say to my children, "No," like Russian government tell to their citizens, to their people, "No, no, no, no. It's prohibited, prohibited." Why? Because government says so and people want to do it, want to try it by themselves to find out the answer why. If I as a mother explain to my children you're not supposed to be doing that because [some reason] or you can't do it because it's appropriate, it's normal, now it's up to you. You have a choice, do it or not do it. Of course he's not going to do it because he knows why. If government explains to its people the same thing as I did [to my children], no problem at all. Explanation about everything. If you cannot do it, why? People knows why, no problem at all.

I'm thinking to finish university and get bachelor's degree at least and to get a job as a nurse or physical therapist and help people. I want to help them really from my heart. Every day I have a dream: I'm in the hospital in white suit and uniform and some patient sits in my office and I speak with him and I help him and I treat him. And finally I meet him outside of the hospital a couple of weeks later and he says, "Thank you, nurse. You helped me. My health is good now, and I am happy. I'm going to live." [I want] to become a good person here, too, to show my personality I am good. Somebody take advantage from my heart, from my soul, take it and use in some way in something to make improvement or something better.

ELENA LIVES with her husband, son, and father in Vernon Hills, Illinois. She has changed her focus of study and is currently pursuing a degree in early childhood development and working in a day care center.

MY NAME IS TENZIN JAMYANG *and I came here* **23 MAY, 1993** *around 1:00 in the afternoon. In fact, I think it was nice out at that day. I was 21. I'm 29, so it's been eight years.* **I CAME FROM DHARAMSALA, INDIA,** *where the Tibetan settlement project is in India.*

EVEN THOUGH I WAS BORN AND RAISED IN INDIA, the Indian government somehow they never allowed us Indian citizenship. And our parents, since they escaped from Tibet in 1959, since lack of education or lack of ideas or whatever, they never thought of making us as an Indian citizen. And so, even though I was born and raised in India, I never had an Indian citizen. I am pure 100 percent Tibetan.

Actually, Dharamsala is kind of like a city and there is a place called McLeod Ganj, which is the main point, which is where all the Tibetans live in. So McLeod Ganj is the Little Lhasa. When we first fled Tibet in 1959, it was hard for Tibetans to survive back in South India and Central India because the weather was so hot that Tibetans couldn't survive. Because of that, lots of Tibetans had died because they cannot survive with that weather. So Dharamsala is in the Himalaya ranges. It was in high altitude. It think it's around 6,000 feet. So, it was better for the Tibetans to live in the mountains as where they're from. And Tibet is a very cold place, a cold country. And Dharamsala was kind of like that place. It was cold and it was suitable for the Tibetans. For His Holiness [the Dalai Lama], the Indian government, they gave him a quarter in McLeod Ganj in the high mountains. And all the Tibetans, they just followed him. Where His Holiness goes, they wanted to go. So that's how McLeod Ganj became the town for the Tibetans. All the Tibetan exile government headquarters are up in McLeod Ganj.

They say around 100,000 [Tibetans fled in 1959]. Actually, my dad, he was really young. He was around 15, 16. He didn't know much about Tibet even though he was from there. Geographically, he is from southwest [Tibet]. The place is called Lapuk. Lapuk means "a cave." So in that village there was only maybe 15, 20 families lives in there. They didn't have school. They didn't have anything in that village. It's just very remote place. They had some animals and they had land where they grow rice and wheat and stuff like that. But it wasn't a major busi-

ness or anything like that. Just to survive. Basically they didn't have anything! [Laughs.] No business, no jobs, nothing. Just grow stuff there and eat from there and that's about it. He cannot read. He cannot write.

Sometimes he would tell me stories about what Chinese would do and how they came in. In one story he was telling me about the Chinese, they had candies, wrapped up candies. And in that candy there was a picture of one Chinese guy giving a candy to somebody with the right hand and the stick on the left hand. And that symbolizes that, "We will treat you nice for right now and later on we're gonna tell you who we are." And my dad would tell me stories like that. I heard little bit from my dad. He tried to escape Tibet with three of his friends. He said it was pretty rough walking on those mountains trying to hide from the Chinese. Eventually when they got close to Nepal in Tibet somewhere, Chinese, they caught all three of them and they took everybody to the jail. But somehow, my dad got to escape from the Chinese and he made it to Nepal and then back to India. My parents, their border is close to Nepal and it wasn't like the other Tibetans who tried to escape from Lhasa or Kham. Those regions, they are hard to get to. It takes days and days. For our parents, where they lived, it was very close to Nepal and it was just probably a day or two trip.

Actually, my dad, even though he didn't go to any school in his life, he didn't have any exposure of the world, but my dad he is really in some word, he was very intelligent person. He's a great person. He never creates a problem in any society or even in general wherever he

With his family, India, 1985

lived. He just does his work and whatever he does, he does it good. She [my mom] is very religious. She just does prayers all day long, just day and night. She likes to help poor people. Even though she doesn't have enough, she always likes to help and do stuff for other people.

When my dad and mom, when they first got married, we were very, very poor. I think my dad and mom they were making like 20 cents in Indian money, which is probably less than [one-tenth] of one cent American. This was long time ago. I think it was 1960s. They did the road work, road construction. It's very hard. You have to break those rocks with the hand, with a little hammer. It's very, very hard. They make like a quarter of a rupee a day! And it was very, very, very tough. And they saved little money from the beginning and then eventually, like 80 percent of the Tibetans back in India, they survived by selling sweaters.

Let me tell you how that started from my parents side. They heard people selling sweaters. First, they will do the knitting themselves, the sweaters. One sweater a day, two sweaters a day, three sweaters a day, and then take that out on the market and put it out and then sell it. And eventually one Indian guy said, "Hey, don't do this with your hand. There is a place where you can buy all this ready-made and you can just sell those just as you are selling right now." And all the Tibetans, they went to this place. This was in India, in Punjab, the

place called Ludhiana. That's where all the Tibetans went and they start buying. And they can just see all the sweaters, whatever they were doing with their hand, it was done by machine and everything was ready to go. And people start saving some money from road construction work and then take that money to the factories and then buy from there and sell them to different places.

They did this work, still doing it. I remember my mom was telling me that she worked so hard and one time the blood was coming out of her mouth by not eating enough and just working, working, working and selling, try to make some money to survive and feed all the childrens. We have actually six. I have five sisters and myself. So we were six and we didn't have any other resources besides that, selling sweaters. And it was hard at the beginning.

At our home we didn't have any heating system, even though the place where I live gets really, really, really cold in the winter time in the Himalayas. It was hard. Sometimes we will burn fires, charcoals in the middle of the house. We had four rooms, but the fire will be only in one place. So if you want heat, you have to come to that charcoal and stay there.

Actually, we didn't have a bathroom. For bathroom what we did was, we had to walk little bit, like maybe 15 to 20 feet away from the house and there's a little canal with the rocks and stuff like that, and we did it right there. So, it was open-air [sewage]. [Laughs.] The rain comes and then takes it away.

Actually, when I was young, I used to sleep sometimes with my mom and sometimes with my dad because we didn't have enough beds at that time. And as we grow older, we had our own beds, but in one bedroom we had three or four beds and everybody would sleep in each bed. Back there it's totally [different]. Over here, everybody must have one bedroom. I don't know why. [Laughs.] Until you get married, I don't know why you wanna have one bedroom privacy. I don't know, you're doing something weird to have your privacy totally from your own family. I don't understand that, but it's human nature. You want what you want.

In America everything is so easy to get. You work a few hours a day and you get what you want. Back in India, it's not like that. You work months and months and the money you get, you can barely survive with that money. I think in that way, people are little bit spoiled here. I don't wanna say that, but people are little bit spoiled because everything is so ready for them. Whatever they want, it's just like that.

[Snaps his fingers.] I could not imagine by working hard five months, you can have a very good car here. It's possible here. That's what I did to get my car. [Laughs.] Back in India, you can work all your life, you cannot have a car. That's for sure, unless you do some stupid business or you do some weird things. By working, there's no way you're gonna get a car in this life.

I went up to 8th grade and that was it. I regret that I didn't finish my school. In a way, I regret. In a way, it was how it was because the school I went to, it wasn't a kind of school for me. From that school, some kids have become doctors, some kids have become journalists in Tibetan community. They did great. But somehow for me, from the beginning from my childhood from my first grade, I had a very tough schooling. I wasn't learning enough and the teachers weren't good. And I was naughty. I wasn't paying attention to my class. And I didn't know exactly how to study at that time. They [my parents] were uneducated, so they thought I was doing good in school. And I think I was fooling myself.

But I was very naughty until I was maybe 6th, 7th grade. Suddenly, one day everything changed and I became different person. I became very quiet. I saw this guy sitting in the corner of the desk and he doesn't talk to anybody, he doesn't mess up anything. He just sits there whole day long. He doesn't do anything, he doesn't bother anybody. And I talked to myself and I said, "Why I'm different from that person? He's so quiet and he doesn't do anything, and I'm the one fighting with the girls, just chatting with the girls, most of time spending time with the girls." And I said to myself, "I need to change my attitude. I cannot do this. It's not a good thing what I'm doing." And suddenly I changed. I became so quiet. Everything changed that day and I started meeting with that person and sitting close next to him and I did what he was doing. But I realized that he was the same as me. He was very uneducated. [Laughs.] But the good thing was he was very quiet. And I liked being quiet and not bothering people. But my attitude suddenly changed from there. And since then until today, I'm just generally very quiet and I just don't like to do what I used to do when I was young.

I just feel very, very sad when I think of how I missed my opportunity of schooling. I blame 50 percent only on myself and 50 percent on teachers, on the school and the atmosphere. Even today I think of it. I was young. If I had a teacher and if I had a guardian who would tell me exactly what needs to be done, I would have done it. And the school was hard. It's not just studying over there. Surviving was hard in

that school because food was so poor that I don't think any American kid would eat that stuff! But we didn't have any choice.

I was like 16 when I quit my school and I started a business. My dad had a friend who used to own a video parlor where they would show movies and rent videotapes. At the movie theatre, you would fit at least 100 to 150 at a time. And they were selling that business and actually, I forced my dad that I didn't wanna go to school, I wanna do the business. And we bought that place, the video parlor, the video theatre. And I start my business from there. I just did my business until I came to United States. And I think I did better by doing business than going to school at some point, because when I took over the business, I spent all my time. I worked from 9:00 in the morning till 2:00 in the night. So I just work, work, work all that five years. I didn't do anything else. I didn't go to school. I didn't do anything.

I enjoyed doing business. I enjoyed doing something myself. I went to school for all these years and I didn't learn anything. And by doing business, at least I'm supporting my family. And my parents, they had to put less stress on themselves for surviving all the kids because I'm doing business. It was more relaxing for my parents for survival stage.

Until I decided to come here, I didn't know anything [Laughs.] about American and I didn't wanna know [Laughs.] about America. I have no idea what America is all about. Even though I watched a lot of movies, but I never put my mind into it. It was different than most of the people. People wanted to come to United States. People knew about United States. People thought America is a land of opportunity and this and that before even they came to the United States. For my experience, it was totally different. I had no interest in America. [Laughs.]

But suddenly what happened was one day I was running my business and one of my friends just came to me and said, "Hey, there is a filing for people going to America. They're gonna do some lottery."

And I said, "Really?" And America was just a name for me at that time. I had no interest, nothing. And I said, "Oh, OK." I didn't wanna fill up the form. I didn't wanna go there. I didn't wanna be in America. [Laughs.]

After I had that conversation, I went home. I ate. And my dad told me, "You should go and fill that up. There is a form going to America."

And I said, "For what? It may be a great country and whatever." And as lots of corruption goes in any Asian country, I thought even if we get a chance, we won't be able to go. Somebody else is gonna go instead of us. Corruption will just take it away. I just let it go. And that day I told my dad, "Forget it. I'm not going. I have no interest." And I went to my business.

And a couple days went by and one day I went home again. I had my lunch. Then my dad got really angry. He said, "I want you to fill this up and take it down right now." I think it was 1991 when they were collecting those forms. And my dad got really angry. He said, "Everybody's filling this form."

And I can tell you, he probably has the same idea as I have: "What is America? Why do you wanna go to America?" [Laughs.] He probably doesn't know much. He just wanted to do what everybody else is doing. And I did fill up the form and I went down there. And this was the last hour and the last day of collecting these forms. And I went there and they were almost done. Everybody was packing up and I gave my form. I forgot about it.

That day when they were pulling out the names, I didn't wish for my name to come out. I was hanging around at my video business just looking around, and one of my friends was walking on the road and he just looked up and he said, "Hey, Tenzin. Your name has come out in the lottery."

I said, "Forget it, man. Don't lie." I didn't even trust him. I said, "No, forget it." But then I thought, "Maybe. You never know." [Laughs.] So I said, "Maybe my name has come out." One of my aunts, she works at Tibetan Home Department, and I called her. I said, "Did my name come out?"

And she said, "I think so." And she looked and she said, "No, I'm sorry." It was somebody else. It was reverse of my name. My name is Tenzin Jamyang, and the name of the person came up was Jamyang Tenzin.

And I said, "That's what I thought!" And then I hang up and then I just forgot about it.

Then again, somebody else comes and goes, "Your name has come."

And I said, "Get out of here. It was somebody else. I just called. It wasn't me. It was somebody else."

He said, "No. No. I swear it was your name. It was Tenzin Jamyang."

I didn't trust him. And I just went down to the office, which was probably a mile or two down. I walked two miles. Over there, we walk most of the time up and down, up and down. So I went down and looked at the list and I found that person's name, Jamyang Tenzin. And I said, "These guys are lying." And then I said, "Let me take a look again." And then I looked down carefully, and I found my name. [Laughs.] It

was down there. All the way down, I found my name. And I couldn't believe. I said, "Oh, man. I'm going to America!" [Laughs.] It was funny.

When they say, "America," to me it was just a blank. It was just an empty land. It was nothing. It was just a blank. I never thought of big tall buildings and people busy walking, making money, dollars here and there. It wasn't that for me. To me, America was a blank emptiness. That was it. Then I went to my dad and I said, "My name has come up."

He was so happy. He said, "Alright!" [Laughs.]

I wasn't happy or I wasn't sad. I was just as I was, shocked in a way that my name has come up. I'm not shocked because I'm going to America. [Laughs.] I was shocked that my name has come up and I'm doing something different in my life. Because I went to school, I start my business, and that was my life. And now I'm going to America. [Laughs.] That was third part of my life. So little change going in my life that was different. And even though my name came up in '92, I had to wait, I think, one year to submit my paper and do this and that.

I didn't put much pressure, I didn't thought about learning about America [Laughs.] as other people did. They wanted to learn about America. They wanted to see and read and stuff like that. I never did any of that. For a year, I was just excited that I'm going to America. And then, I started looking at some of these movies. And I looked and I see how America is, and these high rise buildings, and then those things start coming in my mind.

It was funny that when I first thought America, now this is after when I'm watching movies and thinking about coming to America, I thought it was 100 percent white people. [Laughs.] I thought it was completely white people wherever you go. I didn't know there is all these different people from different countries and different cultures. I thought America means just strictly white people walking around up and down doing business. And I thought, "Oh, I'm going to a white country. There's only white people and I'm gonna be there. I'm gonna act like a white. I'm gonna learn and do a lot of stuff." That's what my mind was going.

And then one day my name came up and they said I had to go to the training where they will tell you how you behave in America, how you behave in airplane. They were talking about how to use a bathroom in an airplane. [Laughs.] There is a bathroom, the door opens like this. In airplane, you can do this, you cannot do that. Things like that. They did some kind of training. They explained to us that we have to take shower every day and you have to put the deodorant. One thing they told us about: Don't get late at work. Never get late at work. If you get late, you're out. That's what they told us. [Laughs.] We [Tibetans] are always late. If you ask somebody to come at 1:00, they will show up at 2:00. So if you want somebody to come at 1:00, you wanna tell them 12:00 so they will show up at 1:00. That's how it was back there. So that's what people were concerned about. That I remember very clearly. [Laughs.]

First they told me I'm going to Salt Lake City, Utah. And I said, "OK, I'm going to Salt Lake City. I don't know what the hell that is!" [Laughs.] I was doing my paper work here and there. And then all of a sudden one day they told me I'm going to Chicago. I said, "OK. I'm going to Chicago!" [Laughs.] It didn't make any difference. And I asked my friends, "Which one is better?"

And some said, "Chicago is better. It's big city."

At his video store, India, 1996

And I learned little bit about Chicago, how the city is structured and how the people are and mostly the weather. I heard back there, the weather is crazy here. You gotta very be careful with the Chicago weather. And I came here and I saw it and it is scary sometimes. You have 60 degrees today, and tomorrow you have snow with minus. So, it is crazy weather here. Besides that, Chicago is a great city. I love this city and I feel good that I got to come here in Chicago.

Since it has to go through government to government thing, I received a letter saying that I'm going to Chicago. There was an organization in Chicago, it's called the Tibetan Association of Chicago, and they had lots of American friends who were willing to support and willing to help Tibetan people coming as an immigrant. I think it was close to 100 Americans. To come here, everybody must have a sponsor letter that when they come here, we will support them, just for the government official use.

And I received a letter saying that I have a job as a bus person in Melvin B's. It's a very famous and very downtown young generation kind of bar and restaurant. They said I had a bus boy job and I thought I was going to drive a bus! And I told some of my friends, "Hey, I'm

driving a bus there." I thought it was a bus person. [Laughs.] That's what they said in the letter. It was a letter from Melvin B's saying that Tenzin Jamyang hiring at Melvin B's with the tips included and the minimum wage $5 an hour as a bus person in Melvin B's. I still have that letter. So I thought I was gonna drive a bus, but it was different when I got here. Just cleaning tables and picking up plates and stuff like that.

I start calculating that $5 into Indian money. And I calculated that $5 an hour at the exchange rate at that time was, I think it was 30 rupees [per dollar] back in India. So $5 an hour into 30 rupees, 150 rupees an hour and I said to myself, "Damn, I'm rich!" [Laughs.]

For a construction worker back there, it'll take two to three days to make that 150 for construction worker, and I'm making that an hour and one day if I work eight hours, how much is that? And that's probably more than whole month of that other person's job in one day. And I started calculating that and I said to myself, "Oh, man, I'm rich." [Laughs.] It was surprising when I first saw that it wasn't very much. When you come here it was totally different.

After a month or two preparation for getting ready to United States, this was the day or two before we were leaving, we had a special audience with His Holiness [the Dalai Lama]. He gave us a statue of Buddha and he gave us some *changye* and *maniribu*. *Changye* is protection. You can put this in your car, you can eat it in the morning. When you have that with you, you are safe. And *maniribu* is same thing. And lot of Tibetans experience that when you eat *maniribu*, you're not gonna get cold. It stops cold. It's more like a religious thing. It's like a seed. It's herbs.

He told us that, "We are struggling. We have a very hard time. Our country is gonna go down if we don't do anything now." And he told us that we are going to America not for survival. For survival you can live anywhere in the world. You can survive. We are going to America as an ambassador of six million Tibetan people. That was his speech mainly about.

It is always special [to have an audience with His Holiness] because for Tibetans, we believe him as a God. And in a way, I think he is more than a God because God is something you cannot touch, you cannot see, most of the time in most of the religions. And for us, he is more than a God because he is someone we call God and we can still see him on top of that. And being around and being close to that kind of God or that important person, being close to that, it's a very good feeling for Tibetans. Even in Tibetan beliefs, you are very, very lucky to be born even when His Holiness is around. It shows that you have luck and you have that kind of merit to be born in this century or this lifetime when the God, or the Buddha, His Holiness, is alive. If you are not lucky, you won't be born and you won't be able to see His Holiness. And that's why we believe him as a God. And it was very proud moment and it was very pleasing to be in front of him. It's very touching.

Until the day I was leaving, I was OK with everything. I was ready for the change. I don't care. I am going to America. Even if it's like the hell, I still don't care. I was just going for the change. I thought I was doing something good, even with the pay and everything. I was looking forward to a brightness. Until the day I was leaving, everything was fine. I wasn't sad or anything. Little bit, but not deeply. But the day I was leaving, whole day I was thinking about my family, my dad, and it was very, very sad. We had prayer at home before we left. My mom, yeah, she was very sad. She was very, very sad. She didn't want me to leave. I was kind of sad whole day because now I'm coming to the point where I have to leave my family, my parents. And my family, I'm the only son, and my dad loved me so much. Even though we struggled here and there, we had arguments this and that, but still he loved me so much in his life that I cannot imagine. When I think of that, I wish I get the same dad in my next life. So it was sad.

Time comes when we were going to the airport, and my whole mind and heart was totally down. Everything was changed. And at the airport, when we walked, my dad advised me. He always forced me to study. In life he wanted me to study, study, study because I never did. And he still told me the same thing, "Go to America, work a little bit, study." And I still think about it and it makes me very sad. And he advised me, just don't do any bad things. He didn't say particularly don't do this and that because I really don't waste my time on doing something unreasonable, so he knew that from the beginning. So he didn't say much, but deep inside he was very, very sad and I was very sad.

In India it's different than America. You cannot walk inside the airport. You have to wait outside. At the airport, we walk inside the terminal and it was a very sad moment. I walked inside. I looked out. My dad was standing there just looking at me. And it was very, very sad. And I cried. I just couldn't say anything and I just walked by from him.

I was still little bit nervous getting on the plane. It was just really unique experience, getting on the plane and just flies in the sky and then lands you where you can never imagine. Actually, I think we slept most of the time in the plane. We didn't talk much. I think there was like 13 Tibetans just going straight to Chicago.

Actually, I looked down from the window and I saw Chicago down there and I was surprised because I never thought or put interest about knowing the United States or Chicago. So I looked down and I saw those houses with the trees just in a row. Houses maybe miles and miles just in a same row and the trees in the same row and it goes miles and miles. And I looked down and I said, "Oh, my God, look at that!" [Laughs.] And then I saw the lake. I'd never seen actually in my naked eye right there, there's water like the sea and then there's the city right there. And I was surprised to see that. And then I was surprised to see all the houses and the roads from there. I said, "Oh, my God. Look at that." It was pretty surprising.

When we landed, we were very nervous. Now we're in America!

Giving a speech at the hunger strike for Tibet, New York City, 1995

[Laughs.] And we got here around 12:00, 1:00 in between. And when we got out of the airplane, I was so nervous. I said, "Oh, man. What the hell?" I was very nervous. As soon as we came out of the airport, we see some of the American friends waiting for us. And it was a very good feeling when you come out and there's people waiting for the Tibetans. And on the way from the airport, we were driving and I looked out the window and I was surprised to see all this green. It's a big city and everywhere is green and cars going fast. *Whoosh, whoosh.* And the noise, the car's noise was very different because cars were going really fast. And I looked around and I said, "Oh my God. Where are we?"

Right now it's nothing. We've been here and we know everything and it doesn't make any changes. But the first time when you come here, it was May, so everything was green and the weather was sunny, bright. And everybody was happy because of the weather. Everybody was smiling. And I was like, "Oh my God. It's a good thing. [Laughs.] I made a good decision coming here."

We just went from airport directly to Malden [Street] and Wilson [Avenue]. That's where all the Tibetans were living in one big building which was fixed by some company and made it ready for the Tibetans. And the first month was free and then after that you paid the rent.

When we walked in the building, it wasn't like a luxury compared to American luxury. But coming from India and looking, first of all I was surprised with the bathroom. One apartment had one bathroom and that was very surprising. [Laughs.] And the room was so clean. They were painted and it was carpet underneath. And I never had carpet in my life on the floor. [Laughs.] And the kitchen was very nice and clean with the water running. The tap was right over there and the cabinets. It's more like luxury back in India. And it was a good feeling. "Oh, man. Look at this! We live here now. Oh, it's a good feeling." It was a very unique experience. The phone was ready there and you can talk to people right there. If I think deeply, everything was kind of surprising, having everything ready.

I had two roommates and we shared, I think it was a one bedroom apartment. It's a little bit different because I never lived with anybody besides my parents, but then still it was OK because we were all Tibetans. We all young people so it was different in a way.

It makes me laugh actually, in a way, because now we are spoiled. Now I'm into this melting pot and now I'm part of America and going back and thinking about how I saw and how I experienced the first time at the city looking down from the airplane, surprising myself, and

driving and seeing all the cars going fast, and seeing all the grass green, people happy. Now I'm an American, so now it's little bit kind of funny when I think about what happened back then.

One of the sponsors from one of my roommates, his name was Penpa Tsering and his sponsors' name were Dan and Jenny. Both of them, they took us to the lakefront. This was first or second day, I'm not sure. And by the lakefront I looked around and I was surprised, "Oh, my God! There is this ocean here and then there's the city and there's sand in the middle!" Like in Bombay they have this kind of beach and buildings, but I've never been there. Even if you go in India, you might have those things, but it's not clean. Water is dirty, the sand is dirty, and the road is dirty, and the buildings. [Laughs.] And people walking around are still dirty. It was totally different because the water was so clean and green. And the sand was totally clean. The buildings were high and clean. And I just circled around and looked around I was so surprised. And I told Dan, "This is unbelievable. It's so nice!"

One time, this was bad, somebody got shot right behind our apartment. I didn't see the bodies, but my friend saw two guys shot each other right there at Malden [Street]. That was scary. No gun shootings at all [in Dharamsala]. I never heard about it, and to tell you the truth, I never saw a gun. This was very different hearing people got shot down there. It was just strange. Another one, somebody got shot in the apartment in that building. Somebody was inside and somebody shot it right through the door in that building. So it was scary.

I was very nervous [my first day of work]. I made a lot of mistakes. I went out there and somehow my supervisor, I don't think they knew where we came from [Laughs.] and what we were like, he just put me on a job and that's it. He said, "OK, Tenzin. Take this towel and you're ready." [Laughs.] He put me there and I didn't know anything what to do! I never picked up plates from anybody! I never picked up glass! I never filled up water to anybody in my life. I never worked for anybody and this guy gives me a towel and said, "OK, Tenzin. Go. Just clean."

And it was not just cleaning when I think about it, not like back in India, you go out there and just start picking things and putting water. Over here, the things have to be done differently, even though people would say, "It's just water filling. It's just cleaning table." But if you think about it, it is not. It is very different. There is a way to do things and you have to learn before you even do it. People always say, "Oh, bus boy." Bus boy is a dirty job, but there is a way to do it. Even though it's a dirty job, there's still a way to do it. So, it was very different.

When you go there, there is rules. You fill the water from the right side, not the left side. You pick up the plate from the left side, not the right side. When the people are done, the spoons are upside down. These are little, but all this you have to learn. And they didn't tell me anything. They just said, "Hey, just fill up the water."

And the waiter will come and say, "Hey, my table needs water. Go water."

And then I go and pick up water. I didn't even look at the person. I didn't give eye contact. I didn't give the smile. It's not that I don't like the person. It's not that I'm scared of them. It's just my culture! They want water, they don't want me. So I just go and fill up the water. Now you have to look at the person and you have to smile and you have to let them know you're gonna fill up the water. "Would you like some water?" You have to let them know. Things like that. But if you think, even that water is very simple thing, but there's a way to do it. So it was very strange that I'm working picking up glasses and picking up plates, but I did pretty good.

First day when I walked and I went home after the work, I had thirty something dollars tips, cash, not the hourly $2.50. That's separate. And I had $35 in my pocket and I was like, "Oh, my God. I have $35!" And I calculated it and it was so much in India, like 1,000 rupees! I was like, "Oh, my God. In one day I make 1,000!" Over there it takes months to make that dollar. I was very surprised. I put some of the money to the altar to His Holiness and I said, "Thank you." And I was happy to go to work every day, just go there and show up. And I was always on time. I was never late.

In fact, what happened was one time I went to work. This is very funny. You won't imagine. I went to work. I didn't have any money. I had maybe a dollar or so in my pocket and change little bit. And I used to buy these tokens, CTA tokens, and I had only two left. I put two tokens in my pocket and a dollar and little change and I went to work. And what happened was, I went to work and the work was very slow. Nobody came to the restaurant and my manager, his name was Adam, and Adam said, "Tenzin, it's very slow. Just go home."

And I said, "I wanna work! Come one, just leave me here $2 an hour for 10 hours!" [Laughs.]

"Tenzin," he said, "go home."

I said, "OK." And I barely speak English so I did what they wanted me to do. I left. I went to the train stop which was on Clark and Division [Streets], the red line train stop. So I went there. Now I have only one token, right? I put the token, I went inside and when I came out, I was out again! I was by the stairs for the Clark Street! I said, "Shit, man! How did I come out here? I was supposed to go down." Somehow I made a mistake. This was maybe week or so in my job, maybe two weeks. So now I'm on the Clark Street again. I just walk up the stairs. I was embarrassed. I walk up the stairs. I said, "Shit, man. I have no money now." I have a dollar and a quarter and a little change. I didn't have $1.50. Now I have no money and I have no quarters. I said, "Shit man, that sucks!" So, you know what I did? Guess what I did. I walked! I'm pretty good with the geography in my head. And what I did, I walked straight towards the lake and I end up somewhere nearby North Avenue and I still went straight! I didn't know where I was going. I was focusing on the lake. I went straight on the lake! And then I got by the sidewalks on the lake and then I made a left. And I kept going straight north until I hit Wilson [Avenue]. And then at Wilson, I made a left again and then I was there. It took me three hours walking! [Laughs.] It was like 12:00, 1:00 in the afternoon. The weather was very, very nice. It was unbelievable and I just walked. And I had a good time walking, three hours of walk. That was funny. [Laughs.] No money, no tokens, and I only needed maybe a quarter or so, and who I'm gonna ask for a quarter. "Hey, give me a quarter!" I cannot do that. [Laughs.] So I just walked!

So, every day I felt better. Every day I was looking forward to work. Even though it was a bus boy job, still I was making money and I was happy. As the days and months go by, I was happier because it was easy, just easy job, easy money. You eat good. You live comfortably. So it was good. Actually, I was more in work. I was more thinking about money I think. I did that job and at the same time I had another job doing same thing at TGI Fridays. I worked for maybe couple or months there as a bus boy. In the morning I worked at TGI Fridays for a couple of months and then in the evening, I worked at Melvin B's. And at that time, it was just work, go home, work, go home, work, go home. I wasn't interested in other things that much.

After that, what happened was Melvin B's, they closed down. They don't close, but no business during the winter time. After end of September, October, this place, nobody comes in there. They're open, but very few people comes in and there's no way you can survive on that. And at TGI Fridays, I worked for a couple months and it wasn't for me. It was very loud. It's a very loud restaurant and you have to be very quick on everything. Then I quit both jobs.

One of our American friends, he knew that I had a video parlor back in India, and he thought I might be interested in this. And he took me one day to Facets [Multimedia] and introduced me to the manager down there in the shipping department, and that guy was Indian. He was a very good person. So he interviewed me and he asked me about what kind of job I did back in India. And I told him I had a video business. That's how I got this job. I was a shipping clerk, two years. At that time I had another job at the East Bank Club. I was doing bus boy plus banquet server over there at the same time.

So all these years, I had almost two jobs for three years, four years and I had saved lots of money. I saved money because I don't go out, I don't drink, I don't smoke and I don't waste money on anything. So, I saved a lot of money. I was able to support my family. I sent money home and they were happy getting the money. And one time, I went on vacation after two years back to India. I met my parents. I was very happy and now I was used to American things, and I got tired. It was two months vacation. After like two, three weeks, I was just tired. I wanted to come back. It was boring because over here, you work every day. Over there, there's nothing you can do whole day. Just drink tea, and there was nothing else to do. And it was not for me doing nothing just staying there [so I came back].

Meanwhile, deep down inside, I was always thinking about Tibet and Tibetans. I have great feelings about Tibet and Tibetans. It is maybe crazy sometimes, but that's how I feel. That's how I feel like where I belong. Even though I don't know much Tibetan, reading, writing, religion anything, but I have all my heart goes toward Tibet and Tibetans. And since my childhood, I always had that feeling inside me.

I was working at both jobs and all of a sudden, one person, he used to be a Tibetan Youth Congress president in New Delhi, a while ago maybe five, ten years ago, and he was very [committed] to Tibet. And before I went on vacation, this guy used to just go around to apartments and talk to people. And one day he came to our apartment, and we had a conversation, like four guys were talking about Tibet and what to do next. And I'm happy that we have this kind of person in Tibetan community. He talks about Tibet and Tibetans and fighting for freedom and all that and I felt good being around with that person. We had a conversation and in the conversation, he tried to see where I am going and what my ideas were. And I didn't have much idea. I didn't have too much to talk about Tibetans. I didn't do much. I didn't have much knowledge. But during the conversation, he talked about doing

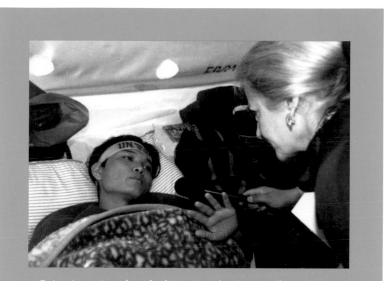

Being interviewed at the hunger strike, New York City, 1995

some kind of demonstration against Chinese in front of the United Nations, or maybe in front of American big offices with a big demonstration which will effect and move everybody, Tibetans or supporters all over the world. And in that conversation, he talked mainly about doing some kind of hunger strike or doing really strong demonstrations against Chinese by the United Nations. And I liked that idea so much, because before even he started that conversation, when I was back in India, I always wanted to do something which is very effective, very strong. And in that case, if I have to lose my life, I'll probably be ready because I have feelings for Tibet. It's always been there.

And as he started that conversation, it crossed my mind right there. And I said, "I have this feeling to do something like this always with me. Do you really think you can organize stuff like that? Do you really wanna do stuff like that?"

He said, "We can try. If I do something, I'll let you know." And the conversation ended there.

And then one day he called and we talked for a little bit. And I said, "Are you really organizing this thing?"

And he said, "We're working on it. I think we have a couple of people and we were waiting for you, whether you were ready or not."

And I said, "I'm on. I'm in. What I said before, that's my decision.

If you can organize it, I'm there. Don't worry about it."

And he said, "OK. You make me feel good. We do it now."

So two of the chief members came here, and they give speech to the Tibetans here, and they said we have a few people going on hunger strike, if you wanna donate some money and the purpose of the hunger strike and how it's gonna go. They explained and everything. And the guy came to me and he said, "Are you ready for this?"

I said, "Yeah. I'm always ready. I was always ready for this. This was my dream before you came here. It was something I always wanted to do."

He said, "OK, that's great."

So he gave me a time to show up in New York on a certain date. This was on the fiftieth anniversary, Golden Jubilee of the United Nations. This was September '96.

So they left and now I was getting ready. I got my medical check-up from the Touhy Health Center. I didn't call my parents. I didn't call my sisters. I didn't call nobody. I just went to New York and we started the hunger strike. So I went on a hunger strike in front of the United Nations head office. We had six Tibetans there. And we made some saying that every one person stands for one million Tibetan people. So we have six million Tibetans and we are six people there, one for each million.

It was right on the street, sidewalk. We had our carpets at the beginning. We bought some sleeping bags. Even during the night, we were right there. We had signs, "Six Tibetans on Hunger Strike," and we had five demands. All five demands were made by His Holiness, actually, on one of the meetings in some European country.

I felt so good that my dream was coming true. It was my dream for long time. I always wanted to do something for Tibet as a Tibetan. If I didn't do that, I will still feel empty in my life. Even if I become a millionaire, it doesn't mean anything to me if I'm not able to do something for Tibet and the Tibetan cause. So I'm glad. I'm more happy that I did that than if I was something else. So during the hunger strike, I never felt sad. I never thought about my family. I was happy that I made that decision and I'm there at that time. It was hard at the beginning because you're hungry little bit. We had water. Sometimes just hot water, sometimes water with sometimes sugar, sometimes lemon, sometimes something in the water. That helped.

It was better than anything else. I felt so good that I didn't get hungry at all. All that time, can you imagine? Thirteen days, I didn't get hungry at all. Today if you don't eat for couple hours, you get hungry,

"Oh, man. I'm hungry." On that day, I don't know what it is that I never got hungry. And I ask other people and they have the same experience. They were never hungry. There was one American doctor and one Tibetan doctor and they did check-ups on us every day. They come in every day 9:00, 10:00 [A.M.] and they did how everything was going.

We didn't talk much. There were a couple older people and three of us almost we were the same age. It was 23, 24 and 26, and the girl was like 26. And the two older people were 45 and 48. Older people were praying all day long. We just sit there and pray sometimes. Sometimes we just joked. But there were cameras from all over. All the news medias were there from all over the world. In fact, I heard that in the Hong Kong television, we were on television even after we were done, after a month. They were still showing six Tibetans on a hunger strike and our cause and what's happening.

When we first made the commitment, we said that we would never stop this hunger strike until we die or until they meet the demands. And we pretty much decided on that. But we had one agreement, that if His Holiness wants us to stop, we have to because we didn't have a choice. And this was politically and morally and everything it was a better decision in a way. Because in a way, if you don't stop when His Holiness says, "Stop," then we're not following his order. Because he's our leader. He's the one we are going with. And the other thing is if we don't stop, the Tibetans may go against us. "They're not following His Holiness order. What are they doing?" And then our support might go down. So we had to make agreement that there was three ways to stop this: Unless they take the five demands, or we die, or His Holiness can stop this. There was only three. And we were there and we had lot of requests from all over, the senators from New York City and all the Tibetan supporters, they were requesting us to stop but we never stopped.

But on the day 13, we received a letter from His Holiness saying that, "You have achieved your goals and we need you more alive than dead." So he requested us to stop the hunger strike and so we had to stop.

I lost 13 pounds in 13 days, a pound a day. The main experience about this hunger strike was that it was like a miracle. We were never hungry and everything went smoothly. And after the hunger strike, everybody was fine except that one girl. I heard she was not doing good after hunger strike. She had problems with her stomach and the doctor was saying it has to do with the hunger strike. Besides that, everybody is fine.

Being alive, I might be able to do some other stuff. My purpose was since I'm not well educated and I don't know what to do in a way, so this was one of the ways. This may not be the right way, but this is not the wrong way either. So, it is a way. Just like anything else. You have to do something. So this was one way which I accept. But being alive, you can do more if you know what you wanna do, if you know how to do it. But if you don't know, what is the purpose then? What are you doing being alive? As His Holiness said, "We need you more alive." That means he wants you to do something when you're alive right now. Since then, I really didn't do anything. So, what's the purpose of all these five years? What did I do? Nothing. So, if we die over there, it might bring up some stories, it might change something inside Tibet and with the exile government. And the U.N. might do something after we die or something. So, it goes both ways.

When I did this, I really don't know whether I'm strong or whether I'm weak. I may be weak because there's no other way I can think of besides killing myself. And I'm strong in a way. People cannot imagine doing stuff like this for themselves. So I don't know whether it's strong or weak.

After hunger strike, I came back and I got my job back, both of them. They took me back. This was second time. And now my parents want to see me. They want me to come back. Then after a couple months I went back India.

I did [have an audience with His Holiness in India]. Other hunger strikers wasn't there, but the Tibetan Democratic Party members were there, so we went together up there. I just cried all the time. He was saying something. I didn't hear. He was proud of what we did. He said it was great and he said a lot of things, but I just cried all the time just right by him.

I came back and I tried to do a little business selling Tibetan stuff. I used to do this when I first came in '93, I came with a lot of Tibetan

With a friend, India, 1996

stuff, just like Tibetan clothing, and Tibetan items like flags, and Tibetan ritual items and stuff like that. Just like most of the people did try to bring stuff and sell stuff here. So, it went OK.

I never went back to my both jobs because I felt bad doing it three times, going back. And this time I went to get another job. I went to work at the Four Seasons Hotel in downtown. I worked as a bellman over there and then the doorman for three years. It was OK. It's hard for me to act like very nice with the people. It was very hard just to be, "Hey, how are you?" It was hard and I'm not good at that. So, I quit after three years. I was driving taxi at the same time when I was working at the hotel. It was hard to work and drive and work and drive. Then I went to cab driving. So since then, I'm driving cab. It's been three years.

Actually, I made some money last year. I bought a house and I kept that for a year and a half, and I sold it and I made very good money on that. So with that money, I was going to put down and buy another building with a storefront and open up a Tibetan store with a café. I'm not good in business. [Laughs.] I know that, but I keep trying to do business since my childhood. I always try to sell something. But I was looking for the building for a long time and I couldn't find it. And at the same time, I'm worried that if I start something and waste a lot of money and if it didn't work out, I'm gonna be stuck because I don't have other qualifications. I don't have any skill. I don't have any knowledge about other things how to do.

And then, one of my American friends, she called me one day. I asked her if she can help me with opening up a Tibetan store. She said she can help, but she said she is looking for a partner to start a business. And I said, "No, I'm not looking for a partner. I cannot do partner business." And eventually, I couldn't find a building, but then at that same time, she opened up a store. So, then she asked me if I want to rent a space in there. I thought about it and I said, "Yeah, why do I

With His Holiness the Dalai Lama, India, 1996

wait for a long time not to have a store?" And I said, "OK," and I went with her. Now I rent a space there for $200 a month and I pay 15 percent of the profit as a commission and it's nice right now. A little store inside the store. It's called Tibetan Lungta Arts. Lungta means luck.

I'm just thinking about this idea of opening a Tibetan café where you go in and everything will be Tibetan inside, the walls, whatever we're selling. Wherever you look around, it will be Tibetan atmosphere. And you will hear Tibetan music. You can have Tibetan tea, salt butter tea that is. And you walk in there, you'll meet lots of Tibetan and you'll see lots of books about Tibet. And you can watch and rent a lot of Tibetan movies. And you can learn almost anything about Tibet as soon as you walk into that little Tibet store. And I'm thinking about in the café, it'll be mostly catering like Tibetan *momos* [dumplings], *thukpas* [soups] and other very nice and tasty Tibetan items which a lot of American friends will like, I'm pretty sure. And things like that. And there will be a screen where you can watch Tibetan movies like once or three times a week. I don't know when it's gonna come out. It might not come out. It might stay there in my dreams, but this is how I wanted to do it for quite a long time and thinking about it.

In a way I'm happy that I'm in America, in a way I'm kind of sad. Little bit lost. I don't know how to explain this. Because my mind sometimes is as an American. Just by driving sometimes, I just do the thing what American people does. Somebody crosses you, you give finger. Things like that. But since I'm Tibetan Buddhist, I try to control myself every day. As soon as I get in my car and I start working, I say and I think of myself as a Tibetan and I control myself not to do what lots of American people does. Driving here is just crazy. People do all stupid things. I just wanna be Tibetan. I don't wanna be American. I mean, I'm American naturally because I'm working and I'm living here. But at the same time, I don't wanna do and I don't wanna take those negative attitudes. I don't wanna make other people sad because of my problem. If I have a problem, I just wanna keep it myself. I don't wanna let other people suffer because I'm not happy. I don't wanna drive reckless because I'm not happy.

I learned a lot [from driving]. When I'm driving, I'm learning, too, at the same time. Because on 12 hours of work, I listen to radio all day. And I don't listen to music. I just listen to talk radios and news like WBEZ and WLS, the talk radios and that's it. Maybe once in a while I get really tired and I have music for maybe 10, 15 minutes and then go back to news. And that's where I practice my English, too, at the same time. Every time the newscast comes out and I hear the news, then I try to mimic the pronunciation and I try to say the words as they go on. And so, basically I'm happy when I'm driving because I'm learning at the same time. But I do this only when there's no customer in the car. [Laughs.]

Tibet [is my home]. I feel 90 percent towards Tibet. I feel more towards Tibet. It's not because just the land. It has to do with the religion. It has to do with the people. It has to do with my genes. So, I feel more towards Tibet. But I am [a United States citizen]. I became a citizen last year, 2000, July 15th. It was good becoming an American because until now, I was citizen of nowhere. Deep down inside I felt myself Tibetan, but Tibetan citizenship, nobody accepts it anywhere you go in the world. We don't have a passport. So I didn't have any passport until last year! So it was a good feeling that now I have a passport. Wherever I go, "Hey, I'm an American." I can use that passport. So it was a good feeling.

Sometimes yes, [I feel lonely], but sometimes I'm used to it. Because back in India, I was on my own since I was six years old. I went to school, which was a boarding school. I quit my school. I did my business and I was never home. I was always alone in my life. I never relied on anybody else in my life. Even my parents, they feed me and they clothe me, but I was on my own since I was very young. And that's one of the reasons I don't feel that lonely.

I don't have very close American friends. I don't have one. I know some people, some Indian Americans and some Americans I know, but I don't have very close friends. Because sometimes, it can be hard for us as we are not very young and we don't like to do what American people like to do, go out and drink beer all day long. A lot of Tibetans they drink, but they drink at home. They don't like to go out and drink, waste money. I don't think any of the Tibetans have a lot of American friends. It has to do with the cultural difference. Tibetan people, they like to have a good time at home. Eat good food, call your friends, listen to music, drink as much as you want, but only in your home.

I have changed a lot in many ways. I look at situations differently now than before. Before, if I see something, I don't question. I just thought as it is and it doesn't bother me or it doesn't effect me. And I have no curiosity that much of anything. If it is there, it is there. Now, I ask questions and I want to know, "How did this come out? How did this happen? Oh, where to go? What to do?" Things like that.

The other thing is that now recently I try to read some books. I never did. Now I'm trying to read some Tibetan books, and His Holiness's books, and spiritual books and stuff like that. I'm proud of being Tibetan and being Buddhist. I shouldn't say I'm Buddhist before. But now I'm learning and I'm going into it and it makes me feel good. I wanna learn more. It tells me I wanna learn more about Tibet and Buddhism and everything. I never practice my religion that much, but deep down inside just like I have feelings for Tibet, I have feelings for my religion. And as I grow older, I want to go deep down and search and do more of Tibetan Buddhism. That's one of the reasons I'm trying to support Tibet and trying to devote and trying to do something for Tibet in whichever way is possible, because of the religion. Because it's so pure. I don't go deep, but just looking on the top of this religion, just little things here and there, makes a lot of sense to me. I just wanna get into it and do it till the end of my life. Right now I'm young and I'm just doing what young people does, wasting time and doing stuff here and there. But eventually, I really want to get the Tibetan Buddhism and just go as deep as I can.

I just think differently than before. One big change is that I never talked before. Now I talk a lot. When I see as we meet, I just talk. Before, I don't talk to people that much. I was very close-minded and I just don't like to talk, and I would think what people would think if I talk, if I speak, what they might think. And nowadays, I just kind of forget about that. I try to do the right thing and focus on what I wanna do and try to achieve the good thing, don't think and waste time on bad things and something you don't want.

I'm getting married soon, probably this year. I'm thinking about it. She's a great girl. I know her from my childhood. She's Tibetan. I know her very young and she knew me when I was five, six years old. I met her recently back in India. And I think I'll be happy with her. And I'm thinking about having my baby with her. [Laughs.] She will be here. I'll bring her here and raise my child, but still I don't know whether my child's gonna grow up here or back in India or Tibet. I don't know where I'm gonna raise my child because generally, educationwise, America is great. There's a lot of things to learn about. But then at the same time, there's lots of lack of moral understanding, and children shooting children, children killing parents. Those are unbelievable and those are unthinkable and those things are rising in the United States. And I'm sad sometimes where the country is going in a way. So I don't know if I want my child to be raised in this society where they have no respect for parents. So I might send them back to India or something for their betterness.

One thing. I think I always feel bad and sad that I'm not able to educate myself in education ways. When we first got here, if we knew, we would have finished the school and be somewhere else. It was a bad thing that we thought we were adults and we just went on. We had to work. We had to make money. We [should have] thought that we were young. We [should have] gone to school. It was not time for us to work until 25 at least.

But I have no regrets in a way because so far in America for me, life has been great. No problems. I made good money. I bought a house, sold it. And I got to do a great cause, great thing for Tibet and I'll still do it in the future. In a way I'm happy to be in the United States to learn about things.

TENZIN IS MARRIED AND HAS A BABY DAUGHTER. He owns a building and a small convenience store in Chicago. He is still trying to open his café.

I AM **RUBÉN MONTOYA** AND I AM FROM COLOMBIA.

Exactly, I am from Medellín. I have been in Chicago since last **JUNE 1999.** *I have been in Chicago for 10 months, almost, and I am 40 years old.*

I'M MARRIED AND I HAVE TWO DAUGHTERS of nine and three years old. The younger is Susana and the older is Laura. My wife is Gloria Patricia. My kids, my daughters, are lovely. They are very pretty. They are very kind. In English I didn't know how to say, but they are very, very good persons.

I love Medellín. I am so much regionalist. Antioquia is the first state in Colombia. I think Medellín is the first city in Colombia. It's not the biggest, but it's the best city in Colombia. It's not so big like Chicago, but it's a very good city in all of the aspects. It's a beautiful city, beautiful city. We have a better train than Chicago, a new train, very beautiful train, very clean, very good. We have many valuable things. We have very good universities, very good schools, very good professionals, very good sportsmen. We have very good architects, not famous architects, but very good architects.

I was born in a small town called Palermo, I think three hours from Medellín. I was born there because my parents were teachers in this small town. Both are teachers of elementary school. They met at that town. One year after they met, I was born. That town was a very beautiful town because it was peaceful. It was very beautiful. It was between mountains and small rivers. The landscape was wonderful and people were peaceful, too. Very kind. I was only just two years in this town because my parents were moved to another towns. And we were moving many times. My mother taught in a school, she was moved, and we have to move to be close to the school. But after, we moved to other towns close to Medellín. Like when you say Evanston is close to Chicago. In Medellín, we moved many times in different neighborhoods because of the same reason.

We were seven sons [children]. Four men and three women. I was the second. A sister is older than me. We had a very good childhood because at that age we don't have any problems like today of drugs, of guerrillas, of this kind of violence. My parents didn't have that kind

of problems.

They were very, very good teachers. The best. Both were the best. My mother was excellent in all the ways. My father, he is alive still. He's in Medellín now, but his temper was very harsh, very hard with his son, with me. My mother was more kind, more polite, more gentle, but they were very good persons.

When I was six years, my father began teaching in a private university, the university where I studied after. I was a very good student because my father was teacher, my mother was teacher and I have to be a very good student. I had to be the best because I studied in the same university as my father.

In my high school when you are in 10th level [grade], you receive information about all the careers, all of the professions. And at that moment, I loved architecture, the design. I liked to draw. I liked painting with simple colors, with regular colors. And I liked painting with pencil in plain papers. [I started] when I was 13 years, I think. I don't remember if somebody suggest me I paint. I think it was born with me.

The architecture was like drawing and I think for that reason I liked architecture. I like drawing, but I never received the classes of drawing. When I choose architecture, I was sure, completely sure. I don't remember exactly how it was, but I fall in love with architecture. Do you say that? From the first moment, from the first time I saw that drawing, the information about it, I told myself, "This is my profession. This is my career. This is the best for me. This is that I can do. This is that I would like to do."

The first year at university was very difficult because I didn't know anything about architecture. I only liked the drawings, the buildings, the design, but I didn't know anything about it. The main study in architecture is design in Medellín in this university. And most of the students had a relative architect, their fathers or uncles were architects, but I don't have anyone.

I lose [failed] my first matter [subject], design. In architecture in each semester you have several credits, several classes. One of these classes is design. It's the main class in the semester. When you lose design, you almost lose the semester. The first semester I failed design, but in other classes I was almost the best, very good student. I didn't understand what are the goals in this class. Many of my colleagues knew the goals of the design, but I didn't know. I felt so bad. I can't explain my exact feelings, but I took strength and I told by myself, "It's no problem. I can do it next semester. I will do it with more dedication, with more strength. I will be more concentrated." I knew I could do it. I didn't resign. At the next semester, I was the best in design because I told by myself, "I have to do this class like the best because I like it. I am capable. I can do it. I like to do it. I would like to do it like the best." My other years were very, very good. I was a very good student. I didn't fail anymore, any classes. I finished my university on good way. I graduated in 1982.

The situation was difficult at this age because, in Colombia, there were many architects. I thought that it was not very easy to work in my field, but that was what I loved. However, I was working one year before I graduated in my field. I began to work with a small company of architecture. I was designing houses and buildings. And I always had work in architecture. I worked with different companies in different ways, but always I worked in architecture. The field was very competitive, but I think I was lucky.

The architecture field was so competitive that, for that reason, I was to change the companies several times because in one company, the work finished. I had to find other jobs. I worked in six or seven companies. I worked for a year, a year and a half, two years, eight months because these companies didn't work any more designs. The situation is like waves. Sometimes it's good, sometimes it's bad. Sometimes there are many works. Sometimes there are a little work. Sometimes there was money, sometimes there was no money. I designed for the commerce, for the residential, for the factories. I designed all of the architectural buildings. For me, it was interesting all the projects. In this profession, my feelings were that the situation in my field will be very

difficult. I will never have stability, but I love my profession. I have to work in what I love.

One day, my sister-in-law told me that in the government there was a position to design hospitals or health care centers. The payment there was not very good, but there was a possibility for stability in there. And I thought that and I liked the idea. I liked to design health care centers. It seemed to be interesting for me and I began. I began to work with the government in 1989. I worked with them seven years. All the projects were very interesting. I loved this work. This job was in Medellín, at the building of the government of Antioquia, but I had to travel two or three or four days in the week to the towns. Towns were four, five, six, seven, eight, nine hours by car. I had to travel by car, by boat, by horse, by everything. The experiences were very, very rich. All of the days were different. One day I have to travel at this town. Other day I have to travel at other town. Other day I have to stay in my office designing or correcting projects. I have to do any activities in my profession. I managed the projects. I designed the projects. I supervised the projects. It was very rich and interesting for me. Most of the times I have to add the hospitals, to grow the hospitals, or remodelate the hospitals.

I knew that it was very dangerous to travel in the roads of my state because I know the guerrillas were in all of the territory of Antioquia. But at that age, the situation was not so tension [tense], so difficult. Guerrillas didn't have so much power. That situation increased the years after because in Colombia, many regions are red regions. These regions are called in this way because the guerrillas is around the regions. The red areas exist in Colombia since 1960s, I think. In these areas it's strange to see a policeman, because the law are the guerrillas.

The guerrillas were born, I think, in 1948. They have grown up in all of the territory of Colombia, and they exist because of the situation in Colombia. Because for many years, there are many *desbalance* [imbalances]. There are a few rich people. There are a lot of poor people in Colombia like in other countries of the world, and for that reason, the guerrillas was born. And the guerrillas have grown up for so long. Each year the guerrillas is more powerful and the state and the government is, how is the opposite, is [weaker].

I found the guerrilla fighters five times in my travels, but they respected the health workers. Only just two or three years [ago], that situation changed. They lost the first or initial respect toward the health workers. At the beginning, they respected the health workers.

They used to stop the buses or cars to search the dates [data] of the

In front of one of his building projects, Colombia, 1997

people inside their cars, the information about the people, "Who are you? Where are you work? What are you doing here?" And you have to answer them completely because if not, they can kill you. Do you understand me? Because they think that you can be a spy of the government. You can be some member of the government. You have to answer them, all of their questions. But you answered their questions, you don't have any problem. But they were stronger, they were harsher after that. In this last two or three years, they have lost the initial respect.

I worked since 1989 to 1996. The architecture office was closed in '96 because the responsibility would be of the municipalities, not the state. The towns had to contract these jobs. I became like a contractor. And I continued working in the same work, in the same activities, but by myself in my own office because people of the hospitals knew me. And they need me. They called me and I followed designing and supervising the constructions.

I came to United States in 1997 [the first time]. I only wanted to know this country, to visit my sister-in-law. She had told us that Chicago was a beautiful city, an interesting city for its architecture, for its people, for many reasons and my perspective when I came first time was that, only knowing the United States, especially Chicago. I don't remember that I had other reasons.

When I came the first time, the expectations were more than I had

thought because I didn't think that this city was so beautiful, so interesting. I saw the first time people of many countries, many languages. I saw an architecture very, very beautiful for me. Many kinds of buildings, many kinds of styles. And I saw something special—the respect in the United States for people, the respect in the United States for pedestrians. In Colombia, we don't have that. When I saw people crossing the streets and two, three, four policemen keeping for the people to cross safe, that was impressive for me. Policemen in Colombia don't do that. They only are for the robbers, criminals, but they don't do what policemen doing here.

My older daughter was very happy in Chicago the first time because she went to this park, Great America, and she went to Disney World. In 20 days in Chicago we went to many, many, many places, many beautiful places. We don't have any problem. We don't have any difficulty and we were happy in this visit to Chicago.

I appreciated the fields [parks] for the enjoy of the people. I was impressed mainly around this fountain close to the museum of art, [Buckingham Fountain], because we crossed the streets to the lake and I saw that park and that street very, very, how do you say, cared [for] in a very good way.

In general, people here respect the law, respect the rules. In Colombia, no. People don't respect the rules, don't respect the law. Most of the people is against the rules. Mainly in Bogotá it's terrible. People don't respect the rules, the norms. For me and for my family and for many people, that's the main reason to appreciate this country.

I didn't think so [about living here] because I was very happy in my country. Even if we have problems in Colombia mainly because of the guerrillas, of the violence, but Colombia had been a great country for me. I had my job there. I had my family there. I had all that I love in this country. The first time I came here I only wanted to know something new, but I was very happy in my country. I didn't think that I could live here at this time.

When I had two years working in this way in Colombia, one day I went to the San Antonio hospital. It is in a town called Cisneros, three hours from Medellín. In the middle of the travel, I was sleeping. I was traveling in a public bus. In the middle of the travel, I was awoke for an individual that pointed his gun in my face. I was scared. I comprehend that it was a robbery. He robbed my belongings. He put all my dates [data] in a kind of notebook and they continue doing the same with the other passengers.

When [this] individual asked to another passenger for his dates, personal information, this individual didn't want to answer him. Then, he shoot him in the head one time. This individual was just one seat behind me. When I heard that, I was so scared, terribly scared. Do you understand me? He fell to the floor of the bus, and they continued robbing the belongings of the other passengers and telling words and sentences against the government. Two minutes after, they shoot other time to this individual. They shoot two times. Ten centimeters or one feet of distance. I think less than that. Five inches. In the bus there were a few people, I think eight, nine people only. It was early in the morning, at 7:00 in the morning. They knew the road. They knew the situation. They knew how these things [happen]. It was very terrible. I think so they wanted to kill him. I think because that individual didn't do anything bad. He only didn't want to give them his data. It's a reason to kill him? I think that's not a reason.

When they shoot the second, they abandoned the bus. Nobody say anything, nothing because people were scared, very scared. I looked several times at this guy, but I couldn't do anything for him. It was a knot in my throat. I was thinking in my family. I was thinking that thing could pass to me. I think these 30 minutes were the most terrible in my life. I thought everything bad. I thought that the same thing could occur to me another day. I have lived in Colombia all of my life, and I had heard several stories like that, but never had occurred to me. I just heard stories about.

My wife told me I had to leave my profession or my works in the towns, but I told her that I love what I did. I loved this work because it was interesting, but also because from these towns they called me to work. In the city, the field was very competitive. And people of the towns, management of the hospitals, knew me. They needed me and

With his wife, Gloria Patricia, and daughters, Laura and Susana, Colombia, 1998

for that reason I couldn't leave my work in the towns. In the city I didn't have so much possibilities to work. It was a short discussion at this night, but we were discussing many nights, many nights. A lot of times. I think each night.

I thought that it was the last experience, but I was wrong because after that, I had a terrible experience also. Because when the shooting [happened], the threats are not direct threats for me. It was a terrible experience, but not against me. It was against mainly other persons. But in this year, I received a terrible call that it was a direct threat toward me, against me.

It happened in March 31, in 1999. I was in my study. I was figuring out a project of other hospital, a hospital for a town called Caicedo. In the morning, after 9:00 in the morning, I received a phone call. A man, a strong man, told me that I should know who they were already. In a few words, they threatened me. He told me that I was in a list of the guerrillas' commanders, that they didn't want to see me in the municipalities, in the hospitals, that they knew all of me, all of my data, they knew my daughters, they knew my wife, they knew all of my belongings, and they could do something against me or my daughters or my wife. They wanted not to see me anymore into the hospitals or into the towns in Antioquia. They wanted I left Colombia. And I tried to tell them that at this moment I was not official government worker, that I was working for myself and I was working just for the community, that I was working just for the people that contracted me, that needed me. But they told me that I was realized already and they have *avisado* [warned] me. I was warned for [by] them that I had to leave. And they hung up the phone and I was more scared than the first experience, because this one was direct threat against me and my family.

There was no words for that. They told me that they knew all of my things, all of my daughters, all of my wife. The guerrillas in Colombia knew all of data of the people. They have informants in many places of the cities, of the towns, of the roads. They know everything about the people.

My wife [picked up] the phone and she heard the conversation. She was not in the study. She was in the bedroom and she heard the conversation. She was too scared, extremely scared. I was, too. And what can happen? We have to leave. I love my work. I live of this work, but first is the life, first is the security for my family, for my daughters. I told my wife, "What do we do? We have to leave Colombia."

Some days after, we talked in my sister-in-law that she lives here. She lives in Evanston. Patricia called her. She told her the story and she offered us all of her collaboration, all of her help. And the other days we were doing arrangements to leave Colombia, to leave our things in the better way. Who will take care of our house, of our car, of our things? We have to ask for the U.S.A. embassy the visa for my young daughter because Patricia, Laura, and me had visas. We had visited the U.S.A. two years ago. We had been in Chicago in 1997. But Susana didn't have visa. Thirty days after, we got the visa and in June 3rd of 1999, we left Colombia and we are here.

Two months after we left Colombia, the guerrillas put a bomb, a car bomb, three blocks close my house. That day, three people were killed, 20 houses were demolished, 15 cars were demolished. Two months before we left Colombia, other car bomb was put for [by] the guerrillas one block farther. And last week, the guerrilla put other car bomb also three blocks of my house. Two people were killed and some houses and several cars. This situation in Medellín is very, very difficult.

It's terrible, because all our life has been in Colombia. Colombia is a very beautiful country in the most of the ways. Just for the guerrillas and for the drugs dealer and for the corruption, but people in Colombia is very good people. Many things in Colombia are very good. We loved our jobs, our works. The schools of the children were very good, private schools, very, very good schools. Our jobs were very good. All our family, our parents, our relatives are in Colombia. I think all our dreams are in Colombia. Leaving Colombia is not a very good idea, but in this moment this was the reasonable idea.

All our family, Patricia's family and my family, went to the airport to say good-bye. It was beautiful. I think they felt we wouldn't come back. I think. Now, I don't know.

I feel so bad [in the plane] because we left all of the things that Patricia and me had gotten with our work. We left the things that we had dreamed. We had left our relatives. It was a very bad travel. It was a hard travel. It was so long. We felt never we would get to Chicago. We never felt that two years after [our first visit] we would have an experience like that, but here we are.

When she [my sister-in-law] was at the airport, what do you guess? She embraced with Patricia. They were crying. She went with her husband and with other friends from Chicago, but it isn't the welcome like two years before. It was so bad, but they were very comprehensive [understanding] with our situation. Each day that happened was better for us, but this day, the travel, all of the things are not very good for us.

I didn't think nothing, anything. I only wanted to take a rest for several days. I wanted to have my mind clear and I had to think what must I do, what should I do.

We didn't know what we do, but the first thing that we thought was we have to study English because here, if you don't know English, you almost can't do anything good. And we wanted to know English. We wanted to learn English. It was the first thing that we did. And we began in Truman.

I only had learned English in the high school, 20 years ago. I only remembered some words, some sentences. One month before we left Colombia, I studied by myself English, remembering words, sentences, grammar. I feel better [now]. I know I have to learn a lot of English, a lot, a lot. I would want to have a better listening. If I would have a better listening, I could speak faster. I could do more things, but what option do I have? I have to spend my time learning English. I have to do an effort to learn English. I think I am good in my grammar, but when you want to put your grammar in front of you, you find that you don't listen good. It's the first thing. And the only experience that I had in English was in Truman because I was not working. I think you learn most of the English in your work. All the day you are speaking with other persons in English. I was not that experience. Only in the Truman in two or three hours, because in my house, we speak in Spanish. Even my daughter told me, "Papi, don't tell me in English. In my school, all the day is in English! At my house in the night, in the afternoon, I want to hear Spanish."

The second thing is our legal situation. In this field, we didn't know what we must do, what we should do. And somebody, I don't remember who, told us that we could ask U.S.A. government for political asylum because of our threats and we thought about it. Somebody told us about an attorney that he had experience in these cases. We went to an appointment with him and he convinced us that we could ask for political asylum. And we asked for political asylum. We will have an interview in one month. After that, I will have a more clear concept about our situation and then I will figure it out.

I think we could have other options here. It's not the end of the world. I think that was experience that it can let [allow] new experience here. It can go up in other way here. We can learn many things here, not only the language. We can work in other fields. It's difficult for me to work in designing, what is I love, but I can work in my field.

Five months after we came to United States, we moved. We wanted to live alone as a family. For my sister-in-law, that situation was not good because she wanted to stay with us, but we needed to be as a family alone. We moved to Chicago in the same place we are living now. This was great for us because at this time it was the first time we were living as a family in the United States. We could see the situation clearer and we could plan our future and we have been planning our future since that date.

When we moved, only Patricia was working. She began working as a baby-sitter and I remained without work. I just went to Truman school with my youngest daughter and I was painting by myself. I painted three or four pictures. I was studying hard English. And I thought that I wanted to get a job, a job in my profession. I knew it was very difficult. I thought I couldn't get a job in my field, but I was lucky because I found a job in my field as an architect two months ago.

I found a job by my sister-in-law. She knew an architect, a Colombian architect, and she remembered that one time she went to his office to ask for a job, but at that time he didn't need workers. But she told me, "Why you don't go to his office?" I went to his office. I told him that I needed work in United States, that I was an architect, I have worked in health care centers in Colombia for 10 years, my experience was for health care centers, and I knew to draw in AutoCAD. And he decided to give me an opportunity two months ago. He needed I had my legal situation good. I told him that in two or three months I could have my situation figured out.

I am drafting in AutoCAD some kind of projects. I am drafting now a coliseum for basketball. I was drawing residential houses and day care, different projects.

I was very happy when I got a job because I didn't thought that I could get a job in my field. I thought, "I was working in architecture in the United States, in Chicago. That is the architectural city in the world!" I was impressed for that and very happy for this reason. I

thought that God had been very great with me. I thought that.

I wake up at 6:00 in the morning. I prepare several things before I leave home. I am leaving home at 7:15 with my two daughters. I have to bring the older to Evanston. I leave Laura at 8:10. She begins to study at 8:30. Next, I go with Susana, my youngest daughter, to Truman. I leave Susana in Truman day care. Then, I go to my office. I am traveling all the day by train. When I leave Susana at day care, I take a train to my office in downtown. I work in this office from 9:00 in the morning to 12:30 or 1:00 in the afternoon and then I return to the Truman College to take my class in Wednesday and Monday. I am studying in Truman, English as a second language, from 12:30 to 4:00 in the afternoon. At this time I have to leave because I have to pick my daughter up at 4:00. I return to my class with my daughter for a half hour more and I am leaving my class at 4:30 and then I have to leave Truman with my daughter to go to Evanston to pick my older daughter up at 5:00 in the afternoon. And then finally, I left from Evanston and by train I am getting home at 6:00. When I don't have class on Tuesday, Thursday, and Friday, it's the same routine but I don't leave from my office at 12:30. I am working since 9:00 to 3:15 more or less. I am working in Saturday since 9:00 in the morning to 3:00 in the afternoon. Sunday is the day that I am with my family. Just a day. On Sunday we can leave home to visit somebody, to visit some place, and at noon we go to church at Broadway [Avenue]. It's very important, very important. We always go to church, always. We feel the need to pray to God, to thank to God every Sunday. It's a very important thing, every Sunday.

We have done [made] very, very good friends in United States. I think really friends. We were [have] American friends, really American friends, I think better friends than many friends in Colombia. We [have] Mexican friends, very good friends. We [have] Colombian friends, of course. I think this is because people here is lonely, is far away from home, from their parents in Colombia and they need company as we need, too. When people move far away, they need to share many things. They need to share thoughts, senses, feelings, many things. And for that reason, people is more, how do you say, close, here. And the friendship is stronger here. I think it's for that reason.

I think Truman has been a very good way not only to learn English, but also to meet other persons, Americans and teachers and people of the other countries. Some of they have been interesting people. We have met people of the other countries, European countries and South American countries, and we have met Colombian people, too. Many people are in the same situation. And many people have the same problem that I have told you before. They are lonely here. They need some people to talk, to share some things. I think the break time is important at the Truman because it's the time you can know other people.

Lonely here, no, because I have my family. Every day I have my family, fortunately. I need my other family, my brothers, my father, but I have my most important family with me, close to me.

[My daughters] like Chicago, but I think they like more Medellín than Chicago because they went every Sunday to their grandparents' farm. They had many friends in Medellín. They had their big house in Medellín. They had their big bedrooms, one for each one. They had, how do you say, dolls and toys. But the problem is more than they can imagine. Many times she [Laura] has wanted to return Colombia because she miss her school, her classmates, her grandparents, but I have told her that it's impossible for now, that we need to remain in U.S.A. for a time that we don't know how much, how long.

I am thinking many things, many projects here. And who knows, I can figure out something in one month, two months. I always dream, always dream because I am an architect. Architects dream many times, and I believe I can do important things here, but I don't want to dream more without getting an asylum. Because if I don't get an asylum, my family don't get an asylum, I think the dreams can fail and it's worse. It's better for us that we can get the asylum first. And if we get that, all the doors in Chicago can open to us. I think that.

I am too nervous. I am feeling this, to be nervous, since 30 days ago

With his wife, Gloria Patricia, Chicago, 2000

because it's the future of my family. It's not only my future. It's the future of my family. If judge says, "You can't remain in the United States," it's like a [slap] in my face and not only my face, in my family's face. I am very nervous. I am stressed because it's an important decision. I am thinking about it all the day. Patricia doesn't sleep good. She has problems with her sleeping. I think much of her problem is for that reason.

I have dreamed to remain in the United States, to live one, two, three, I don't know how many years here. I like this city. I like this country. I like the way people live here. People respect the law, respect the rules. This is a good country to be while [until] in my country the situation is better or when in my country guerrillas don't threaten the people.

I love my country, but I can't live in my country. I always want to go to Colombia, but I can't go only for that reason, the security. Colombia is for me a beautiful, great country. I'm totally sure of that, of come back to Colombia, to return Colombia because I believe I can be useful to my country. Many of the professionals are leaving Colombia. Colombia needs all of these professionals. When the situation change and it is safer, I think to return Colombia.

I think that it can take two, three, four or more years to change the situation in Colombia. In two, three, or four years, you can see how long you can remain here, how many things you can do here. I think I could do interesting things here, too. I believe I could be useful here. But I don't know now how much could I get here. Only the future in one year maybe could say that. I don't know. I have a big project here. If this project progress, I could stay here for many years. Who knows? Who knows? I don't know.

| *111*

RUBÉN AND HIS FAMILY RECENTLY BOUGHT A HOUSE IN CHICAGO. He is working as a real estate appraiser. His wife, Gloria Patricia, is a real estate agent. They received political asylum in the United States and are planning to stay here.

MY NAME IS EMIR HUSKIC I'M COMING FROM BOSNIA. *I'm 31 years old now. I came here when I was 27 years old. I remember that. That was* **7 JANUARY, '97.**

MY NAME ACTUALLY IS MIDDLE EAST NAME BECAUSE MY NAME IS EMIR. And in Bosnia, we have main population is Muslims, but actually we are not so related with Muslims from Middle East. We have 100 percent different culture because we are European. Before war we had, they say, communist system. But that is not communist system like Cuba, Russia 50 years ago. You could go everywhere.

And there in that time, religion wasn't so important. That means people is not so religious. I'm Muslim. I like my religion, but I went in a mosque twice, like when is Bajram, Muslim holiday. That's all. I'm not praying. I'm not religious. I was always Muslim, but not Muslim with religion because I can say I have my own religion. I believe I need to help you, I am asking you can help me because I give you hand, give me hand. Do not think I'm Muslim and favor people who is only Muslim. I don't care for that. I don't care! That is reason why I came here. Because after war, it's very important who you are. Especially in a war, they abused religion. They put religion in focus. But I have different thing because I have education. In my country, people with education think same way like I think, because they don't care for religion. They care for education, they care for economy, they care for their family, and they care for friendship. If you are good person, I will be friend with you.

That's my ego. You know what means ego? It's means me, person. And actually, now when somebody asks me, "What you are? Where are you from?" I'm making a joke.

Because I say, "I'm from ocean, from water." Because after too many troubles, I don't know who I am.

I am from northwest Bosnia. It's small city. It's not big. It's almost like on border with Croatia. Exactly my place where I grow up, it's almost like village. That is Ponjevici, but you can say Cazin. Because if you say Ponjevici, that is really small place. But that place belongs to that city. It's not big and we had to go in another place in school because we didn't have like high school in that city and we didn't have

college. When I was student, I had to leave my parents and live like 50 miles away.

I was nice kid. And you know, I never had problem in school. And I had good respect for my teachers. They like me because I was quiet. All my life I'm quiet person. I'm not person who like be, how can I say in English, on stage or maybe in group and show I am special or something. No, always I was quiet.

My father and my mom, they don't have education. My father finished three years high school, but he finished that when he was 35 because he didn't go in school regularly. And my mom, she doesn't have education, but they know what is education because they told me, "I didn't go in school because we didn't have chance, because we didn't have money. I have money, you have to go." Because they knew how education is important for person. Because you are 100 percent different person. And they know that. They force me to do that.

He said, "You have to go and finish college."

I said, "OK, that's fine." But he want put me in a school system to be teacher. I said, "OK, I will take history and geography because I like history and geography and be a teacher for that."

He said, "No, you know what? That's not good because it's better for you if you are a classroom teacher and teach kids from 1st to 4th grade because it's easy find job."

I said, "No, I don't like it." I'm quiet. I'm nice person. I have nice personality for that, but I have feeling I can't do that. I can't.

And when I start study for that kind of job, every year I was more interesting in general subject. I was preparing myself for classroom

With high school friends, Bosnia, 1988

teacher. And second year, when I start going in schools, I had mentors who is going to teach me how I supposed to teach kids, I got more interesting for that. And I found out I can do that. When I finished school, I like it.

In my group, that was special group because usually my school had 30 students in group. But that year we had big problem. We didn't have enough teachers in country and they decide to extend class. My class was 110 students in group, and we had seven mens.

That was a little bit unusual for a classroom teacher. If you go to study history or geography, there is like 50-50. Fifty mens, fifty womens. But it wasn't anything. And I was making a joke. They always say, "Ladies first."

I said, "You know what? This is special group. In this group men supposed to be first because you need appreciate us. It's only seven guys and hundred three women!"

I finished my university on time and I was good student. I didn't work and I had time to study. And I can tell you, education in my country is really, really hard. It's not like in this country, [where] it's much easier. We couldn't work. During the day, you have to go take classes, afternoon you have time for lab. At night is for study. You are done for day. Because any kind of university if you go, you have lab. If

you study science, you have lecture and afternoon you supposed to go in lab because you will know what's going on. It's very hard. And we had oral test and we had written test. If you take written test and you pass, you have to go take oral test. If you not pass oral test, you need repeat written test. It was tough, but it's good. You have somebody pushing you. You supposed to study, study, study, and you have knowledge. When you finished, "Hey, I studied psychology and I can explain you that," or "I finished college for math and I can show you that because I'm not embarrassed if you ask me question." That was good.

I finished in October, 1991 and I start working in November, 1991. I taught kids in my place where I grow up. It's next my door. Just across my street it's school. It was small group and they made combination—1st grade and 3rd grade they put together. It's very hard. And that was fine. I liked because I just finished. You know, when you're fresh, you are going to show your friends, coworkers who you are. And they were my teachers. You believe that? All my coworkers, they taught me. When I finished school, my teacher in that time was my boss.

I like it. Kids are fine. I like discipline. I was so strong, they were so quiet, but we made a deal. When it's time for game, it's time for game. Enjoy. When it's time to do something, you supposed to do and done. And they like me. I like kids and I enjoy. I can't complain anything about that.

I got two checks, only two checks. Actually, in that time they start war in Croatia between army from Serbia and Croatia. And after that, they didn't have enough money to pay us. And we didn't get money like from December to May [1992]. We finished school year early because in April they start war in Bosnia.

I knew what's going on and I wished at that time to leave that place, but I couldn't because I didn't have enough money. If I had money, I could escape that place and go in Germany and be refugee there. But I didn't have money to escape that place. We could know what's going on, what's going to be because we had TV. On TV you could see everything what's going on in Croatia, what's going on there. People killing people, burning houses, that stuff. Of course I was scared, concerned, because I lived day by day. You never know what's going on tomorrow, what's going to be.

I can tell you my main opinion about war in ex-Yugoslavia. Because 1990, they decided to change politic in ex-Yugoslavia because we had communist system. They say we need more party in government. But that time they make big, big mistake. Instead make big multiculture parties, they make national parties. Like Muslims, they have their party. Serbians, they have their party. People from Croatia, they make their national party. And they start talking so nasty, so bad stuff, things about other nationality. And my grandfather told me, "Hey, here will be big mess. That's not good. That's not good." And he was so scared because he knew what's happened 40 years or 50 years before that period. And all three groups made big mistake and they helped start war. I can say Serbian people made biggest mistake there, but I can't say Muslim and Croatia, they didn't do anything. They helped. I'm talking about only nationalists. They start war. And Serbia had power. They made biggest mess there because they had power. But can you just think about if Croatian people had same power, it will be same. If Muslims, it will be same, exactly same. But they had power, then they make mess. And you can see on TV in U.S. or Germany or everywhere, you can see on news what they made because they had power. But could be same if somebody else had same power.

In my place, major nationality is Muslims and only one percent was Orthodox [Christian] and some others. And they [Orthodox Christian] left place. They left place because it wasn't secure for them because they couldn't believe anybody.

I couldn't do anything because we had two different groups: people who think they supposed to go and people who think that's not right. They lived there 300, 400 years and now they supposed to leave their place? That is sad. And I was talking about that and they made fun with me, "Who you are? Are you them?"

When they left their place, people who hate them, who is very national, they burn their houses. And I said, "Hey, that's not fair. Why you burning? Why you stealing their property? Why?"

They say, "This is not yours. Take your business. Who you are? Why you staying behind them?" or something like that. And you just put yourself in dangerous case. It was very bad. And after one month, we got people from other city came in our city because they were small group with Serbian. And that start big mess, man. People moving, moving, moving. And they are losing everything. And people stealing, burning. That is start.

I didn't go in a war because nobody called me. The police didn't come to pick me up. I was living day by day and I was guessing nobody is going to call me because I was guessing, "Hey, school is school, war is war. But you know, kids they supposed to go in school. Doesn't matter it's war. Somebody needs work with kids." And I was

thinking they are not going to call me because hey, I work with kids. Doesn't matter there is fighting line, but kids they supposed to go in school. And January '93, they send letter. I supposed to go and I had to go. Because if I didn't go, they could send police. No choice, no choice. I had to go in army.

I didn't have a chance that time [to leave]. But January '93, when I got letter, I didn't have choice. No way. No way. There was circle around us. Serbian army was around us. And in January '93, they gave me gun. Go fight.

That wasn't my war. Still I have same thing. That's not my war. For what? For who? And especially in my place, we had nice relationship with neighborhood, with Orthodox [Christian]. We had special communication, good economy with them. But government from Sarajevo, they knew that and we are not ready to fight, generally. And they try send people from other places there just make morale to fight. And I had couple discussions with people from other places. I said, "You know what, sir? You are in a wrong place, in wrong time. What are you doing here? If you think like that and these people is not thinking like that, you are wrong person in wrong place. Hey, why do you come here? You like that, enjoy? You could enjoy that?" I had couple discussions with that people. And they send in all generals. They were from other places, not from our town. They don't care. You can't talk. You have to take gun. You have to go with group. Done.

I was burning inside in myself, but I couldn't change anything. I couldn't change anything. I hate that people. Still I hate that people. Still I hate that generals who put me. Maybe I hate them more than people across the line.

And many times I was thinking I hate one guy, he was in personnel. And I ask him many times, "OK. Can I go home and work in school? Hey, you have too many people you can call." Many times I was thinking, "Should I hide bomb in his office?" I hate him, man. I hate.

In 1993, we had chance to sign not temporary peace, permanent peace. We had guy from our town, he had power. He said, "Who like peace, sign 'we like peace'. We will sign a permanent peace with Serbian people and stop fighting. We'll start doing economy, production, that stuff." And 80 percent people in my place signed because we didn't have any other choice because we were in circle. In my town, that is in northwest Bosnia, all around it was Serbian army. We didn't have choice. We couldn't go. We didn't have choice and we tried to sign peace.

But in that time, government in Sarajevo, they didn't like that. And they had people in my town, I told you they came from other places, they had power. They were generals, policemen. And they start beating people who signed it. We went in a city and protest, like meetings, "We don't like war." And they start shooting people, kids, women. They start fighting with us and we didn't have chance. And we split the circle in two pieces. And I left that army and went with that guy who had power, and I change army. That was army who make peace. We signed peace with people around, with Serbia because we don't need war. We need stop. We need start working. We didn't have army because we just signed. And we bought guns from Serbia and we made our army to protect ourselves. It's really crazy. Yeah, we bought. It's a little bit crazy, but business is business. In war, they have business.

When they split this line, my home was over there on other side. And they had bigger power because we didn't have guns. And they push us little bit there and I had to leave my home. And there were my mom. She was over there, and when they push us from this line to this line, they kill my brother. He was in army. They killed him. He was 22 when he died. And after 15 days, they gave us his body. They brought body on line and say, "Take his body." Like when you're buying stuff like sugar, guns. It's like that. Business.

They robbed my house. They took everything my father was doing 30 years buying stuff, making house. They destroyed that. They steal, or if they couldn't take with them, they use gun and shot. If they couldn't take fridge, it's heavy, they use gun and destroy fridge, TVs, that stuff what was heavy.

My mom, she stayed home all the time. She never moved. They took everything. She was looking. People is coming taking stuff, and she was just watching because you couldn't say, "That's mine," because they will kill you.

[They say], "Hey, your kids are there. Your kids are our enemy. You are our enemy. Be quiet or we'll kill you." She never beaten but they took her to talk them about us. "You have kids there. What they are doing?" She was in so dangerous situation.

And one guy, our neighbor came in her door. He knocked the door and he say, "You know what? You have kids there. If they not come today or tomorrow, when we catch them, we will kill them." He's neighbor. He's not Serbian, he's brother Muslim.

November '93, I lose my brother and after that period, I was soldier. I was working for army in office, in personnel stuff, doing the paper stuff. Because I lose my brother, I say, "I'm not going to fight again."

They had respect because I lose brother. I had excuse. And they put me in an office.

In morning, August 21st [1994] they started pushing us, pushing us to force us to leave place. And my [other] brother came with my friend, actually he was my teacher, he was my boss. They came in front of building where I work to take me out and go. We were going with car to Croatia. And that was so late. This army was already there in town. And we were in car. My friend, he was driving and I was his passenger on right side and my brother was back side. And I saw soldiers. I said, "Guys, put down heads." And somebody shot windows in the car. And thanks God my brother, he took my order. He pulled down his head. Thanks God they didn't shoot him. And that was couple seconds. I said, "Oh, God. I'm injured."

And he said, "Oh, me too." And I was injured by bullet in my left foot and he was injured in right foot. And it's so funny. We had same size of shoes. And when we went in refugee camp, they give us same shoes because he needed left one and I needed right one. Do you believe that? It's funny, but it's true.

In August '94 they push us, and we had to go in this place in Croatia. We moved from Bosnia and we were there in refugee camp. And in December '94, people decide go back. They took guns again. They bought guns from Serbia, go back fight. Yeah, go back in Bosnia. And we start fighting here and push them back. And they start doing the war, American and Serbian. Americans help Muslims and Croatian push Serbian back. And Serbians had to move from these places which belongs Croatia. They had to move and Croatian people came here and they move us. We had to move again in Croatia. That was August '95.

That's big mess. You can say nothing because you have too many different groups. You have people who like fight. Why? Because they are criminals. They were poor. They are stealing. You have to watch. He's taking your TV. Taking TV, put in car, but not his car. He stole car also. Go over there and sell somebody else. They like that. Some people is sick. They like fighting. They like killing. You have people who doesn't like that. You have people who is scared. You have people who is crying every day. You have too many groups.

Of course, I was praying, just saying, "God, do not make of me handicapped, you know, bomb and take my legs. If I died, OK. It's fine, but God do not make me handicapped from bomb, I can lose my eye or legs." Because when you see that people, it's making you so sick. Because I was watching kids, six months, they never walk and they lose legs. How you can feel about that? Man, it's killing.

I married in time we had fight. That was May '95 in Velika Kladusa, that's my wife's town home. And I went in refugee camp with my wife. It was like honeymoon in refugee camp. It wasn't good honeymoon, but...

August '95, we had to leave that city again and we went in a refugee camp. And after that, from August '95 until June or July, I'm not sure, '96, I was in refugee camp. That's not refugee camp, actually. That is street six kilometers long with maybe 20 houses there. Who was lucky, he took house. Who wasn't lucky made tent or something.

I was living in one house, but that house wasn't finished, no windows, no nothing. We put plastic on the window. We had holes on the wall because it wasn't finished. We put toilet paper in holes. We got some help from UNHCR [United Nations High Commission for Refugees], it's international organization to help refugees. They gave us food. You know how is food? It's spaghetti, that cheap stuff from storage, 10 years old. They gave us blanket. It was so terrible. We were living on the roof. It was so cold. I was there with my wife, with my father, with my brother, with my uncle, uncle's son, and it was one other guy with us.

Couple months I didn't do anything. I was preparing our places, going in a forest, bring something, make bed, use stuff, use wood. Always try make life easy. It's house there, but you don't have bed. Winter, it's terrible. We got some wood from forest. We cut wood and make fire. Like here they call fireplaces. My father is so handyman and I helped him and I know lot of things. He planned our place nicer. And my wife, she worked for the International Red Cross. And in December '95, I got a job like a teacher. International organization, they brought big tents and they try open school under tent in refugee camp. And I work there until we have to move that place. And I got money. We got money for that and that help us.

I lost a lot of cousins. You care about that. Thanks God, you don't have that experience, but people is stronger than they thought they are strong. You are burning and you are suffering, suffering, but you can't take that. Because you are crying, just thinking about that. It's happening. You can't change it. You didn't finish thinking about one trouble, it's coming another trouble. They are becoming like regular days, regular life, usual life. But you are becoming stronger in your personality. Just you have to. It's like, how do they say people who is sitting in yoga. It's like that. And in refugee camp, I found my teacher. He taught me

With his wife, Zejna, in the refugee camp, Croatia, 1996

psychology. I say, "You know what? You are psychologist. It's easy for you because you can help yourself."

And my teacher told me, "It's easy when you're giving advice to somebody else. Psychology is psychology, but it's very hard to help yourself."

When I was in refugee camp, we had problem because they didn't give us status like refugees. And we ask international organization, "We are refugees. We need have papers like we are registered like refugees. We need chance to leave this place. This is not for living." We were here three months. We had protest. After couple months later, we protest again, say nobody care for us.

Some people escaped that refugee [camp] because they had money. That's black business. They say under the table. "I will give you $5,000. Can you give me a ride to Germany?" It was like $5,000 to $7,000 per person. I didn't have that money.

They made movie about us. Netherlands, they sent one group with cameras to make movie about us. International journalists, they came there and make stories. "Hey, we are sick about stories. Give us hand. We need to leave." And I was sending letters for Netherlands embassy. I sent papers to Norwegian embassy, Australia. Everywhere I sent papers, "We are refugee. Is any possibility to take us?" Nobody cared.

I say, "OK, I will go everywhere. I'm not going to go back." And my father was so mad at me because he was in refugee camp. He knows everything is trouble, but he didn't like to go. He always thinking go back, go back. He has property. He lived there all his life. His father is there. He want to go back. I say, "No, I'm not going back. I don't care for anybody. I'm sick of this trouble. I'm sick of Bosnia, Croatia, this refugee camp. I'm never going to be back." And that hurt my father because he's not going to see me again. And I was thinking, "I will go everywhere, everywhere. I don't care which country, but I won't go back."

My father many times didn't talk with me because he was so mad I decided to go. But I was mad at him at that time because I was trying explain him, "Father, do not live in your dream." But it was hard explain him. When he went home from refugee camp, when he saw what's going on there, he was so happy why I left. When he saw real situation what's going on there, he changed mind. He was so happy for me.

And in April '96, they start opening programs for refugees if you have any papers from U.S., Australia, Canada. And in June '96, I got papers from U.S. because my friend, he left refugee camp in May '96 because he got papers from somebody else, and he sent papers to me. And I had two interviews with American officer in Zagreb. And they ask us, "Why do you want to go in U.S.?"

And we couldn't say, "You know what? I'm sick of this trouble or I like money." We said, "It's dangerous. I don't like go back because it's dangerous. They killed my brother. Who knows? They could kill me because I was their enemy. I was enemy because I don't think like them. They will kill me because they killed a lot of people there who went back from refugee camp." And thanks God, I passed the interviews. I came here in January '97 with my wife.

That was exciting because at that time I knew I have a chance. It was something what is going to take you away from that terrible place. Because I lived there in tent, and no life, no nothing. And I remember here, when I came here, it was exciting because it's not a tent. I have hot water at least. I have bed. I'm not talking about my life before war. I had better life than here. But that is something else.

In one hand, I was excited because I will leave refugee camp. In another hand, I was so concerned because I never been in U.S. I'm person who is thinking about everything. It's not only refugee. I will leave refugee camp, OK. That is not only one problem. I will solve one problem, OK. And I think about job. What kind of job I can work there? How is life there? Can I live day by day? Can I save some

With school children in the refugee camp, Croatia, 1996

money? I know I will work bad job. Can I go in school, find better job? Can I make progress in my life? Can I send some kind of money my parents to make them happy, because they will know if I send them money that means I have some money. How is economy there? How is system? OK, I have my wife, she speaks English, but we don't know system. Hey, bank system is different. Economy system. Transportation is different. Everything is different. I was thinking about anything. But you know, I had people there [in refugee camp] without education and they just like go, "Take me away. I don't care what's going on."

And they were so happy sometimes they make me crazy because, "You're not thinking about anything, just go! You're thinking about America. You're thinking about movies. Hey, that's Hollywood!" And they make me sick because, "I am happy for you because you will leave refugee [camp], but how you can think like that. Think a little bit. Hey, you have bigger family than I have. Are you concerned? Are you going to have school for your kids?"

I didn't know what's going on here, what kind of life I will have. Forget it. I was watching movies, movies, movies. Real life is real life. And I didn't expect too much about this country. I didn't expect. When I came here I was lucky because I wasn't shocked because I didn't expect life will be like a movie, like Hollywood stars.

I never think I will find good job or easy job. OK, I am worker.

I will clean street. I will do anything and I will have my home. And I'm not going to be in dangerous situation and nobody's going to ask me, "Give me your paper. Who you are?" That kind of stuff.

International organizations, they help us about everything. They provide buses for us because it wasn't only me, one person. It was three buses in same time. It's big group. They came there and they took us from refugee camp to Vienna in Austria. Refugee camp is not big and it was crowded. People know each other. Almost we knew everyone and where he go. But like in bus, we were talking, "OK, where you going to be? Which city? Who sent you papers? Who is going to wait for you in airport there? Who is there? Oh, I know him! He sent you papers?" It was discussion about that. And after that we took a plane from Vienna to New York. From New York I change another plane to Detroit. From Detroit I change another plane to Chicago.

In Chicago airport when I came here, my friend came there to pick up us because he sent paper. He was our sponsor. He left refugee camp, and I know he didn't have money. When we came here, he came to airport to pick up us with his car, and I saw his car. He has car. I said, "Oh, he has car." He was here only eight months. I said, "Oh, OK. If he could buy, maybe I will be able to buy car." That was good point because I know he didn't have money. He made that money here. And I was just relaxing, "Oh, it's possibility to buy car."

And he brought us in his apartment, it was small apartment, to give us chance to live couple days. And he show us, "I live here in this building. In this building has couple vacancies. If you like you can find apartment here. If you don't like you can find apartment in other building. I will help you. That's up to you. Or if you don't like stay in Chicago, you can go to another state." But we know each other. And I found here small place. It was a studio, small, really small. But it was really fine for us. We don't have kids. OK, we stayed there. And after 15 days, we change that place, changed that studio. We went in another bigger studio. Still studio because we didn't have money to pay expensive rent because we were getting money from Public Aid to pay rent. They gave us $400. They don't care if you find apartment for $1,200 or $1,500. They only give you $400 to buy and $200 for food stamps to buy food. World Relief, they gave us some kind of furniture that was old, but it was good. For start it's fine. We have to appreciate that because I didn't pay. And day by day, somebody gave us plates, somebody gave us this. Actually, we had two mattresses. I put mattress on mattress because we could sit on this. And I made picture and it's so

sad, so sad place. But we have that picture for reminding us how we had that place. And I have been here, in this building almost four years. I change couple units, but always in same building.

I came here without any English word. I couldn't say, "Hi," nicely. I was just scared and shy. Because I knew I don't know and can't understand anything. It was difficult for me. I never studied English, I studied German. That was difficult and that was scaring for me because I say, "I don't like languages." I don't like it and it's hard for me to take that and learn. But, you know, month by month, at least I can communicate. My English is not perfect, but we can make communication. If I come in your office, if you are working in office or maybe bank, if I come there and say anything [nothing], we can't do any job. But I say, "Deposit. Account. Open." Something like word by word, no grammar or nothing, you will understand I want open account! We can make deal! But if I come there and show you money or something, you are not going to understand anything.

It was difficult. For everything I had to call friends. And thanks God we met nice friends. They're so nice. They help us. We got some money. We need open account. We don't know what is account because I never been here. They took us in bank. They explain us. We came there and they say, "OK, what kind of account you want to open?" It's another confusing situation.

"What kind you have?"

"Oh, we have saving account. We have checking account. We have checking with zero limit balance. You need have $300. If you have this one, your benefits are this. This one is better than this one. You can have this one, but you need have certain amount of money." It's hard! And that is my experience.

Then I learned everything and I sent papers to other families. I brought them here. I was sponsor for somebody else. And when I start talking with them and explaining them and they are not catching everything, I was mad! I said, "Hey!" It was funny like I was born here. I know everything, "How you don't know that?" I just forgot how was difficulty for me.

That [finding a job] was big problem, but you know many jobs are good and you don't need communicate with somebody and you can work your job. It's not high level job, but it's fine. It's housekeeping or that kind of job. You don't need speak. And I had friends here. They came here before me and they were working that time and they gave me promise they will find job for me. They will be reference. They will ask boss. And I found one job in one company, it's housekeeping company to clean offices in downtown. It was second shift. And I was working 20 days and I say, "No, that's no good for me." Not because it's cleaning, but it's second shift. And my wife work first shift. I said, "I'm going to change. I am going to find something in first shift." And I remember I change my job and I had more money in that job than another one. I said, "OK, I'm going to lose, I think it's 50 cents per hour, but I'll be with my wife." We don't have kids. We don't have anybody. We need be each other. I don't care for that 50 cents. That was Hotel Radisson in downtown. And I was working there from July 1997 to March 1998.

And after that I got a job in school. I was lucky. That was lucky. That was luck because I went in one school in my neighborhood. They have Bosnian kids. And I went there, asked them, "Do you have any job for me? Do you need any help?" And I knew they had two Bosnian teachers in that time. I was so happy. I knew I wasn't teacher, I was assistant, but anyway that's my field. It's school. School system. I like that. How can I explain that feeling? It's like I was born again.

And I was working on that position from March 22nd, 1998 until February 2000. That is Nettelhorst Elementary School. It's [near] Broadway [Avenue] and Belmont [Avenue]. It's nice.

And I'm still there, but they changed my position. In February they put me in a computer lab. And I'm running our computer lab. It's new stuff. Everything is there. It's good job. Actually, I like this job. And I will try reach my certification and get more money, but I don't need change job because I like it. It's very nice.

But I'm going to try get degree. At least two years degree. If I decide make two years degree, that will be I think computer information system. But many days I'm thinking I can use my credit hours from my country and go maybe two and a half years, and get bachelor degree. That will be much, much better. More money. More education. And that will be difficult for me because I'm still thinking about real job, what I'm going to do. It's not only going school, finish school, but I need know I will do that 30 years, 20 years. If I decide take something what is really boring, not interesting for me, that will be very hard for me. It will be tough. And it's the reason I'm taking computer classes, general. I need that classes. I decided to be hardware engineer, or programmer, or computer information.

Especially this semester it's very hard because they didn't have schedule good for me. And I'm going in school Monday and Wednesday. And every day I'm taking three classes. Four thirty I supposed to be in Truman College. From 4:30 to 5:45 I have one class. It's Computer Information System 116. And I have 15 minutes break. Actually that is good time to change one classroom to go in another. From 6:00 to 8:40, 8:30 depend of labs, I have another class. It's computer class, Computer Information Systems 111. And from that class, I supposed to go in English and stay there at least 40 minutes, 30 minutes depend. And I'm dead tired.

Monday, Wednesday, and Friday I am happy. Tuesday, Thursday, and Saturday I'm not happy. Actually, I'm joking because one hand I'm happy. One hand I'm not happy. I'm happy because I escaped that place. I don't like that place. It's my country and I'm trying to forget everything. I'm happy. In another hand, I'm not happy because I'm living very hard tough life because I need money because I need pay my utilities. I'm 31 years old. I need think about future. I don't have pension. I need think about saving money for future. I need think about education. It's now time. I'm not going to go in school when I'm going to be 50. I need kids because I'm 31. Everything. You don't know what is more important for me. I'm just thinking. One day I said, "Monday, I'm thinking like this. Tuesday, I'm thinking like this." Then I say, "Monday, I'm happy. Tuesday, I'm not happy." Because Monday, maybe I'm thinking, "Oh, fine. I'm not there." I talk with my parents and they say there is trouble, no economy, no life. I'm happy. Tuesday, I have my real situation. I need go in work. After work I need run home, eat something, drink coffee, go in school, take one class, go another class, come home 9:00, 10:00 [P.M.], make dinner. Ten o'clock, I'm still doing something. I need to do my homework. Go in bed at 12:00. Wake up in morning 5:30, 6:00, tired. Life is tough, but generally I'm fine. I'm happy, generally.

I'm not satisfied with what I have today. I'm thinking about tomorrow. Many times I'm pushing myself too much. I'm not thinking about tomorrow, I'm thinking about 10 years forward. Because many times my wife say, "Hey, calm down. Think about tomorrow or next week. Do not go so far."

I think I will go there [Bosnia] but very short, short time. I wish go now to see my grandfather because if he die, I'm never going to see him again because he's going to die soon. But situation there is not good for me yet. Nobody is going to kill me. Nobody is going to beat me. Nobody is going to put me in jail. But I still don't have feel. I can't tell everybody what I want because some of them, they need talk with

With his wife, Zejna, on Michigan Avenue, Chicago, 2000

me. I need tell them what I really feel about them, what they do and that's wrong. That's wrong.

I'm embarrassed to live and I'm mad to live with them because they don't have any character. I can go there because I'm clean. I didn't do anything wrong. Nobody can say, "You took my TV. You took my car. You did this. You did that."

I will be citizen. We got a green card. That's like permanent resident. And next year, we will be able to apply for citizenship and I think we will get that because we came here legally, everything was fine. All papers went smoothly. We didn't have any problems about that.

You know what? I'm not going to have that feeling all my life I'm American because I know I'm not American, that's one thing. And when I say something, all people who is American will know I'm not American. And doesn't matter what kind of feeling I have, they have different feeling. It's two reasons why I'm not going to have that feeling. But I have feeling I belong in this place. I have that feeling for sure, for my thinking about life, about everything. I belong in this place because I like progress, I like work, I like honest. I don't care

what kind of person you are, what kind of religion, what kind of color. I need your personality. If your personality is fine, we can be fine, we can be friend.

I change many feelings in my life. When I was student, when I finish my school, I never think go some other places, never. One year later, trouble. I had different feeling. My God, this trouble never going to stop. I'm going to die. Come here, another feeling. Oh, God. I'm starting from zero. How I'm going to make better life because I came here with two bags. You know, it's hard. And many times I told me wife, "OK. Now is fine. We are healthy. We're still young. Economy is good. But you never know." We have phrase: If you were bitten by a snake, you are afraid of other small animals because you have bad experience. Now is just fine. I think everything is possible. Everything is possible and it's changing faster than you think. I never think about bad possibility. But here also, you never know. Still I'm not thinking about that every day, but sometimes came in my mind.

I can't tell anybody what he supposed to think, but I think they [Americans] need be proud because hey, you are able to take somebody, help somebody. It's better to help somebody than be in case to be helped. My father always taught me all my life, "If you have some money, you have to help somebody. It's better than be in case somebody need to help you."

I was in case and I couldn't help myself anything. They come there say, "OK, we will give you visa. You can come here, but at your expenses." I didn't have money to pay ticket. I didn't have money to pay bus from refugee camp to airport to pay ticket for airplane. I didn't have money to support myself and my family here couple months to get job. That is good appreciation because that is good start. We paid that back. I'm not lazy. I'm working. They're taking my tax. And maybe my tax go to help somebody else. And I'm from Bosnia. Thanks God we don't have anymore refugee. That's fine. It's over. But we have refugee maybe from Kosovo. We have maybe refugee from Ethiopia. We have from Somalia. They are taking my tax. Maybe I will pay for them. We have people who were born here and they don't make work or they are sick or they have public aid. Maybe, maybe my money go there. Who knows? Maybe your money came to help me.

| 121

EMIR IS STUDYING AT TRUMAN COLLEGE for his associate's degree. He continues to work as a computer lab manager for the Chicago Public Schools.

MY NAME IS DENG DENG AGOT I'M FROM SOUTHERN SUDAN. *Deng actually means rain, but we use it for someone who is respected, looked up to in the community. I'm 24 at this time. I came to the United States I think, what was it,* **SEPTEMBER 25TH, 1995.**

THE REGION I'M FROM IS CALLED GOGRIAL, CLOSE TO 3,000 OR 4,000 PEOPLE APPROXIMATELY. My tribe is Dinka, and we have multiple tribes in the south. But traditionally, the lifestyle of my tribe is that most of us raise cattle and sheep and goats. But there is a division in that, which is that some of our parents raise the kids and send some of them to school in the cities, and some of them stay in the villages or in the rural areas to take care of the cattle and take care of the older people also.

So, we have two kinds of life, also. But the person that go to the city and go to school, after school during the vacation, they still come back and spend their vacation there [in the village], so you can't lose your tradition. Because you can be caught up between the western civilization and your traditional culture. So, you come back and stay for six months. You go to milk the cow and take care of the cow. You release them. You mind them. You take care of them night and day.

My father had cattle. I took care of cattle during the break time. There are certain things you do based on how old you are. If I was 16 or 17, I could do most of it, like take the cow to go eat, and after that bring them back and put them down, because you have to tie them down and then you have to milk them. These are the skills you need to know to take care. Actually, I didn't learn all of it because I was little and I was not to the age where I have to do this, but I see people doing it. I would just sit down and then see the other person doing it. They would do it and then give me the milk to drink it. At the time, when you're milking the cow, you can call the child and then milk the cow right in your mouth. And it's fun. It's something real good. We don't sell the milk or sell the meat. What actually we do with the cow is that we just use the milk to drink.

There are two ways people used to do it [raise cattle]. You can go in the cattle camps where you are away from your house completely. You're just there with a few people that are taking care of the cows far away in the bush where you sleep there, you take care of them. People stay with them for a period of time, like six months or so. And there's another way where you can leave them in a house. They have a big room where you can put them in and in the morning release them. First you have to milk them and then release them. When you release them, you have to go and mind them and then after that, 6:00, you bring them back. That's the kind of life. You have to be a certain age because anything happens. A lion can just come jump between them, so you have to be a person that physically you have to run a couple miles to go call the people and come so they can rescue the rest of the cows. Sometimes lions have a tendency to come in and attack and eat the cow because they are vulnerable.

It is a very valuable asset to us. We value it like people value U.S. dollar in this country. So that's how important or equal it is to us. The main thing we do with the cow, is people get married with the cow. People pay dowry for the cow, so I think that's one of the main importance of you having the cow. Because if you don't have it, I think it would be difficult to get married, particularly for my tribe, the Dinka.

If you're getting married, not the girl's father, but the man, you're the one that pays the dowry to the girl's father. It's not like you're buying the girl, but the point is you're trying to pay for all the services or the pain that the mother and father went through. These are the paybacks. You have to pay them back for what they did to raise the child.

Our house was not like this, where you have a high rise story building. I think there was no third floor in the city I came from. [Laughs.] It was just first, second floor. My house was a four room house. You make it like a cone where you have the top part coming like this. [Shapes his hands with a point on top.] On top it's like this and then under it, it's round. And it's built by grass. And we had four houses like that, but they face one another. We put them in a circle. So my father has a room, the children [have one], the other room for the girls and then one is the kitchen where you cook inside and do other things. So that's how it was. We call it one house because they're all together close, and you have the circle around where people sit in the evening and just talk or when you're eating, you have a dinner, then you sit in the center and then eat. After that you talk, and then when sleep time comes, then you go to bed.

We didn't have electricity, no telephone. We didn't have no TV at that time in that city. There is no TV station. Everything we got was from the radio in that little city. We draw water from the well. At that time I liked it, but now I think if I go there, I would find it difficult to live there after [Laughs.] getting used to all these electronics and cable TV and all this stuff. But at that time, I didn't know anywhere. I thought that was the only place existing on earth.

I think my mother is a well loving, kind person. She was the person I always remember most. I think I grew around my mother. She was the person always around me. I got that connection. And my father was always traveling, going to different cities, and he was not around actu-

With two older brothers, Sudan, 1983

ally when I was growing up.

In the city, actually, my mother used to have a little business. She used to have a liquor store. It's a traditional liquor where she used to make herself and sell it. So that's mostly what we were surviving on for some time to what I can recall, because my father at that time was not working. He was a business person before. Actually, the business there was just a store where he used to bring some goods from the cities, most of the needed things like the clothes, salt, sugar and these sort of things where people in the interior need most. Those are the things he used to sell, and some of this is the ground peanut. There is something called *dura*, like wheat. These are the staple foods for the southern Sudan mostly, I think. And then what happened during the war, his things were taken away by the government troops. So he didn't have nothing to do at that time and he didn't have money to begin another business. So my mother was the only one actually supporting us. She was the person that was providing for the whole entire house. So she used to make this traditional liquor and sell it, and then that's where we get our income from and that's how we survive and send us to school. It was not the real poor life, but it was something to keep us living until something happened someday. She didn't have education. She does not read. She does not write, but she just used her common sense to do this business, even though most business requires some education.

At times we just eat one meal a day. Another time we eat two meals a day. Another time we go to school without lunch, or have without something for allowance for lunch or whatever you need in school. So you have to live like that. Even sometimes we used to cry. You say you don't wanna go to school because you don't have lunch break money, but that's part of life. You have to adjust to it and live because sometimes you see your mother doesn't have it, but she tries her best to give you whatever you want, but she cannot give everything that you need every time. So it was kind of difficult.

It's not too expensive or too rich life you live. It was simple life. You didn't demand anything more than what you can get. Whatever you get, if you get it, you'll be really happy with it because you don't get something whenever you want it. It would take time for your father or your mother to get it to you. So when that time comes and that gift be given to you, that's the greatest thing you can achieve and you always value that, too. Because here [in the United States] you almost get everything when you want it, so I don't think it brings that much joy. But when you want something and you don't get it right away and it takes time, if you get it I think you're gonna be really, really happy with it. You appreciate it more than just walk to the store and having it right there. You appreciate food.

I used to like school, actually, when I was small. I used to get a lot of awards and gifts from school. We used to sit, actually, under the tree and then read, write. Sometimes we write in the ground on the open field. We didn't have a classroom at the time. From 4th grade to 6th they sit in the classroom. But the first grade, you don't have a classroom. You sit under the tree or sit in the open field, and then the teacher first would teach you how to write ABC, which were Arabic at that time. We used to write it on the ground in the sand [with your finger] exactly. So that's how we learned how to write. You have to write it and then the teacher would come around and see whether you write it correctly or not. If you wrote it wrong, they beat you and then you have to write it correctly.

You start when you're seven years. As long as you can talk clearly, you're eligible to go. But it was not based on age actually because some people can be eight, nine, and they can't talk well. So you cannot go until your mouth and your tongue become clearer in speaking. Then you will be allowed to go to school.

The war started in 1983. There are a couple things the war is about. It's about sharing the power. Secondly, it's about dividing the religion from the state and about misusing of the resources by the north, by the government.

My area was affected I think around '85. We used to hear gunshots every night because the military was afraid of the rebels attacking them. So therefore, what happened was that they used to shoot at night, almost every night. In my city, it's a little city, so if you shoot from one end, you can hear from the other end. At night we hear gunshots, *boom, boom, boom,* here and there. So, we moved to a bigger city, which was

about 120,000 at that time. We moved to the bigger city, and still there were gunshots every night, too. [The city] is Wau. The region is called Bahr Al Ghazal. That was in '85, I think.

I lost two brothers during the war. My elder brothers were killed by the government in the Sudan, and another one got lost during the war. We don't even know where he is right now, whether he's still alive or dead. I have two brothers right now alive and two sisters.

We were going to school and sometimes the school would stop, because the war would interrupt and people were moving from other smaller villages. The school would stop and the people would live in the school for sometime, the displaced people that come to the city. They were accommodated in most of these schools. I think I was in the 2nd grade at the time, so they would close the school and then we stay for sometime and when they reopen, we go back.

At school, you see, there was not a normal life where the kid would be happy, go to school, you come back to school. Every day was just a hustle day. At times you got one meal at night. The war just disrupted the economy and everything and hunger was all over. To get a meal is very hard, too. Even you have the money, but you can't get it. If you got one meal, you can stay until the next day. But mostly with the kids what happened was we have those trees like mango trees and you just go and hustle on your own and get something. If you get one or two, you eat it and you drink water. That's how survival was because if you depend on the meal at home, you're not gonna survive on it because it was hard to come by. You find fruit trees and whatever you can get your hands on. And sometimes you walk miles to go in the bush and find some fruit and take some, eat it and come back home. It was just survival. That's it. It was not eat and enjoy. We were going to school sometimes, sometimes not, because even sometimes you don't want to go to school because you're hungry. And at that time, nothing get in your head. You're thinking about when you're gonna get a meal today.

Every day is a hustle day. Every day is a struggle day, because you just pray and live to see the next day. You go to bed with that mind and you don't have a clear conscience that you're gonna wake up tomorrow alive or dead. It's not just you fear that you don't know how you're gonna get food. Of course, that fear is there because you are a child. And secondly, the war was going on and there were rockets landing in the city, so you don't know if next day it's gonna land in your house. You never know.

So I didn't have where you go out, you play, you go to school, you come back, everything at home is set. Everything was not like that. You just wake up thinking where you're gonna get your meal. Go climb the tree, find some fruit to eat. That's pretty much how we spent most of our time in the daytime, looking for food in the tree. And sometime if you get enough, you will sell it and get some money, buy something. That's pretty much it.

When you go through a lot of difficulties and problems, you just live through it, just trying to survive. That was the main thing. That's why sometimes when you see the kids in Africa holding guns, it's not that they choose to, but the society and the environment dictate what you do. So you become like a grown person when you're holding that gun because you can do pretty much everything that you want to do. So that's the kind of thing that's going on.

First, I wanted to join the rebels. There were a lot of people who went there, even 11-years-old people. Smaller kids, they were going there, so I thought it was something new and everyone was going and I was the only one left there, so they were calling you, "Sissy," when they come back when they look at you. My equal was going, so I thought it was something we all should do. My friends said, "We're fighting for our country."

So therefore I said, "OK, we all gotta fight, too."

My mom said, "You're too little and you're not going anywhere." She said, "If you go, I'll kill you!"

So I got afraid, and I forgot about that and I said, "OK, since you said I'm not going, I'll go somewhere else." Because there was no life at all in that city left anymore for you to stay there.

Actually, I didn't wait. We were on break from school [in '87, when I was 10 years old]. So he [one of my uncles] was going for treatment in the north in Khartoum. He was going to Khartoum because he was sick. At that time I didn't tell my mom that I was going anywhere. In that city when you see the plane coming, because the war was going

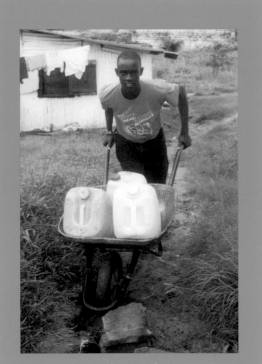
Working at home, Liberia, 1994

on, the plane would come and spin around for five or six times to get lower to go to the airport and land. So when I saw the plane, I ran to his house because I knew he was leaving. I went to his house and he was putting some bag in the car. So I went and helped him and his son and went to the airport. When we entered the airport, there's a stop sign outside with the military troops at the gate, and he was with the police. So what happened was that he told them, "Those two are my sons, so let them in. They're just taking care of my bags, so let them in for me."

So the officer said, "OK," and let us go.

We went to the airport and we stayed there waiting for the plane to unload because they were bringing some military ammunition. So after they unload the plane, there were a couple injured people. So they put them in the plane first. And then after that, he told me and his son, "You carry those bags in the plane and then you go back home."

But I was thinking about to go somewhere. We went. We took the bags, and then I came back and I started thinking about whether to go back or take my chances. I just was with those clothes that I had and shoes, that's all I got. I sat there and I was thinking because I was scared also because they have the military around you with guns, holding them like this.

People were just getting in the plane and I was the only one sitting by the plane and no one luckily asked me. And I was afraid to get in because if I got in they might ask me, "Who are you going with?" Because you must have somebody with you. Most thing I was afraid of was that I thought one of the officers was gonna ask me, because they were surrounding. The military was so tight and people were around the plane holding the gun. So that was the most scary thing to me at that time.

And so I was standing there and then I was thinking whether to go, take my chances to go in, or go back. I said to myself, "If I go back, I'm not gonna get this chance anymore." So I just closed my eyes and walked to the plane and then I just went in.

It was very difficult to make that decision, but something just came to me and said, "Try your luck and just get in and see."

So when I sat down, I was just trembling and scared that somebody was gonna ask me. People came. They sat by me because it was just two lines, on that side and then on this side, and in the middle they got all the bags and some other stuff. So I sat down and I was just bending my head down, not looking at anybody's eyes, and luckily no one asked me. And other people came. They sat by me and they covered me so nobody outside could see me anymore. And then the plane took off.

I knew that whenever we landed, I would look for him [my uncle] right away, but I didn't want to show myself openly in the plane. Probably I'm afraid he's going to say something. [Laughs.] I didn't know what he was going to say, so I said, "Let me wait and see when we land, then I'll show myself to him and see what he will say."

He didn't see me until we landed. Then I showed myself to him. I was afraid, too. He was surprised. And when I came to Khartoum, I didn't know nobody except my uncle that was going, and he said, "Oh, did you come?"

I said, "Yes, I came."

He said, "Why?"

I said, "I just wanted to come."

He said, "OK, fine."

So I came to Khartoum and he put me in the hotel. When you come from the south and you're part of the government, they will put you in a hotel. He was police officer. I stayed with him for a couple time in that guesthouse. So I stayed there and then a few days later, he was hospitalized, so I used to go to the hospital.

I used to visit him in the hospital, and I think he spent like a month and then the sickness was not getting better. It was just getting worse and worse every day. So what happened, the hospital said, "We cannot make it and we have to release you from the hospital." So he was released, and then he went to another hospital. And then I think two weeks later, he passed away.

I didn't do nothing. I was just sitting down. I didn't know nobody, so I was just living in that place. I didn't know nobody in Khartoum, actually, to go to and assist me and maybe go take me to school and all of this, so that was the hardest thing.

I stayed in the guesthouse. The government officials that came from the south and stayed in the guesthouse, if they need something, they will send me and go and get it. And after that if there's anything left,

the pocket change, they will give it to me. And that's how I make my living. And I used to just be there. They would send me, "Do this. Go do this for me. Go bring this." And I would go and get it for them. I used to sell cigarettes. I buy it and I sell it to those people. But it was illegal for you to sell cigarettes at that time. So when you get caught, you go to jail.

So that's what I did for a couple months. And in Khartoum, it was very scary to live there because if you go to the market, there was a squad that was responsible for if you don't have a work ID or student ID card, you would be taken to somewhere in Port Sudan to go dig salt, to work for free. If you don't have that ID, you would just be thrown in the back of the truck and you go to that place, Port Sudan. So your movement was kind of restricted. You go at certain times and come back. It just was targeting most people from the south. They don't want them to be in the city. So I think that was the main objective of doing that.

It's very difficult for somebody to digest that and believe that it's true, but in time of war, if you go to where I came from, hopefully one day you will see the hostile society where we came from and where we live. You just have to try your own to make something out of nothing. You try to make some way for you to go, to pass. So, that's the kind of thing. You begin to think on your own whether this is right, whether this is wrong. You don't know. You just wanna try it and see. You begin to move away from your parents because they probably have a little one, and you have to swim on your own to survive. The care of the parents was there, but there was not enough support that goes with it.

It didn't come to my mind at that time that I need to steal. I didn't put that in my mind that I should take something, even in Khartoum. That was some of the frustration because I could not get nothing. Nothing comes easy. At that time I have to work, like standing outside to sell cigarettes at the time after I got a little money from those people after sending me. And most of them used to ask me, "Who you come with?"

That was the most question I was asked and I didn't have no answer for it. I just said, "I came myself." And they would just try to help me. At that time I didn't call or I didn't talk to them [my parents]. I just sent a message later that I went to Khartoum by somebody that was leaving.

At times I felt bad. Sometimes they tell me that, "You're crazy to leave your parents and come to this city where you know nobody." At times, I was thinking about her [my mother]. That's what bothered me.

But at certain times, I was just thinking why I came here in the first place. Because I just get confused. It was a big city and you don't know nobody. I used to go outside and see cars passing, and I just don't know what to do. So, it was difficult at the time.

I stayed there in '87 and I think I spent from February to October, and then there was somebody that knew my [another] uncle. He's my mother's smaller brother. My uncle was in Liberia at that time. He went to study medicine. And he graduated and he was working in Liberia. So a friend of my uncle was in Khartoum. So he asked me, "Why you came here? Who you came with?"

I said, "I didn't come with nobody. I came myself."

He said, "What are you doing here?"

He asked me those questions and I said, "I just came to see if I can get away from the south."

He said, "OK, now what is your plan?"

I said, "I don't have any plan."

So he said, "OK, do you wanna go to school?"

I said, "Yes."

There was a school close by. So he took me to school and he said, "You can be going to school and I will try to talk to your uncle if he can send for you in Liberia."

So I said, "OK." He went and he registered me in the school. All they needed was just somebody to recommend you to get in. So he took me there and I just got registered and I start going to school. He bought me some books and I began school.

That was one of my happy times because I didn't want to let him down. And most of the time, he used to help me also, bring me some money. So I was going to school and I didn't have problem at that time. So a few months later, I think he wrote a letter to my uncle saying, "Your nephew is here. He doesn't have nobody. And he said he was coming to you, but he didn't have money at all." [Laughs.]

So my uncle took some money and he sent a ticket by someone. After that, my uncle's friend came and he told me I was supposed to leave two days later. He shocked me. He said, "You're leaving tomorrow night."

I said, "Where I'm going?"

He said, "You're going to Liberia to your uncle."

And that was it. So I was surprised. I was so happy to go because where I was living, I didn't know where I was going, actually, because there was no one that I was related to and I was just by myself in the city. I even wanted to go back to the south because at one time, I didn't

With friends at the airport before leaving Monrovia, Liberia, September 24, 1995

do nothing and I didn't find anything, so I decided I'd better go back to my mom and see what happened there. I was so lonely and I could not get along with anyone.

I got on the plane and we just fly. I think we passed a couple African countries. We landed there [in Liberia]. And that's all I remember. I was sitting by the window, just looking and thinking what I'm gonna wish. I didn't even talk. I was just quiet the whole time. We left from 6:00 in the morning and we reached Liberia around sunset time. So we landed and some people came for me. We took a taxi and we went to the house, and my uncle's daughter was there, too. So when I went there, I was happy and so excited. I was a little confused. I looked at the place and it was much better than where I was from.

My uncle actually took me to school and they tested me for mathematics. And then I passed it, so they put me to school. I tried to catch up and I had a tutor at home. When I came home from school, he would teach me. And in 1989, my uncle decided, "The only way you're gonna catch up and learn English faster is to go to the mission." So he sent me to a mission school in the 6th grade.

I didn't speak nothing at all. No English, nothing. I didn't understand a thing. In the school, I was so dumb and stupid. I looked stupid every day because I didn't understand anything what the teacher was talking about. And it was difficult time for me to adjust and learn another language. It was hard. When he sent me to the mission, I tried every day. I used to wake up like 4:00 and try to memorize because I didn't know that language. So the only thing I did was to memorize and read very, very hard.

In Liberia, I started going to school, and after that the war came in 1989. So we stop school and we were sent back home. I was just confused. Everywhere I step, that's what I thought, everywhere I go they just start another war. And it was not a stable life that I had been living. There was no stable life. And my uncle decided this is getting risky for the kids, so he sent us to Sierra Leone. Nobody there. He just sent us. He said go there, try to find a place, and he will send us some money to go with and then we can live on it—his wife and three kids, my uncle's daughters, and then me.

We tried to go to school for six months. And after that, the rebels came again to Sierra Leone and started fighting. So I think it was like within six months, the war started again, coming to the city we were living in. So we have to move to the capital city, which is Freetown. When this rebels came in and they started fighting in Sierra Leone, they were just driving people to the city. Thousands of people were just moving to Freetown. So my uncle said, "You guys got to come to this city." And maybe he try to send some money so we can come back to Liberia because Sierra Leone was not safe anymore.

So we came and we got to Freetown. We spent three weeks and my uncle, he went to the NGOs [nongovernmental organizations] but he didn't have enough money to buy a ticket for us to come, so he bought four tickets and then he said the rest of the people will come by ship, because there was a ship that was bringing the refugees to Monrovia, which is the capital city for Liberia, from Sierra Leone. Because the war was getting worse, so Liberia become safer than Sierra Leone now. So we were coming back to Monrovia because there was a peacekeeping force there just in the city. So he told us, "You gotta come back to Monrovia. That's the only safe way now."

We got in the ship and we spent a day and a half and we came to the city Monrovia. When we came, we went to my uncle's wife brother's house. He was there and another sister and family, they were there. So we came. We joined them. And we stayed there to '91, and there was no school at the time. We didn't do anything. All the schools were closed. Just what was concerned is to survive. That's it. You didn't think about learning at that time, because the war was still going and was not far away, so we didn't think about someone teaching you at that time. Even though I was still trying to catch up with English, but still no one was teaching nobody.

In '92, the government school opened, and I went to school. Even though I didn't finish the 7th grade, they gave me a test and I passed, so they put me in 8th grade. And then from 8th grade I passed to 9th grade in '93. And in '93 I went to 9th grade. They gave a national exam for 9th grade, for junior high to go to high school. And then I passed the test and I went to another government school.

So at that time, I started playing basketball. I used to like basketball. When we were there, if there is NBA final, they used to bring in a tape. And I used to go there. You pay money to get in to watch it. If I see the poster outside, I'm just gonna find time to come and see it, no matter what. So that was a good time, actually. It was the best. When I passed 10th grade, I was taken by one private school called College of West Africa, it's a private high school. I was playing basketball and they gave me some scholarship to play.

That helped me a lot. I was also asking the U.N. to accept me as a refugee, and give me refugee status in Liberia so they can give me assistance. And then I think a few months later, they accepted me and they were giving me allowance of $50 U.S. a month. It was the end of '93 to '94.

That $50 helped me a lot, because it took the pressure off my uncle because he was taking care of a lot of things. So pretty much I used to buy some clothes and some school material that I needed. I continued to go to school. And even though my English was not that perfect, I was still trying to catch up, so I was reading a lot and studying.

The Sudanese that were living in Liberia, they applied to the U.N. in Geneva, as a group. So they applied and they wrote and said, "We are a certain number of Sudanese and we want the U.N. to accept us as refugees and resettle us somewhere, because our lives and our children's lives is not safe anymore in this country." So that's what happened in '92, and it took three years before the reply came. When the reply came, they contacted the United States Immigration. Within six months, the Americans came and they did the interview, and then we went for the medical check-up and we went for orientation and then we left. [Laughs.]

I didn't put too much attention because I just wanted to come here and play basketball. [Laughs.] I just wanted to come to U.S. So whatever they were saying, I didn't take it to be serious because people say, "Oh, United States is not good, especially those big cities. Chicago is the worst city to be in. It's divided into two. The north is the white. The south is the black. There are a lot of killings every day. So that is the worst city to be in."

But all I wanted, I said, "If I have the opportunity to go there, I wouldn't mind because I just want to see basketball, I want to play basketball." [Laughs.] I said, "Whatever you said, I'm just gonna listen to it, but I'm not gonna base my decision on that. I already made up my mind." I just decided, because they told me I was coming to Chicago. I said, "I'm going to Michael Jordan's city. There's nothing better than that." [Laughs.] I said, "Wow. That's great." And Chicago was famous at that time, so it was good to be here. There was no discussion whatsoever. All we wanted was just to come to United States, and no matter where you were placed, it's not any problem. It doesn't matter. I was very excited to come here, especially Chicago.

I think I was fortunate to have that opportunity. I was thinking that it was based on the decisions that I made, but now I think it was just a miracle. I was lucky to pass through all these stages, and get lucky to find people who asked me, and then they helped me along the way until I came to the United States. And sometimes, too, it's based on your respect to the older people. I think without that, I could not have been here, too. So that's what helped me out. I used to stay around the older people. They send me and I never say, "No," and I respect them also. And I think about a memory when I was small, there was old man who used to come to me and said, "If you respect your elders, you're gonna be blessed, and you will go to a place where an ordinary person would not go. Because if you don't have respect, you will not get that blessing that you need to go somewhere farther in your life." So I think

With two friends, Chicago, 1996

that helped me also. I just realized it now.

That was a good flight. I was so excited. When I was leaving at the airport, they came and my uncle's daughter, she paid one guy to take a picture. It just was one picture I took and then that was it. When I was getting off the airport, I looked down and I was surprised to see that I'm leaving to go another place again. And I just waved to my friends and I told them I might come back some day, but now I don't know. Some of them are in the United States, but I've not met them since.

The group that came from Liberia, only four of us came here and I think the large number came to Dallas. They sent some to Texas, Arizona, Seattle, Chicago, Kansas City, and Portland, Maine.

We came separate. Three of them came first, and then I was the last to come. I was happy the whole time that I'm coming to United States. There was no doubt about it, I was happy. But when I landed here, I saw things were different than I expected to be. [Laughs.] I thought this was sort of heaven, to say it all. Even though I didn't expect that money grow on trees in this country, but I expected it was not hard to get money. But even though it is not hard right now, at the time when I came and you have to go to work in the snow I said, "No, this is not what I expected." [Laughs.]

When I landed, I don't know where to go. Nobody was there! There was miscommunication or what I don't know. I just got down from the plane. I saw people walking. I followed them. So I went to the desk and I asked whether they know the Ethiopian Community [Association]. And they said, "No, we don't know."

So I just start spinning around, walking around thinking I would get to know them because Ethiopians, I know them in Sudan. I came outside in the parking lot and I didn't see nothing. And I went back in. I wait there for like an hour, two hours. Finally, I went back to the desk and finally the guy came looking for me, too. So he put me in the car.

So we reached at home, I think, 9:00 or 10:00 [P.M.]. So we were living I think at Argyle [Street] and Winthrop [Avenue]. They [other Sudanese] were outside at the door waiting for me. Then when I got in, they started making fun of me. They said, "Oh, go inside." I was so excited. I thought that what we see in TV in Africa, that's what we're gonna see here—everything is set and TV is on. But when I got in, the mattresses were on the floor. I start looking around. [Laughs.] I was a little surprised, but United States, what can you get more than that?

That's the illusion I came with when we see some movies, you see video, you see TV and telephone and other stuff. When I came to United States, I didn't have it, so I was thinking that this is not the United States probably. [Laughs.] I'm waiting to go there! [Laughs.] So I thought that was not it. I didn't know you have to work for everything to have it.

The next day, we went to the hospital by Wilson [Avenue]. I think we go a couple times to go for check-up and have to take multiple tests. They found TB, skin TB, so they gave me medication for six months. I think it was from the milk, because we drink the milk directly from the cow without purifying it. No pasteurization. So that's where we get most of it from. Three of us, we got skin TB and one guy didn't get it. I guess because he didn't drink that much cow milk because maybe his parents were not wealthy, which means that they didn't have cow. So they were fisherman and stuff like that.

And then, a friend took us to another place, where they call the Vietnamese Community [Association]. And one Somali was there called Hussein. He said, "There is a hotel downtown that want people." He was good caseworker. He said, "OK, what I will do, first I will open up a file for each of you guys. And then next week, you'll come. I will take you downtown. Then I will find a job for you guys." So we went. He took us to Hyatt Regency and we got interview. I think we did everything the same day. We got interview, we fill out the form, we did orientation, and the following week we started.

I started as a steward. You wash dishes basically on the machine. We got a big machine I never seen before. [Laughs.] You take the dishes and throw them in and when they come out on the other side, they're clean. So that's basically, what we did. And then sometimes mop the floor, wash the floor. That's part of stewarding. So basically, you get your feet wet because you play with water a lot. [Laughs.]

I think what I learned from that was that it was so hard for me to look at that and waste food actually. I didn't want to do that, but it's

part of the job. I just think if I could have a way to feed people back there with all this food, I would have done it. But there is no way that you can do that. But there is so much food that is wasted in most of the hotels in the United States. It's not given to anybody. Even some food comes back and nobody touched it and it's your job, it's your duty. You have to waste it. You can't do nothing with that. So that was a difficult thing. Sometimes I would just look at the food and stare at it and think, "How many people will this save at this time?" But it was part of the job. You have to waste it. That was a difficult part working in the hotel.

I'm thankful when I get food. That's why when I'm eating I don't like to waste food because I know very well what it was before. People they come here and they taste something, "Oh, I don't like it that much," and throw it away. Here because you have it in your hand, you don't appreciate it. Everything is so easy. Parents work and when the kid comes home, of course he goes to the refrigerator. He finds something. But we don't have it there.

When you get something, you don't know how valuable it is and how good it is. But from where we are, we used to walk to school barefooted. You don't have shoes. You just have a short dress and a T-shirt. You walk back and forth. My school was not too far away. It's like a mile in Sudan. Even in Wau, we used to walk to school. It was like a

With his cousin, Dallas, 1999

With friends, Chicago, 2000

mile, but you have to walk. Everyone else walks. Some people walk more than we do. They walk and they come from far place, like five, six, seven miles. So that kind of struggle. You have to wake up every morning, take your books, take shower, you go to school. And maybe 2:00, 3:00 you come from school. You look white and you're hungry. You just come home to find something to eat. Sometime you come, people sitting down. Their look alone will tell you there's nothing to eat. So what do you do? Just put your book down and go hustle for food to eat.

The first two months was really difficult because we didn't have no TV, we didn't have no telephone. There's no program, nothing to do at all. So we just wake up and what did we do? Nothing. We just wake up and sit down. We cook. We started getting fat because we just eating and do nothing. [Laughs.] I didn't gain that much. Within the course of that two month, I weighed 158. That was the highest I went. [Laughs.] I'm like 148 [now]. [Laughs.]

There are a lot of [difficult] things—using the telephone, using the transportation, going to use the vending machines, those things that we never had before. So those things are very hard. Sometimes you just act like you know it and wait to see somebody doing it, because you don't want to make yourself shame and asking somebody how to use. So those things were hard. And life itself, it was very difficult to adjust to

a place where you just don't expect things to be the way they are. And you have to live. So I think the hardest thing was the weather, part of it, the life itself, the culture, trying to be Americanized, do like they do. Eat the same food, McDonald's, [Laughs.] go out and do things faster, which we didn't get used to. [Laughs.] I'm kind of slow person and I don't want to get in that fast pace.

How about time? Because we didn't believe in time. Right now I'm believing in time because I have to, because it's good and it makes things work better. In Africa we don't set a real exact time. We just say, "In the afternoon, in the morning, in midday." That's all about time. We didn't have a specific and precise time, like you gotta be 3:00. You say 3:00, we will come 4:00. So we didn't value time, but here you have to value it because time goes for money. You don't want to sit down and do nothing, because you're wasting a lot. It's kind of concerning money.

After work, first thing we bought: telephone. And our bill went so high because it was something new and we didn't know that much about telephone. Nobody knows. We just got it, we paid the first installment fees and we started using it. And at that time the bill came to close to $1,000. Just one month I'm talking about! [Laughs.] Actually I didn't do that much calling but my cousin, those guys, they did a lot of calling. The only place I called was my uncle in Dallas and my uncle's daughter in Seattle, Washington. I didn't know nobody. [Laughs.] And those guys were calling back in Liberia, they were calling Sudan, and in United States and in Canada. So the bill went so high. And even when you go to pay the bill at the currency exchange, people look at you like you're crazy. And we didn't understand that point. You learn from your mistakes. [Laughs.] That's the process. I think we're going through the process of learning.

Truman College was right here close by. So what happened, a friend, one guy, he came by and he was going to Truman. He came and said, "Oh, there is a college right here. You guys can come, and I will take you guys there and just take the test and you can go to ESL, or go to four-year university if you want." And for me, I was in 12th grade when I left, so I just wanted to go.

After the test, they showed us the result. It was just English I think. And then after that, we started. They put me in level 4 in English. And the other guys, they put them in level 6. And then we started going to classes, ESL every day.

And then in September of '96, my friend told me, "What are you doing? Go take the test for free credit classes because ESL is just wasting your time. You're not going to get nothing out of it."

So I went and I took the test. And I passed not that high. And they placed me in English 98 and Math 100. So that's how I begin from there taking all the free credit classes. I think I started in '97.

Actually, I'm kind of afraid to go farther right now. But from asking my friends and other people, they told me, "You got the potential. You can make it." But all along I never had a solid background of education, and this problem still bothers me up to now, but still I just want to try my best and do what I can and do the best I can to proceed. Actually, I want to go to university. I want to do computer information systems.

First when I went to Truman, I decided I'm gonna do accounting. I did it almost halfway and then I changed my mind. I said, "I'd better go to computers." I did both of them at the same time. So now I think I'm qualified for both accounting and computer information systems. After the graduation, May 17th [2001], with an associate degree in computer information systems, I want to go to Chicago State University. I still want to follow up if I can play basketball, if the school can take a chance and give me scholarship. That would be great. That's what I'm looking for, or just take any sport, to run, or play soccer. I will try and train again and see if I can get any scholarship to play. I will use financial aid and just continue my education.

I will be the first person in my family to graduate, even I'm not the oldest. I'm very excited. That's one of the things I would say. This is my first, and I think my brothers and sisters, none of them reached to this stage I am right now.

What I like the least, I think I didn't have fun [Laughs.] like I'm supposed to. I see friends going out to the movies, theatres, going out with friends and that's one thing I don't like that much about myself. I'm depriving myself, I don't know for what reason, but I deprive myself from that, not to go out. I make myself really busy, but there is no way I can make it less busy because I don't have a choice.

Second thing I don't like that much is sometimes, when you go to a neighborhood, people look at you. There is a connection between the whole entire black people. Not even the white, but those people from Asia. I had an incident. When we lived in that house, we used to go to this Vietnamese store. Almost all the time we used to come buy clothes, socks. Every day we used to speak to them nicely, but they used to be afraid. Every time we come in, they would just turn and get close to the telephone, every day. So one day she just came and she asked, "Where are you guys from?"

So we told her, "We are from Africa."

And she laughed and she said, "OK." The next day when we came, she said, "You know what? We used to be afraid. We thought you guys were people from the South Side, and every day we used to be afraid of you guys. We thought that you gonna rob us. That's why always when you come in, we didn't smile, we didn't give you that much of attention."

But we said, "No. We just came here."

We make friends of them after that. We used to talk every day and they said, "You guys are so nice, and we didn't think like that before." So people generalize and you've been judged or you've been targeted for something you're not and you didn't do. So that's the connection.

We all come to this place and people begin to judge you. I think it's mostly based on the color. So people will just look at you no matter whether you are African, you just came, or you've been here. We're all the same in one line, which is that we've been judged, which of course isn't [right]. But I don't care about that. I just don't go by it. If you look at me, whatever you judge me, I don't mind.

I think I make a lot of friends and I'm really happy to be here. I don't have that much of Sudanese friends, but others like Indian, Pakistani, Bangladesh, Chinese, Japanese, Americans, other Africans, Mexicans. I have a lot of friends, and even from the Middle East. My uncle used to say that popularity brings content. I don't buy that and I don't go by that, but I just like being friends to people. And most of the time when I walk with my friends in school, everyone says, "Hi,"

And my friend say, "Why people know you so much?"

I say, "I don't know. I'm just friendly and just talk to people."

Here people live apart. There is no connection that much to tie together as a family. So the gap is widening every day. And the only place you meet maybe by phone and that's a few minutes, and that's it, which of course I don't think is enough to keep relatives together. The mother, father, and brother relationship and after 18 you get out of the house and all of these things, they're kind of strange because back home, you can be twenty-something as long as you're not married, you can stay in your mother's house. So, relative relationship of father, son, brother, and sister relationship, I think it's not here that much.

Right now, I think America makes me to define myself and see things in a wider and a broader point of view than I was before. If I was to grow up in Sudan, my mind-set would be different than it is right now. So I would consider myself a Sudanese American because I still love my poor little city. I still like it.

Many people want me to marry a Sudanese, but if I find somebody that I can relate to, we have a common ground, who can understand me and I understand them, then it shouldn't be a problem.

The best part is I learned to appreciate life. Now I know that I can someday help my mom. And I think the only thing I don't appreciate from myself, is that I think I wasted my time and I didn't achieve anything within the course of the six years I've been in the United States. I don't think I achieved that much. To me I'm thinking that I did not get anything. Maybe I'm too greedy for whatever I'm looking up to or whatever I'm aiming at. But I think that I did not achieve anything, I don't have the education that I supposed to have, or I don't have any money. That's what I think, that I didn't have anything. But I have learned. I have learned. That's one reason which makes me eager to get something, because I learned. And I want to value time and I want to make something out of it. So I thought I didn't make nothing out of it. But from now on, I think I'll make something. Now I'm beginning to think and reflect back, and try to at least adjust my life and make something out of it from now on.

Sometimes I just think that life here is very easy. If you can't make it in this country, I don't think you can go any country and survive there. Trust me. It's very easy and it is straight and forward. You have to make a living. If you want to be good and better person, you can be a good person here because everything is accessible to you. You have all the opportunities to be where you want to be. So if you don't make it, I don't think you can make it anywhere else.

I'm trying to take the good part and mix it with the culture and make some changes [Laughs.] in order to be good. I don't know if I'm making mistakes, which I am, but not too many.

I'm excited to become [a citizen]. I don't think it adds anymore to what I have right now. I think from my point of view, it's just for protection purposes. It will play a major role in that, I think. Maybe for job purposes, yes, it will make a difference.

But what scares me the most is how to raise a kid here. [Laughs.] That's my biggest problem because when I was raised, when I made a mistake, I got beaten, I got punished. And I respect that and we grow up like that. It limits you to do certain things. Even though there is no flexibility between a father and mother, the discipline they bring to you, it makes you to grow up. The discipline, you grow with it and sometimes it benefits you in life. So if you do wrong, you gotta be punished. So I think I believe in that. And that's what scares me

At his graduation from Truman College with his cousin, Chicago, 2001

most. How you gonna do this in this country where if you beat your child, there's 911, the relationship with the police and all that? So it kind of scares me a little bit. I was beaten and I didn't find it so offensive or a crime.

You got hit by a stick. At times if there's no stick around, you get beaten by belt. So that's punishment. So we took a lot of punishment, but it was part of discipline. And we could not say anything. If you don't want to be beaten, then you walk on a straight line. I was not beaten that much because when I was small, I was quiet. I didn't get that much trouble. But a couple times, my friend got me in trouble and I got beaten with him, because you gotta punish both of you if you do something wrong.

To me, it was strange [that it's illegal]. Even up to now it is. But I think it's culture. So, I think they should have a little bit of exception to exercise your culture. But it's what you call the melting pot, where you want everybody to come in and melt in the American culture and American society. So that's the sort of thing taking place, which of course is very difficult for a parent from another country. Mostly African parents right now, they get in a lot of problem with this law that you can't beat your child. Your child does something wrong, you just talk to them.

[Visiting Sudan] has been in my agenda for a long time, even though

I keep postponing it and setting it to another date. That's been in my mind for a long time now and I want to make it happen. So hopefully things will work out my way and I will get it. You have to pass through a lot of struggle and difficulties, but I think it will be possible.

But hopefully within two years from now I'm thinking about going there and see if I can see my mother. Since I left, I didn't speak to her. Since '87 I didn't talk nor a letter. From '87 to '98 there was no contact whatsoever [with my family]. Even I tried to write a lot of letters, they didn't get to them. I do [think about my family] when I'm lonely. I do. The person I think most is my mom. Maybe I'm selfish, but I think she was the closest person I'm close to. And my brother, I contacted him in '98 I think. I didn't speak to my father or the rest of them except my brother in Kenya. Right now I guess and I believe that they know [where I am], because I told my brother and then I think he sent it by message.

If I tell you it's safe, then I'd be telling you a lie. It's not, exactly. It's like a no-man's-land. It's a hostile society right now. You have the rebels and you have the government in some part. It's been divided into pieces. The government is here, the rebels are here. So it's just people here, people there, and between, anyone can take over.

But there is constant thinking in my mind that I have to see my mom, from being away for a long time. And I don't know how I'm gonna get there. Even sometime when I think about it, I just get confused how I'm gonna pass through these military people and all of this to get there. But I pray and hope that one day, I will make a step to get in a plane and say that I'm heading to southern Sudan.

I still can picture her, even though I don't have a picture of her. She might be old because of the struggle she's going through right now, and hardship, and that can make you old before your time. I hope I'm gonna see her. I have that confidence she's there alive. I do very much.

DENG IS LIVING IN PORTLAND, MAINE, where he is studying for his bachelor's degree in computer science at the University of Southern Maine. He has not been back to visit his family in Sudan yet.

MY NAME IS **SERGIO SOARES** I COME FROM BRAZIL. *I am 50 years old. And I come for United States in 1996,* **AUGUST 1996.** *I born in Brazil, Rio de Janeiro, in July 22, 1948.*

ALL TIME I THINK ABOUT THIS, TO COME ONE DAY TO STUDY. My idea was, yes, college. I think about college. It was a dream for me in this period. I think only the Disney [World] and to come to study! I think about university. But in this period my father doesn't have any chance to send me, because we are five brothers, and if you send one you have to send the other. In this situation, I forgot because I think it's not possible for me. I have to go by myself. When I have opportunity, I'm going. I think about this.

I have a graduation in business administration [in Brazil]. When I went for university, I had exactly idea what was my way. I decided to go to the business administration, and I continue in the same way for all time. And I start to work young. And I get a good opportunity and I work for three big companies in this period from 20 to 46 years old. I work for one car company to build cars—car makers, truck makers, manufacture trucks. And I work for this company for four years. I work to one publisher company in magazines in Brazil, and then I start to work to the Souza Cruz, a subsidiary of British American Tobacco from England. I work for Souza Cruz for long time. I work for 18 years in this same company. And I work in different parts of the country. I was planning supply manager and I was happy during this time when I did work for this company. I was working for the company to supply the company with products, different products. I look for fertilizer to grow tobacco, spare parts, and the raw materials; and I was responsible to plan and buy materials for this company. I had one accountability, only my accountability, it was around $100 million per year. And I work in five different states. I was one top manager, like senior manager over there.

I worked more than I stayed home, because we spent a lot of time to take a plane to one city to other city. My job, I had to travel all the time. Maybe 90 percent of my time I was traveling to look for things in all part of the world. It was not hard work, but had a lot of stress. I had stress all time from the work, from trips. Because in this period, I didn't like to fly and I had to fly all time, but I did like the work.

I never think about this [coming to the United States]. I was happy over there. I had a good life. I don't have to think about nothing. Only my job and my family. I was happy. It was fantastic because I had one beautiful big house. I did construct a beautiful house in Rio de Janeiro, two blocks from the beach, and I had a good life over there. We had one house in one other beach, two hours from my home, and to spend the holidays and the weekends. We sailed. Brazil have a lot of weekends during the year! I can receive people all time, and my family, friends, and it's a permanent party.

My hobby in Brazil is travel. I and my wife traveled during one month a year. All time I did some travel for one place inside of the country or outside of the country. I crossed the South America for east, north, west, every direction. For me it's more important in my life. When I was a kid I think it was possible. In the first time when I saw the world map I ask, "Why I cannot go to this place over here by car, or by horse, or by camel?"

And ask people about that and people say, "No, it's impossible. No way. You have to cross the Amazon forest. There are Indians. People going to kill you."

And I grow up and I think, "Why I cannot do that? Why I have to by boat? Why I have to go by fly? I have to go by myself." This is my idea.

I think this all time. If I have opportunity, I'm going to cross the China, or I'm going to cross the India, or I'm going to cross another country. I need that. This is my life. When I told you I have to do

His three children asleep, Brazil, 1981

something different, maybe it is miles travel.

I like to know people. I like to know different place, cultures, jobs, what people is doing to live, what the people think, why these people live in this place, what's fun here.

And this opportunity you have when you have a trip, when you look for different place. It's very, very different what you have in your life. You are in your apartment. Everything is the same every single day. When you move to Israel to Jordan, to every place, you can see new things. You can motivate your life to do different things.

[The first time] I came to America it was interesting situation because when I was in Souza Cruz, I come to Mexico to give training to people in Mexico, in Monterrey city. When I finished my job, I had one first class ticket to come back to Brazil and I told the guy, "OK, could you change the first class to economical class and give me one way for Florida, to Miami?" It was possible because the ticket was very expensive, first class. The people change, and I come to know the United States. It was my first time. It was in 1982. It was very interesting because I didn't speak any English.

And I arrive in Miami. I didn't have any hotel. I did not book hotel. And when I arrived in the airport, I looked at one big screen with the name of the hotel and the phone number. I picked up the phone, punched the button and the guy answered, "What do you need?"

I didn't understand anything. I told, "I am in airport and I'd like to

go hotel."

The guy told me, "You have to pick up limo in front of the airport."

"Do a limo run all time?" I do not understand. I wait for three hours and I do not find the limo. I call again.

The guy, "Look, the limo! It's written the name of the hotel."

I think the limo was wait for me, but the limo is running all time! So, I arrive in hotel midnight. In this time I look for one piece of advertisement in the desk of this guy and there was written, "Tour to Disney every day, 4:00 at the morning."

It was 12:00 midnight. I told to the guy, "OK, how much is it?"

"OK, you have to pay $100 and you go to Disney. The bus come here in front of the hotel 4:00 at the morning."

I think, "OK, I have to sleep for three hours only, but it's very important for me to know Disney. I'm going." I pay the ticket. 3:30 [A.M.] the guy called me. I sit in the bus and went to Disney.

When I arrived in Disney, it's very, very incredible for me. I went to the Epcot Center. I stayed there all time, look, look, look everything. But I forgot to put my watch in the same time of the Miami. I was one hour after the Miami time.

The guy told, "OK, 9:00 [P.M.] everybody here to take the bus to Miami again." And I arrived at 10:00. So, in this period, I lost [missed] my bus.

I didn't speak English. I don't have any information where I was! It was incredible. I don't have any chance to look for opportunity. I think, "No, I'm going to call to Brazil to my family to ask for help with them." And I went to the phone number. I punched the number to collect call.

And when my mother was called, [the operator said], "You pay for phone?" My mother didn't understand.

And I told her, "Say, 'Yes!' Say, 'Yes!' The person need you to say, 'Yes!'" But she doesn't understand me. My mother hung up the phone. So I was there lost for the night. I found one guy who was speaking Spanish and explain. I speak Spanish. And I explain with the guy about my problem.

The guy, "OK, maybe you have to take another bus. One commercial bus crosses this street over there in few minutes. Maybe you go fast and take this bus to Miami." I went over there and the bus coming. And I took the bus, but the bus stopped for diverse areas.

When I arrived Miami, I didn't understand where I was. And I saw one cab. I went to the driver. I told, "OK, I have to go to my hotel, but I don't know the name because I went in hotel midnight and I didn't receive any paper, I lose everything. I have only my passport over here, money, but I don't know where is my hotel! I have to go to the airport because if I arrive airport, I can see the screen and then I can see the name of the hotel."

And the guy asked me, "Which airport are you look for?"

"I don't know. [Laughs.] Let's go to the more important one and then if not, I go to other one."

And he asked me, "Where do you come from?"

"I come from Mexico right now."

"OK, maybe you are going in the big one. Let's go to there." And we went.

When we drive, maybe drive for 10 or 15 minutes, I saw the advertisement [sign] of my hotel. I told to the guy, "Stop, stop. There is my hotel! I have to go." [Laughs.] I gave him $20.

He said, "OK."

"I'm so happy. Thank you very much." I went to the hotel. [Laughs.] My first experience.

It was funny because I'm optimist. I thought this is a good opportunity to learn things. It was very strange for me, because I have a big experience in the world. And over time, you arrive in one different city, you have to take the name, the card, of the hotel, everything. But I was so excited about this situation to come here, I forgot completely the safety law. I think, "I am in hotel, the bus come here to pick up, the bus come to leave me in front of hotel, I don't have any problem." But I forgot the watch. I forgot the time.

This was a stupid situation, and it's funny because if I ask to talk to the people, the people say, "You're a stupid guy! You have experience to travel. How you do this big mistake?" Oh, somebody makes mistakes. I did. But it's funny because I learn too much.

In the second day, I think to myself, "Now, I can go to any place in the United States. I can resolve my situation. I know everything in here to talk about things." [Laughs.] It's very interesting. I'm optimist guy. Every time when

His wife, Maria Clea, Brazil, 1985

something happen, I think a good situation's coming. If I had a bad situation, I think, "Maybe something's good in this situation. I have to learn about this." I am never unhappy, never unhappy.

I come here [again in 1996] because many, many, things happened my life during this time.

In 1991, I had one car accident with my wife, and my wife died. It was one weekend and we decided go to the one Japanese restaurant. And I was with her, and on expressway one car come fast and crash us in our back in high speed. And she died two days after in hospital because in this period, the hospital was in strike. Hospital was not working because the doctors was on strike and doesn't have any help for us. And she stayed for many hours waiting for help. And when the doctor come to help her, it was late because she had brain problem.

I broke inside of me a lot of parts, my arms, I broke my ear, and I had to take plastic surgery in my face to rebuild my face. I had different surgeries for many times during six months. And during this period I didn't work, I stayed home.

My son was 10 years old. My daughters, 15 and the other 17. My daughters respond well. My son had problem after this, because during this situation, he never cry and he never talk about his mother. It was very hard for him. And he is very sensitive. It is so hard for him because he was together with her all time. He was youngest and she was good mother, excellent mother—the mother who help the son for everything, help to school, help for everything. It was a big loss for him, big loss.

It's hard for me, too, because I think of this all time. I can't understand what happened. It was so fast. My idea is some people come in wrong time, in wrong date, in wrong period, in wrong space. And people come here for short time to do something and go out for different reason. These people, they are special people, like the people who do dangerous things, like the people who go to the mountain. They are different peoples. And sometimes the people die, but do not die. They go to the other side of the line and come back.

We cannot understand why. I think I went to the other side and I come back because when I had the same car crash, I think I died. I feel dead! Suddenly, I come back. I make this question for me, "Why I? Why not her?" Because I think if was her, will be best for everybody because I had a big insurance. If I dead, maybe she and my child will be in good, fantastic situation right now because I had a big insurance. And I do not understand why I and not her, why her, not I. No idea. Maybe something is right about this, I had to stay here. Maybe I can help my child more than her. I'm not sure about this. I can't understand. Sometimes I ask to myself why I am here, what I'm doing in this situation.

When we started together we were small. She was 14 and I was 16 and [we] never went separate for long, long time. She did three universities. She was economist, she was a lawyer, and she was a teacher. She teach math for high school. And she had private kindergarten, day care for kids. Do you remember I told about my house, the big house over there? She changed this house in one big day care. She was dynamic. Good mother, good person. Completely happy woman. If you read her letters, you do not believe because she wrote very well, beautiful letters, beautiful books. One day I'm going to put everything together. She wrote things very interesting about the spirit. For her it was so important because she discovered herself.

When I lose her, it killed me, it killed me. I stay six months inside of the house. My life changed completely. It's very interesting. I am an optimist guy. Every time when something happens, I think good situation's coming. If I had a bad situation I think, "Maybe something's good in this situation." I have to learn about this.

I decided do not travel anymore because I decide to stay with my son and my daughters at home. It's hard, because my problem is I was not prepared to take care them. It's very hard for a man who travels all time, and I didn't have any experience to care child. Relatives stayed in my home to take care them. My uncle and his wife stayed over there to help me.

And I went to the company and told about this. And after six months, everything changed in the company. And when I come back to work, I found different situation over there.

I told them I cannot continue in the same situation. I had to look for a new opportunity.

When I talked this, the president told me, "Yeah, it's a hard decision for us, and maybe you have to quit because we don't have any space for you in different area." And I told them in this period it will be too hard for me because all people is over three legs. One leg is your health, the other leg is your family, and the other leg is your job. When you lose one leg, you disestablish your life. I lose three legs at the same time. I lose my family, and I lose my job, and I lose my health because I had to do some surgery to complete. So, I don't have any leg in this period, and I told them about this, and, [there was] no chance for me because no area to change.

So, in this situation I think myself, "I have to do something. I have to eat. I have to take a business."

My brother is a nuclear engineer. My brother talk to me, "No, I'm not going to still work for nuclear plant. I'm going to do my own business." And we start one wood company. We bought one small company and we increase investment over there. And this company still increased all year. Increase, increase, increase. We were well. We buy wood from Amazon forest, and the guy send wood and give us in Rio de Janeiro. We cut and prepare to do furniture, to do house, to do everything.

I never had any information about this [before]. We found this company from one friend. This guy decided to sell this company and it was in a good place near my home. I don't have to drive for any place, and I can learn about this, and I went to Amazon to learn. I stay over there for few periods, and I learn about wood. And I bought machineries and I start work. And we increased, and we started one transport company because in this period we had to pay for transport. It was very expensive. Sometimes the transport were more expensive than the wood. And I told my brother, "Maybe we can buy trucks and we can create a new company, about trucks company, and we can bring things to Amazon and come with our wood." And we do it.

We transport oil for Shell and Texaco to Amazon, and come with wood. We started nice and I liked to drive truck. Sometimes I was to Amazon to buy wood and relax, because it was very nice to drive to go to Amazon. We spent about 15 days driving from Rio to Amazon to go and to come back. It's long distance, around 3,000 miles to go, 3,000 miles to back, but very beautiful trip, very, very beautiful trip. And we started with two trucks, big trucks.

In this period, one of these trips, I take one truck and I had one accident with my truck and I fell in one *rio* [river]. I was completely full with oil. I completely destroyed the truck. The insurance paid, but the truck was destroyed. And when happened, my daughters said, "OK father, you cannot do this anymore. It's not your job. You have to look for us. We are alone. If you die, what we're going to do?"

I told, "OK, it's real situation. I'm not doing anymore." And I finished.

And in this period, I start a new job in the same line. We started one construction company because I have wood. I know how work with wood right now. I can contract to people when you need to construct your house or rebuild. We start increase again. In this period we are in a good situation again.

And one day, it was in 1994, I worked late. It was around 8:30 in the evening. I bought one new car for my daughter and I told her, "Do not go with this car to the school." She was in the Japanese school to learn Japanese. "And go with the pick-up because the pick-up has insurance. In this new car I didn't have time to pay insurance. Tomorrow I'm going to do this. I'm going to close our business and then go home. That's it." OK, she went with the pick-up and I stayed with her car. So, when I closed the door to go out, one guy with a big gun is waiting for me. One gangster kidnapped me, and put inside of the car and go to a strange place, and put something in my eyes. I can't [see] nothing, and put one gun here. [Points to his side.] Two guys in the car.

And he told me, "You have to pay for your life right now."

I told him, "I don't have nobody to negotiate with you my life because you are wrong. You make mistake. I don't have any money. I am worker. Nobody can talk with you about me. I have only my son. He's young. How you going to take money?" I think he made mistake.

With his daughter, Paula, and sister-in-law at his beach house, Brazil, 1989

Maybe he was looking for another person, not me. And I was $5,000 in my purse.

"You have money, you have to pay money. You have to pay money right now. Go to the cash station." He saw my card in my purse, "You have to take money right now."

"I don't have money."

So, the guy put one gun again. "If you not, we going to kill you right now. You have your car. You have everything. And you have your cellular telephone. We are going to look for your house, telephone house, and going to kill your son or your family."

And I told him, "OK." What I'm going to do? And I have two accounts. One account of my company and account of my private account. And I went over there. I had $5,000 with me. I gave my car, my new car, and I gave more money from cash station. The total was $25,000. And I stay with this guy for eight hours. And after this he put again one thing on my eyes and leave me in one different place.

I had opportunity to pick up the gun from this guy for two or three times, because the guy was so nervous when I stayed with them. And I removed the things in my eyes, and I saw the gun, and the guy looked outside of the car all time to look for police or something like this, and the gun stayed in front of me. And my intention is pick up his hand and take his gun, but I didn't have courage to do this. And this makes me feel bad because I didn't have courage. Yes, I think I die. Why I'm not picking up his gun and try to create opportunity for my life? And I stayed quiet. And it was so hard for me because, I think I don't have courage, because I do not take the gun. And after I think more, more and more. I think, "No, I had a good decision." Because if I did, in this period, I was not sure about this guy going kill me or not. But now I know I had a good decision. But the same time, my brain thought, "You don't have courage. You are not a hero. You're weak." But I'm alive. [Laughs.]

When happened this, it was big and too hard for me, because during months all day during my sleep, I think about this. I can't sleep more. It start make a big pressure. And the company stayed down after this because it was small company to pay $25,000. It's money to pay suppliers, to pay everything. We had no money like this. In this situation I had to sell my house, my beautiful house, which I construct for long time.

All this moved my brain, started move my emotional condition, and I started think about leave the country. I think I cannot continue to live off nothing. I lose money, I lose my house and I have to go out. And the other situation was the corruption over there.

I have to explain about corruption. My son worked with me over there. And I put his name with employee. And he started work with 14 years old. So, his name is over there. One guy from work department went over there to look for paper to look the name of my son. He told, "This guy doesn't have 18 years old. He's small [young], but no problem. But you have to take one specific paper to authorize him work."

I told, "But I am the father. I'm authorize him working."

"No, but you have to take this paper over here."

"But I am his father. He's work with me over here."

"No, if you not, you have to pay $1,000." And he looked for one fire extinguisher. One fire extinguisher was empty. "Oh, you have to pay $1,000 more because the fire extinguisher doesn't stay full." And he went into the lockers, where employee put lockers. And I have 15 employees and I had only 10 lockers. "You have to put more five lockers because…" When he finished I have to pay $5,000. And he told me, "OK, no problem. Give me $2,000 and I'll forget it." All time I had the same problem. All time.

[My friend], he came [to the United States]. This guy, who I work for right now [in Chicago], is very interesting story because this guy, I contracted this guy to Souza Cruz! He was my trainee over there! I hired this guy and I started train this guy. And he came. After few years, this guy started to work in one cleaning company in Boston, and I called him. I provoked this. He's owner about this company. I talked with him. And he has difficulty to look for manager right now because the country is in good economic situation. And he needed take people who trust. And he put advertising in newspaper, interview, but he cannot find people with same character like me. And he needed people who speak English, and who speak Spanish, and who speak Portuguese. And this is very hard to look for this, and who has experience, too.

They invited me, "OK, I have a good opportunity for you here. You can help me. I need you. Could you come?"

I told him, "Yes. I'm not in a good situation over here. I'm going to close my business. I quit. I quit Brazil. I don't believe in this country. I don't believe in government. I don't believe this country can reduce the corruption. No, I quit. I have to stay happy. I don't have to [can't] think I'm going to lose my money the next day. I buy a ticket. I'm going. That's it."

His father with the logging truck, Brazil, 1993

The family asked, "What are you going to do there?"

I told them, "I'm going to change things to do, because in this situation over here, I don't have anything. I don't believe more stay here. When you do not believe, you have to look for another place."

They said, "OK, let's go your way. You have to look for a new way. That's it."

And Igor [my son] was here in this period. He was in Minnesota in the high school. "I'm going to there and I'm going to live with Igor."

I am alone with my son in United States [now]. It's very, very nice. More I am doing it for him. And I have to work to help him. He's a good guy. He's happy to live with me, and I am happy with his decision how he's living.

So, this company is my sponsor. When I came here, he was my sponsor to legalize my situation. He gave me the work permit. And he is my sponsor. I cannot work for other company before I receive my green card. I don't have any intention to change.

We had two situations. One good situation for me, one good situation for him. It's a business, and I think the life is a business. The relationship is one thing. But now I am working for him. He's the owner. Now, this guy is my boss. He pays me and I work. That's it. Alright. We have a good relationship. It's different, not like before. I am employee. The world change and the life change. I feel well.

I arrive here one day. Two days after, I started working. September 9, 1996. Normal day, yes. Like I was in my home. Only the different thing is now when I start to work tomorrow, if I receive some money, I have the money to do something. In Brazil right now, if I receive the money now, I can lose the money next day. That's it. The difference is that.

When I come, I stay in my boss home for four months and I started one [English] course in Elgin. And one teacher over there, I told her, "Oh, I'd like to change, move to Chicago. And you have any idea which college I can look for to help my English?"

"Oh, I have this information." He gave me the Truman College name, and I come here and it was easy. I started there in level 3, and I was fast. It was good. I am completely comfortable when I stay there [Truman], completely comfortable. I am happy. I am so happy all time. I improve all time, I know. And it's very important for me. Now, it's hard for me to go to the school because sometimes I work to 2:00, 3:00 in the morning. But when I go to school, I am happy. I'm going to improve my English. I have one decision. I have to go because I like go. If I not go, I'm unhappy, something is wrong. It's very interesting, this. If I do not go to school, something is wrong with me. The day started wrong. I know this school. I like the people. I know everything. It's like one house. I am comfortable when I stay over there. It protects me. It's my feeling when I stay there.

I work with American people all day. The people correct me all time. "OK, thank you very much. I make mistake."

I have a friend, he told, "I'm going to fire you because you cannot speak English well."

"OK, fire me. You have to wait here and look for me again, because nobody going to work for you. You cannot explain well!" I told him. [Laughs.]

My problem here, I think is the more important things for everybody who comes from another country, is the relationship, the relationship. Look, when you go to make new friend, it's very hard. I try to go to the single bars to look for a girl, to dancing, to things like that. When we approach to start talk about your life, if you do not speak a good English, the most of the people don't like talk with you! It's different in other countries. In Brazil, if you talk to a different people, the people like to talk with you to learn. But here, no. The people don't have patience to speak slowly or to teach you about things. And then, most of the people go to this place stay alone, come back alone. It's

hard. If you ask to immigrant people, "What is your most important problem over here," the people say, "The relationship. I can't have a relationship." In this situation, the people look for the same, to make a private relationship when you can. For me it was hard because I can talk with the people for a few minutes, but I can't maintain or improve relationship because the people is thinking in another things.

And now I'm going to stay home on my computer. [Laughs.] A friend! I have my computer, and I improve things to cover this empty space. But it's still hard.

When I started use the Internet too much, I reduced my contact with people. I have to change that right now. I have to decide if I'm not going outside of my home, it will be bad for me in few months. Because now, I like to come to my home to look for things outside by Internet, not with my eyes, about the Internet eyes. And I am losing things. I am losing friends, I am losing time, I am losing everything. I have to modify my system of life, fast. And when I ask about the situation, I think, "No, I have one door. If I cannot go to the China right now, my door is the Internet." This is my problem. I am using the wrong door right now. I have to change my door. I have to open my door and close the Internet. That's it.

The people here is more closed. The people think in themselves. I have American friend and ask him, "Do you know what is happening in other country?" The people doesn't know nothing what is happening in other country. The people live and think in shopping, and your dog, and your food. Most of the American people don't think about the world. Only this thing, I think, is different. Not 100 percent, but most of the normal people, the common people. I am teaching people to improve new opportunity of the life, open brains, [and they teach me] about America. I like exchange things. I can teach you that, you teach me that. You can live in good opportunities.

My responsibility is with accept the culture. This is more important. I'm not going to live here if I do not agree with the culture. The first of all, I have to accept that. Now I have to live like American people. If I have this opportunity, I can stay happy because I am American people. I think like that. When you think, when you construct your life, when you accept the culture, it's very easy. I'm not going to fight with nothing. One day, Igor talked with me. We went to pick up something, and he stopped his car and received a ticket. I told him, "That's it. You are learning. This is the culture. You learn the culture or you cannot live here."

I'm going to become a citizen. I think that. This is my objective because I don't have any intention to come back to Brazil to live there. I have intention to go to Brazil to vacation, to stay with family, and that's it. But if I have to construct something it's in this country, because in this country you can plan. You can have opportunity. You can have help. If you want to do something, you can do that. But I am Brazilian. I have to stay Brazilian.

It was so happy for me, this opportunity, because I believe in this country. I believe the opportunities. I like the freedom. I like the human rights. I can go to street if I'm not agree, "I do not agree with that. I am going to look for my attorney to look for my rights." I can do that. This is very important. I believe that. I have to respect the people, but people have to respect me. This is more important things which I think.

The people talk about freedom, but the people do not understand exactly what is freedom. You have to stay in a freedom place, but it's important that the other countries, the other place have to be freedom, too. If not, you never will be freedom. If the people there don't have a good country, a good life, they come here to damage you. It's like in Brazil. Do you know about *favella?* It's where the poor people live in the hill. The ghetto. It's different things when you live in the ghetto. In Brazil, the ghetto is the top of the mountain. There, you stay there in the ghetto, and you look at the people in the top of the building. The people are there, good food, swimming pool, beautiful women, beautiful place, everybody drink. And you are in a poor house, no food, no drink, nothing. You look there. You want to go there. If you do not go there in peace, maybe you are going to there to rob them.

You [the United States] are a bad people for the others. You are. You think you have good things, you have a good intention, but the people when they look at you, "No, come on. Let's go. This guy is American."

I think Americans need to learn about that. For me, I understand that more. I know the bad countries. I know the freedom countries. And I know what the people think about that. You cannot be free if the others is not free. This is the situation.

His mother and family, Chicago, 2001

I feel comfortable in Chicago. It's my life. It's my space. I am in other country, but here is my space. It is important. When you have this, you can move your life too easy. I don't have money to spend like I spend before, but I have money. I organize my life. In Brazil it is impossible. You can't see a few years in front. You have to see your one day after. In United States, you can plan your life. Fantastic. I have a plan. You don't have corruption to construct a future.

I have to try now. I come here because I believe in this country. I believe in the serious country and if you work, if you are honest, you can take a good life. You pay your tax, you do your job well, you have a good life. I come here to stay here. I do not come here to make money and come back. I come here to stay, to do my life, to turn my life.

Now I am to buy a building to rebuild, and I'm going to live in one flat and I'm going to rent the others. Maybe I have to do something new. A friend of mine, he came from Brazil and he lives here a long time, he ask, "Why are you buying one building and you have to work a lot to rebuild it?"

I told him, "Two things is important for me. First, I am sure I'm going to make money doing that. And second one, I have to do something to do different. It's opportunity right now. Look, this building, I rebuild in United States. I did something."

I have to talk with my son. My son have to talk with his son, "Oh, you know my dad? My dad did that."

I don't like when the people born, the people grow, the people study, the people create a family, raise a family, and die. This for me is completely unhappy life. If I do not do something different, I am going to die unhappy. I have to do anything different. I have to construct anything. I have to leave something and the people say that, "Oh, Sergio Soares did that before, or Sergio Soares wrote about that, or Sergio Soares constructed that." I have to do something different.

I am 50 right now, but my brain I don't believe that. I am not 50. For me, I am starting. All time I am starting. The age is not big deal.

With his son, Igor, and daughter, Sabrina, Chicago, 1997

I have to do another thing different. I know how to sail. I sailed in Brazil. My idea is, I'm going to prepare to do this trip. I'm going to buy a boat, maybe next year. And I'm going to learn with a course, I can see this in the Internet. But my trip will not go from United States to Brazil only. I'm going to do different things. I'm going to see different place. In Brazil, [they] have place you can arrive there only by boat. I have to know the Fernando de Noronha Island. It's my objective. I'm going to stay there for few days. Because all nature live there, and I have to know this place.

I never show nothing about my past life. Because if I show, the people do not believe, if I show the picture of my house, or the place I live. The guy who is my boss, who invites me to come here, he was my employee before and he knows my life. He is from the rich family there. We had a good relationship in Brazil and he knows my house. He went in my house every time. For him, he understands about that.

He left his good life over there to come here to work hard, too. For him it's more easy to understand that. But he asked me how I am feeling. And the answer is: I can construct again. This is simple. I'm not thinking about what happened there. I can do again. It's not difficult. And I am going to do. [Laughs.] If not this year, maybe the next year. I am sure, completely sure about that. You have to create opportunities. That's it. When you have this thing it's very easy, the life. I can stay here. I can read a book. I can sleep well because I know tomorrow I'm going to do again. Simple.

One day, I was driving to work and I was playing a song and I thought, "Wow, it was a bad day for me because maybe I'm not going to buy my apartment," when I received the information about the mortgage broker, but I am singing. I think, "Why I am singing because I have a bad day?" And I answer to myself, "Oh, because tomorrow I'm going to resolve these things. It's not a big deal." [Laughs.]

The problem is you need have courage to do that, because when you leave your family, it's so hard. When you start that, the first year is hard because you think in your family. This is very difficult. And the people depend of the family. The people can come here for short time to make money, come back. But I'm not talking about these people. In my situation, my wife is dead. I don't have anything, anything. I have to rebuild my life. My kids, my children, I don't think about that because they can come when they decide. They're adults.

This is my life here. It's not more than I explain here. It's simple life, but it's a positive life. And I think if I'm not doing right now, I'm going to do tomorrow. And I'm going to prepare in that my first step is this building which I am buying. This building will be my step to create a new opportunities, or new buildings, or money to do anything different. This is my objective, and I'm going to do that, maybe in small time. I am preparing my plan to the future. And I stay very happy when I sit in my computer to look for things to complete my plan, to construct my new life and release my plan.

SERGIO OWNS AN INDUSTRIAL CLEANING COMPANY and lives in Lindenhurst, Illinois.
He is shopping for sailboats to sail to Brazil. He is the father of a new baby girl.

MY NAME IS LUISA CARDENAS I'M FROM CHILE. I CAME IN '93. *[I was born] November 10th, '49 in the south, Puerto Montt. It's a big city. It's together with sea. It's a port.*

I REMEMBER MY CITY ALWAYS BEAUTIFUL IN THAT TIME. BEAUTIFUL. Always the sun shining. Have the mountains, the lakes, rivers, the sea. It's beautiful. Always I remember my father and my mother when we went to the beach, when I went to visit my uncles in the fields. A very, very good time.

My mother is a kind of people serious, but she has always *paz* [peace] inside, always. She believes in God. She always hope everything will be good. My mother is very good. It's like me. Is my better friend.

I remember my father, a great person because he had a lot of imagination and strong. He was strong, decided, determined. My father was different, very, very different. My father always was laughing, was *alegre,* happy.

Always in my life I think I learned from my father and my mother: Everything you want to reach, you can. In my life I think everything I can reach.

They got married very young, very, very young. My mother was almost 15, my father 17. My father when I born, maybe 19. When they got married, they had nothing. When they got married, they didn't have a store. They was a people who buy in the street. They make money, they buy a store, a little store. After they make more money, they bought bigger store. My mother and my father worked in the store. [Laughs.] Food, vegetable, fruit, clothes, everything. Always I admire my mother and my father because they did reach a lot of things.

Other thing, my father and my mother always was talking with my teacher, going to the school. Always they participate in the activities in my class with my teacher, with my friends, always. They are very, very good parents. With my friends they are very nice.

I liked to sing in the choir. I was the better voice in the choir when I was nine years. In that time, I start to learn to play the guitar. A friend of my father give me a guitar. I like the music. I like all music. I cry when I hear the symphony orchestra. I can cry. I like it. My three

uncles, they have a guitar in their house. My father, when I was 11, he bring a teacher at my house to teach me notes in the guitar. Many, many hours. I remember my uncle Armando, my uncle Chano, they played together the guitar. They sing and play. I like it. Other uncle who lived in other city, his name is Juan, he played the guitar, too, and his son played the guitar, the accordion and *arpa* [harp]. I remember always when I was very, very young I was singing and I like it always.

When I was 12 or 13, [I stopped playing because] one day somebody, a friend in my class, told me, "Luisa, you play the guitar and I sing in the theatre."

I told her, "It's OK." She sing, I play the guitar. We practiced before. When I went the theatre, I began to play the guitar, but she forgot the song. She sing another tune. I was very, very embarrassed. I decided never I play the guitar! [Laughs.] At home, I told my father, "I want to play piano. I want to learn."

He told me, "I don't think so."

"Why?" I told him.

"Because never I can buy a piano."

"OK." When I was 16, I get my guitar again. Never I left my guitar. [Laughs.]

I studied to be teacher. We give test and when we were 12 or 13 years, we went to the school. Finish the six years, we were a teacher. Nobody had a problem with me, my teacher, nobody. I was a good student again. I wanted to be a teacher. I wanted to [be] teacher for me and for my parents. Always I was planning to do activities, artistic activities. I organized different activities in my class. I graduated in December. In March I was working at the school, rural, not in the city.

The name of the place is Correntoso. In that time when you was the first time a teacher, you can't work in the city. Every people go outside, and me, too. [I was] excited. We were prepared for that.

I was lucky because I met a school, a modern school. A beautiful building, new building. The principal in that school was intelligent people, good people. Together, we work 10 teachers. I was very lucky. For five months I was substitute in that school. And one day, I call somebody and he told me I get my real school. Another place so far from my home, a little, little place. One teacher, just me. This school is on an island, a small island. Not electricity, nothing. In that school has 10 children. Those children for two years didn't have teacher! When I get this school, when I walk in the road, a little road, the children when they saw me, they *esconderse* [hide]. I told, "Hi." Nobody said me, "Hi." They were embarrassed. That time was very difficult for me. I get a depression because I was alone. Nobody speak with me. I sleep in a room. In the corner was my bed. Nobody speak with you. It was very difficult.

I was teaching. I was cooking. I was making the housekeeping. Everything I did. [The children were] between six and twelve together [in one class]. [Laughs.] Some morning the principal, he told me, "Luisa, come my office because I have a news for you."

"What happened?" I say.

"Come. I tell you." When I get the office he say, "Luisa, sit down."

"What happened?"

"Luisa, do you want to come back the Correntoso school?" The first school.

I say, "Why?"

"Do you want? Yes or no."

I say, "Yes!"

"OK, Monday you can go."

I say, "You are kidding."

"No, it's true."

I was very, very happy, happy! The next Monday I go there. I stayed for five years in that place. Electricity, everything. We can make many activities, a modern school. Very, very beautiful.

That year in February I got married, in '73. When I was studying, for my summer holidays I went to my uncle's house in a place at the north. I met my husband in that uncle's house. He was a friend of my cousin. I was 19. After four or five years, we get married. I was working in that school when we got married. He worked in other city. By bus, almost two hours [away]. Every time we were separate. We met just the

With her two daughters, Maria Luisa and Maria Angélica, Chicago, 1999

weekend, Friday to Sunday.

In September [1973] was when Pinochet get the power. September 11 was the military pronunciation. That day was the teacher's day in Chile. Monday the 10th, I went to school because I had to help the children to make the celebration to the teachers. When I went to get the bus, nobody else. My other teachers, always we went together in the same bus. That day nobody was in the bus. I ask, "Why?" In that time everything was confused. Nothing worked normally. So I went in the bus. Just me I get the school that day. I live near the school. Very, very close. In the morning before 7:00 I was listening to my radio, the news, and I think something was bad because it was different. At 7:30 maybe, I heard the first news when Pinochet or somebody else was talking about what happened in the country. When I heard that, I cried because I know what happened with that. Every 15 minutes in the radio we can hear about what happened in the country. The military were talking.

They say in the radio, "Nobody go to work. Nobody go to school. Nobody leave your house. Stay. Every people stay in their house." So, I think the worst for my father because my father was a *concejal* [city councilman] in the city. In that time, I know about what happened if somebody get the power. Every of us know about that because we had a group, we talk about, we read other experience in other countries. We know what happened about that. The first thing, I think my father was dead because I saw before that day in my country, I saw a lot of *violencia* [violence]. One day there was a group of women in the house. [They] had a picture of Allende. I saw a lot of people walking in the street. When they saw the women, they stop the march and I saw when they began *tirar* [to throw] stones. When I saw that, I stopped, and I stayed in the front of the door in other house. I saw everything what happened. Somebody get a revolver, a gun. He began to shoot [the women] through the window. I listened to the women who was screaming. Very, very confused. I saw in their [the crowd's] face *odio*, hate. For that I knew they can kill.

I went where was other teacher. Her husband had a truck. I heard on the radio there isn't buses, there isn't nothing. I went where my friend was. I say, "Please, bring me my house."

He said, "I can't. I can't. You heard the radio. I can't!"

"OK," I say. I went my bedroom. In that time I was five months pregnant. I put in a bag some things and so I walk to my city, 32 kilometers. I walk and walk and walk and walk and walk. I left at 9:00. I get to my house 4:00. Just I drink a glass of water. Somebody in the middle of my walk gave me a glass of water. No cars. No people. I was walking in the road, so I was crying, crying, and crying. I was very angry because I know we didn't do anything bad. "Why was happening that?" When I get five kilometers before my house, were the military. I was very, very angry.

They say me, "Stop."

I say, "Why stop?"

"I need to see what you bring in your bag."

"OK," I say, "Here it is!" I throw.

One of them told me, "Be careful. Be careful."

I say, "Why be careful?"

So they saw my bag and say me, "OK, go ahead."

I remember one hour before I get my house, my shoes, I lost the soles. I was walking in this way. One hour before I get my house, began raining. When I get my house, I open the door and my mother said, "What happened?"

"Where is my father, mom?" My mother hug me and the water of my clothes fell in the floor, a lot of water in the floor. All of my clothes were wet. My father wasn't in the house. He went to my uncle because every people was thinking the military would get them.

My mom tell me, "Your father is with your uncle. Don't worry about." So, every people was afraid. My mother was crying.

The next day when I was alone in my house, maybe it was 7:00 in the evening, I heard the door. Somebody knock in the door. I went to open. Before I open I heard a click, when the people put the machine gun, to prepare. I opened the door. My house was in the corner. I opened the door and all the street was the military. All of them were with the machine gun ready to shoot. One military told me they had to review the house. "OK," I said, "go ahead." Looking for I don't know, arms or papers. He asked for my father. I said, "I don't know." They stayed in my house two hours.

You know what? Never I was scared. I was angry. Angry and frustrated. Scared, no. Angry, every time angry, angry because I knew what kind of people was my father, my mother, my other family. My father every time was thinking how to help other people. He always wanted to build not to [destroy]. I couldn't understand that. For that, every time I was angry, very, very angry.

My father always before that was a happy people. Every of my friend want to go to my house because my father every time joking, joking. My friends always enjoy, laugh, always say me, "Luisa, your father is a nice people. Your mother is a nice people." He was an active people. For example, he organized a team of football in the country, in the different countries, soccer in different countries. A lot of people know my father.

After that day, my father changed. My father changed his personality. After that day he can't move from my house. The military get my father and put in the jail. I don't remember how many days. They say, "OK, go." Again the jail. A couple of days or months, I don't remember, they say, "OK, go." My father was sick psychologically. We, too.

I think never my father was the same person. I remember my father worrying, not happy. You understand me, different. I saw my father looking at the window, look and look at the window. I think he lost his happiness.

My sister came United States together with her husband [in 1976] because her husband was in jail almost three years. He was president of the young people's organization in the city. They give the chance to go outside of country. From the jail, he went the train. The military take him to Santiago. In Santiago, he stayed in the jail. The military take to airport.

My brother was young in that time. He went Argentina. [He was]

19 or 20. My father, my mother, and me stay there alone, sad. My sister never came back to Chile. My brother never came back to my country. He lives in Argentina now. I think that made my father lose the happiness. Our family always was very, very united.

[Pinochet] has the responsibility. He destroyed my family. They didn't kill nobody, not my brother, my father, but destroyed my family. My father was a people who always fight in the life. He was very, very optimist people. He was a people who looked always ahead, so I told you, I think after September 11 [1973] my father was other people.

Maria Angélica born in November 25 [1973]. My husband lost his job. Then, always I thought when my first children born I was [would be] very happy. Nothing like that happened, because every people was worried about my father, about my sister, about everything because all of my family was worried about Pinochet, about other people.

When Maria Angélica born, always I was singing to my daughter. I make my own song. I sing. I sing with her when she was very, very baby. Always I was talking to her, singing and telling stories. I remember she just looked at me. [Laughs.]

[I started teaching again] in the same school until Maria Angélica was a couple years because I was waiting for my second daughter. I liked that school. I lived with my daughter in the country, in Correntoso.

When Maria Luisa born [two years later], I changed my city. I moved back to my city. After that, I was teaching science and music in the city. I live with my mother, my father, and my husband.

I remember one day, [my sister] sent me a paper in an envelope. I received it. I open and I see a paper about immigration. I was angry. I call my sister, or she called me, I don't remember. I told her on the phone, "Why you send that paper? I don't want go to United States."

She said me, "Luisa, don't be angry, don't be angry because some day you can decide to come United States."

I say, "I don't think so."

She told me that day, "Luisa, fill, fill, fill the paper. Send the paper. You never know what happen."

I say, "OK, [but] you know, I don't want to go United States."

She said, "I know, [but] you just fill."

I did.

The life in that time was very difficult. I give example. The principal in the school one day say me, "Luisa, I want to organize a choir." That was the first time I work with a choir. I didn't know how. I practice with the children, practice, practice. I can't.

I went to the principal, I say, "Mrs. Olivia, the children, they can't go to sing in the festival."

"Why not?"

"Because they can't learn the song."

So, two or three weeks after that, I receive a letter from the principal in the city. "Teacher Luisa, come my office."

When I go I say, "What happened?"

"Why you didn't present the choir." I explained to him. But he said, "Why?"

"Because the children didn't learn."

He told me, "Your principal say different thing."

"What she say?"

"You didn't want the choir."

"Why not?"

"Because you are against of the government."

I say, "What?"

"She told me that."

I say, "It's not true."

So I had a big, big problem with the principal in the school. That day, I cry.

He ask me, "Did you support Allende?"

I say, "No, no I *did*. I *do* again if he stay here. I mean it's not past, because my ideas are the same. Now is the same as the past."

He say, "That is dangerous what you say."

I say, "I know, [but] I'm honest because never I did nothing bad."

So, he told me, "Luisa, you are very young, so I see you are very decided [determined]. You are very honest. Don't have *miedo* [fear]. I hope you always be honest like you are now."

So after the meeting, nobody speak with me. Nobody say nothing. I was a big depression. I lost in one month, maybe 10 pounds.

In that time, if you was support Allende, nobody can speak with you because every people were scared. For example, if you support Allende, and if I was your friend, so now I'm not going with you because the military can get you.

My father died '84. My father died from [a heart attack]. Nobody was prepared of that. My mother got a big depression. Me, too. She cried every day. Me, too. She fight with me, and I fight with she. My father had a store. My mother couldn't [run] the store. Then, my sister told me and my mother, "Come to United States." My mother say, "Yes," because she think that was the way to forget, to change. Then, my mother come to United States. When my mother come, my father was dead one year. I was alone with my two daughters, with my husband. I feel really, really alone. Everyone of my family was far from me.

In October '91, I went the doctor. He say me I have cancer. After the treatment, I get again a depression. Then, the doctor say me it was better for me to stay together with my family. My mother say me, "Why not come United States?"

I say, "I don't know. I don't know." So, I began thinking about that. After five months, I decided to come. The plan was, I come first with my two daughters. I say my husband, "I want to go United States. What do you think?"

He say me, "I say, 'Yes,' what you decide." I say it's better for me because I was very, very depressed. I was thinking staying together with my mother was better for me.

I come in '93 with my two daughters, and my husband stay in Chile. It was better he wait in Chile, because in my country I had my house.

So, I remember especially a friend, a teacher in the school where I work, when I went to the room to say good-bye. His name is Ramón. "Ramón, I'm going."

"OK, Luisa. Just a minute. Children, the teacher Luisa is going to United States." All of the children were listening. "Luisa, I want to say I think you will have a good life in United States."

"Why?" I say, "Why?"

"Because I know you. I think where you go, you reach all you want." I say, "Thank you, Ramón."

"It's true. It's true, Luisa. Because all of us know you."

Always I remember to Ramón.

That day I left my house about 2:00. I was very nervous, excited. A lot of friends and my daughters went the airport. I remember many people in the airport, my uncles, my cousins, my husband, the friends of my daughters, a big group in the airport. I saw my daughters, they are happy, excited! I was a little happy, a little sad, because I was thinking I would come for three years, four years, no more. Never I think I stay a long time in United States, never. So, for that, I wasn't very, very sad, no. It was different. I remember the friends of my daughter. They are very excited and happy, "Oh, Maria Luisa, you go United States. Write me please! Don't forget me, please!" Everyone was very, very happy.

I remember I was thinking in airport, "When I come back? What I do in United States?"

They was waiting for me in the airport. When I get the airport,

With her granddaughter, Gabriela, Chicago, 2000

I saw my mother over there and my sister. My sister and my mother come to me, hug me. All of us were crying. My mother was very, very happy. She say me, "Luisa, this was my dream. Now it's real." My sister, too. They were very, very happy. I was happy. I don't know how describe the feeling. Maybe nervous, but I was very, very happy.

The airport. Wow! It's enormous. Here the train in the airport, the buses, a lot people. I see from the window a lot the airplanes, ready to fly. Other thing, different people. Chinese, Japanese, American people, Hispanic people, how they speak in the airport. I heard English, other languages. I don't know what they were speaking. That, I like. That thing was surprise for me here.

The expressway when you see the Chicago Loop, that was beautiful. One day we were going to downtown in the expressway, my daughters, too. We were in the expressway. Over there I can see all the buildings spectacular, super, super beautiful.

Was a surprise for me, the trees in the street, because in my country I didn't see enormous trees all in the street. Remember I came when the leaves are green. For me that was very, very beautiful.

The stores. I was surprised. When my mother bought something, she bring to her house. If she didn't like, she return. Nobody had problem, "OK, it's OK."

I said my mother the first time, "Mommy, you can do that?"

She say, "Yes." Because in my country when you buy something, you buy it! That's all. You can't return. Maybe you can change, that is all. That was a surprise for me.

I thought the American people was friendly, because when I was in the street the first days, many people, "Hi. Hi." In my country, no. You say, "Hello," when you know people. Never you say, "Hi," to people who you didn't know. That was a surprise.

I was helping the summer school in the church June, July, and August. After that, I was a baby-sitter for American people a couple months. [Laughs.] I laugh because she speak with my sister, because I didn't understand nothing. Then my sister say me, "Luisa, this lady say when the children sleep, you can sleep, you can take a nap." [Laughs.] That was very strange for me. That was very, very funny. She say when the children was sleeping, I can take nap because she want the people who care for their children was [to be] very, very relaxed and not tired to continue to care for their children. That is strange because all people say, when the children are sleeping, you must clean the kitchen, other things, not say, "Take a nap!"

After that I went to work in the factory at 5:00 [in the afternoon] to one in the night. I didn't like that. Fill the [containers] with the popcorn in the line. I wanted to make money, [but] I don't know why, one day I say, "Finished!" Four days or five days. I thought this is not the place for me, but I say, "I must work." I don't have other chance.

I was a little happy because I feel protected by my mother the first months. I was not sad. Always I was thinking I stay a short time, not a long time, always. For that, I wasn't sad.

I go back Chile in '94. I went to Chile because my house, my things. I went to fix many things. In that time, I sell my things. Not my house, my things, because in that time I saw it's very difficult [when] I come back my country. In that opportunity, I think it was really when I left my country, really. Because I feel different. I had been in this country. I knew it was difficult to come back. My feeling was different. In that opportunity, I was very sad because I knew what mean to leave my country. My daughters began to study here. I saw I couldn't cut this study. I looked in the future and I think I can't go back with my daughters again to Chile. In that time I saw it was more easy for my daughters to study here.

When I come back again, I get other job of baby-sitter. I went to work in Lake Forest to be baby-sitter, two children. That job I like.

Leading her church choir, Chicago, 1999

I remember that family. When one day I see that family, I want to say, "Thank you." Because it's nice people.

They is people who say you, "I need you for my children. You are not under me." I know I was under them, but their attitude said, "You are important for my family because you care my children. You are important for us." [After] two years, the man lost his job. When he didn't find other job, he said me, "Luisa, you don't stay because I stay here. I can care my children while I find other job." I think in that house I learned many words because my job was to take the children to the school and to take them to the different activities—karate, basketball, soccer, tennis, every day. So, that was a good time for me. Bobby was six and Christina was eight. The day when Mr. Bob say me, "I'm sorry, Luisa. I'm sorry," he gave me a big hug, "I'm sorry, Luisa."

I went to looking for a job to housekeeping. They say, "No," because my English was very, very bad. Other job, no. So, one day my daughter say me, "Mommy, go to the school. Go to the school. Learn English."

I say, "No, because I need work."

"Why?"

"Because I need help you."

Maria Luisa say me, "I can study, I can work. You study!"

I say, "No." [But] when I can't find a job, I say, "OK, I'm going to school [until] I find a job."

My two daughters say, "Yeah, mommy!" Maria Luisa buy the book. They were very happy when I decided to study last year in May.

I feel bad [about my English]. Let me explain. I like to speak with people. I like. I like when the conversation is serious about political, about book, about music. I like to talk about that. In English, I can't express what I feel. So for that, I don't like speak English. I think some day, when I learn to speak English fluently, maybe I like. Now, no. I prefer don't speak. I know I need to practice. I don't have where to practice my English. I need to practice. If I get a job where I must speak English, I think I do better than now.

One day I went to store to see the TV and VCR. I want to explain the [salesman] about what I want. [Laughs.] I laugh now because she say me first, "Hello, how are you?"

I say, "Hello." I want explain what I want. She was looking me. I try explain again. The face was changed. First she was smiling. After a minute, [she] say me something I don't understand and she went away. [Laughs.] I go my house. I feel bad, [but] now I laugh.

So now, I think I lost my time. The first thing I had to do was learn English. Now I know. Always I like to study, [but] I didn't want because I thought my responsibility was to support my daughters, not studying for me. Now I think that was wrong, because I saw the English is the most important thing in this country.

Never I feel United States is my home. I don't think [go] back now, no, but I don't feel United States is my home. It's strange. I don't know how I feel. I know I won't go Chile to live, but I don't feel American. I don't know how feel American people. I stay here, [but] I'm Hispanic people.

Since the last year to now, I think I need to have friends because I would like to go to the concert, for example, the theatre, where I don't want to go alone.

Last summer I liked it, the first time I liked Chicago. I feel different because I went the beach, I went the lake almost every day. I enjoy. I stay in the beach from 3:00 [P.M.] to 6:00, to 7:00 alone. I have my music on. The sun shining. Very beautiful, beautiful time. I was quiet. I have a lot of peace inside. I don't know why. Maybe because never before I went the lake. I don't know. It was different.

[I would like to be a citizen] to have rights for example, to elect the president, the representatives. I want to have a voice. That is interesting for me, citizen. I think every people have to be interested in the happening in the city, in the country. If you are a citizen, you can say what you think when you vote. If you are not citizen, never you can say what you feel, what you think.

The American dream for me is leave many things which you have in your country. Maybe a good life. American dream is leave many things, many friends, many good times, is work a lot, is feel many times frustrated. That is for me the American dream.

The future, I want to have my house. I want to have a good job. When I say good job, is to work doing what you know to do. That is good job for me. If you was housekeeping in your country, good job is a good work doing housekeeping, right? I was a teacher. A good job for me is working as a teacher. That is my dream. Always I work with children between 10 to 12, to 13, to 14. Now, I want to know more about the little kids. I want to study the music for children between zero to five. It's interesting to know how they get the music when they are very, very young babies.

The religion is important for me, very important. I believe in God. I think every people need God. I need God. I go the church every Sunday, almost every day because I do different things, the choir, work with the children, I sing in a group. It's good for me go to the church. I conduct the choir. I use my guitar, especially with the children, when I sing with children in the choir. You know what, my mother always laughs when I say, "Mommy, today the practice was beautiful, wonderful." It is for me, the maximum. It's better than somebody give me money. When the children sing well, I'm very, very happy, very excited! That is a thing which I feel very, very happy, the music.

My father, he would be very happy because we are together. Maybe he would be saying to me, "Go, Luisa, go! It's good for you."

LUISA IS NOW STUDYING FOR HER ASSOCIATE'S DEGREE at Truman College and plans to get her bachelor's degree in education. She continues to work with the children's choir at her local church in Chicago.

MY NAME IS # ZAYA KHANANU **I WAS BORN IN IRAQ**, *city called Kirkuk. That's north of Iraq. I enter United States was exactly end of* **JULY 1994**. *It's about 25 or 26 of July.*

ZAYA IS A FAMOUS NAME IN ASSYRIAN BACK HOME IN IRAQ. It's called for one of the famous sons who came from Jerusalem to spread the Christianity north of Iraq. I was born in 1962 in a family all Orthodox Christians. In that city [Kirkuk] we practice our religion. We have our own church, and of course we can practice learning Assyrian, which is Aramaic language, inside the church. Actually, the majority of that town is Muslims, Arabs, and Kurds. We are very minority in Kirkuk.

My parents, they are from north villages from Iraq, but they moved to the city Kirkuk, which very rich in oil companies, and my dad start working in the oil company as a driver. My mom, she was household, taking care of my sisters and brother.

I'm the middle son. I have six sisters, one brother. I really felt like I'm a lucky person because the oldest two sisters that I have, they always following my homework, teaching me in math, Arabic, all this kind of stuff. Always taking care of me. Whatever I want from them, I can get it easy. Even my mom she's not there, they always there to help me and help my younger sisters.

We have rented house, of course. And it was a big house and we have a big yard over there. We growing up chickens and every domestic animals sometimes. My dad actually is good in farming, so we always plant a lot of vegetables and fruits because we have a big yard. I loved that house because I learned a lot about different kinds of vegetables and the time they grow up, the time of harvesting, and a lot of information about the fruit. We were middle class level. We had television, we had recorders, we had a lot of toys. We play a lot and we always play soccer in the backyard. We were very happy, to be honest. We live simple life, very happy, and we never felt that we need money because the money was enough for us for food, for clothes, for school supplies, for everything.

I learned from my parents that we are Christian and we are Assyrians. And I have to be very careful at school when I'm talking to my friends about Christianity and something else, because my parents told me we are kind of discriminated and it's not allowed to talk about the religion. So only what we have to do is just to listen whatever in class from the instructor and not to discuss with any very strong religion subject.

When I went to the high school, there is religion class we have to take, which is about Koran. And always when the time comes for the class to begin, as Assyrian and Christian, I have to leave the class because I didn't want to listen. At that time, I have hard time because instructor who is teaching Koran instruct me to stay in the class and listen, even I wasn't interested in learning Koran. But I have nothing to do. Otherwise, everybody will make fun of me.

Well, to be honest, yes, I was very good student. And if I not get like an A in class, I will come crying at home and I feel something like I'm guilty about what I have learned. I liked school since after I finished primary school. Then I realized what the students are, why we are in class and why we are taking classes and why we are learning.

The last year of high school I was planning to go outside of Iraq and study outside of Iraq. Let's say United States or England. I was planning to go and get my degree from there. I couldn't get a chance to go outside because two major reasons. The first one, after high school I wasn't involved in the political party that allows you to go outside to get degree. The second thing, we don't have financial support for that.

Students while in high school, before you go to any institute, any college, or any university, they ask you to be in the political party like Arab Ba'ath Socialist Party, who is leading there the government. So, if you are not involved in that one, you have less choices, options than the others who are already involved. None of my family were in that, even my father. At the same time, I'm not against it, but the thing is, I don't like it. I never have benefits from it. I can give you an example.

As a university student, Iraq, 1986

Friends of mine, they were in the same high school. After we finished high school, this is how the system is work if you get a good GPA average. So I get 81 perecent. The system is allowing me only to go to the colleges that taking this average. But my friends, same high school classes, they get 55 percent, 60 percent, and they went really to medicine classes because they were in political party, or they have middle person or somebody mediate them to that system.

I always planned to go to engineering or to medicine. I love to be a doctor and I like to be any kind of engineer. I had that knowledge. I can afford academically whatever colleges for medicine or engineering, because I was good in physics and math and chemistry. Then by applying the application for university, I put all my engineering school in the top. Then after that, I listed the agriculture schools. But they ignored all the things and put me in agriculture school.

I became angry. Then I was upset at home with my friends and we talking, but what I can do? If you talk in public, then you will be very punished and you will dismiss from all educational options that you have. I said, "You know what, I'm gonna go with my GPA wherever the system will put me there."

Then I went to agricultural university in Nineveh. And I finish

four years college there successfully. I study forest and soil. This is the department.

The war with Iran was start at that time at the end 1981. [I was] 18. If you fail in high school, so there is no choice. You gotta go and serve in military. So that's why I was very careful with my studying to get a higher GPA to go to a good school. Now once you get a GPA good and you are eligible to go to any college, then whatever college years you have to finish, then back you serve to the military.

The end of high school I was so worried not to fail because otherwise, I would be kind of not a human. Just completely not a human, completely I would be like any victim. The war takes you for nothing. Because we knew that the war was only fighting two countries just for a little kind of border which have been years there. Nobody concern about that border. That's why I was very worried about that, and the decision that I made to go to college is really I had different approach to my life.

[Saddam Hussein] was the one in charge. He was in charge as the president in 1979, and the war start 1981. And we knew right away from the first two couple months in the war, we knew that the war is gonna last forever.

[I had] a lot of friends who served and my cousins who served. Some of my friends, they get killed in that war. I can't describe that feeling because it's very scary if you see something like that. You realize that death is there in any time, if you are civilian or you are in army, military services. The death is there. Anytime can take you. That's why we were very careful where we to go, what to do, and what kind of life we have to choose.

I finished college and I graduated 1987. By the time I finish, I had to serve to the military. I had to serve unless I have to escape from the country. I have to go north of Iraq. There is illegal ways. The Kurds who is living there, they can take you out with a certain amount of money, and it's not very secure. So you can get killed, or you can get stealed, or somebody can do something just for your money.

I thought about it not to serve, but then my dad sat with me and talk to me. He says, "If you escape, if you run, you know how the government are. They gonna send letters to us to define where is your son. He took advantage finishing college and everything, and he don't like to serve to the country." So, I realize that. And my father and my mother, sisters, probably they will be questioned to this and probably my dad, take him to the jail and spend couple or three years to the jail till I will be back, or probably forever. So, I have to sacrifice. I have to make my sacrifice, even I know that this war is nothing has to do with me, and I'm not that person to go there and just kill whatever enemy. I have no enemies.

I had no choice what to do. What I said to myself, "Everything is gone, so I have to adapt myself to the situation, not to be killed by easy way or by foolish way. So let's learn about this to be a good soldier, how to protect myself in the war services, army services." I had a good knowledge about everything, and I had a good knowledge about respecting people, knowledge about any subject matter. So I said, "Military is a good chance to learn different stuff."

Then right away, it was three months, they took us to the intensive services in military centers. We were learned how to be tank driver. So I was a tank driver. I learned how to use the weapon, all the kind of weapons. I learned how to protect myself from the chemical weapons. I learned how to drive a tank, how to lead a tank if there's any other soldier in the tank is missing, so I can take his place. So they send soldiers in different sites. At that time, in the end of 1987, I was chosen to serve in the south of Iraq, which is very hard environment. I never had experience in that. It's all deserts and flat. It was really very scary to drive a tank. I really felt very frustrated, disappointed when they sent me to the south because I have no experience in the south. I never visit south cities since my life. When I was a kid and in high school and graduate from the university, I never visit any city south of Baghdad. So I have no experience because these people, they were completely different culture. All Shiite. Even not Sunni Arab. All the south is Shiite. Again this is a different environment to me. I have to be very careful, to adapt myself, not to contact very much with this kind of people, even I knew we all speak Arabic.

It was one city before Basra. We call it Al Amarah. When I was transferred to that place in different unit, one of my friends, Mohammed, was with me. We were from the same Kirkuk city. We knew each other. So when we sent there, we were kind of completely lost. We don't know what to do. Then once we set up, we spent then about 35 days without getting back to Kirkuk and let our family know where we are. It wasn't kind of scary because we are soldiers. We were trained OK. First, second day was kind of scary. And then we said, "You know what? This is the life. We have to manage. We have to adapt ourselves. This is a new environment. We never face it before and we never have any experience, but according to our army training we are

prepared." We faced the situation, but it was a big impact on my general life, seeing the death every day. And you don't guarantee anytime, because you know how the war was before. Iran always making a big huge attack on Iraqi units and soldiers and back and forth.

The very front line close to them is about one mile. And that one is all soldiers without tank. We were in the tank unit so we were behind that mile about half mile supporting them. So we were always close. Binoculars, you can see wherever the other side is. We were always attacked by the different kinds of missiles and bombs all the time.

You just feel like you will be dead any moment. You sleep nights sometimes. You sleep in between afternoons, but you gotta be very aware, very awakeness for the next day and see any attack or any operations around there. But I never feel like I have human rights to live. I'm just there to occupy physically any little position like a tank driver and to be killed and dismissed and that's all. And you feel completely like you are not a human.

As soldiers, we have all something in common that we realize that we are here for nothing. We have all something in common that we have to protect ourselves first. Because each one has a family, so we always being very careful. Some of them are very careless and very crazy, because they've been in the military for several years.

With Iran war, I stayed till when it's over, August 8, 1988. Eight years, with a disaster killing hundreds of thousands of people. Soldiers, they were died from both sides. And just for nothing.

We didn't leave. We did every basic operation for 30 days, then take seven days break, go back home and come back again till 1990, August 2nd, when Saddam invade Kuwait.

One month exactly before that order day, we knew that all the military and republican specialty forces [Special Republican Guard], they were doing a big operation on border of Basra and Kuwait. We knew that something's gonna happen. So we were all afraid, and we were all doing preparations to see what the next events will be. And once we heard that order by the public radio, then we all were shocked. Again, a big disaster is coming. We didn't believe that eight years went with Iran, then another big war is gonna happen. And we knew that the whole world would be involved.

To be honest, all the soldiers, they were with me. They felt guilty about this because this is different kind of project to do because we don't believe in this. Why we invade innocent people? Why we kill innocent people? Why we kill innocent civilians? Just for the oil? We said, "It will never finish. And really we are going to die and we are going to die for nothing."

So, August 24th we received order to drive there. The first day, we drive. The whole two days we are driving, take a rest at night, and we drive the whole morning and the whole daytime. Every couple days we stay one place. Then we receive an order to move forward. Then we move forward. And to be honest, we were driving not in the desert. We were driving inside the city and destroying the whole highways and all the streets inside the city. And we were seeing big houses, big buildings, they were all destroyed and fire inside. Some of them they were completely burned. We just saw it. That's what the republican army had done.

The people, they were yelling on us. The women, they yelling on us and saying, "You gotta get out from here. You are dogs. You are not a human anymore." But some of them who did, I saw get killed. We were hearing shooting inside the city every night.

Within seven days, we were receiving seven orders. Then we moved forward till we were into the border of Saudi Arabia.

They [Iraqi soldiers] steal a lot. Glasses, clothes, jewelry from different shops. Everybody was breaking shops and get things and sell them. When they get permission from their officers, they said, "Broke this shop and bring whatever is here."

I just want to tell a story when I received a message from one of my big officer of my tank unit. He called me morning time. I was sergeant. So he called me and said, "Pick up two soldiers with you." Then I picked up two soldiers with me. And he took us by his own car, which belonged to the tank unit, just a civilian car. He took us. He drove us about three miles inside Kuwait, one of the small cities.

Then I ask him, "What we are here for, sir?"

He said, "You just shut up right now. You have to obey any order."

And I say, "Yes, sir."

Then he said, "Break the door, the main door of this house."

I said, "I can't do that. I'm human. I never broke the door any of people."

He said, "Broke the door right now or you're gonna be punished." Then we just broke the door, me and the two soldiers, the main door. We broke it and we get to inside. Then we broke another door to get inside the home. We saw a fancy remodeled kitchen. Then we removed every single plate, all the cabinets, and glasses. And we put it back in his car. Then we took out two TVs and VCRs. Then he went exactly to the living room. He checked all the jewelry there. And he went to the bedroom and he found two, three gold jewelry and he took it. Then he start put everything on the truck. Then he said, "That's enough."

Then I was so ashamed. I just feel like so ashamed about this because I never had done in my life. And I was always, when we went back again to the unit, the whole way, you don't believe, I was praying. I was just asking Virgin Mary and Jesus just forgive me for this because it wasn't my interest. That happened and I never forget that day. I was all day kind of upset with myself and just blaming myself for what I have done. But again, I have no choice. I have to obey it. So he took everything to Baghdad.

We were all prepared to the big invasion of the world, not only United States. We were informed that United States and England will invade Kuwait and gain it back, without any Arab army units they will participate in that. But we were prepared for that. This time I really scared about it. We were living in hope that all these diplomatic solutions from Russia and France and from Jesse Jackson sometimes come by Iraq. We were hoping all this until January 16, 1991.

January 16, we were hoping all the day that the peace process is still on. Then once at night time, 2:00 morning January 16, we were outside sitting and talking. We were all shocked when we saw the whole missiles go through the sky and burning the entire place there. Then we said, "Oh, my God. This is the end. That's it. This is the end." Explosion all in the air.

Then I just feel it. I said, "That's it. This is the moment I can just tell we are going to face the death. There's no way to escape it. There's no way to be away from it. We have to face it because we can encounter a big problem with the world."

And from the first day, that night, I start writing a letter to my family describing them every moment, what I feel and what I'm seeing. That letter, I had it with me and every day I put it in my pocket here. [Puts hand to breast pocket.] Then I said, "I will be dead one day and they will take me home. Then they will read my notes." I explained to them. I was talking to my mom, to my dad in my letter, and tell them that I still miss you. I still have that letter.

Then next day morning, I don't feel like to eat or to drink something. Just completely shocked. My mind is completely lost. I don't know what to think about. Somebody just give us order, "Don't do this. Do this. Listen. Don't do this way. We gonna fight. We gonna win the war. We gonna do this. We gonna do this."

Of course, I say, "This is all false statements. This is just generalizing whatever is not true."

We didn't sleep till the morning. In the morning time, all the fighter jets, all over the Kuwait country just bombing every military spot in that desert. [Some are] American, some of them are from the Gulf countries. Every military spot on the desert, they just bombing. They just start bombing, and missiles come from Gulf, because we can see the explosion bright from the ocean. Then we just count six, seven seconds. Then you see the bomb. Everything is shaking there. The entire ground is shaking and the bomb is somewhere around. And we just keep going creating new shelter for us. And that shelter of course is in desert. Then after couple minutes, one bomb is hit in that area. All the shelters are destroyed and we have to again rebuild the shelter again and again.

We didn't move. We just stayed. Everybody stayed and hold the position, each unit where it is. The tanks, we have the special machine gun on the tanks that's the long distance in the air, start shooting the fighter jets. At that time I was a tank driver, but if the shooting guy is not available, so my friend or I should replace that position to go up in there. But never happened with me because always there is available guy for doing that.

Once we realized that Desert Storm was going to start tomorrow, it was exactly February 10. One of my friend, he was a soldier, but he work as a medical support for us, and we were the only two who are educated. Others, they all drop schools and volunteer for army. They don't like educated people to be in army. We were very close friend together, and we sit one night and said, "Let's do it. Let's go back. It's night time." I said, "OK."

We just escape our units and just go back through Kuwait City till Basra, then take our way. I'm going to north and he's going to Baghdad. What we had made for us, a fake release note for three days. It was a

Graduating from university, Iraq, 1987

fake one, and we gave it 50 percent if you will be caught by the secret soldiers or nobody will ask and go. So, we start walking night time, from 10:40 exactly night, till 7:50 morning we reach Kuwait City. So we were walking all these nine hours from Kuwait–Saudi border to Kuwait City the capital. Just walking, walking. By that time, we were attacked three times believe me with the jet fighters because they were tracking that road by missiles. Three times we were completely dead, but again something by the God, we just get surviving. Then by the time was 11:30 morning, we sit in a bus and that bus was going from Kuwait till Basra. And that bus start driving towards Basra city. Then at one checkpoint, there was secret army there asking for all IDs and release note to go. Then they got us. They said, "This release note, we have to call." When they call and check, that is a fake one. And they took us and put in different car and take us to the prison. We weren't in the prison actually. We were in, you know this metal cabinet of the big truck. It was set on the desert. We put in that one about, you don't believe, about 55, 60 soldiers. And it's about 30 feet long and 10 feet wide. Then they were taking each soldier, by cover eye with any fabric and lock him up in the hands, and take him to a room and start beating them. And when they came back, we just saw them. Everybody who was coming back start crying. And about half hour beating. We don't know what kind of beating they used.

Then when it come to my time, he called my name, "Zaya Khananu."

I said, "OK." And the guy took me and he covered my eyes and he tied my hands in the back and he just was walking with me, sometimes pushing me along. The image is in my mind. When I get out from that cabinet, the metal cabinet, he walk me straight first. Then we make a left turn about four minutes after left turn we were walking. Then we went down about two minutes, downstairs. Then we stayed there on the right side. He put me in my room. Then, by myself what I think at that moment, I said to myself, "Now the guy who's standing next to me is gonna start beating me. I don't know what kind of tools he's using or what kind of stick he's using, but I'm gonna be beaten any second." So I'm just preparing. Don't be surprised or anything. Then the guy who was sitting on the table was officer. I have to call him sir. Still my eyes are covered, my hands are tied on the back. I can't do anything. I'm just waiting for any knocking me down or I don't know what kind of beating.

Then the officer, he told the guy, "Pull out all his documents in his pocket and his pocket money and check out what he has." Then one of my document, I still have it now with me, it was a small document showing that I am agriculture engineer, which I am agriculture engineer back home. Then he said next question. By that time, I was kind of waiting for knocking me down or hit me by the stick or something else. Then he said, "Are you agriculture engineer?"

I said, "Yes, sir. I am agriculture engineer." By that time, believe me, I was praying to Virgin Mary again just to get me out of the situation clear, nothing wrong with me.

Then he said, "You know what, Zaya?"

I said, "What, sir?"

He said, "Because you are agriculture engineer and I am agriculture engineer, too, I will let you go this time."

I said, "Oh, thanks God. Thank you, Virgin Mary."

Then he said to the other guy, "You know what? Respect him. Do not do anything for him. Take him back to the way and make his release note from here that he's released from the prison. And take him back to his own unit." It was something unbelievable. I have strong belief that when you pray for Jesus or Virgin Mary, believe me, you will get out of any dangerous situation easy. Then I was released by that night at the same time. All of them, they been killed. We heard. They send a note for all the units that these guys, they were escaping this time, this date, and all they get killed. My friend, he escaped someway because he gave all his money to one of the soldiers and he let him go back to our unit.

We stayed there until February 27th. Then we receive an order to escape back to Iraq from the head of the unit. It was so stupid order because at that time, the Desert Storm start, and all over the Kuwait I can see nothing, only all the petroleum points are all bombed and start blowing up and making sounds, horrible sounds. And a huge intensive smoke come over us. Just you can reach it anytime and we don't know what's going on. Then the head of our units, he just call all the soldiers

In front of a tank in a museum, Jordan, 1992

around him and he said, "Listen, we start losing everything. We just received an order to go back to Iraq. Escape. I have no plan how to escape, but I want you to do. Everybody should just escape and survive."

Then I told my friends, "You know what guys? I'm gonna stay." At that time, I knew how to speak with them in English. My English was OK just to translate anything. Then at the same time, I had my uncle's address and my sister's address in Chicago. So, I got all this information, telephones and addresses that might help me.

Then all the soldiers with us, they said, "Yes, you are right if you wanna stay. But make sure. After we are escaping and all Americans are replacing this area, this area will be easy target for Saddam Hussein to just target all the chemical bombs. Then you will be killed."

Then at this moment I give it 50 percent for that. Then I say, "I don't like to take anymore chances. This is one chance just to see my family first. If I can see my family, then I don't care about the others, even if I will be safe in Americans, which I prefer." Then I just went with my friends.

Then all my friends, soldiers, we just decided to run in one tank, even it was extremely, extremely dangerous because all jet fighters, they start bombing any tank that's escaping from Kuwait. Even not tank, even any other parts that hold missiles and bombs. But we have no choice. We cannot walk. It's gonna take us forever to walk, or probably we might be killed in the middle of the streets. Then we drove the tank back. We were seven of us. We face about three, four missiles coming to us while we are driving that tank. To be honest, I prayed a lot. I always pray and always recognize Virgin Mary to any kind of dangers or any happiness that I have and I thank that. At one part of the city, we start receiving shooting from the building in Kuwait. Those are Kuwaiti people who were there. By somehow they knew that Desert Storm is start and Iraqi soldiers were escaping. They start shooting us. And we escaped from that, too. We were lucky survivors.

I drove from 7:15 night. At 8:30 we reach that point because we need gas for the tank. It was a back point of our units where all kinds of papers, documents. And we saw one tank of the gas and we guys, we just pulled over our tank. So, our tank was full of gas. Then the other guy, he took the tank because I don't know the direction inside Kuwait. He took the tank and he was driving so fast, about 45 miles per hour. And we were just looking to the sky if there's any missiles coming towards us, because we were going to be killed in any second. Then by that time, we reached the center of Kuwait to take a highway to Baghdad. Then we saw that highway, they call it Al Mutlah. That highway was unbelievable. All soldiers were killed, all tanks were exploded and all the trucks and everything were exploded by the fighter jets.

And the other civilians at the same time, they knew the dangerous situation, they start driving their families' cars to run out of Kuwait, at least to be refugee in south of Iraq. So what they use is a civilian way, a trick way around the ocean. At that time, the jet fighters didn't bomb these civilians. So what we do, we just step into them. Then we took the desert way with the civilians just to get out of Kuwait. We driving the tank, but on the desert very close to the main street. But again, we start getting missiles from the jets. We stopped three to four times, if I'm not mistaken, and we throw ourselves on the desert because our tank was an obvious target for them. I stopped the tank, get out of there and just lay on the ground because we know three or four missiles are coming toward us. You were on the ground and you feel that the ground is start boiling. Making sounds. You cannot hear any other stuff. And you hear when the missile is exploding on the ground.

We drove from 7:15 [P.M.] as I said, till 6:20 morning we reach Basra city. I never forget all this because I went through a dangerous situation in my life, the most dangerous moments and minutes I just saw in my life. I can tell you what happened in this trip exactly from 7:15 night till 6:20 morning. What happened exactly I can tell you.

When we got to Basra, at the moment we reached the border, believe me, what I saw, the most horrible sight in my life. It was a little small bus. That bus hold about 25 passengers. And this bus was hit by a fighter jet missile at the moment we just reach, probably couple minutes or five minutes before. That bus was hit. Believe me, we smell like kind of something, meat is burning. And all soldiers we just took a look at that bus is all burned, and soldiers became this size, kind of a toy trying to escape from the window. And all were burned. All black toys like this. Small toys inside the bus. When I smell that meat kind of burned, at that time it was the fourth day we were without food, without drink, then we start throwing up, all the soldiers, because we never smelled this kind of smoke. It's very weird. Then, to be honest, I cried at that moment. I remembered all my family and I just start crying. I said, "What would happen if we were just reaching this bus at the time when these people were leaving and we were hit with the missile, too." I just cried for three, four minutes, then I stopped.

When I tell that story, I feel I want to cry again. If I smell it, I will throw up again because at the moment, I just feel that all these soldiers, they have families in the same situation that I am. And they will never go back to see their families and they were trying to see their families in the same situation I put myself. I was trying to go see my family. I don't know should I be dead here, or I can see them next day?

I was angry, to be honest, in both sides because mistake happen with both sides, American side and Iraqi side. If this is the situation, we should be escaped and released from Kuwait in a professional army war rules. We are leaving so why they are keeping killing people that are releasing? We are releasing because we need to be survived to see our families. When we are escaping, we cannot fight back more because we are leaving everything and we just want to survive and they are shooting from the back. That's what they were doing. And why this bus? The bus is not a tank. It's an easy target.

All the fires on the oil fields, all of them [we could see]. It was something really dangerous and horrible. You can't stand it because the smoke is so strong. You can't take in a pure breath. You just wanna get out of that area. And at the same time, the winds, I can tell was southeast, going from that area to south of Iraq and going up. So that's one of the reasons we realized that Saddam Hussein didn't hit Kuwait with the chemical bombs because it will effect with the winds and go back to Basra and Iraq.

In Basra we stay one night. Then the second day morning, my friend he said he was going to Baghdad, too, which is my half way to go to the north, so I gotta go to Baghdad first. I said, "OK, I will go with you."

Then we walked. We walked about the whole day till night. We reached the other side of Basra because there is a big river inside the Basra. At that part, we sat in like a destroyed area, buildings, whatever. We stayed there. We had a small radio with us and we hear the news that the war is stopped, everyone is holding fire on the both sides. Then we were kind of a little bit relaxed. Then we just cross the river by a little small boat. That boat holds only three people, but we sat on it about six people. There's no choice. Then we reach the other side, then we stay one more night. Then the second day morning, there was a bus, a lot of buses. If you are lucky you can get one. And they were taking soldiers and put them in Al Amarah city. Then we had a bus and we were inside Al Amarah city. Then, all the civilians, they were all crying there, waiting for their sons, relatives. Then I stayed there. One lady, she said, "Do you wanna eat something?"

I said, "Yes, please." Then she gave me a little cheese sandwich with a cup of tea. Then I just ate that one and drink the tea.

Then I step aside where the highway go from that city to Baghdad. And you just wave to anybody. Nobody is stopping and taking you to there. Then, by accident, this happened again. The sun was going down till 5:00 P.M. One of my friends, I know him from Mosul city north of Iraq, he was an officer driver. He was driving his officer from Al Amarah city going to Baghdad, escaping again. And he was driving Land Rover pick-up. I was just waving for anybody. I was very hopeless. Nobody will stop and take me with them to Baghdad. Then, he stopped the side far away from me, about half kilometer, he stopped that Land Rover pick-up. Then I was running. Then the officer said to the driver, "Why you staying here? Are you serious? Are you crazy? We gonna hit. It's very dangerous to stay."

"Sir, it's my cousin." Then he start yelling at me, shouting, "Zaya, come back here." I just run to that truck. I put all my stuff inside that truck. I reach Baghdad it was 4:15 A.M. morning.

Baghdad was all dark. There's no lights, nothing. Then, that guy he dropped me inside the main parking lot that's taking buses to different cities. Then I thanked him very much. Then they left and I start looking for a bus to go to Kirkuk, the north city. Then by that time, I stayed till 8:00 A.M. morning. And if you drive from Baghdad to

Kirkuk city, it's about three and a half hours driving. Then was by 9:30 A.M. morning, there was we call organization agency for army. They organize all these soldiers. They knew that we were come from the south and we were in the war. So they organize us in the parking lot and they bring buses to where you go. So they put each one into different buses. Then I put in a bus. Then at the time I reached Kirkuk was about 1:30 P.M. afternoon. Then I went to my home.

By the way, when I was walking to my home, there was no cars, so I walked about hour and a half from bus station in Kirkuk to my home. I was completely exhausted. I can't walk anymore. Hungry with everything inside. I don't think anymore. Just I wanna see them. Then when I rang the bell, the first person to open the door was my mother. She just sit on the floor and she start crying, kissing me and crying. That's it. I start crying again. And everyone start crying, kissing me and crying. I said, "OK, OK. Everything is fine."

My mom, she started touching every part on my body. She said, "Are you injured?"

I said, "No, I'm OK. I'm fine." Then, my dad, and my sisters, they all coming out and they crying. Then my neighbors they came. We keep relationships with the neighbors. All neighbors they came and ask for me and crying. I didn't take a shower since, you don't believe, it was at the end of October, I remember. I didn't take a shower October, November, December, January, February, till I reached home was the first week of March. My face was all dirty and black from the gasses and smoke outside. They didn't believe that I'm there and I'm still survive

To be honest, it's still unbelievable what I went through. It was just close from death, kind of one minute close to death. I saw a lot of soldiers they were dying inside Kuwait City on the side of the streets, in the middle of the secure areas, buildings, but we didn't care because we just want to go straight and be survivors.

When I was at home, I stayed about one week in Kirkuk city. Then, the Kurds started invading the north of Iraq. They were protesting and invading the north of Iraq. Now my family is in dangerous situation. We were kind of thinking to escape or not to escape, the whole family. We say, "No. We're not gonna escape. We're gonna stay in our house with my two uncles' family." Then the police officers, the army, they just escape from Kirkuk and leave it for civilians and Kurds. When the Kurds invaded, it was night time and we were all scared. My feeling was merged with my family feeling. We said, "You know what? We are all going to be killed all in one time." Then at that time, of course, all the roads and access to Baghdad were all closed, all kind of threatened. If you go outside, you will be responsible for your life. You might be killed in the middle of the street before you reach any station to go there.

And they stayed until two weeks exactly. And during these two weeks, there was a lot of missiles and bombs come outside from Kirkuk city from the government side just targeting all points of Kurds. We all were scared. And there were innocent people killed by that because missiles can be missed, bomb can miss any point. Until March 15th exactly morning, the Kurds start escaping from Kirkuk after they have destroyed the whole police stations, water supplies, and electricity supplies. They destroyed everything and they start stealing the computers, cables, papers. Whatever is belonged to the government, they steal it when they were running back out of Kirkuk city going back to north. And all schools they were burned out. And supermarkets they were all broken and taken all the things inside.

When the army was in, they start announcing in the city and in everywhere that if you are military soldiers and you get stuck in this city, just go to this police station and get a paper, a document, and you can return back to your official unit army without any government charge. Then I get that document. It was signed by the official officers of Kirkuk. Then I went back to my unit. It was exactly, if I'm not mistaken, between March 24th, 25th.

I had to go back to the Iraqi army again because we were just released to be survived. And they give me a period of time to go back to my army to reorganize. What I thought, I said, "This is not gonna be finished. This is not gonna be end unless I will escape totally from Iraq country. Because as long as the government is there and they still asking us to contribute in army services, so it will not be end, will not be finished. That's all. There's no life."

We went back to the south and our unit was reforming. I stayed there till July 1st when I was released from the army. In July when I released, I decided to do two things in my life. I lost five years without nothing. First of all, I said, "I have to get out of Iraq and get another chance for education and better life." That's one of my major decisions. And the submajor that I have in my life I said, "I should stay and go for work, find a job and start my master degree in Iraq." Two ways to think about them and see which one is more effective, give me more professional acting for future.

I talked to my family. They said, "Well, it's all up to you. You've been suffering a lot from all this stuff. And we know you are educated.

You graduated from a good school. If you wanna continue, that's your choice. If you wanna just marry and stay in Iraq, that's your choice. If you wanna get out of Iraq and do something else, that's your choice."

I decided to get my travel documents ready. When they found everything was clear, everything is OK, they gave me the travel document. It was issued in that year, 1991 August. And my travel document was stamped. It said all countries except Israel. But it didn't work because the only option I have to travel is by bus to Jordan. So I just travel to Jordan by bus. It took me 18 hours, central of Baghdad to central of Amman. In my pocket was $200, American dollars.

The time when it comes, they [my family] were in Baghdad to just say good-bye and I was leaving on my bus and they all start crying. They said, "If you are not sure being there, just see, relax for a couple months and come back."

I said, "OK. I will." Ninety-nine percent I was thinking that I will never get back to Iraq. I said, "Whatever is in Jordan, I don't know what's in this country. I'm gonna explore it. So whatever situation will be there will be better than in army situation, or living in the middle of Kurds, or living in the middle of Shiite down in the south of Iraq." So I will say, "These are new people. I know their language and everything. I'm a smart person. I'm educated. I know how to find my way, but I need a legal official way to get to the United States." That was my goal, to reach the United States.

I didn't know anybody there [in Jordan]. I just was there and start asking people where to find a hotel. But after second, third day, then I found a lot of Iraqi people, especially Assyrian. They were there before me six months, three months searching for same way to get outside. Then at that time I tried to go to German embassy because I have my uncle live in Germany. I tried to go to different embassies and I applied, but I got the same result. All rejected. I said to myself, "I will stay six months till I find my way just to travel anywhere." Money wasn't my problem because I think at that time my sister, I was sure that she will support me with the money I need, even $1,000, $2,000 to travel just outside Jordan, any country of Europe. Because I know, if I reached Europe, any kind of Europe, then I can get refugee, political asylum for temporary life and then I can reach United States.

The U.S. embassy, I couldn't apply at that time because they ask for conditions. First of all, they reject all Iraqi applications. So at that time, I wasn't eligible for immigration status because my sister, she is the only one who is living in United States, and if she would do the legal document for immigration status it would take seven to ten years. It's kind of hopeless.

Again I went to United Nations one day and I ask them for any asylum. They said, "We've been receiving thousands of people from Iraq, so we don't know what to do with you guys and we don't have any political asylum here, so please try different way."

I have only $200 with me. I spend it for three times meal a day and travel from this side of the city to the other side, then I start thinking just to work. The good thing about Jordanian people, I met the indigenous people of Jordan and they were Christian. They have different thought about Iraqi people than the others. One start giving me just one kind of job in a big supermarket, just starting working with this stuff. Open boxes, groceries. Fill out this order. And the owner really liked me a lot, and he said he'd rather want to keep me there.

The thing was, at Jordan in August and beginning of September when I start working, I said to myself, "Thank God. Today is September. Take me seven months back in February, I was like dying in Kuwait without food, but today I'm working. I can have a food. Thank God." So that's kind of very patient. I have big satisfaction in my personality. I just satisfied whatever situation is there, just to adapt myself to that time till I will get better things. So I was kind of happy working.

When you change your life a little bit, you shift your gear, you start working now, you have a hope. So you wanna keep it because you start improving yourself personally. You are working, you are being responsible for your job, you are responsible for your money that you are taking now, even wasn't that good paid. At that supermarket I was working from 8:00 morning, you don't believe, till 8:00 P.M. And I get my salary monthly and I get 60 dinar Jordanian which is exactly about, you don't believe, $90 or $91 a month.

After six months, the Jordanian government they have issued that none of the residents will stay more than six months unless you renew your passport. So you gotta get out of Jordan and come back to Jordan again. So what I did, I said, "This is a good idea. I have no obligation. I have no criminal charge, so I can go back to Baghdad, see my parents again, see my family again." And I took some money with me, what I saved from my work.

Then I told my boss that I'm gonna leave for just temporary two weeks. He give me vacation for two weeks. And then he said, "You know what? Good luck and come back again. You still have the job."

Then I was kind of happy. I still have something in Jordan to come back and work and go back to Iraq and see my family. That's what happened. I did that two times. Then last time when I went in Baghdad, I think this way. I said, "I will never get out of Jordan for any kind of embassy legal visa." Because most of the Iraqis, they were traveling from Jordan to Yugoslavia at that time illegal way, illegal visa transfer. And some of them, they stay in Yugoslavia, they run away by the border to Greece and Italy, they get asylum. I said, "I don't wanna go through this. I had enough in my life."

Then last time when I went back to Baghdad just to renew my passport, I went to any embassy that is open in Baghdad. But unfortunately, only Cuban embassy was open. Then I went there, Cuban embassy, and I applied for a visa. They said, "What you wanna do with this visa?"

I said, "Well, I wanna go to Cuba."

They said, "Are you serious?"

I said, "Yes, I'm serious."

Then they said, "You have to pay 200 Iraqi dinar."

I said, "That's fine. Here's 200 dinar Iraqi." I said, "I'm going with my wife first time to Cuba."

And they said, "How you get the money?"

I said, "I get money from my sister. She's American and she's citizen."

They said, "OK, that's fine." They gave me the visa for two people for three months. That's good.

The reason I'm taking this way because before three months ago, my first cousin did the same thing from Baghdad and he was living in Spain. I said, "This is perfect." He got political asylum in Spain. I said, "This is perfect. I'm gonna try."

Nobody knew about that plan before. By secret he sent me a letter to Jordan. He said, "This is an easy way. Go do it this time."

I said, "OK."

When I went to Baghdad, then I met with the person that I love for five years. So we were always keeping in touch, my girlfriend. She was my dad's second cousin. She said, "Are you going serious this time and you don't ever come back?"

I said, "Yes, do you wanna come with me?" Then we decided to go together. Within month, I made her travel document ready and visa for Cuba ready and we had a wedding ceremony, just one special evening night. Then second day morning, we traveled together to Jordan.

Working at a shop, Jordan, 1992

The Spain embassy in Jordan, I went there. I said, "I want a transit visa to Spain because I'm going to Havana. So my way will be taking Iberia travel."

They said, "OK, go get your ticket first. At least make us sure that you are going to travel and using that, then we will give you the visa transit to stay six hours in Spain."

I said, "OK." Then I went to the travel agency. I made all arrangements with him. And I paid for two persons a round trip ticket from Amman–Madrid–Havana, Havana–Madrid–Amman. It is, you don't believe, $2,850 for two persons. Then, I just submit my documents and my ticket to Spain embassy.

It was Monday. They said, "Stop by Thursday." And my ticket is showing that Friday, July 23rd is my travel day if I get the Spain embassy OK.

I said, "Is that guarantee I can get it?"

They said, "No. They will discuss your status, search on you and see what is going on." At the same time, I attach with my ticket a six hours stay in a big hotel in Madrid airport, not outside the airport, in Madrid airport. That was kind of to make sure that we are OK.

Then on Thursday morning time, I went there and I asked for my all documents and if it's signed. They said, "Yes, you got it." And I got the transit visa for six hours only.

I was so happy at that time. My wife she got scared. She said, "Probably we're gonna get back and lose all this money."

I said, "Well that's fine. This is the first try in my life legal way. As long as it's legal, I will never get upset about it."

She said, "OK."

Then Friday morning, I took my wife with the small suitcase for us, one suitcase for us. And I just bought a book, "How To Learn Spanish in Five Days." Arabic [to] Spanish, five days. We got into the airport, and everything was checking around us. The Jordanian security agencies in the airport, they were checking our document, "Are you going seriously to Cuba?"

I said, "Yes, I'm going to Havana."

He said, "What are you gonna do there?"

I said, "It's my honeymoon. I'm not gonna spend it in Jordan."

He said, "OK guys, just be careful." He asked me, "Do you have any address in Havana?"

I said, "This is the address of the hotel I'm gonna stay in Havana."

He said, "OK, that's fine."

I was so nervous when I sit in the airplane, Jordanian airline. I was so nervous. So the airplane start flying from Amman. Then my nervousness and everything is OK, but my wife start being nervous because this is the first time for us travel by airplane.

Happy, nervous, unbelievable. Talking sometimes small issues. I don't know what's gonna happen. I was so happy. Smile all the time. Four hours till I get to Madrid. Then at that time, I told my wife, "Do not pay attention to anybody, any Spanish security in the airport. Just pay attention to my face. Smile and make some joke around me. Don't pay attention to them, because if we just pay attention and make our eyes contact to their eyes, they will attack us easy and say, 'These are different.'" And I'm look like pretty middle-eastern person, but my wife she is blond, so she is totally kind of European or Russian.

We reach airport, you don't believe, it was 6:00 afternoon, beautiful sun in Spain, Madrid. One day before, I called my cousin. I said, "Wait me outside the airport." Then he was waiting there. Now, how we can get outside the airport? In this case, I put two options in my way. I said if I get caught by the Spanish police in the airport and they will check my documents and everything is legal, but they know about me, at that time I will ask for political asylum and I will tell them the truth. But if things are going OK and smooth till outside the airport, then I will shut my mouth and don't speak anything.

I picked up my bag. I was hugging my wife and she was talking to me different language and smiling. And we both say, "Hi," to the police officer who was signing our document. Then we didn't pay attention to him. Then we start again smiling and doing some fake joke about us. Because this way, you will let him feel that these guys are OK.

Then he said, "OK."

We just heard that he is stamping our document, stamping our document *boom, boom,* on the table. Then we start talking. I felt very secure. I was so happy inside. Then I took my document. We said, "Thank you," by English.

He said, "Thanks."

Then, I don't know what to do. He didn't guide me to where is the hotel. But this is my way. After stamp the documents, I supposed to go to hotel. This is what the way is. Stay six hours in hotel then get back to the airport and take the plane to Havana. Then I went to counter. I said, "I have reservation for the hotel. Please would you help we with where the hotel is?

He said, "Oh, yeah. Go outside the airport."

I said to myself, "Oh, my God!"

Then he said, "From that you make a left turn. If you wanna take a taxi, it's gonna drive you like five minutes. If you wanna walk, it's two blocks away from the airport."

I said, "OK. Probably I'm gonna walk."

He said, "OK." All this was in English. At that time, I speak English very well.

Then one policeman followed us. Again, I didn't pay attention to him. I know that he was behind us, walking with us, checking something probably. Then I was talking to my wife, and smiling, doing some jokes till the main gate of the airport. Then I asked him, "Where is the way?"

He said, "*Esta es la puerta.*" [This is the door.]

I said, "OK, *gracias,* thank you, thank you." I was learning some words by that book in the airplane.

When I was outside, beautiful sun, a big smile face of my cousin. He just hugged me. We were kissing both of us. Then the taxi was waiting for us. Then he took back to Madrid. We were so happy. Then the third day, he took us in the morning, 8:00 morning, he took us right away to the Red Cross organization.

[We asked for] asylum in Spain. My wife and I, we just sit and we have interview with one representative there. And he say, "What's your situation?" He start talking to us in English. He said, "OK, you don't need translator. You are OK."

Then I translate all my persecuting story since from Iraq and how I get there. And I said, "This is my only chance. I know the Europeans, they know human rights. If I go back, this is what's gonna happen to me. And we are very young couple married and we want to stay. We want at least any chance to better life."

The historical moment in my life was when I put my first step in Spain. I never forget that. It was kind of somebody just with a long arm, they took you from that place and put you in a secure, with a freedom, with everything. To me it was a paradise.

Then at that time, we went back again to my cousin apartment. After couple, three hours, they called us back and he talked to me. He said, "We're gonna give you a resident hotel for temporary, like a month, with a three times meal. And we're gonna give you some pocket money to help you."

I said, "OK, that's fine."

"And we're gonna send you to school."

That's a good thing in my life. I said, "Wow, there's a school, too!"

They said, "Yes, school for free language."

I said, "That's perfect. That's what I want." Then that's it.

One month there, then they send us to a big center. All were refugee and immigrants from different countries. So at that time, even I was in Spain, European country, I face people from Togo, people from Haiti, people from Cuba, from everywhere. So we start facing nations. At that time again, we start how to deal with different people, different cultures.

The hotel was north of Madrid, about half-hour if you ride the train. They called Robledo de Chavela. And it was really beautiful village. Green everywhere, mountain, waterfall, river. It's a beautiful civilized village with every accesses. Cars, streets, electricity, television, everything. We were so impressed about this. Then every morning five days a week, Monday through Friday, I have to take a train 9:00 to get half-hour to the different big city, not Madrid, but the city close to Madrid where is my school. It's San Lorenzo. It's beautiful. It's a big castle of one of the princes of Spain at that time. I love it. I love it. And Luis was my first instructor and he's really good teacher. And I spend with him seven levels of Spanish. Reading, writing, spelling.

I did work. I was working as a barber, hairstylist, cutting people's hair, because I used to do that back at home in Iraq. I used my skills again just to get extra money. [I did it] for fun, first of all, because I have a lot of leisure time. If I cut one person's hair, so he give me like 500 peseta, about $4 or $5. Then it was OK. About every day I will do three, four, sometimes nothing, sometimes five, sometimes six. So that's one of the jobs. Then the other jobs, I found weekend jobs only Saturday, Sunday, washing dishes in restaurant. I said, "This is a job. So whatever it is, I am very satisfied with it. As long as I'm happy, I'm getting my money legally, I'm getting everything by my heart, I work hard for this amount of money, that's OK. Even it's not good money, not decent job, but that's fine."

They gave me political asylum, a free transportation ticket and 3,000 peseta a month, which is about $30 to $40, which is good for any kind of food, bread, and stuff like this because we have three times meal in hotel, so we don't need that.

After six months, I start apply for United States embassy. It was [through] Catholic Charities. And they asked me for different documents. I bring those documents to them and they were OK. It was June 1994, they gave me the date of interview. That was a big time in my life when I was living in Madrid. I was living OK, happy, now again back to stress and nervous. Why? Because I didn't reach my destination goal yet, which was United States. So in order to reach United States, this is a big exam in my life. At that interview date, I might 50 percent be rejected, 50 percent accepted. So I really was worried about that.

I asked my sister and my parents to send all the documents that Catholic Charities requested for me to start open my file. When I get all of them back, affidavit and everything, then the Catholic Charities asked me to write a persecution story, why I left Iraq and why I wanna go to United States. Then of course, I listed all these historical events in my life and exactly what happened and the dates. I still memorize them. I'll never forget that. And I put all of them in one whole four-pages story and I submitted to the Catholic Charities. Of course, I did it by my English. Then they gave me appointment to interview with the officer in the embassy. And at that time, we felt like kind of frustrating, because a counselor come every six months to Spain to interview people and go somewhere else. So we wait six months. And we were so afraid because, you know how the propaganda is there, "Oh, he will dismiss all the Iraqis family. None of you will pass the test or

interview. You guys gotta be careful. Don't lie to him."

I said, "This is true story. And this is my situation, and this is the reason why I wanna go to United States." Then I list everything in my story till at that date of interview. And we went there. At the interview date, I sit and I spoke to the interview officer, which was American lady. And that's it. There was another translator, interpreter person with me, for some kind of rules and legal residence and everything that I don't understand. She just translated to that officer.

I got the result back after a couple weeks, and I was so happy about that. Then they ask us to go to the special clinic belongs to the U.S. embassy to do all these tests, blood test, for all our results to be OK. Then after that, we complete all this process and we get the visa to United States.

The first time, I just said, "My God, I can't believe it, but this is the situation. This is the true things." We are in the airplane and we just start flying to overseas to come to United States. "And that's it," I said. "This is my last destination. Hopefully I will stay here."

It was exactly around 3:30, 4:00 evening, afternoon. It was sunny hot day. And we spent in the airport about two, three hours to do some papers arrangement and all legal documents they give to us. Then they put us in the different plane to come to Chicago. And we arrive at Chicago at 11:30 P.M. We get some delays because it was a very rainy stormy day in Chicago in that time. Then I met my sister and my all aunts, relatives in Chicago airport. Once the door opened, my sister jumped in my face kissing me, laughing, kind of crying, bringing all these flowers in my face.

My sister left Iraq 1979. Then I didn't see her till 1994. Her face changed red, crying, kissing, laughing. She couldn't just realize that I am there. It was unbelievable for her. She was touching all me saying, "Oh, you became big!" Of course it's very strange to see her. Even we have photograph from United States and everything, but to see her physically, it's kind of unbelievable.

The first day we were all invited to a big dinner with all my family, relatives, my uncles, my aunt. After first day, second day, I start discussing with my sister what to do, where to go. And the organization that made all these papers legal, we contact her and she said these are the options. So we went to her office, it was in downtown, and we fill a lot of applications. Some of them to find a job, some of them to be like legally residents, you know how this process is going to get social security, ID card, and all this stuff. And they gave us some public aid supplement at the beginning for the first couple months. Nobody can find a job and work right away. And I received all this government aid till September 1994. About three months only. Then I found a job. I work as a clerk in a 7/11 food stores. And that 7/11 was and still owned by one of my relatives. And I work there a year and a half. I lived with my family for two years. Then I moved out by myself.

Both of us, in the meantime, we select Truman College to be our first station of continue our language and education. First, both my wife and I, we start learning language. They put me first in the ESL level 5 after taking the placement test, and she was in level 3. She finished level 3. By the time she was to finish level 4, she found a job, so she couldn't come back. She start working at Carson Pirie Scott and she's still there, but I continued. I talked to my instructor in class and he said, "You speak very good and your grammar is very well if you wanna skip."

I said, "Well I'm gonna go to level 6 to improve more." And I assigned to come to school four days instead of two days a week. After I finished level 6, then I took placement test for credit program. Then I start my classes. It was in the year 1996, I start the first course in the credit program at Truman. Then I continued till 1998.

My financial aid was approved and I get my first GPA course was 4.0. I get As all my classes. Then I was qualified for scholarship. Then I got scholarship from Truman College. Then I got a letter confirm that I'm qualified for work-study program. I said, "Yes, I would love to start any job at Truman even it's work-study. I know my qualifications not that good but at least I can do work-study, 20 hours work as a work-study." Then I quit the job at 7/11.

The first time I start as a lab assistant. It was the first time in my life watching computers, do everything by computers, and learn by my own. After that I spent about not exactly two years, but year and nine months with the work-study. Then the communication chairperson, he hired me as a technician because at that time they badly need somebody else, so I was around, available, and I have a little bit experience. Then I stayed there till one year with the computer technician. Then my very knowledgeable supervisor, she came. She directed the lab and she realized everything is going fine when I'm there. She gave me a lot of projects to do, like creating workshops for students, developing some software programs for different departments to use. She found me like very hard work person and knowledgeable with everything about computers. Then she hired me as a computer lab manager. Then again I

With his wife, Chicago, 2000

was so happy, but still it is hourly, not full-time but hourly, which I accepted. So, I'm happy about what I'm progressing in my workforce in the United States. Starting with the work-study, then technician, then lab manager.

Working with the computers, I realized I really like this stuff. It became my major interest. It's a good feeling. So then I decided taking more classes in computer, improving my work experiences and apply my skills, abilities to improve more, develop more. Then I find out myself, I'm really good in this stuff. I'm really understanding this. Then I decided computer science to be my major.

I finished Truman College. I get my associate's [degree] from Truman College in two years. At that time, I earned 60 credit hours and they gave me extra certificate of advanced skills I had gained. May 15, 1998, I graduate from Truman College. It was a big jump in my life. You know how you shift gears in your life, so that was when I shift my gear. This is education part that I'd done, but I'm gonna continue and transfer. Education to me wasn't ever an ending step in my life. Continuously I took courses, continuously I get education like taking classes in Spain, proving myself that I still have ability to learn. In Spain, I just discovered that this is what I am. I never stop education. Even I went to United States, I will continue my education to get a better job, to get degrees from United States.

Truman College has a big impact in my life. When I graduated I was so happy about that, just being graduated from American institute. I spent five years at Truman, not just studying of course, but working at Truman, studying at Truman. When somebody asks me about Truman, I just give him a beautiful impression about Truman because Truman is one of my fantastic happiest stations in my life. I find myself successfully. I find myself building up my personality.

This is very exciting story. I stayed at Truman College two months and I didn't know Mohammed was in Chicago. We serve as good soldiers in our unit back home in Iraq. It was in 1987 when we start serving in the same unit of tank. So we were together, too. We spent all this time together—three, four months. And one day I remember, I never forget that day, Mohammed and I, we became very, very hungry. There's no food in that desert. The food suppliers from the army, they didn't get us like after two days. But that day night, we were looking for a piece of bread and we couldn't find. Finally, Mohammed find a piece of bread. It's almost like a rock in his box of tools for that tank. Then I said, "Mohammed, how we gonna eat this?" We weren't able even to walk because we were starving like two days without food.

He said, "We're gonna eat it." Only I remember he just boiled a water with a little stove, a little fire, and he put tea on it. So at that time, this remind me, whatever situation we went through, we always have help from each other.

But when it comes to the attack with the United States and allied forces, so Mohammed was in the front of our unit tank fighting with the first. Mohammed units was the first victims. They get prisoner of war. They caught by United States army. They became prisoners at that time. When I reach back the town that I live, his parents asked me where is Mohammed. I didn't explain to them what happened to Mohammed's unit at that time. I explained that everybody get exploded to different directions and we don't know what we to do, and I saw Mohammed when he was running. Probably he will come after couple days or three days or one week he will be here. But I knew that Mohammed was like war prisoner soldier. He caught by United States army. I never heard from him. His family, too, they never heard from him because you know how the connection between Iraq and Saudi Arabia wasn't OK.

Then one day I was walking by the second floor [at Truman College] and just behind me, somebody just calling, "Zaya!" When I turned my face around, I just saw Mohammed. We just running, believe me, together and we start hugging each other. People somewhere around they were laughing, but we were so excited. Then I took Mohammed with me that day and spent three, four hours with my family. They were so happy about him.

He's still here. He's a good guy. I still see him all the time. We contact each other. We keep in touch by phone, by seeing each other sometimes here at Truman or outside. It's amazing story of my life. I never expected I would see Mohammed back again. We lost each other exactly on February 21st, 1991. Then we met back again here 1996, September something. It's amazing story.

I have big plan in the future. First of all, working in my master [degree]. I'm still putting a lot of goals and plans to reach my destination to get a master's degree in telecommunications and networking at DePaul University. I already applied for that and I'm still waiting for the result.

I can see my future every day. It's there, but I start to climbing the mountain to get into the top. But my steps are so clear, and I found some hard time to climb to the next step, but that hard time it's all about time consuming, but nothing hard to me about logic or intellectual. It's all hard time consuming, patient and time consuming, because of my involvement and my obligation to my family, three part-time jobs, part-time student. To be honest, I used to adapt myself in hard situation back home in Iraq and in Jordan and in Spain. Then fourth time in United States wasn't that hard to fit myself in one situational problem. [I have] pretty good background handling some situation that I have.

I would like to thanks this government. That's why I would like just to work for American government for any job they can benefit from me and I can do a good job for them. My dreams job is working for National Security Agency, for example. Nothing like as a spy, but to benefit from my skills, to benefit from my ethnic education background. I owe the United States a lot of favors. I have to pay them back, and for all those who understand what refugees are, and how refugees can be successful in different country, and how United States is really rescuing immigrants who are really suffered before and still suffer outside the United States from war, bad economic resource in that country, and religion problems.

I'm proud of myself. I'm proud of I have a good family. They are helping me with this, especially my wife. She devoted a lot of time to me to work part-time and study part-time. She's very well understanding the situation. She's going for full-time job. And I'm proud of myself to be continually taking classes and being in school and improving my English skills.

Becoming a citizen to me, first of all, is to have rights and to have protection. Of course I'm so happy to get that citizen status or certificate. I'm so happy not to exaggerate that this is American citizen. It's powerful to me as a human and really the land of rights, not to show off it. Let's say, if I'm going back to Jordan or any European country, not to show off to the people that, "Hey, I have American citizen." Its happiness is inside. You have responsibilities to your community, to society, to your neighborhood, not to abuse your citizenship status doing illegal stuff. Doing legal stuff with it, it can bring some advantages to you and you can benefit some other people in society.

I passed the [citizenship] exam and the oath ceremony is in next couple weeks, March 21st, 2001, 12:00 [noon]. It's historical moment. I feel so excited. Since I received the letter, every day I just remember I have oath ceremony on 21st. I'm gonna be there. I'm gonna dress like this. I'm gonna stay and watch people and what they do.

To be honest, the United States is my home because United States is the land that I decided in my life to stay in and to live in. So I consider United States is my home, but my birth place is Iraq. And I belong to that Assyrian culture and I belong to that ethnic group. And I have native language Assyrian.

A human should live in a society that gives you some rights, at least to practice your beliefs. That's one of the things that you can get. To speak out whatever you feel. Then when I got to United States, I found more options and I found more opportunities in my life. But I'm still keeping my culture strong, keeping my family close to me, and take advantage whatever opportunities are offered here like education, being

Receiving his U.S. citizenship, Chicago, March 21, 2001

in good future career.

As a country of birth, everybody like to go back home one day and visit relatives, visit the city, visit everything that you miss. If there's any chance or any opportunity to do that, I will do it. If there's no fear of it, if there's no scare of it, so I will do it. Not today, no, because as the government exists, so you can't make any decision like this right now. I don't wanna be killed. I don't wanna go same situation, and especially people that are living there with anger and they all are in need. You go there and you see them. They are suffering from diseases, from hunger. That makes you sad. I don't wanna be in that situation again and see those people are suffering.

Personally, I have made some changes in my life. See, back home, we feel about other members in our family, every day we have to see them. But now on, I can't do that because of the job, because of a lot of pressure from the school, a lot of pressure from the outside. I don't have time to do that. And especially I'm married, so I'm living separate home. It's difficult, but I have to do it. I have to adapt myself to that. I have to accommodate for different situation in the United States. But I call them every day.

I'm changing from things I learned in United States. Be patient for the things I cannot get it today, because probably I need to improve more because I know it's completely different system of education, life system, economic system. So anything I cannot get it today or tomorrow, I have to tell myself I gotta practice till I will get it. So in this case, I have to be patient.

I learned open-minded looking at the different cultures like African Americans, African people, different other cultures in the same way because we all are human. So we all are in United States to get this chance to live, to practice our human rights.

As I told you before, as Assyrian Christian, we were persecuted. I'm just generalizing. We were persecuted by Arab Muslims there and many times we were subjected to violence in different ways. So I was closing myself not to involve in the relations with more Muslims and Arabs, because I know what they are thinking.

Well, the thing is [I'm still] not very open-minded with the Muslims because I still have that background impression little bit still in my mind, judgment about them. But while I'm dealing with them in school situation, being in class, my classmates, or other outside the education institution, how they can help you when you ask for the help, then in that case probably will take me more years.

When I was living in Spain, I said, "Oh, my God. I just wanna see myself in the United States, doing this and that." And when I came, I saw everything working fine for me. Only disappointment because there's some kind of discrimination here. There's some racism here that's going on, sometimes when they just take a look at your face. We still need to build some bridges between all these nations to understand each other. Because when they take a look at my face, they say, "Oh, he's from Middle East." But they don't know about my background. They don't know about my religion. They don't know about my other culture, ethnic group, whatever story that I have. They judge, "You are from Middle East and probably you don't like other people, or you hate women." Whatever Middle East impressions they have.

The first time when I came to the United States, it was my first job, and I had a big accent in English and some of them, bad customers, they say, "You go back to your country. You don't understand nothing.

Why you are here?" I ignore them. It hurts that time, but then I realize these people, some of them are not educated, so I don't have to deal with them again. It's the matter of respecting yourself. It matters how you present yourself to Americans or anybody else. If you present yourself as very polite, they will accept you as very polite. It doesn't matter your face or your skin.

The worst thing [in the United States], I'm sorry to say, but sometimes there's no respect. Children to their parents, there's no respect. Children being outside the whole day, getting in the streets, troublemakers. Business, education are high. Respect is very low.

My life is like everybody's life. There are stations. You have to go through these stations. You gotta travel from one to one and you have to accept it. Life is not easy. Life is not all the time beautiful. There are good situations, bad situations. But at least when I went through a bad situation, when I get out of it, at least I have to learn a lesson, not to be in that trouble or to avoid being in that situation again. Of course, I have sad days in my life, not only days, probably years in my life. But again, this is the life. We are all human. At the end, I feel very happy, satisfied. Thank God what I'm doing, what I'm receiving from the outside.

In this country, this is my last station. I hope so there's no more station than United States unless there's a moon, to go to the moon and living there. [Laughs.] I have to use everything in my life, but not to abuse them. Use for my benefit. Treat everybody the way I like everybody treat me. Consider other human around you. Consider other people. Living in peace and harmony, that's all what I need.

ZAYA IS STUDYING FOR HIS MASTER'S DEGREE in computer information
systems at DePaul University in Chicago.

MY NAME IS OSWALDO MEDINA *I'm 26 now. My birthday is May the 3rd and* **I CAME FROM MEXICO**. *I came to Chicago about four years and a few months ago. I'm not very sure about the date. It was* **FEBRUARY, ABOUT THE 5TH, I GUESS, FOUR YEARS AGO, 1995.**

I FEEL OLD ALREADY, really old because I never really cared about doing something for myself. I used to live just the day, and not worry about what is going to happen tomorrow. And then now, I'm really worried about my future because, I don't know, maybe it's because I'm getting married and now I care about what am I gonna do tomorrow, and if I'm gonna have money later on in my life to have my family, to have kids and to get a house and all that stuff. And I look at myself and I'm 26, and I'm just starting to get my responsibilities in life.

I came from Mexico from a kind of big small city. It's called Ciudad Hidalgo. This is in the state of Michoacan in Mexico. The first thing when anybody asks me about my city, what I think is the way it looks from far, like when you are in the mountain, because there is a lot of mountains around. It's like kind of in a valley, so it's kind of down and there's a bunch of mountains around. It's a beautiful little city in the central part of Mexico.

We have all kind of people. Most of the people is really nice. People work to go on with their lives. I think in my state, most of the region is about wood. They do like chairs, tables, and all this kind of works with wood. Those things where you put your clothes in, not a closet, but the ones that you can move. They're called *roperos* [armoires]. Those things are really famous in Mexico.

My father is, I'm not sure what's in English, in Spanish it's *herrero*. He does windows, doors with metal. It's like a welder. He does all that kind of stuff. I never get really close to my father when I was in Mexico. I don't know, somehow it was kind of hard for me and for him, too, because we have like the same character. So, I don't know, we're like kind of weird. We're like reliant [reluctant] to show our feelings. Now, I totally changed. I feel like a totally different person. And I miss my father like never before. I mean my whole family. Everybody likes my father. I have a lot of cousins that they see him as a second father. And he's just a really great person. He's always trying to help

somebody else. It doesn't matter what it takes to do it.

My mother is a beautiful sweet lady. She's just so sweet. Her whole life is her family, just taking care of us and my father. She doesn't work. She stays home. She works in the house.

My father came to Chicago long time ago. So, we were really young and my father was here. He was here in the late 70s. I just remember I was really young. I think he came twice. And he did really good over here. He started like most of the people in the kitchen washing dishes. And when he left to Mexico he was a sous-chef in Hilton restaurant. It was something really big. And my mother was studying also, because she wanted to do something with her life. She took, it's kind of a course in Mexico to become a secretary and accountant assistant. She never worked because the day she graduate, my father showed up in Mexico, like a surprise. I remember, we were going out of the church, because in the graduation we went to church, and I remember seeing my father coming towards us. My mother was just like screaming, she was so happy. Maybe I was seven.

I liked school. I was really good at school. My grades were really good, really, really good. I've always liked math. I still love math and everything related with that. And then when I went to *secundaria,* which is like high school over here, I didn't really know if I wanted to keep going in school, so I kind of slowed down a little bit. And then I went to *preparatoria,* which is maybe college here, junior college. I didn't

DJing at Ojo de Agua, Mexico, 1999

[graduate]. I didn't like to mix with anybody there. I was always in the back of the classroom. Everybody was there and everybody was like in those little crowds, and I didn't belong anywhere because I didn't want to. I didn't really feel like going with these people or these people or that people. I didn't care about what they did or what they didn't. And it was when I stopped school. I started hanging out with people outside the school, and these people didn't go to school. Not getting in trouble, just hanging around. I knew I didn't want to be in school, but I didn't know what I wanted to do. I didn't have any plans for my future for my life. Like I told you, I just wanted to live that day. I didn't wanna to know what time I was gonna wake up tomorrow, what I was gonna do, what I was gonna eat, what time I was gonna sleep. I was just living it like that.

I used to work in a body shop fixing cars, everything but paint the cars. And then, this happened. I used to be a really good dancer. I think I was the best in my town and around. Dance music, like some Michael Jackson kind of moves and stuff like that, just dance, and all that kind of dancing like Paula Abdul, Janet Jackson, kind of thing. So I was really good at that. I used to go to clubs Friday, Saturday, and Sunday. Sometimes I used to start dancing since they open until they close, for four hours. You know what they used to do? In the middle

of the night, the clubs close at 10:00, open 6:00 to 10:00. And the club that I frequented the most, they used to cut the music like 9:00 and ask everybody to clean up the dance floor because I was gonna dance over there for them. You can't imagine myself. I can't stand being in front of a crowd, but I used to do that because all my friends used to hang in a corner of the dance floor. So, the whole time I just face my friends at the corner and I didn't pay attention of the rest of the people. We're talking about 300 people in the club. It wasn't a huge club, but it was a lot of people if everybody is staring at you. So, they used to play a song and I used to improvise something, and I just got on the dance floor and dance around until two, three minutes and that's it. And they start dancing, everybody again. I don't know why, but I used to love dancing. And I was skinny like you have no idea. You could see my ribs! You could count my ribs totally. Really really skinny. My pants size was 28. I feel really good, and mostly because people used to tell me that I did it good, so I feel really confident with myself every time that I have to go to the dance floor.

At the same time I started studying again what my mother studied. I wanted to be a secretary and accountant assistant, and at the same time, I was dancing the whole time. And then this guy which was the DJ knew me already 'cause I was always there. He used to love the way I danced, so I was like his number one dancer. And one time I was there early when they opened, like they usually used to do, and I was watching him putting the records. I didn't have an idea what the headphones were for and stuff like that. So, one time he asked me if I wanted to learn to play the music or to do it. And I told him, "Yeah, why not?"

So he told me, "Come next Friday and I'll teach you." I went next Friday and he just told me, "Oh, the records are here. These are the ones that I need the most. These are the ones that I need the least. And these ones, I don't really need them. So if I ask you for a record, you look for it here, and clean it up with fabric and give it to me."

Well, I did that for a year and he never really told me what to do or how to do it. I kind of figured out by myself by being there. I just watched him for a year. I just clean the records for him for a year, pass it to him, he pass it back to me, and I put it in its place. So I came familiar with the music.

What happened is that after a year or so, somebody opened another club in a hotel, but it was gonna be a different kind of club because they were gonna open at 8:00 [P.M.] and close at 2:00 [A.M.]. It was something totally different. So they called this guy, his name is Juan

Jose, Juano. So he told me once, "You know what? They're gonna open this club and they need a disc jockey. Do you wanna try it?"

And I was, "Yeah! Why not?" So he set me up with this guy and I went there and I talked to the owner, Tito Martínez. The name of the place was "Ojo de Agua" disco, and I talked to the owner which later on became one of my best friends.

He told me, "You know what. I have a disc jockey for tonight, but come next week and we give you a try and let's see."

So, yeah, I went next week and I went to the DJ booth where they have the system and stuff. It was just like a box with some records over there. And it was a chair with a turntable and another chair and a turntable and a carton box in the middle with a mixer over there. It didn't really look like a DJ booth, but it made noise. So, he told me, "These are the records. This is the mixer and you do the rest."

It was a terrible night for me 'cause I didn't know the music, I didn't know the crowd. And if you're a disc jockey, it's like a nightmare 'cause you don't know what to do. It was a totally different crowd. And I didn't know the records. I knew maybe 10 or 20, but you cannot play 20 records for five or six hours. So, I have to go through the records while the other song is almost over and come up with something else. And at the end of the night he told me that I did a really good job, that he really liked me and if I wanted the job, the job was mine. So, he gave me some pesos and I started working. I start working Saturdays. But it was good money, not in the beginning, but later on the club took off.

I was just the DJ, not even a DJ because I never hear that term. I mean, I hear that in Mexico, but I never realized that I was one. I never realized that I was a DJ. People used to ask me, "What do you do?"

I used to tell them, "I play music at Hotel Ojo de Agua. I'm the one who plays the music there." So, people have an idea. But I never call myself a DJ, and I never have a DJ name, either. I think I was like 19 or 20. Because of that job, that's why I came over here.

Well, I finished this course that I told you about before, secretary, and I tried to place myself in a job. But in that time, I already have started to let my hair growing and I didn't really look like a person that you wanted to be your secretary. So what happened is that I never worked in that. My work give me a really good money. Some people used to work in a shop doing like *roperos,* or stuff like that, and they used to do like 150 pesos a week or something like that, and I used to do that in a single night working as a disc jockey. So I didn't really work in anything else, sometimes the body shop.

Time passes, and goes and goes and goes and I started growing up and it was kind of boring over there. I wanted to do something else. Then, one day one of my friends came from L.A. He told me that it was really nice, blah, blah, blah. And he was my best friend and he told me that, "You have to go with me, blah, blah, blah. It's gonna be great and we're gonna make some money, blah, blah, blah."

You know what, I never wanted to come over here 'cause I was doing really good over there. So, I didn't need to come over here. What for? Nothing really impresses me. Nothing really was like, "Oh, I wanna go. I wanna see this and this." No, I didn't care about it. I was just like, I wanted to go and if I can make some money, just go make some money and I come back and that's it. So I ended up going with him to L.A.

I told my father. And it was terrible. My mother was just crying and crying and crying, because you have to come as illegal. And it's a lot of dangers, and it's a lot of stories, and my mother couldn't handle to hear that.

There's a lot of people that offer you to take you there. They drop you off at the door of your house, or the address that you wanna go in L.A. or in Chicago, or anywhere else, it depends. But that time we pay like $300 for each one. This was '92 or something like that. Three hundred dollars, and either you can go with him in the bus, in a three-day-

With his grandmother, Mexico, 1999

175

ride, which we didn't like it, or you take the plane and you meet there in Tijuana in the hotel. And that's what we did. We took the plane and we met him in Tijuana. And then from there, he takes care of the hotel room and some food once in a while. And then he crosses through the border with us. He knows people at the border, people who lives there, people who every day goes 10 or 15 times across the border. So, they know where is the *migra,* [immigration officers]. So they know which spots are hot or which spots are really good, so you don't have any problem. In five minutes you're in the other city, safe and stuff.

Actually it's a lot of people who does that. Like I told you, it's something that happens every day in my town. There's a lot of people that offer you to take you here. It's not like I told somebody in Mexico, "I'm going and I'm gonna go illegally." Everybody comes illegally from Mexico, at least the most of the people that I know. Half of my town is here. If you know anybody in my town, that person has a brother, a father, a sister, a cousin, or some kind of relative that is here in Chicago, specifically. So, it's not a big deal to come illegally. It's like whatever. It's something like everyday life. I know people who go there every six months. They come six months over here. They go to Mexico. They stay a month and they come illegally again and after six months they go and they go back, go back, go back bunch of times in the same way. It's not a big deal.

It worked terribly. We tried crossing a few times and we got caught, so they just take us back. And we try again, they take us back. We try, they take us back.

Sometimes it was kind of nervous 'cause you're trying to hide, but it's not that big deal 'cause when they grab you they don't do anything to you. They just put you some plastic in your hands and they put you in the truck. And you go and you fill out some questions. Sometimes you spend a few hours, sometimes you spend the night over there, and then they just drop you off again at the border. They don't put you in jail. They don't do anything. There's not even a jail.

With his brother just after arriving, Chicago, 1995

Just think about, this is Tijuana right here where you are with me. And right here, a few blocks up, that's the border. It's just a huge wall. It's more a fence. Of course, you're not gonna try right here. But you go outside the city. You walk, and you go kind of outside the city and where there is not a lot of people. But in the middle of the street there is the fence. And in the other side, well, in the other side of the street is the other city. And that's the United States and this is Mexico. It's really dumb, kind of dumb. Makes no sense really. But anyways, there's a bunch of holes or you can jump in the top, whatever you prefer to do.

All the time we did it at night. One time it was really funny because we were walking and walking, we were like four or five guys and we were walking and we could see far away was like two people also walking. But we thought it was like another two guys, but no, they were immigration agents that were just following us. And we were walking and walking and walking and then some other ones came in trucks, so we started running. And I start running with my friend and we needed to jump a fence and he jumped a fence and I was wearing a jacket. And when I jumped, the jacket got stuck so they caught us. The funny part of this is that the guy was laughing and we didn't understand why. So we sat over there and he was laughing for like five minutes. And then he told us, "Come on. I wanna show you something." And he showed it to us with a flashlight. Three feet away from where we jumped it was a huge hole in the fence. That's why he was laughing, because we didn't see the hole.

It's a game, and they don't even treat you bad or anything. That was my experience. Some guy [immigration officer] even gave us some french fries and some pop and stuff that he was eating. He asked us if we wanted some. He was eating in his car. What I'm trying to tell you is that they're not mean with you or anything. It's just their job. Even some of them told you, "It's my job. That's what I have to do. You do what you have to do. I do what I have to do. And I'm just gonna drop you there and you just try again later. If I don't see you, good luck." They even tell you, "Good luck next time."

So, the last time that we tried we walked a lot. We really, really walked a lot. We have a walk for the longest time. I don't know how many hours we walked. And finally we did it. Then, put us in a van and took us to L.A. That was it. They drop us off in front of the house where we were to go. And we paid the guy and that was it.

We got there at night, Mother's Day. It was a Sunday. Everybody was asleep already. We slept in the floor that night. The next day, he gotta go to work, so he took us to work and we started working the next morning. The same thing—body work, body shop. Basically, they gave us work over there right away. Cash, just cash.

So, it was nice. Even it smells different. I don't know how to tell you that. If you go to L.A., it smells totally different than if you go to Chicago. I don't know why, but for me it smells different right away. And it feels different. Everything is new for you, the signs, the streets, the lights, the stores. Everything is just totally different.

It was great because I even have a job right away. So, I like it. So, I was there and we start working. I was doing like $200 a week. And it was a lot of job. I did have a lot of job. But I didn't have a lot of options. And I was living with my friend. Every morning from the house, from Compton to East L.A. we take the highway. And you can see all the buildings really close from downtown L.A., and in the other side there's like the huge sign of "HOLLYWOOD." It was really ironic that I never got to go to Hollywood Boulevard or anything like that, and being there. Nothing, nothing like that.

They didn't do anything in weekends but sit outside the apartment and drink and drink and drink. And next day Sunday, drink again. And next day, Monday, to go to work. I never went anywhere. Just one single time another guy took me to Long Beach. But we were like 20 minutes far from the beach, and I just went once. And it was terrible for me 'cause the lifestyle of these people, I didn't like it. I didn't like the way it was. I ended up hating L.A. I just wanted to go back.

I was really disappointed because that's not what I wanted. I wasn't even doing money because we have to pay rent and food and gas and the ride. And when you're working, you have to buy your food over there because you're working all day. So, I never had money for anything. The most exciting thing to do was once in a while go to the swap meet to buy some clothes. And that was it.

I stayed there from May until December. I went back to Mexico in December. And I was just happy to go back.

Then I spent another year over there in Mexico and doing the same, just DJing. But then I was just tired being there. And then a guy from Chicago went to Mexico. I met him in Mexico when I was working in Ojo de Agua. He really liked the way I play. So he told me, "Anytime you wanna go to Chicago, just look for me and you have a job."

Every time he used to bring music over there, a few records for me to play it over there 'cause it was the hot music over here and he wanted to put it over there. So, this time he brought like 10. So, he asked the owner if he can go to talk to me. So, he came and he told me, "Can you play this music?"

So, I took his 10 records and I mixed his 10 records one after another, after another, after another, after another. And when I finished, he came up to me and he told me that he never knew a DJ that, without knowing the music, mixed the music as good as I did. So he really like it and he keep telling me to come to Chicago and I have a job with him. So I took his card and I told him that I was gonna think about it. I didn't wanna come here at all anymore 'cause I have a really bad experience in L.A.

So, I got bored again. There was just nothing for me exciting to do down there anymore. So, I decided to come over here, and then my brother decided to come with me, too.

This time we took another plane from Mexico City again to I don't know which town, I think it was Nogales. I don't even remember. This time it really took us a while to cross. Every time just was getting worse. It was like more people trying to catch you in the border. And every day is more and more and more and more 'cause there's more people trying to cross. So, this time we tried a lot of different places. One time we just walked for five minutes and we were already in the other side. There was like a bus that goes to another city more into the United States. And he put us in the truck, like a van, kind of bus to go to another city. And in the middle, almost there in the city, immigration stopped the van to ask for everybody for identification and they got us. And they got us a lot of times that time. A lot of times. And then the guy who crossed us started telling us that, "Now, everything was more expensive." They always do that to get more money from us.

So this time we tried for a tunnel. It was called "The Tunnel of Death." You can't imagine that, because a lot of people got smuggled, robbed down there sometimes. Gangbangers are there and they know that they use the place to cross. And supposedly a few people die over there. You can't imagine that. It was like a sewer tunnel, but it's not this like round, tiny place where you hardly fit. This place was like maybe like your apartment wide. Maybe like 12 feet high and I don't know how many feet wide. But it was big. But it's empty. It's not water. It's nothing there. So, we tried from there and we tried a couple of times. And finally we did it. We run through the tunnel. And this was already early in the morning, like 5:00 maybe. It was already clear. It was like February [1995].

So, it becomes a channel so we keep running, running, running, running, running and we end up in the back of a hotel. And somebody have already paid for an apartment in the hotel. And we were like, I don't know maybe 40 people in the room. And everybody was smoking. You can't imagine that. It was just overcrowded. But anyways, after that, they went and they picked us up and they took us in an apartment complex and we stayed there. This was in the city of Phoenix. We stayed there for a really while because from there we were gonna fly to Chicago. We were supposed to take a plane to Chicago. But because the guy asked us for more money and we didn't have more money, we have to call here and see who of our friends or aunts was gonna borrow us money. So we have to stay there for another week or week and a half, something like that. Finally, one of my aunts sent some money, so we took a plane. It was another adventure because in the airport there is more immigration agents.

We were really dirty by this time, so somebody borrowed [lent] me a shirt like the one that I'm wearing right now, a T-shirt. And I took a shower and I kind of cleaned up myself a little bit and we were ready to go. So, this guy took us to the airport and he told us, "Just stay with me, stay with me. You're just gonna go and sit over there. Until the last call of the plane, you're gonna go there and show your ID, Mexican ID because we didn't have anything else, just to check this is the same name of the ticket. And you just go into the plane and that's it."

So we got in the plane at night and we arrived to Chicago in the morning. It must've been like 4:00 or 5:00 in the morning in February. I was wearing a T-shirt, let me tell you! So the plane arrives. While you're walking through the door of the plane, they have these stairs, like this kind of tunnel where you go to the terminal. I couldn't believe how cold it was! It was really cold, like I feel my pants wet. So, we went to the terminal and my cousin's husband was waiting for us, and my uncle were waiting for us. So we see him and we just follow him out of the O'Hare. And my uncle is out there right away in the car. Just me and my brother. So, from the door from the airport to the car—

oh, God, it was frozen. It was like crazy. It was totally crazy! My uncle give me a jacket. He was wearing two huge jackets. He was inside of the car, so he give me a jacket right away and my cousin's wife, I think he give my brother another jacket, too, right away.

We were driving and like I told you, it smells different right away and it looks different. Everything. When I was in L.A., all the streets, all the highways, they are like totally new. They are amazing. In L.A. everything looks new. And I came here and we got to the expressway right away and everything seems so old. Some bridges look like they are gonna fall anytime. That was my first impression. Over here it seems like it's been here forever. Like the streets, some of the houses, they're looking more used.

And you know what another thing, everything seems too white 'cause the salt in the roads. And you know how it gets when there's no snow anymore, the street looks really white? It looks like that. And it was really cold, really, really, really cold.

So we went to my aunt and my uncle house. Everybody was getting ready to go to work. They went to work and we stayed there, we took a shower and we slept. I stayed with my aunt that day, and then the next day we moved with this friend of mine and another friend that we met while we were crossing, and he offer us to stay with him.

I was worried, because before I came here everybody used to tell me about the gangs in Chicago, that it was so dangerous to be here. And I was terrified when I got here. When I was living with my friend, the first few weeks, even to go to the corner to buy cigarettes, it was really scary for me and my brother. We used to be watching everywhere and everybody. And it was like that. It was really tough. Of course, it wasn't like that at all, but you have it in your head that that's the way it is, that you cannot wear this color or this other color hat or stuff like that. It was so scary for us. And we were there just trying to get a job, and without money. We didn't have money at all. I got here with a quarter in my pocket. So, it was tough. It was tough. I didn't have money to eat. We used to do our laundry like twice or three times a week because we just have like a few pair of pants, and a few pair of socks, and we have to do it. And my cousin give us some clothes and stuff like that. And they were really nice. My aunt help us a lot, a lot, a lot. My aunt, my uncle, my cousins, they help us a lot. I think if we owe somebody, it is to them.

So, I called the guy right away, the guy who want me to work with him as a DJ. I called him and he told me, "Where are you?" He asked me my address and he told me, "I'm going to pick you up tomorrow." He picked me up and we went down to buy some records and stuff like that.

So the first week I just went and I looked. It was at Marina Towers. Underneath there was a club. What he does is that he rents the places and then he promotes around. He gets DJs, and sound systems, and lightning. And then he charges people to get in the party and he keeps the money from the door and that's what he does.

So I went there and it was totally amazing for me. I mean it was totally different. The people was different from the people from Mexico. They looked different. Somehow they looked fancier than the people from Mexico. And the music was different.

So, I don't think I got to play the first night, but they paid me anyways. I got like $30, I guess, or something like that for my first night as a DJ. So after that, they start telling me, "These are the CDs." I never used a CD player to mix. I have to use a CD player. So it was totally different and I have to learn everything again, what people likes to dance, music that I never played in Mexico that they used to dance over here. And I start playing for him. It was only Saturdays. Just Saturday nights.

Maybe I was doing like $150 a week or something like that. But it was better, lots better. And then I got a part-time job cleaning out a shop. I used to go there and clean and take the garbage out twice a week. But it was some money, too.

So, by June or July, something like that, they told me that I needed a DJ name 'cause they need my name to put in the flyer to promote the parties. And they asked me who I would like to be called. So, I talked with my cousin. I was driving one time with my cousin in his car, and I was talking to him about it. By this time I was already thinking which was gonna be my name. So, I thought about that if we think about something small, something like when people like the music, when they hear the name, next time they're gonna know if you're playing it's gonna be good music. And they're gonna like it. So, I became with a name,

With his friend and boss, Frank, Chicago, 1998

with "DJ Diablo." Devil. I just figure out. So, I told my cousin that day in the car, "What do you think?"

And he was like, "I think it's kind of a strong name, to use it."

But I like it and then I told my boss. He's like, "Do you want it to be just 'Diablo,' or 'Diablo the DJ,' or 'DJ Diablo?'"

I go, "Whatever, just 'Diablo,' just 'Diablo.'"

So it came up to be a concert around those days of a Spanish band called Caifanes, really good, really good guys. And so they did like maybe 10,000 flyers and it was when they used my name the first time, "Diablo." And I have the flyer, by the way.

I wasn't thinking about school at all. I knew I needed it. I never speak English before. I mean, I guess it took me a while to start. I say a few words when I need it in a store or in a train, I mean in the bus or something like that. But let me tell you something. I know people that have lived in Chicago for 10 years and they don't speak any English because there is everything you need. You can go in a store and they speak Spanish. You can go a *taqueria* [taco stand] your whole life and they never gonna speak to you in English.

Of course, I wanted to learn and I feel bad, because me working in a night club, people used to come to me and talk to me in English, and ask me about if I can play this or that, and I didn't know what they were talking about and I feel embarrassed. And I'm not the kind of people who likes to be embarrassed. So, I knew I needed to learn English. I just didn't know how.

So I guess after a year here, I start going to school. Lakeview [Learning Center]. I register at Lakeview. Actually, I like the school and it was gonna be free. And I was like, "Well, I have a lot of free time. Why not?" So, I start studying English and I think I was doing OK. I stayed there for like a few levels. And then it was problems here and there. And I didn't wanna to be in school anymore. And then with job, I was trying to get another job always. And then it was too cold, I guess, too. It was like frozen to go out. And I couldn't handle it. And then I stopped for like six months I guess, and then I met my girlfriend, my wife, which is an American girl, a *gringa,* how I call her.

She used to go to Marina Towers. I know one friend and she introduced me to her and all her friends. We went out. Oh, I was so nervous. I'm nervous now that I'm thinking about it. I was so nervous. So I pick her up. She was so beautiful. She was just amazing and I couldn't believe that this woman was going out with me. So we went out and we started talking. It was really hard 'cause I wasn't really good in my English. So we went out and it took us a while to try to communicate ourselves. My English was really poor in those days. That's when I find out that my English was really poor. So, I went back to school. I went back to school because of her. I knew that sooner or later I was gonna learn English. But then when I found out that she didn't really speak Spanish, it was gonna be really hard. And I really wanted to be with her, so I went back to school. This time I went back to Truman.

Then when I started going to school, I think Kathy was my first teacher. One amazing thing at Truman is that teachers are always trying to, not to push you, but [encourage] you to go ahead with what you want. And over there they started telling me that I could do a lot of things if I wanted to do. And I realized that if I wanted to do something, I always was gonna find somebody to help me there. It was just like all the people there just wanted to help you. You weren't even asking for anything, but were always there offering you some kind of help to do something else for yourself. So, I started realizing that I could do more than just learning English. Then she told me about this program that, if I take a test and if I do good in math and English, I was able to take college credit classes. And I was like, "Wow!" So, I took the test and I did good. So, they told me that if I wanted, I was eligible for taking credit course.

After the first college class that I took, I got an A in the class. So, it seemed kind of easy, not that hard. I mean you have to work for it, but I really like that I can make it. I can do something like this. I can become whatever I want to become. If I wanna be a doctor, I can be a doctor or a lawyer or whatever I want. So, like I told you, people just opened the doors for me that I didn't even knew existed in Truman. So, I decided that I wanted to do something. I wanted to do something, and I wanted to do money 'cause I wanted to have a family, and I didn't want to be worried about what my family is gonna eat or things like that.

So, I also used to have a friend and I used to frequent this guy, and he used to do flyers for clubs in his computer, and he learned by himself just playing around with his computer. And I really like it, but I wanted to take it more seriously. I don't want it just to be in my house and I'm doing this and that. I want to do something out of it. I wanted to do my career of it. I wanted to become a graphic designer, or I don't know maybe a computer programmer, something but with computers 'cause I really like computers. I'm about to buy my computer hopefully, maybe in the next month. And I wanna finish a career. I wanna finish a good career.

Out of two years and a half that I've been in Truman, I didn't have to pay anything. And, God, it's a great incentive. It's a great opportunity that you have and it's for free.

After I met my wife, I started thinking differently 'cause I was looking around and, not that it's bad, but most of my friends, I used to see them working in shops or restaurants and I used to think, "It doesn't seem like it has a lot of future there. What if something happened to them? What if someday they cannot work anymore? What is gonna happen with them?" And I realized I didn't want that for me. Another thing of me that is I've never liked to work in a shop or in a restaurant. First of all, I don't like to have my hands dirty. It's like some vanity thing or something, but I don't like it. And I don't really like either when people gives me orders. And in my job, my boss has never told me an order. He asks me what to do, but it's not an order. He's more

On his wedding day, Chicago, August 19, 2000

180

asking me than telling me to do it. I mean, he never told me how to do my work. He asks me what time to get there, but he doesn't have to tell me anything else.

I start thinking more seriously with [my wife]. I realized that I really like her to be in my life. One time even, I broke up with her. It was really hard for us because at one point I realized that I wanted her really bad in my life, but in conversations she told me that she couldn't possibly go to live to Mexico. And up to this point, my whole idea was to be here, do something, and go back to live to Mexico. So, I got into a point that I didn't know what to do and I was just, I guess I was confused and I was really afraid of thinking about never seeing my family again, or being with the woman that I wanted to be in my life forever. So I just broke up with her. And I was really confused for some time. And then, it was really hard for her.

It was really hard for me. All that thinking, it was just driving me crazy. But somehow I realized that in some point of my life, I needed to take care of my own life, and that I also needed my family in Mexico, but sooner or later here or in Mexico, I was gonna be far from them if I wanted to do something with my own life. It's still really hard for me to even think about that I'm not going back there, but I need to do something with my life. If I'm always gonna stay thinking about what to do, I'm never gonna do anything. So I just realized that I'm gonna try to be there as much as possible, but I know that the rest of my future is gonna be here. I realized that, I thought about it, I went back with my wife, and I start thinking about going to school and going to school, going to school. And every single time it seems like I have more chance.

But it was one detail over here and that come up later on: How am I gonna go to a university? I need a social security number to go to university. And then I started getting tickets because I don't have a driver's license. And some day I'm gonna end up in jail 'cause I don't have a driver's license. And so, she thought about it that we should get married only so I can fix my situation, and later on get married in a formal way, the way we wanted to do it. I didn't really like the idea, but as the time passes, it seems like every day I needed more to be in a legal way in this country. It became a problem not to have a legal residency here. Plus, I didn't want my wife and her family to think that I was only using her to become legal in this country. I want everybody to know that I wanted to marry her because I love her and I want her to be my wife. And she used to tell me all the time, "Let's do it. Let's do it."

And I told her, "I don't want to. I don't wanna do it."

Another thing she wanted to marry me was so I could go to Mexico and see my family, because she sees how I cry. I cry in front of her telling her things about them. Up until I met my wife, I never really have a communication with my family in Mexico. I used to talk to them once in a while, really far apart the times. And then like I told you, I totally changed when I met her. Everything changed in me, totally. I started calling my family. Until now I'll call them almost every week. Every Sunday I call my mother, or any other day that I want, I just pick up the phone and I call my mother, my father or whatever.

It's really hard to be here. I used to cry a lot, almost every other day before. After six months I used to cry a lot because I just, I didn't have any idea when I was gonna see them again. And it's really hard. Even now I feel like crying. It's really hard to think about it. Then you think about the time that you spend with your family and me, I didn't get really close to my father or my mother. I never even get to tell my father or my mother that I love them. I was the kind of person that never show his feelings. And now, every time that I talk to them in the phone I make sure that I tell them that. But it's really hard. It's really hard. You have no friends. The people that you think is your friend is not your friend. Some other people help you, but you don't really have anything in this country. If you think about it, you don't even exist in this country. Legally, you don't exist in this country. So, you cannot own anything 'cause you can't. You can't. They just close you all doors. You cannot get a driver's license. You cannot drive. So, obviously, to get a job is almost impossible. And even if you get a job, how you gonna get to your job if you cannot even drive? And you're not gonna find a job around the corner. So they make sure to close you all doors. And you have so many problems here, trying to survive over here. And then you have all these memories in your head. It's just really hard. It's just really hard. You cry a lot. I cry a lot.

And it seemed every day harder for me to be here without the social security number, without a driver's license. So I needed to be legal in this country. So, we talk about it a lot. We talk about it a lot, a lot, a lot, a lot. So, I decide that I want her to be my wife, that I want her to be the mother of my sons and all that. And finally, when we decide to do so, it's really hard for me because it wasn't just going there and get married. It used to be like that, that you go, you get married and then you apply and that's it. But now it's not like that. When I went with her, I couldn't get married her and apply for my citizenship or residence. The laws in immigration, every single day are changing. They're just trying to make it harder and harder and harder for anybody to come to this country. So the best way for me to do it is that I have to go back to Mexico, and she needs to apply for a fiancé visa for me.

We flew to Mexico. We spent about 10 days with my family. She was really nervous. She really liked my family, my family really liked her. For me, you know, I have it on video when I just got there. It was just like crying and hugging. And my father and mother were crying and I was there hugging them crying, too. And my wife was recording it crying, too. And then I flew to the border, to Ciudad Juarez, to pick up my visa.

We enter here, and we have three months after the date I enter, January 28. And when we were to cross the border, the officer asked her for an ID, and she showed the ID and I showed my papers. So, she told me, "You have to come over here." So, she went to a parking lot with the cab driver and I went to an office. And they make a bunch of papers and signatures and fingerprints, and then they just give it to me in less than an hour, like 30 minutes or something like that. It was nobody there. No line, nobody around. Just the officer over there and like one of those things in the supermarket that you push to get in to count the people. And before you pass the thing, you show it to her and she did not even take a really good look. She was just like, "OK." And I went to the parking lot, and we went to the airport and that was it. It was ironic, the way they do it.

And we got married in March. We set the date and I ask her to marry me. I gave her the ring and we went to DuPage County, the courthouse. It's by her house. It's far, far. And I took my brother and my friend that live with me now, which is one of my best friends, too, and her mother and her father. And that's it. We went and we get married there. Like 15 minutes, I guess. I have it on tape also. That's a real wedding, but what we wanted to do was to keep that really apart from people knowing that we get married just to fix my papers or my situation here. We don't wanted people to know that. We don't wanted her family to know or anybody. So, what we wanted to do is that, keep that for us, this wedding for us, and the other wedding is when we're gonna invite everybody and let everybody know that we're getting married. And now we're going ahead with the plans for the ceremony, for the religious ceremony. We're looking for the sight, deciding, so many things that she need to look for. I just have to say, "I like it. OK. It's OK."

Discrimination is really great almost with everybody. I've feeled that. I've feeled that in restaurants. I have feeled that in the street. I have feeled that trying to get a job. You feel people looking you down, like you're too low for them. Even with another Latinos. And I think another Latinos are worse than any other people. They're just mean, and they want you to know they're mean, and they show you that they're mean. And it feels bad. It feels really bad. I've never wanted to become a resident or anything like that in this country because I have a resentment that, although a lot of people help me in this country, I've always have a resentment towards the most of the people because they always look you down. And I've always been really proud of who am I or what am I. And I'm from Mexico and I've always said that. And I didn't wanna become a resident of any other country because I'm really proud of being Mexican. I feel like they think like they own America, the United States people that say that the United States is America. It is not America because Mexico is in America, too. And it's not in South America. It's also in North America. Every time that I hear "America", what are you talking about? America is a bunch of countries. It's a lot, a lot of countries, not only one. If I would have been born in Europe, like in Italy, and I tell you welcome to Europe because you went to Italy, Italy is not Europe. Italy is Italy, and Europe is all those countries. I just think it makes no sense to say "America". Like the World Series. It's like what, a bunch of teams from the U.S.A.? There's a lot of people who play baseball, not only United States, and it's the *World* Series? I have no idea why they do that. Like in soccer, they play the World Cup and all the world plays. And in baseball, they play the World Series and only the United States plays. It really makes no sense.

For the longest time I was trying to get rid of my accent, but I don't think I wanna do it anymore. I always wanna keep my accent. I wanted to get rid of my accent because like I told you, people looks you up and down when they think you're lower than them if you're an immigrant or somebody else that is not from this country. But now I don't think I care about what people thinks about it. I just wanna be myself. I'm really proud of being here and learning another idiom [language]. I'm going to school and doing good in school, doing better than a lot of people that I see there that I know they're Americans. And I'm doing better than a lot of people that should be easier for them.

I'm gonna become a citizen because I need to, but I'm always gonna be Mexican and I'm always gonna say that I'm Mexican. And now that I almost fixed my situation, I don't go around telling everybody, "Oh,

With his wife, Jackie, and son, Diego, Chicago, 2002

you know what? Now, I have a visa. And look I have a work permit." I don't care about those things. I have them because I need them, because I have to have them, but I don't really care.

I think I wanna vote because it's a lot of people here that doesn't think that Mexicans or immigrants can do nothing much but work in the kitchens. There's a lot of people that think like that. I want a lot of people to know that we have power, too, and that we're a lot, and that we deserve a lot of things that we don't have. And I want them to know that we know that we can do it.

I couldn't stand to talk about Mexico before. Too emotional. It's too emotional still for me. I spent four years without going there, without seeing my family. It's really hard. I mean, I spend my whole life with my family. I've always lived with my family. My whole life I've been sleeping under the same roof with my brother. We sleep in the same bed and in the same room for 24 years. So, we were really close. My family is a really close family. Everybody's right there, right there always. And it was really hard. It's really hard to leave all your friends, everything you know, to go a country that you don't speak the language, you don't know the people, you don't know the customs. You just don't know what is gonna happen. You just go with the wind. And like I told you, I got here with a quarter in my pocket, and it's really tough.

There's people here that treat you really bad, that look you down. But there's another people there that help you a lot, like friends, and like my teachers, trying to open doors that you didn't even knew you can go through. All that makes your life better over here.

My boss, which is also my friend, Frank, he's been just great. He helped me since the beginning. He always helped me. He was always there for me for years and years. I can tell you about at least three years that he was always there helping me, every single day, every single time. He never let me spend a penny while I was with him for years. And I'm talking to you that I used to be with him every day, going here and places and there. And he always helped me. And this other guy, Oscar, which is another DJ, I don't understand why he was like that with me. He always helped me. He used to take me shopping. He used to invite me to eat. I'm talking to you that I was here a month, no, I was here a few weeks and he was already offering me, "I have some clothes for you that I wanna give you," and inviting me to places and taking me out and trying to make it livable for me.

I've never been better here than in my country. I mean, I live good. I have a nice car. I have a nice apartment. I have a nice life. Of course, my wife is the best part of my life here. But if you put that on the side, nothing is better.

I think every person who comes over here has a different story to tell. Most of the people who come to this country, it is for necessity because they don't have anything in their country and they need money and stuff like that. And people that is here because they need money, because they don't have money in their countries, they may live better than in their country, if you see it in a way about economically. But in any other way, you don't live better here than in your country.

OSWALDO IS WORKING AS A COMPUTER LAB MANAGER at Triton College in River Grove, Illinois, and continues to work as a DJ. He is looking for a job in web design. He is married and the father of a baby boy, Diego.

MY NAME IS # HARALLAMB TERBA **I WAS BORN IN TIRANA, ALBANIA** *in November 21st, 1965. I came here exactly in* **MARCH 25, 1996.** *It was afternoon, 5:00 Chicago time, but my watch say 12:00 in the night because it is seven hours different from my country to here. [Laughs.]*

DURING THE WORLD WAR TWO, my mother's family was separated because my grandfather came here to the United States. He had three daughters. My mom and her twin sister were 10 days old. They were little babies. They lived in a village near the border with Greece. He leave by himself because, at that time, the men came in the United States, they work for five, six years and they come back again. When the World War Second was over, the border were closed so they stayed separate. [My aunt, their oldest sister] was in school in Greece at that time and, when the border closed, she didn't have any other opportunity and she decided to go with her father [to the United States]. My mother [and her twin sister] with my grandmother stayed in Albania, and my grandfather with my aunt stay here in the United States. So, they stayed separated with each other for 50 years.

Because the communist government, which took place in Albania after the World War Second, was afraid because my mother's family escape the border, they took them from the village they were living and put them in a camp, which was the same like a prison because they were not free. They were surrounded with a soldier. They worked there. They worked hard for five years. Meantime, the communist system took everything, every property that they had in the village, like sheeps, goats, everything, the land, the house. After five years, they get the opportunity to come in Tirana, but not in their village. So they came in Tirana. They have a hard time to find a job because they [the government] consider like they were against the government. Finally they found a job, my mom get married with my father.

During all that time, my grandfather tried many ways to come in Albania to see two of his daughters and his wife. [We never spoke to each other] because in Albania they have telephone, but they couldn't talk with the United States or the other country. Once a month, every month, they send us the letter and check, and with their help we got a beautiful home in Tirana and our life, it was OK because we got money from here, from the United States, and we live very well comparing with the other people. Just we get $400 per month, but $400 per month, that were a lot of money. Two hundred went to their [the government's] pocket and two hundred came to us, but we fight for that. My mom went to the government and say, "Why? My father is Albanian. He left from Albania many years ago. It's not his fault that the border were closed. He is working in the United States. He just want to support his family, or let us to go there!" And that's why they let the money. Another way, they get benefits from that money because, comparing the dollar with a lek, a lek was nothing, the Albanian money. So, they get benefits from that, but they didn't let my grandfather and my aunt to send dress, things like that, or medicine. My grandmother was sick, and finally with fight with the government, we get the medicine from here and for that we have to pay twice. They pay here, but we have to pay in office there the same price that they pay here.

So, we got letters, we got pictures from them. This was really the first time I think about the United States. I think, "I want to go there, I want to live there." Because I see that in Albania I don't have a lot of cousins, I don't have a lot of relatives. They all were here.

Just I get the idea from my family, from my grandmother and my mother because they always talking about the United States. I remember when we get the letters, I took off the stamps, the United States stamps, and I collect them in a book. I always, you know, I got in my mind it was here in Chicago. And my mom always told, "There is my father—your grandfather; my sister—your aunt." But it's not only this. They have their first cousins here.

Finally, in 1981, my aunt get the permission and she came with her son in Albania and they stayed only three months. They don't let them to stay more than three months. It was the first time my mother saw her sister. And my grandmother saw her daughter. She [my grandmother] saw her when she [my aunt] was 16 years old and now she was 58. I remember that day. It was a lot of crying from both part, from my mom. And I remember exactly that day, because my mom was in hospital because she get some problems with her legs. And they came from United States without notice. They just knock the door. I opened the door. When I saw a big guy I thought, "Who is this?"

He told me, "I am your cousin from the United States. I am Johnny from the United States!"

I couldn't believe that. "How could you came here?"

I saw my aunt just from the pictures, you know. They came upstairs. There was my grandmother. She started crying. And after that we went to the hospital. My aunt say, "OK, we have to go in the hospital to see your mom." And we went to the hospital.

My mom noticed immediately. She saw out of the window and she said, "Oh, come on! This is my sister from the United States. How could she came here?" But, you know, they meet each other. They start crying. They didn't say nothing, only crying, crying, crying. That night my mom didn't sleep at all and tomorrow morning she say to the doctor, "OK, I'm gonna sign out. I'm going home. I don't care about nothing. My sister came. There are a lot of years I didn't see. I'm going home!"

And the doctor say, "OK, you can go."

[My aunt's] son was 19 years old. I was 16 years old. We spent all these days together. We were like brothers. And I learned a lot about America. This guy told me everything about here, the life here, and many times he gets angry about the way we live in Albania. He told me, "Why you not against the government?" He couldn't believe how we was prevented from the right of speaking or thinking. I had a hard time to explain him what happened if you say something, we are going to go to the prison. And our family had some [experience] like that.

They were in camp only because [the government] think that my mom and my grandmother can escape the border.

They stayed only three months. They wanted to stay more, but the system doesn't let them to stay more. I remember the day when they left from Albania. We still were crying. In the airport I was shaking hands with him, and it was the first time that I saw him cry and he just told me, "I believe that you will come in the United States. We will live all together." But this wish doesn't come true because the time I am here now, he is not. He passed away, heart attack, heart problems. He was 32 years old. This is the last time I saw him, just three months. He stay in my heart. I always remember him. He was just my brother, my bigger brother.

After six months, my grandfather get the permission to come in Albania. This was a really hard time for my mom because she saw for the first time her father. She knew that she has a father, but she knew him only from the pictures. It was very hard for my mom. She say, "I have a father but I don't know who is my father. I want to say, 'Daddy,' but I can't say. OK, my mother takes care for me. She did everything for me, but I want the love of my father." So, it's very hard to know, to have in your mind that you have a father, and you couldn't meet him. This was very hard for her. For what? There was no reason. Just

With his mother and wife celebrating their arrival, Chicago, 1996

the politic reason. And for he, it was a very hard time. I remember when he came in our home with my mom he said, "I remember a little girl, and now I saw a woman in middle age."

To be honest, I know he is my grandfather, but he was like a strange person. I always know, always in my heart was the idea that a part of my family is in the United States, and I want to go there and I believe I will be here in the United States, but I don't know when. And when he came I thought in myself, "OK, he is my grandfather, but he looks strange to me." Because you know, I had nothing, any love, anything. Just, he was very polite with me. But you know, little by little I learned. I accustomed to that idea that he is my grandfather.

When my grandfather came in Albania I asked him, "What you see from the plane?"

He told me, "I saw a lot of ships."

"What?"

"Ships. These bunkers looked like the ship from the plane." So there were so many of them. Even outside of your home that you live there were just bunkers, bunkers, bunkers and they were built to be against our enemies. First enemy was United States. So they were really ridiculous, really crazy. This idea of building all these bunkers everywhere in Albania and they cost a lot of money for building them. Concrete and steel. Everywhere you go you see only bunkers, bunkers, everywhere. They are empty now.

He stayed exactly three months. He wants to stay more in Albania, but they didn't let him to stay more. Just three months. And for my mom, this is the first and the last time that she saw her father because he passed away when he came here in the United States many years after, in 1989, before the revolution in Albania.

My father, he was in Italy before the Second War. He was a young guy and my grandfather, his father, had a store in Tirana. He lived OK. My father, when he was young, he lived a good life. He came from a family that, before the communists it was, you could say, middle class. He get some money, but when the communists came, they took everything! He came back in Albania, but after the communist he lose everything. His family lost everything. He have to work hard and live.

[My mom and dad] are people who work hard. They were peaceful people. They wanted to live in peace and harmony. They wanted freedom because they were people who worked and worked to get a better life just by their work, but the system don't let them.

My father worked for a wood company. They makes furniture. He makes the furniture and he designs the furniture. It is ridiculous, because he designs furniture for the leaders of the government. This is ridiculous! He hates them, but in other way, he has to do a job for them.

My father wanted to come to the U.S. He always talked to me about the communism, "It's the worst regime that all world has now. We are not free to say nothing. We are not free to express ourselves. We are living like in prison. We are doing what they say. We are not people. We are like the animals. Animals do what the other say." Just tell me all that stuff. He always talked to me like this. He always advised, "But please don't say anything outside because our life, it is going to be in danger. But keep in your mind that one day we are going to be free, and we are going to go where we want to live."

I was child when he talks to me like that, and I thought sometimes, "What he's talking? What's he saying we are not free?" But he just gave me examples.

He say, "People in west or your grandfather, my father-in-law, he lives in the United States. Their life is better than ours. They work and they send us money. So we lives from them, from their money. So we work here, but we don't get money to live, to support ourselves, our family. Our money that we get from here are not enough." He gives me a lot of examples like that. "They are free. They have cars. We don't have cars. They have their homes. We don't have. We have to live in the government homes, but we are lucky because we get the money from the United States and we buy our home." About the culture, "They are free. If you see their movie, they are something realistic."

He loves movies, and he took me always in theatre to see the movie and that's why I love movie. I wanted to work for the movie. He told me, "All that movie that came from the other world, it was just cowboy movie, old movie. They stopped new movie because they don't let to see what really happen in Western Europe and the United States." He always told me, "You see the movie, they are free in writing, they are free. Just listen to the music. Our music is like a march, like a band. And our musicians are not free to compose the music what they feel in their heart. That's why the music here it's like a march, like a band. And if you listen to the other music, it came what they have in their heart." He told me, "We say that we are doing fine, we are the best of the world, communism is the best system of the world. Here no one is dying, but when you went out of Tirana, you see where they live. Now compare with the pictures that came from the United States, compare the home. You see where they live, you see where we live in Albania." All these examples would just put in my mind that I have to leave this country.

But anyway, I don't blame my country. I don't blame Albania. I don't blame my people. They were very good people. I blame the government. All that is the government. Because he told me, "Before the communists, I was living very good. My life, it was OK. My father has money. I got money. I work and I get money, but now we work and we don't have. We have to move. We have to go in someplace else and they don't let us to go there."

Really, when I was in high school, I make a friend, and he was my best friend, my close friend and I talk together about that. First, I was afraid about that because I couldn't believe anyone, because my father told me, "In this system, of three persons, one works for the secret service." But at that time we were only two. [Laughs.] He was my best friend. His name is Tom. He is in Albania now. He is working for an American company in Albania now, and we got many things the same together. We wanted to go in United States. We saw only the United States, the land of opportunity, the land of the freedom, the land that we can do what we dream in our life.

Secretly we heard the Voice of America. The signal came very weak, but we heard every day. I remember it was at 5:00 afternoon. We don't lose [miss] any edition of the Voice of America. My father say once to me, "This is not the Voice of America, but this is the voice of truth. And you have to believe what they say, because what they say is the truth." But only secretly. I was in high school at that time and we keep the volume down because we were afraid. I remember that the best position of the radio was in the hallway in the second floor, but it was a little danger because somebody outside can hear. [Laughs.]

There are no church. Nothing about the religion. In 1960s the leader of our country say, "No more church. The religion is the opium for the people. We don't believe in religion. There is no God. We believe in ourselves, in our job, in our work, in our party, in our Communist Party." [Laughs.] They took all the religion book and burned. No Bible. It was illegal before. They took the icons on the church. It was a really wonderful icons on the church, and they burned them. But some people took some of them icons, and they survive them in their home, and after the revolution they bring it back in the church. This was really wonderful.

I just know something about religion from my grandmother. We were Orthodox. She always told me, "You have to be nice with the other people. You don't have to [must not] lie. You don't have to [must not] spy someone else." Things about the religion. Then after when I get the Bible, and study the Bible and I compare what she told me, it was true. It was on the Bible. She learned me to believe in God, in Jesus Christ.

After I finished high school, I went to army for two years. One way, it's a good experience for everybody to stay in the army, but it's hard for a guy in this age. I was 19 years old and I was so far from my family. It was my first time that I went so far from my family. I thought, "OK, everything I have to do what they tell me." There is nothing that I can do what I want, but even I can't stay OK in army. For example, I was in artillery. And they prevent me from be the gunsign [spotter], who make the sign for the target. And they prevented me to stay there because I have my relatives, my grandfather was in United States. So, the only thing that I can do in military was just transport because I have someone in the United States.

They say, "Our enemy is the United States, so how can you let this guy to do that when he has people there." So, that's why I was prevented. I remember I wanted to go to the kitchen to cook for the soldier, and they say, "No, you can't do that."

And I say, "Why?" But they didn't tell me in front, but I learned that they didn't let me to went to the kitchen because they were afraid that I have someone outside in the United States, so they can't believe me that post 'cause maybe I can put something in the food. No trust. So, my experience from the army, it's very bad. I feel separated from the others, even [though] I didn't have nothing in my mind to do something like that. But they don't like me.

When I come back from the army, I met my wife and I start a job. Because I loved movies, I decided to work for that movie company, because it was just one movie company in Albania. And I start working there like a costumer, about the dress. I was the assistant of the designers. After, I start making sounds of the movie. And I loved my job. There was completely different, because I have to work with people who work with the art, and they feel more than all the other what is free. I loved my friends there. I make a lot of friends there because they know what freedom means. They talk with each other. They were not afraid about saying what is wrong and what is right. So, for me this was a very good opportunity. They know that something is wrong with their government. Even they say, "OK, we have to do that" or even they make movie for the government, movie for the communist, but they know in their heart that this is not the way that we have to work. We have to do something else, but they couldn't do that. But with each other they express that. They talk and they liked me. Even the fact that

Celebrating Christmas with his wife, Ana, Chicago, 1998

I have people in the United States, my grandfather, my aunt, and they like me and they wanted to know about that, about the United States. I just told them what I know from my first cousins. I was lucky because I have a real contact with an American, and he was young. They just ask me always, "What he said for that? What he said for that? What he said for that?" And I was telling, explaining.

I was in the center of Tirana [one day] and there was no blue jeans, cowboy pants, and one guy has a pair of pants like that and they [the police] stopped him. It was 6:00 P.M. in the afternoon. It was a time that everyone was outside because people doesn't have nowhere to go. Just in the afternoon they stay outside and they have a discussion about the sport, about the soccer, nothing else. And they saw this guy and they tear his pants in the middle of the street and all the people was looking.

And with the long hair. Same story happened with the long hair. You couldn't get your hair long. They cut the hair in the street. They don't care about that. "You are not our guy. This is not our moral, our communist moral. This is a revisionist moral." And believe me, this guy was really in trouble. Only for the hair, only for the pants.

All these guys were really in trouble because they [the government] were going to their family, and talk with the parents and they have a meeting in the neighborhood, with all the neighbors. This guy have to stay in front of all neighbors and all the neighbors have to say something for that guy, "It's not good. Why you do that? Why you

keep your long hair? This is not our moral." So, even those people understand that this is not right, but they have to say that. Like the public shame. You have to say that that's wrong.

Some of the friends that I make when I was free from the army, they were trying to escape the border and they were dead. They killed them. They killed them, and they never noticed [notified] their family that they killed them because they were trying to escape the border. But they kill them and they throw them in the mountain. And no one knows what happened. And their family always ask for them, "Where they are?" They went to the police station, they say, "My boy is disappeared. My son is disappeared."

And they say, "OK, we're going to found them."

But they know better what happened. A lot of guys died.

I thought about that, I thought escape the border, but I think about my mom. She stayed five years in prison [camp]. But if I escape, she's going to stay for the rest of the life in that camp, in prison. I don't talk because I don't want to make them afraid. The only reason that I didn't do that it was just because I think about my mom.

My mother she talked with two guys [once]. They were American, but they speak Greek. They needed some help, but no one knows their language. Even they [Albanians] know how to speak English or Greek, they [Albanians] turned their head to the other side because they were afraid. But my mom, I don't know, she just wanted to help them. She say, "OK, I can speak with you. What you want?" They wanted direction. She explained them. But after two hours, the police came in our home and took my mom. We were all surprised.

My father asked her, "What you did?"

She said, "Nothing." My father went directly after them in the police station, and there we learned that they took her. Why? Because she had [spoken] with other people, foreign people. But my mom speaks Greek, so she just wanted to help them. She said, "They asked me for direction and I give them the direction. I did nothing wrong!"

With me I had the same thing. When I was in my job working for the movie company, we went in south side of Albania and there was a guy from Italy. He was a photographer, and he went with us because he wanted to take some pictures because Albania is a beautiful country, has a beautiful nature, high mountains, beautiful sea, the Adriatic Sea. After that, one month later we came in Tirana. In center of Tirana is a big hotel, 15 stories. This is the biggest hotel in Albania, 15 floors. And I went there because I wanted to buy cigarette. I was coming down from the stairs when I meet this guy, [the photographer]. I say, "Hello," and we have just a simple conversation, how are you, when are you going back to Italy. We say, "Bye-bye."

When I went down, there was a guy downstairs, and he say me, "Can you come here please for a moment?"

I went there. I say, "What's the problem?"

He ask me, "Do you know him?"

I say, "Yes, of course I know him. He is from Italy. He is a photographer. He work with us for some days. That's why."

He say, "You have to come with me in the police station."

"For what?"

"You are going to learn that when you go there! Can you give me your name?"

I said, "OK, you can have my name. Can I have your identification?"

He say, "No, I don't have anything here by myself. I have in my home."

"But I want to know the reason, for what?" He didn't say nothing. He just called the police. The police guy came and took me in the police station.

They ask me for two hours, "Why you did that? It's something wrong. He's not from Albania. He's Italian. We don't know what he's doing here, for what he's photographing here."

So I just explain, "OK, you can call my institution. Just ask them. They know him." This is my second experience. Just because we can't talk with the other people.

I saw the parade in North Korea [on TV] last month or last two months. When I saw all those people crowding on the streets and carrying all the red flags and the portrait of their leaders, it was the same I remember everything in Albania. In Albania we have parade every year for May 1st. It was the day of the working class and all the people have to go, even they don't want to go there, but they have to do that. And they stay for five hours in line to go in front of the old leaders, even there were a rainy day, because it's May 1st. Sometimes it was a good day, perfect, but sometimes it was really winter. They have to stay there without umbrella, because it's a respect for the leader. This very crazy thing. Even though they don't want to go there, they have to go there. They looks like monkeys, like the robots. But they have to do that. Seven years in prison [if they don't go]. I went there twice from my school. The government doesn't say directly that you have to go there, but it was the system. It was built in this way, that every school,

every factory, have a communist organization, so the leaders of this organization make you to go there. They make a list so they say, "Five hundred for this factory have to go in this parade tomorrow," or from this school. So on this list they sign all the names. If you say something, "No, I don't want to go," you are in trouble.

I always had the hope that someday I would come here. And when I start working for the movie company, we started to believe that very soon something is going to happen, because we saw that everyone saw the difference. Everything it's going wrong, everything it's going down, that something is going to happen, but when, we didn't know that. The first sign came in 1990 when people went to the embassy in Tirana. Many people went to the embassy in Tirana. There was not American embassy at that time. Italy, Germany, some of them to the France embassy. But most of them went to the Italy and Germany embassy and they stay there for 10 days. It was a really bad days. Imagine the guys on the embassy and their mothers were outside and crying because they want to know what is going to happen, because the government say, "We are going to put in prison all these guys that went to the embassy."

At the Germany embassy came the German ambassador and say, "OK, all you guys you are going to go safely to Germany. Even if I will die, I'm going to let you."

And this was true. All these guys went to the Germany, to the Italy, and to the France. And some of them wants to come in the United States and they came. From Italy they came to the United States. From Germany they say, "I want to go to the United States," and they came here.

This was the first sign, and it was really ridiculous that after they left Albania, the government organized a meeting in the center of Tirana and they say, "All these guys were the enemy of our country." But who were these guys? They were from Albania.

Another people went to the ship and went to the Italy. Just one day. Twenty thousand people that day went to the Italy. This was a time that I want to went there. I talk with my wife. I say, "OK, let's get the train now. Let's run to the Italy."

But she was afraid. She said, "No, let's wait two days more. Let's see what's going to happen." But this waiting left us there because nothing happened.

I was excited. This was the first sign that something it's going to happen, that this government, it's not going to stay anymore. And their secret service, their soldiers, their police was like crazy on the street.

They took some guys and beat them, and it was very bad situation at that time. By '91 everything destroyed. It was like revolution which start from the students. They went to the president of the government and they say, "OK, we want from you to let us to create another party, Democratic Party."

He say, "Yeah, but it's not time now."

"We don't care. We think this is the time and we have to do it now. If you don't, we are going to talk with the people and we are going to take the power with force." So he didn't have any other choice and he let to create another party. It was the first time that was two parties, the Democratic Party and the Communist Socialist Party. Another election came.

It was the day, Sunday, that we have to vote, to give our vote for Democracy or for the Socialist. And my grandmother, she was 85 years old at that day, and she told me, "OK, you are gong to bring me there. I have to vote."

I told, "It's OK. The Democratic Party's going to win anyway because all the people going to vote for that."

She said, "No, I'm going to give that vote for that [Democratic Party] guy." And I took her, little by little, it was not so far. And she went there. She told me, "OK, Harry, you don't want to lose any votes." Outside it was a guy. His father was a communist and a spy. He knows what I have in my mind. He knows that I was against. I don't say nothing. I took my grandmother inside the room. And there were the people who works for the vote, the election, and they all stand up for that. One guy just give the paper, take the identification and put her name, put everything and gives us the paper. And she went to the room, but she couldn't see well and she told me, "OK, just sign for the Democratic leader."

And I signed for that and she folded the paper. And all the people say, "Thank you." They couldn't do nothing. She walked, I holded her.

The Democratic Party win absolutely power. It's '92. I was a member of the Democratic Party, and it was just a happy day, just laughs. I remember the day that the Democratic Party won, just the streets was full of the people. The flags of the Democratic Party and people shouting, kissing each other. It was a big, big. big day. And it was the spring, and I remember one of the leaders of the Democratic Party say, "This is the spring of the democracy."

It was some fighting when they tear down the bust of the dictator, Hoxja, in three cities, in Tirana and in two other cities. The police was outside, but people say to the police, "Come on. You are going to shoot me? We are brother. Even you have this uniform, but you are the same like me. We eat the same thing. We live in the same neighborhood. Why you are going to shoot me?"

So that's why there's not so bloody in Albania. But you know, everything it's hard. It's hard to come from one system to another. And the leaders who had the power before, they were still in the same position, but they were in the other party.

My father passed away, but he saw the democracy. He was very happy and he say, "Finally, this is our day." Just he told me, "This is for you. This is your life. Now you are free. I was prevented from this freedom from when I was in your age, and I get now that I'm old. So you have it now." He didn't cry, but in himself like he was crying. His eyes was. My mom was happy, too. She wanted to come here. At that time my grandmother passed away, so I stay only with my mom.

I thought, "I want to go in America. I'm gonna start working." I didn't thought that I'm going to work in my profession, that I'm going to do the same job that I'm doing in Albania, but I'm gonna work. Just I'm gonna go there. This was in my mind, "Now I have all my chances to go to the United States."

My aunt said, "Come on. Just for what are you waiting there? Come on just as soon as you can."

And I went to the American embassy because the American embassy came in Albania. It was a sunny day. They called the names. It was a little window. Behind the window it was a girl, 35 years old. She was very polite. She was American girl, but she speaks Albanian! I couldn't speak English at that time, just: hello, thank you, my name is... That's it. And she speaks very good Albanian. She surprised me. And I just told all my history, all my story and, "I want to go, I want to visit them, I want to go there."

She said, "OK, but you have to come in the afternoon. You have to let your passport here and you're going to come in the afternoon."

From that time I was worried about if they say something, "Oh, you don't have to [can't] go, something like that." But when she called my name and she said me, "Good trip, *bon voyage*," I was so happy.

It was a very, very happy day. I saw my passport with American visa. I couldn't believe that. I thought, "This cut my distance from Albania to the United States. This is my dream. Now the half of my dream is true, because the completed dream is going to be true when I will become an American citizen. Now I have the permission to go there to my dream country, to the country of my father's dream, my mother's dream, my grandmother's dream. I have a part of my family here. I have cousins here that I never know."

After that, my mom went and she get her visa and my wife get her visa. And I remember that everything that we had in our home, we give it to neighbors or to relatives. Everything that we had, everything. I remember I have a bookshelf and I told my mom, "No, I'm not going to give that because I like that." My father make it for me and here are all my books, and I have something from that books. It's a story for me because I have read that book at one time. Even I saw the title of the book, I remember the time that I read it, so I'm not give that, and I put it in one room and I closed it. My bookcase is in my home in Tirana. And when I go there, I'm going to take all my books. I'm going to bring it here.

We made a celebration party five days before we left from Albania. We invited all the people that we knew. After that day, the home was just empty, nothing. And we let the home to one cousin because they came from other city. They wanted to live in Tirana. We said, "OK, you can live there. Maybe we will come one day, for one month, for two months and we can stay in your home!" [Laughs.]

They laughed, "No, it's your home!"

It was Sunday when we left from Albania. It was a sunny day. I went to the airport. I don't have no one in Albania from my relatives. My wife, she has a lot. People cry, but on the other hand they say, "You are lucky."

We went to the airport. It was my first time in the plane. I was little afraid about the plane. I saw from the window, we came from the Adriatic, and the plane went to the Italy. And I saw the Italy, the shape of the Italy like a boot, and we was flying in the middle of the Italy to go to the Switzerland, and I thought, "It is Sunday afternoon. Now the soccer championship is playing in this land." This was our dream, you know. When we were in Albania we always look at the Italian soccer team because they were our neighbor. "Today, now I'm flying over them."

I didn't sleep. I just want to enjoy every moment. That was the first time for me in the airplane. I saw people, the food. Everything it was different from my experience in Albania. It was funny because when the food came, it was the lunch and the girl ask me, "You want something?"

I heard her to say chicken. But I don't like chicken, I like meat. And I thought in my mind, "If this one is going to be chicken, the other one is going to be meat." So I say, "No, the other one. Not chicken, the other one." But the other one was vegetable food. So I have to eat.

With his aunt at his graduation from Truman College, Chicago, 2001

[Laughs.] This was funny about the language.

And I went to Switzerland. And next day we changed the plane and came to the United States. And I remember it was a TV in the plane and showed where we were and I saw the Quebec and the Lake Michigan and just I wanted to see down, how it looks. But I saw only a big part of white. There were ice in the middle of Lake Michigan! And when we went to the Chicago, it start snowing. My mom say, "This is a good sign, because when you go in somewhere place and start snowing snow, the snow means food. It means many things. It's a good luck."

So, we went to the airport. I couldn't get the opportunity to see the Chicago from upstairs [above] because it was cloudy. I went to the airport. "I couldn't believe," I said, "that I am in America." It was just a dream. Officer sat down just start asking us. We don't speak English. I just say, "We came from Albania." I told, "I go my mother's sister." But nothing else.

She put us in one room and say, "You have to stay there."

At that time, one other guy, an officer came and asked me, "You speak French?"

I say, "No."

"Spanish?"

"No," but I say, "I speak Greek."

He say, "It's OK. You have to wait here. We're going to get a guy who speaks Greek and he's going to translate. Don't worry about nothing."

We was worried. We thought, "What happened?"

We stayed there for a half an hour. A guy came. Another officer interview us. We went out. We get our luggage. My aunt was waiting for us. I saw my aunt older. I remember her from 1981, when I saw she was younger. That time now she was older and she looked at us and she start crying. She say, "Now we are going to stay together for all our life. Nothing is going to separate us anymore." And my mom, it was hard, but it was happy. The first time that we meet each other [in 1981] we were happy, but we were sad because we know that they are going to come back and we are going to stay there. But at this time, we were just happy. We met each other, and we know that we are going to stay there forever, we are going to stay all together.

We took a taxi because she say, "It's hard to park in the air terminal. I don't know how long we are going to stay there, so it's better to take the taxi."

When we was coming back from the airport to home I saw many cars. I said, "Hey, I'm in America. I'm in America! I can't believe that. How fast I came here. It was so many years just all my life dreaming to come here, and just for one day I came in this land where my grandfather came, all my relatives. Now I'm here."

The next day I took my wife. I say, "OK, let's get out. Let's see."

My aunt say, "OK, we can go with the car."

I told her, "No, I like to walk because I'm going to see better things when I walk. In the car I don't see nothing." So I took my wife and we went around the neighborhood to Lincoln [Avenue] and Catalpa [Avenue]. I went to the Foster [Avenue], to the Western [Avenue]. Just we went back. Same thing the next day.

After that I met one guy. He was from Albania. He had been living here for two years. When we went out he say, "OK, I'm going to show you something about Chicago."

When I went first time downtown and I saw all those cars, I thought in my mind, "I'm gonna lose [get lost] in this city."

But my friend from Albania that took me there [said], "The same thing I say when I first came here. So don't worry about that." And he was right. He was right with that.

And he took us at the planetarium. From there it's a wonderful view. But when we went to the Lake Shore Drive, I saw the wonderful view of Chicago and I say, "Ah, this is America. I'm here." I was excited. I saw the big buildings. I saw the face of Americans that I saw on TV.

Just a lot of cars. Big buildings. I was happy. I couldn't believe. I was afraid that I was in a dream and I can wake up one moment and I will be in Albania. Just this was a wonderful dream. That's it. And I was afraid that sometimes I'm gonna wake up and, "Oh, this is nothing true. I am in my bed in my country in Albania."

And I never thought that I'm gonna speak English. I just thought, "I have to learn to communicate with people, to have a simple conversation." I never thought that I'm gonna be interviewed by someone else, by an American, in English!

He say me, "You have to go to Truman College. I know that place and there you are going to learn English because I learned English at that place."

And I told, "OK, just show me where is Truman College." And he took me to Truman College with my wife. It was registration at that time. I saw many people. I say, "Hey, why I am here? They are American students. I am in American college." It was unbelievable for me. Everything it was unbelievable. Just a dream. Just a beautiful dream. They register. Then, they put us in level 1.

We come back and we start coming to the Truman College, learning every day, every day, every day learning something. Now I speak English. I don't speak good English, but I dedicate all my English to Truman College because I couldn't say any word when I came here.

After I start in Truman College, I took my wife and I went there in downtown and we start walking downtown. We start going to the stores, and you know everything was perfect, everything was beautiful, and we start hearing that surround us were American people. We just start thinking and thinking, "We are going to be a part of this society. We are going to be a part of this life. But not now, but after little by little." I'm going to feel a part now when I will become American citizen. This is my completely dream about America. 'Cause I want to live here. I want to stay here forever.

People always help me to correct [my English]. They told me, "You're going to learn by your mistakes. Just say." I don't talk with the other people on the street. People talk to me in English now and just I answer them a short answer.

I feel like I understand, but I feel that I have to work more in talking. I understand everything. Even when I saw a movie or different programs in TV or in radio, because in radio it's a little bit more harder than TV, I understand. When I say something, when I talk, after that I recognize my fault, "Oh, I have to say it in that way, not in that way that I say it." I think it happens for the new language.

Going to the grocery store, I like that because you don't have to talk! You just pick everything you want. So, this is good for people who can't speak English. But on the other hand, it's bad because if you want to learn you have to say, "I want that one." And the guy is going to say the name of the product that you want. I was surprised because in my country you have to ask the guy, "I want one pound for that product. I want one pound for that." And here you just pick everything. It was something new.

I was really feel bad when I went to the stores, for the dress stores in downtown. There were the girls, very polite girls, and they came and ask us, me and my wife, "You need some help?"

We couldn't express ourselves. [Laughs.] We don't know how to say. Just we say, "No, thank you."

I try to feel like an American, and I want to feel like an American. That's why I'm talking with my wife. I say, "OK, let's don't talk in our language. Let's talk English! Let's practice English in our home because we are living here." I don't like the idea that I get on the bus and I heard too many languages and I don't hear English. OK, everyone have to speak his native language, but not in public place. Just little bit more respect for this country. We are here. Let's talk this language. Because if the native people saw us and we spoke our language, it's the same if an American is going to come in Albania and they speak their language.

So, I want to stay here and I think I will feel more American. You know what? When I first came here, just because I like sports, I start seeing in TV only basketball, because it was the only sport that I could understand. The second year I start seeing American football. And now I start seeing American baseball. So you see how it came, year after year we became more American. But everything depends on the person. If you want to be American, you can do that. You can be American. You can think like that. You can feel like an American. But I think, it's the language. How good you are going to perfect the language, how good you are going to express yourself, you are going to be more American.

There are many things that make the American life very easy, like credit cards or the bills. Just I saw my aunt. The bills came in home and she fill the bills and she put it in the mailbox. She doesn't have to go there to pay. You have to go and to stay two hours in line [in Albania] to pay the electric bill, to pay the water bill. Even when you go to get your benefits, your monthly fare, you have to wait in line.

And here everything comes in home. Just fill out from the home and mail it. That's it. All these things make the life very easy and gives to people more time. The organization. In that way it's perfect. For example, if you need something, you just call. If you have some problem with the TV, or the air conditioner, or refrigerator, just call and the service is going to come. And in my country, you have to go there to get that guy and to ask them, and they are gonna say, "OK, not today, not tomorrow, after a week."

"But it's the refrigerator."

"OK, but I don't have time and I don't have car." Something like that. It's always something.

We have to work hard. After the first month, you have to work. You have to work because you have to start your life, and I started come to Truman College and I start reading and learning and studying hard to get here where I am. I'm sad that I lost a lot of my years in this system. I wish to be here younger.

I'm in college now. My major is computer information system. I think after I will be graduating from school, I'm gonna start working, maybe for a company. I love working in computer, computer programming, designing and building programs, applications. I think my life is gonna be good. I always think about that. My wife is in school, too. She's taking sign language. She loves working with deaf people. So, I think she is gonna get a good job.

I'm lucky because I have my wife. She is for me my wife, my friend, my sister. She is everything for me. I share everything with her and she with me, so that's why I think I don't feel lonely, because I have her. We are both together now. I think if I was alone here, I would feel lonely.

I miss friends here in United States. I miss American friends. And I have to make more American friends. Having more American friends is gonna make me feel more American. And my language, it's gonna be more perfect. In Truman, I have the opportunity to meet a lot of people from different countries, from different cultures, but you have small opportunity about Americans. It's hard because the language. But I think now I am OK to make that. Our friends that we met here are from different countries, our classmates, friends that we make in Truman. I like that because even they are from the other countries, they have the same dream. They are here. They have forget about their countries. They wanted to be part of this life.

It would be very, very different [if my cousin were still alive], because he was American. I would be in his friends. I would be a part of his relationship. I met one day one guy in front of my home and he was American guy and he asked me, "You are John's cousin?"

And I say, "Yes. I am."

And he said me, "John told me a lot about you. You are from Albania?"

I said, "Yes."

And just we have a simple conversation and he said, "Nice to meet you." I don't know if he's friend. Just that's it.

I know maybe when I'm gonna meet friends from my country, they are gonna tell me if I have changed or not. I think I am the same.

Home is a place where you live. I think about my home in my country. It's the place where you born. But this is the life. The life change. You have to move. You have to try and when you try for the best, it's better for you. I like my country. I like the people there, but I feel this is my home now. I don't feel that about Albania now. I feel that when I was in Albania, I have this thought in my mind that, "I will go. One day I will go in the United States. Everything that I did here it's nothing. I have to get my education. I have to work. I have to do, but everything it's gonna start when I go in the United States." That's why I wish to came here younger.

I think to have my own home, years after. I think about that. It's not important, but I always loved having my own home, my yard. I always loved that because I have been grow up with big home with a yard in front, so that's why I love that. But now I'm living in apartment and everything is OK. I like that.

In the future I want plan for to have children. I'm going to tell my children in the future that they will be American because they will be born here, but I always am gonna tell them from where they are, their parents are. So they have to know about their country because this was the country that grow us, their father and their mother. So they have

Working in the Truman College computer lab, Chicago, 2002

to know about their culture. Maybe I'm gonna advise them that when they go in Albania, to be more Albanian than Albanians are, because Albanians are gonna see them just, "Hey, you are from America. You're American." You know what happens.

America to me means freedom, and the land where everyone can do what he dreams. Dreams come true. It's a hard work to do what you want, but finally you can do that. I came from one country that you want to do something, but no one lets you to do that. You can only do what they say to you. So here, if you want to do that, if you like to do that, you can do that. It's hard. I know it's hard. Nothing is easy in our life today, but you can do that. And this is more important for our life, to do what we want.

195

HARALLAMB LIVES IN CHICAGO. He is studying for his bachelor's degree in computer science and working in a computer lab at Truman College.

MY NAME IS CARLOS GANDOLFO *I am 38 years.*
I AM FROM ARGENTINA *and I remember I came here in July 12th, 1997. I think that was a Sunday. It was a Saturday when I left Argentina and I arrived to New York in Sunday* **JULY 13, 1997.**

IN ARGENTINA, I THINK THAT 50 PERCENT ITALIAN AND 40 PERCENT SPAIN and 10 percent from around the world. My mother and my father are from Argentina. But my grandmother and my grandfather, they are from Italy, both of them. My last name is Gandolfo. It's from Genoa, the north of Italy. And the last name of my mother is De Conti. It's from Italy, too.

I was born in Patagonia in the south of Argentina in 1962. The name of the state is Neuquén. My father is a dentist and he worked there in Chos Malal. It's a very small town. It's 2,000 people. Very small. My mother is a teacher.

I don't remember much about Chos Malal, my first place, because I was so young. I remember *los Andes* with the snow. The small town don't have, how do you say, *pavimento* [pavement]. The street, they have earth. And I remember in the street, it's a canal where goes the water. Here's the street and here's the house and on both sides of the street there are open, we say *asequia* [open sewers]. I remember that was a very nice place to live.

I moved from Neuquén, the name of the state, to the other state, Chubut. March 1969 was when I moved. I didn't like, because I think that when I was nine years or ten years, I went to Buenos Aires. When I went to Buenos Aires I think, "This is my city." I like a big city. Every day I said, "I like a big city, I like a big city." That was the problem. When I knew Buenos Aires, I say, "Hey, where do I live?" Because I was born in Chos Malal. It's 2,000 people. But when I moved to Rawson, Rawson is 10,000 people. Rawson had pavement. Rawson had other things that Chos Malal didn't have. But when I went to Buenos Aires, my mind changed immediately. And I think, "I want to live here." And every year in my life I was thinking about, "I want to live there. I want to move there." But I was young. I needed to finish my primary school, my high school, and then go to Buenos Aires.

In Rawson, I used to study a lot. I remember I was the best student in the high school. In Spanish it's *abanderado*. It's the person who have the flag. Every year we have an important day, like Independence Day, that our country has different parades. And I used to have the flag because the person who have the flag is the person who is the best student in this year.

I remember that I study a lot everything, but I didn't like history and physical education. I remember that was the worst grade in my note [report card]. But I remember the best for me was mathematics, and physics, and *química* [chemistry]. And then when I finished the high school, I decided to study engineering because I loved mathematics, physics, and *química*.

When I was 18, I went to Buenos Aires to study. The university is free in Argentina. It's better than here because if you want to study here, you need to pay every month a lot of money. In Argentina it's free. It's a good point for Argentina. When I started study engineering in the university, it had six years. The first three, we study a lot of mathematics, physics, statistics. You don't study a specific about shipping or electronic. When you finish 3rd grade [year], you should decide

With his mother and father, Argentina, 1981

than 100, that was my case. And then I start the army conscription like a *soldado* [soldier] in 1981. And then, it's just one year. But when I had to finish the year, the President Galtieri started the war with England. That was terrible for me. I finish my conscription in April 30th, 1982. But in April 2nd, Argentina go to the *Malvinas,* it's the Falklands in English, and Argentina started the war with England in April 1982. And then the army said, "OK. Nobody finish the army this year. We need you and need the new people." And then that year, the people who start in 1981, continues with the army. And the people who begin, OK, more people for the war. I was so afraid because I didn't know what happened here. Should I go or not? But fortunately, I didn't go to the *Malvinas.* No, I didn't because I was in Buenos Aires with a general who was fighting with Galtieri and he decided, don't send soldiers to the *Malvinas.* I was lucky. When I heard those words, I was so happy [Laughs.] because I thought that was a stupid war. The general, Galtieri, was a stupid general. The journalists said that, that morning he was drunk and he said, "Ah, I need to be a president for 10 years. And what is the good idea? OK, the *Malvinas.*"

I think there were between 600 to 1,000 people [who died]. The war was very short. It was easy for England. It's nothing if I say 600, but ask the mother of some of them, "What are you talking about. It was my son." It start in April 2nd, 1982 and finish when the Pope went to Argentina in June 16th, 17th the same year. The war was two months and two weeks.

When the war finished, I started to study again. But before finish the university, I start to work in a place where you draw plans. I started to work there one year or two years before I finished to study engineer. Private company. And I was so happy there because when you study engineer, you don't have experience. But when you go to work, it's a little bit different. You need to know another thing. And I was so happy because I learned many, many things working there. At that moment, there was a lot of work [designing boats] for fishing for private company.

In Argentina there are a lot of fishing ships. In that moment, Argentina bought the ship [from] Korea and China and Japan because it was cheaper than construction in Argentina. But if you bought a ship in Korea or Japan or other country, you need to enter to Atlantic Ocean in Argentina and the country needs some *registros* [registrations], a specific thing that the government asks. And we transfer the plan and we need to do the plan for the company. A little thing, not

what kind of engineer do you want, if you want to study naval, or you want to study electronic, or physical, or whatever do you want.

In naval engineer, they have a similarity like architecture and I love architecture, too. And the only engineer that is similar with architecture is naval and civil engineer. I decided to study naval because I thought Argentina has a big country. The third part of Argentina has in contact with the Atlantic Ocean. In that moment, there aren't a lot of *astilleros. Astillero* is the place where the people construct ships. Dry dock of ship yards. In that moment, for example, Patagonia in the south of Argentina, there aren't a lot of dry docks. And I thought that is a good point to study that, because the *mercancía* [merchandise] is transported with ship. Nobody transport in airplane. The people transport with ships. It's the big transport around the world. If you need to send something to Europe or Asia or North America, you need to use a ship. At that moment, by the time I thought, "That is good point. Maybe in Argentina will be a good work." But I was wrong. [Laughs.] Ten years later, "Oh, what happened here?"

I went to Buenos Aires in 1979 and then I had a problem with conscription. In Argentina it was obligatory you should go to the army. They put your number in a big globe and it's like a lotto. If you have [a number] less than 100, you didn't have to do the conscription. More so much. For example, the ship that Argentina bought from China, they had just one bathroom on the ship, for example, for 25 people. In Argentina we need one bathroom each five people. And we change in the plan, in the paper. We redesign the boats, the ships. And we gave the plan to the company and they change. And they could use in Argentina.

That was a terrible idea to buy a boat another country, because the dry dock, they don't have work in Argentina because it was cheaper to buy a boat in other country and not to construct in my country. It's crazy. I remember that to buy the same ship in Korea it's $800,000, and construction in Argentina, $1,500,000. And the company say, "OK, I go to Korea and I buy the boat. It's cheaper for me." And the redesign was $50,000. "OK, $850,000, I have a ship to fishing. I don't want to buy a ship in Argentina." It was terrible for us because every day, company who constructed boat, they [go] broke. And every day I remember I saw that problem.

I have my best friend here in Oak Park [Illinois]. He lives here. He's naval engineer, too, and we talk with him. "Hey, what will happen in two years, three years?" Because the university has about 20 naval engineer [per] year, but there are no work for 20 for year. There was work just for one or two. And this is the problem.

On vacation, Rome, 1991

When I graduated [in 1989], I worked there until 1991. But in 1991, the naval studio closed the door because they don't have more work.

It's terrible. I don't know if you know about that. American people I think that you don't know. When somebody say you, "OK, the next month is your last month that you will work with me," it's terrible.

Because you think, "Oh, what happened? What happen next month? What will happen?" When the naval studio closed, I thought, "OK, what should I do? Change of career, or continue and wait for the change in Argentina?" I sent a lot of curriculum [resumé] but nothing. [Laughs.] There are no jobs for me.

When I lost my job in March, 1991, I started to teach mathematics and physics, not in a school, in my house. That was fun for me because I love to teach. And I taught mathematics and physics for people who were studying in high school. And in September, I went to Europe. I went to Spain. I went to France, England, Belgium, Holland, Portugal, Germany, Czechoslovakia, Hungary, Italy, Greece, and that's it. It was fabulous because I had never traveled outside Argentina. I traveled around the Argentina, north, south, Buenos Aires, west, but I had never been in Europe or other countries outside Argentina. And it was very, I don't know in English. In Spanish it's *grandioso,* wonderful, amazing. It was amazing because I knew different people, I heard different language, and I knew different cultures, and I was in different cities, big cities like Madrid, Barcelona, Paris, London, Berlin, Milan, Rome, and was fantastic for me the traveling.

When I finished to Europe, I went to United States, to New York, Boston, and Washington. I wanted to go to New York because I knew that New York was bigger than Buenos Aires. I told you, when I was young I knew that I love to live in a big city. And I knew that L.A., New York were bigger than Buenos Aires.

I left Madrid and after six hours I arrived to New York. And I take my bags and I take a subway and my first place was Times Square. [Laughs.] And I saw and, "Wow, what is this?" [Laughs.] I remember I talk with, how do you say the place where people go, not YMCA, it's like YMCA [youth hostel]. And I call to the youth hostel at 110th Street. And I went there. Have you been there? It is a big, big hostel. That was my first place in New York. And I loved New York. I love now. [Laughs.] I think that Buenos Aires, Los Angeles, and New York are the three cities that I love. I love theatre, musicals. And when I lived in Argentina I heard about *The Phantom of the Opera, Les Miserables, Miss Saigon, 42nd Street, Cats.* You know what? I saw *Evita* the last year

With friends, Argentina, 1994

in Chicago. Because in 1991, *Evita* [closed] in New York, and *Evita* has never been in Argentina because it's dangerous. [Laughs.]

[I spent] two weeks [in New York]. [I love] the theatre, the people and I don't know, I love the city that have energy. The energy of New York for me is amazing. I don't know if I can explain, but if you go to Times Square or Greenwich Village or I don't know, Chelsea, the energy of the city is amazing. And I love that thing.

When I went to New York, I felt free. How can I explain this one? Because I am gay, and when I went to New York, I felt that the people, I don't know, maybe because I didn't speak English very well, but I felt free. When I went to Greenwich Village or when I went to Chelsea, I saw people who was walking in the street, two men together with [holding] hands, things that I had never seen before in Argentina. And it's impossible now, in 2000. When I lived in Argentina, every time I thought to be gay was the most terrible thing around the world because in Argentina the military government hate the gays, and the other government, too. To be gay in Argentina, every day jokes about the homosexual people. When you say he's gay, he's homosexual, but in the bad way, in the bad mood. It's discrimination. Sometime the people say, "I prefer to have a donkey son or a drunk son or a thief. I prefer all of them than to have a gay son." This is terrible in Argentina.

But when I came to United States, better than Europe, I felt a lot of difference with my country. I saw that thing. I saw two men together or two women together. I went to gay discos or pub discos in New York and I thought, "Why the people live free here? Why? This is the same people like me. But the difference, they was born in United States. They spoke English, but it's people like me. He's a man like me. Maybe he study, I don't know, engineer like me. They work." And I thought, "OK, there's something wrong in Argentina, something that is not for me." And my mind exploded, and every day when I went to Chelsea or Greenwich Village, I was in the square, it's a gay place, a gay square, with two men together and two women together, statues. The men is standing up and the women is sitting in the bench. And I saw the monument and I thought, "Wow! In Argentina that is impossible. The people maybe break [it]!" And I walk in Greenwich and other street, and I saw a lot of people, a lot of *negocios* [stores]. I saw a lot of stores they sell things, many things with flags or clothes, or different things. And I thought the same, "This is impossible in Argentina."

I thought, "OK, in this city you can have a partner, you can live like other people, like my sister or my brother." My sister live with my brother-in-law. My brother live with my sister-in-law. And I thought, "The gay people can't live." That is the point in Argentina. But when I went to New York, I thought, "OK, I can live. I can be free here and I can do the things that I want to do."

The first time, I remember I took more than 96 pictures of the Gay Parade because it was amazing for me. "Hey, what happen here?" I remember the first time. There was a lady. I think that she was religious, and she said, "The word of the Bible against the homosexual." It was funny, but was amazing the first time for me because a lot of people on the street, a lot of people inside the parade. It was incredible. That is impossible in Argentina.

That is the problem in South America, all South America. I think that Argentina is the most *avanzado* [advanced]. It's easier to be gay in Argentina than in Mexico or Honduras or other countries, but it's not easy, it's not enough.

When I came [back] to Argentina, I told my mother and my father and all my family, "I am gay."

I think that the mothers know. I think my mother knew, but the mother didn't want to say, "Hey son, what happened? Are you gay?" My mother crying a lot, "Why? Why? I bring up, educate the same way to your brother and you. What happened with you? What I am going to say to my family? What I'm going to say to my neighbor?"

My father, he is very intelligent. He never told me nothing about that, nothing negative, nothing positive. He didn't tell me, "OK, go from my house. I can never see [you] again."

They changed because I am his [their] son. I didn't change. All my life I was the same people. I didn't wear women's clothes or *peluca* [wig]. [Laughs.] I was the same people and they understand. I think that was hard for them. But the problem is not for them, the people around them. And the people say, "What happened with Carlos? Is he married? Is he… Is he…"

"No, he's not married. He's not married."

And my brother and my sister, they are, how do you say, modern. "It's your life." I think that they saw in me that when I told them I am gay, I change. Because when I lived in Argentina, I had a big building over me [a big weight on my shoulders]. But when I say that, my life change because I feel very free.

[I came to New York in] '91, '92, '93, '94, '95, every year for two weeks or one week. And I returned to Europe four times and every time I went to Europe, I went to New York. [Laughs.]

And I worked teaching mathematics until 1992. One year I was teaching mathematics and physics. And I don't remember if were a lot of money, but are money. And then I started to work in a club *náutico*, a marina near to Buenos Aires in the north, but I didn't work with boats. It was just in office, to change the boat place or work of the office. I worked there 1992 to 1995, three years. The work was, how can I explain? Every day the same work. It's boring. Every day the same work. Nothing new. Every day, go to the club and open the door and wait for the people who go to use the boat and finish the day and nothing interesting for me, but I lived with that money.

When I finished to work, my friend lived in Oak Park. I called them every month and I told them, "I don't have work. It is terrible."

And he told me, "You can come here if you want. I don't know if you are going to work like engineer, but you can come here to work in other thing. There are a lot of work here."

And then I came to Chicago in 1995, in March. It was terrible day, cold. Forty degree under zero. I remember it was terrible. I came in Chicago and I went to visit my cousin. I have a cousin in Madison [Wisconsin]. And I came to New York, Chicago, Madison, and San Francisco. And I loved San Francisco [Laughs.] more than New York in the gay style, but not in the theatre or culture. But when I was here in Chicago, he told me the same thing, "If you want, you can stay here." Was just for a visit. And I was calling with them for two years. And in 1997 I decided to go to United States.

When I decided to come here, I bought the ticket. I had a tourist visa. But when you come to United States, the immigration official say, "OK, you can be here for six months, or three months." It depends of the face. [Laughs.] When I came here, they gave me six months. I sold everything and other things I sent to Patagonia to my parents' house. It was easy for me. [I was] excited.

When I came here, how I feel is nervous and anxious because I didn't know. I went first to New York. [Laughs.] I was there for three weeks and then I came to Chicago, to Oak Park. I lived in my friend's house with his two sons. He's a naval engineer like me. He's working in the same business. But when I came here, I started selling furniture in the 26th Street near *La Villita*. *La Villita* is a neighborhood here. It's 26th Street. Little Village. American people say *La Villita*, too. A Mexican neighborhood. [My friend] introduced me to the owner of the store and I started to work with them. And sometimes we went to the Spanish neighbor and knocked the door and offer the furniture. And sometime with *citas*, I don't know in English, appointment, when you call somebody, "OK, you need furniture? We can show the catalog."

Celebrating his last day in Buenos Aires, Argentina, 1997

Just commission, nothing salary, but was very good for me. Because when I, for example, sold one furniture, I earn $100, $200 or $300. And I remember I lived with [my friends] and it was easy for me. They was very kind with me because I didn't pay anything. I didn't pay rent. I didn't pay nothing, just live there and they pay everything that I needed. I started in the store in September, October, November, December, January, and February, work selling furniture.

And in January 1st, 1998, five months after come here, I rent an apartment in Barry [Avenue] and Broadway [Avenue]. And in February, I started with sell pre-paid phone card, both together. I was selling prepaid phone card, but I was selling furniture because when you start to sell prepaid phone card, you can't live with the money. [My friend] and his *socio* [associate] gave me $10,000 in phone cards. "OK, this is your phone cards. There are $10,000. Go to the store and offer this card." And I started to offer the card every day. I took the north area because the south area is other people, and I started to offer the phone card. [Half] of the day I worked selling prepaid phone card and [half] of the day I worked selling furniture. But when selling prepaid phone card was better and raise, I left selling furniture. And now I sell just prepaid phone card. And that was good for me because I thought that point, "OK. I can't work like a naval engineer now. Maybe in the future, I don't know. I will try, but not now."

It's a good business because in Chicago there are a lot of people from Latin America. And the people from Latin America call every day. [Laughs.] American people they don't use prepaid phone card. I don't know why. You prefer use Ameritech or AT&T, but it's expensive! It's more expensive!

I go to the stores every day and I gave them phone card and I write down a bill and they pay me and when I have money, I go to Oak Park

With his brother and sister-in-law in Times Square, New York City, 2000

and I buy phone card. And I earn between 2 percent to 5 percent. If I sell $10,000, I earn $500. I sell to the store and the store sell. It's a consignment.

There are a lot of cards. Some of them are good for Mexico. Others good for Colombia, but all of them are good for Mexico because Mexicans is the most important people here. But it's a good job now. And every day it's better because all people use cards. I sell a good card that is one cent a minute inside the United States. Think about it! You should think! What company do you use? [Laughs.] How much do you pay for a minute? There is a card with one cent a minute. Latin people use this card because they have family in California or they have family in New York or *la Florida* or Texas.

For my life, I need to be free first and then to earn money. I don't know how explain that. I can't live in a city where I hear every day something wrong about my life, something wrong about my lifestyle. And when I start to sell prepaid phone card, I thought, "OK. I can earn money. And I can live. And I can live free. And that was good for me because I thought that point. OK, I can't work like naval engineer now. Maybe in the future. But I can live in a city that is good for me, in a neighborhood that is not gay, but there are a lot of gay people in my neighborhood." The street, the name is Halsted, there are a lot of pubs, there are a lot of bookstores and coffee shops and there are gyms. I go to the gym that is, I don't know, maybe 70 or 80 percent of people is gay.

I am trying to change my visa to asylum, political asylum. I have a lawyer and she's trying to ask for asylum. The problem is Argentina is not too bad now for the gay people. But I have two friends and they apply before and they have asylum and after a year they have a residence. But now, I told you it's very difficult for Argentina because in Argentina, the people change. In Buenos Aires, the law change every day and five years ago it was very different than now. I have a friend who applied two years ago and he earned the asylum, the same basic reason: He's gay. Depend of the lawyer and depend of the official of immigration. I don't know what will happen. I need to go to the official with my lawyer and apply and maybe he could say, "OK," and the decision is automatic. And after one year I can apply for residence. Maybe he could say, "No." I don't have other thing to do because it's very, very difficult now to immigration. I can have a job or a work, this is other point, but it's more difficult to do this one because to apply for a job you have to demonstrate that other American people cannot do that job, and that is very difficult.

Some people, they don't do anything and they have been here for 10 years, 20 years, all life. But I decided to apply for this one because I prefer to be in legal situation. And I would like, I don't know, in five or ten years, to study something about my career, engineer, or to transfer my degree or something like that. Because if you want to transfer your *título,* your degree, you should speak English very well first and then you can try. And in this case, I need to be legal in this country. I cannot be illegal. That is the point that I decided after two years to apply for that visa.

I'm studying English in the Truman College. I am not happy [with my English]. Sometimes I think that I lost two years and six months studying English. I started to study English in the Wright College, the west, near my friend's house. It's in Austin [a Chicago neighborhood]. And then I went to the Lakeview [Learning Center] and then I went to Truman College. But I don't think that the problem is the college. The problem is mine. [Laughs.] Because I need to study. That is the point. I didn't study. I have never studied. I went to the college, but when I finished the class, I didn't study. I didn't take my notes. And that is a problem. I should have more time to study and I'm sure that if I study, my English change completely just in two months. Because, I speak English now with you, but I didn't study. I'm speaking because I went to the college for two years and when you go to the college, you learn something every day. But the difference, when you study. You study, your English change or everything change. If you don't study, nothing happen with you. I think that is my problem, but I don't have time because I work. The problem with the prepaid phone card, that you don't have time because, how do you say, you are your owner of your time. Sometimes the people call you, "I need card right now!" [Laughs.] OK, I go there. Because if I don't sell, I don't earn. That is the point. I don't have a salary. Every Friday I don't have my check. No. When I

went to New York and when I went to Los Angeles, I didn't earn. That is the point. I need to earn money every day. I need to send money to the bank to have some money saving, but I need to work. That is the problem for my English.

I have American friends, but they speak Spanish very well. [Laughs.] You know what? They want to speak English with me but I have *vergüenza* [shame], something like that when you think, "I can't speak English because I don't speak English very well." Shame. That is the problem to speak English with my friends. When they want to start speaking English, when they ask me something in English, I respond in Spanish because I am ashamed of myself. But I try to watch TV in English. I go to the theatre every week. Every week I see more than one movie. That is the reason I am speaking English now. But I am not practicing.

When I came here two years ago and nine months, I couldn't speak like now. I couldn't speak! I learned everything that I'm speaking now in two years and nine months, but I have never studied.

When I ask somebody, "Where is the street?"

"What? What? What?" [They don't understand.]

OK, I don't speak English. That is the point because I think they are not going to understand me. It's easier for me to be quiet or, "Do you

| 203

With his partner, Martín, San Francisco, 2000

speak Spanish?"

"No, I don't speak Spanish, but he speaks."

"OK, *hola. Tú hablas Español?*" [Hello, do you speak Spanish?]

"Oh, *si. Dígame.*" [Oh, yes. Talk to me.]

That is the problem in Chicago. Because I think sometimes the people they are from Romania, Bulgaria, Russia, they speak English better than me because they can't speak Russian, or Romanian, or other language when they go to the store because nobody speak other language. Sometimes, but it's not usual. But when you go to the store in Chicago, every time there are people who speak Spanish. And this is dangerous. It's dangerous for me!

I would like to buy a house here in Chicago because I am renting now. I want to learn more English. I would like to speak English very well, know more English. I know that it's impossible to speak English like an American, but speak English very well like other people who speak both languages. I know some people who speak more than two languages very well. And I would like to do something about my engineer, my career. But that is the future, not now. Now I need to work and I need to study. That is the reason that I go Monday and Wednesday to try study English. I don't have a lot of ambitions about, "I would like to have $1,000,000 in the bank. I would like to have an apartment in Manhattan, or an apartment in L.A." No, I don't have. I would like to have money to live well, but not a lot of ambition.

I would like to be a citizen because the other problem that I have, I love the politics. I love. I love. I love. When I go to Argentina, I love the politics in Argentina. When I went to Spain, every day I read about the politics in Spain. Nothing important for me, but I love that. I don't know why. Maybe because my family loved that and they loved to read, to listen radio

news. I think the people from Argentina, we love to read newspaper, we love to listen radio, the news, and we love to watch TV, the news and political programs. I think that is a bad idea, but it's the reality of the people from Argentina.

I would like to be a citizen here and to vote. That is my big ambition, to be a citizen. Not for to have a passport for United States, but to be part of you, of United States, to decide about the country. I know that one vote is nothing, but one vote, more one, more one, more one is important.

I don't think about the rights or responsibilities if I will be a citizen. I try to do better every day if I am citizen or not. That is the point. I don't want to try to be better because I will be citizen. I think that is the same. Just for responsibility like to vote, to decide. Not decide about the president of the United States, because I don't know if that is important, but yes, decide about the city, about the neighbor[hood]. We have a congressman in Lakeview. Every neighbor[hood] have different person who represent the neighbor[hood]. And I would like to do part of that.

Do you know what? When there is an election in Argentina, I go to the Consulate of Argentina in Michigan Avenue and I go to vote for Argentina. [Laughs.] That is not important for the election, but I love that. In the last two years and nine months, I went there three times to vote. I would like to do the same in the United States.

I miss my friends. My family, I miss them, but I call them every week and they were here two weeks ago. They can travel because they don't have economical problem now. I am in contact with them every week or every year when they come here. [I miss] something about Buenos Aires because Buenos Aires is a big city, bigger than Chicago. It's a beautiful city. And sometimes I walk in Broadway or Belmont or Michigan Avenue or other street, and I think, "I would like to be walking in Santa Fe." It's the name of the street in Buenos Aires. But not many times. But sometimes I miss that.

With his sister and nephew, Chicago, 2001

When I was living in Argentina, I told you before that the Argentine people have the similar with Italian people about the food and about the fashion. And I changed that. When I was living in Argentina, that was very important for me, too, to wear the good clothes, good shoes, good pants. That is a big problem in Argentina. Because in Argentina if you are fat, or you are so ugly—oh, forget it! The people discriminate. We don't have discrimination with colored people, but we have discrimination with the clothes if you don't have the new one, the last one, if you don't have Armani. You are *esclavo*, a slave to the fashion in Argentina. The people is slave. All people go to the gym because you need to be perfect! You need to be thin. And I changed here because of American people. Here I saw a lot of people that they don't like to be perfect. They eat a lot. They wear different clothes. I changed about that.

I don't change so much, but I told you before, I am feeling free here because it's a problem to be a slave about the fashion, to be a slave about the body, to be a slave about different things. I told you, when I went to New York the first time, I feel free and that was very important for me, very, very important. Maybe you can't understand me, that point. But when you live in a country that every day you heard bad things about your life, bad things about the economy of the country, bad things about the politics of the country, when you go to the other country, just when one of the three things is good, you are happy. And when I went to New York, I was very happy about my lifestyle. I don't know if it was enough, but it was similar to enough. [Laughs.] I don't know what happen with me in 10 years, but now I am very happy here. I have work and I feel free and I live.

CARLOS LIVES IN CHICAGO. He continues to study English, sell phone cards, visit New York, and attend Broadway musicals as much as possible.

MY NAME IS JAVAD KIANI *I am 37 years old. I came here* **23 OF JULY, 1995. I'M FROM IRAN.** *I born in Tehran, the capital [in 1961].*

I HAVE THREE SISTERS AND ONE BROTHER. My family was middle class. I mean from the richness or poorness, in the middle. We had just a room. That room was kitchen for us, it was the bedroom, everything. It was very hard that time. It has a big closet that we put all our stuff over there. We had just a radio. We didn't have a TV. I don't remember it has anything else. It was just a simple room. The food was OK. Clothing was OK. It was not very good, but we didn't feel cold or we didn't feel that we need clothes we don't have.

And since I know myself, I wanted to be independent. I can do anything that I want. Even in primary school. It was funny. Once I wanted to work and I just went to a store and I bought a box of gum and I bought [paid], for example, a penny for each one and I sell it again a penny each one. I just wanted to work. I didn't know that I had to make money! I just think, "Oh, I have to do something." I don't know why, but I just wanted, like my desire. In school, yeah, I go to play with children, I like to play, but when I get more in middle school and high school, I didn't want to even go with the guys, the kids my same age to play always. I didn't want to go to waste my time. They wanted to stay in the street sometime, just talk. I didn't want. You know, I hated to go and just talk. Still I have that desire. I don't want waste my time even here.

I think I got that from my mother. My mother is very independent. She is very sensitive and she was bossy. She loves her children and she tried the best for her children. She used to work for us, because that time my dad doesn't make that much money. She used to work just in house-keeping, and I remember I wanted she be at home. I just wait, wait, wait.

My mom loves to read, but she couldn't read that much. She tried a lot. And she was very stubborn to learn something. Even though my dad said, "Come on. It's enough. You have been to school [just] four years, five years." At her age it is very hard to learn, but she couldn't stop. I think still she is trying. I think as I know her she just try to learn something.

My dad worked for himself, but after that he left and his work was in TV like a mailman [messenger]. In the TV you have to get news from here to put there, bring from here some news, some letters, go to the airport, some news come from the airport, get some news, deliver it to the office. He is very simple. He is very kind. He is very good. To me, he is like a friend for me. He's very happy guy. He's not that much serious. He's just teasing, kidding. As I remember—oh, my God. My dad used to buy a lot of fruit. I don't know why, but he loves lots of fruit. Everything, depend on season. There back home, any season, it has own fruit like pomegranate and orange. I think the winter started that time, and then peaches, and watermelon. Everything has their own season. It's not like here. Here I can find everything anytime.

None of them was religious. They like, but they didn't pray. They are Muslim. In spite of my dad and my mom, I was religious, but not that much extreme. I just pray and I have some feeling little bit with my religion, with God. And I think everything that I earn in all my life, God help me.

I just went to the school, and I liked to be very good student. I just wanted. I don't know why, but I wanted. They [my parents] didn't push me to study. They didn't push me at all. I just like to study to improve myself. They just push me to sleep, but I didn't go to bed like two hours after them, like until 1:00 [A.M.]. I just studying and studying. I wanted to learn English in primary school. It was for me the first time that I draw ABC and go my home, "Oh, I can speak English. I can write English." And I was very happy. And that time I wanted private school, but my dad couldn't afford to send me there.

And also I worked in the summer when the school was closed, and I wanted to do everything by myself, everything. So, that's why right now I'm like handy. I remember story. We lived that house that I told you, just in one room. Then, we didn't have electric that time. Then they got electric, but they wanted to make wiring everywhere. Constructor come, and said we want that much money to make electric for each room. And I remember that I study in school and I know how the switch work, how the light work and I told my dad, "I can do it. Don't let them do it."

He said, "Are you sure?"

I said, "I'm sure."

And I did. I did very good job, and even the contractor look at this and told the helper for him, "Look, you have to learn from this guy!" [Laughs.] I was 15 years old, 16 years old. They teach me in middle school. We had a book about everything. About agriculture. It was about electric. It was about carpentry. Section by section. About weaving, even. I weaved something. But the things that I just gravitate to was just electric.

It [school] was the number one, but during the college when I was at the university, my degree score come down because I should [had to] work until 1:00 in the night. I used to work in TV also. And 1:00, I go to my home. Get there, 1:30. And then I slept until 6:00. At 6:00 I have to go to school again.

During the revolution that time [1979], actually I didn't think a lot about this subject. Actually, I was happy the revolution happened because I thought maybe everything is going good, you know. Because when I was kid, I see all the differences between the rich and you know, poor people. And I see everything. I was in Tehran. Tehran is big city. And I see the people. Some people was very rich. They spend money very easy, and I was not in good [class], so I thought maybe now is everything getting good because they promise

everything is getting good. I said, "OK, this is good. Islamic is good." But you know, they don't use real Islam. They just use the Islam that they want.

Most my priority was studying. Even the people go to political things. I didn't go. I go sometimes to see what they are talking about 'cause that time everything was hard. They just discuss, discuss, discuss a lot. I didn't have that much desire to go to political things. I don't know why. But I most desire to go to scientific, to go to studying.

I studied electronics. My plan was to get my degree in electronics and going to work in Iran. I had plan for myself to improve myself over there. And I did. I didn't even think about the United States. I start working over there. My first job I work for myself. I got a project from the fire department. They had like a siren that is from Motorola. They wanted to improve it, and I did for them. This is right after my education, my degree in electronics.

When I finished that job by fire department, I went to Telecommunication of Tehran and I work in software department. They promise me to send me to Germany to get more software education in telephone switching system. But after one year working, nothing happened and the guy that wants to send us, they changed him in the high position and the new one said we don't need to go there. Nothing changed. I decided to change my job. I went to a private company. They are representative of General Electric and some companies from Germany, Dornier Germany. I start work for them. They send me to Germany for training for lithotripter. It's a machine that you use for break stone in the kidney. I like so much this system and the technology that they use. And I work with that machine. I knew everything about that machine. When I go to repair, to installation, to service, I knew everything how they work. I didn't spend that much time to find the fault. Immediately I go open software, and then find the place and change. Even sometime we didn't have part, and we have to order it and it takes time and they have lots of patients, I just somehow make the machine work. For example, once I went to power supply of computer. It's burned. We have to order it. It takes like two weeks to come from Germany. And I just bought the normal power supply of normal computer PCs, and I changed the pins, everything. Matched it with that one, use the voltage that I need, and it worked very good.

After I came to the Germany, I wanted to live in Germany. Because when I saw Germany, it was so beautiful: clean streets, everything on time, prompt, the train, everything. I said, "Oh, I have to live over there." The transportation in my country is not good. There [in Tehran] the public transportation is like here. I don't say here is bad, but you know, the first year I was here I didn't have car. It makes me crazy here. Buses stop for just every half an hour, 45 minutes, and when they come they come two together. At that time I said, "It looks here like Tehran." In Germany, I just see the timetable at the stop. Maybe just one or two minutes the difference is, they come. Believe me, I don't know how they make it for bus.

I was very happy. It was like something new in my life. I'm going over there to see how is the place. And when I came there, it impressed a lot on me, the rule. It was very important for me. There if you go inside the transportation, public train, they don't ask the ticket for you. They just trust you that you bought the ticket, and you put it in the machine. It was very good for me to look at this people, how they work. They just trust and it's very good. Sometime they come and check, but it's good that they trust you. But sometimes if they catch you, they fine you.

The first time I hate the German language. I hate it. It was very hard for me. I didn't even try it. I said, "Forget it. Don't try it." I was one month over there and I didn't try to learn German. But the second time that I went over there is 1994. And I said, "I have to learn this language. Anyway, I have to. I like to. If I want to someday come here to live over here, I have to."

Then I start learning German. But you know, they are not like here. They have gender for everything. It was making me crazy. I didn't know. I remember a funny story. We were installing a machine, lithotripter, and engineer come from Dornier to help us there. And we have a problem with one of the system. It doesn't go on good. And he just pointed to machine and said, "The problem is him!"

And I look. I didn't see anybody over there. Just looking, "Who is

With his dad and mom, Chicago, 1999

he talking about?"

Again, he just talk, "He is the problem. We have to solve it."

And, believe me, I just make confuse. "What is he talking about? Nobody is here. Why is always pointing some place that nobody is there?"

And one of my friends, he used to be in Germany, he told me, "You know why he used 'he?' Because the things have gender for them. That's why he used 'he.'"

That was very hard for me to learn in German. But second time I start to learning. I start by myself. And I got a girlfriend over there. It was very funny that every time we want to talk to each other we open the book, dictionary, and then I see in German, in English. In English I have to translate for myself again. It was good for me to learning a little bit.

Sometimes I see, for example, in Germany, I saw topless. That was very strange for me. Even I went to Munich. It was a very big park. The name was English Garden. All the people go over there naked, completely naked. Even they don't have shorts, nothing, nothing. "Why they doing like that?" It's very strange for me. I don't agree with that, because I saw they bring some kids over there and the dads and moms are like that, naked, and they play with each other and the kids look at them. But after a while, everything is getting OK and I don't have problem with looking the woman, even naked.

[In Iran] women should wear Islamic cover. I always have conflict with myself why they should cover. Because when you limit some people to not do something, they want more.

I liked the job, but it didn't satisfy me. Always I wanted something that I see improvement in myself. I didn't see that much improvement. I install one machine, two machines, and repair. After that, the company offered me very good situation, money and everything. They promised me they send me United States. I think another horizon for me to learn more, change my job again.

I was get happy because two reason. One of them, I was changing my job. I was working for Dornier for the laser machine from Germany, but this time I'm going to go to the radiology department, another story, another thing. It was very exciting for me. And especially I want to work for General Electric, big company. It make me very happy. Then I want to come over here. OK, another training course, another everything, even a new world for me. I haven't been in United States. That was very good for me. I was very happy.

When I came here it was 1994. I came here, stayed for just three weeks. It was in Waukesha, Milwaukee. It was two weeks, but they extended for another course, make it three weeks. It was very new, huge training center of General Electric.

And the weekend they gave us a car and we came to Chicago. And actually, to be honest with you, I scared a lot because everybody told me, "Chicago is the gangster city. Be careful." But when we came, we went to downtown and everything was good, nothing very panic.

I was thinking, "I can get my job now." If I get this training course, I can get my job anywhere, maybe General Electric, anywhere.

But when I came back [to Iran] after training course, I start working. They send me to some cities to install new machine. We install lots of them in Iran. And then once I was working hospital, my boss came over there and told me, "You cannot work anymore over here."

I said, "Why?" He told me they got a new General Electric representative and everything changed. And that time I was thinking, "Now I should move. This is not good place anymore to stay." And I try to come over here.

I knew the opportunity is good here. I knew that I will have good situation over here. I knew this. I didn't know what will happen. I said, "OK, I will go over there." I have many certificates from other companies. I have from Dornier, Contron, Technolas, General Electric, Fisher Imaging. Fisher Imaging is here. At least I can get job with one of them because they need somebody that has these experiences.

My sisters and my brother, they say, "OK, go. We know that you wanna improve yourself. You wanna be successful in your life. We don't want to stop you."

But my dad and my mom, they don't want even accept this. And they just keep telling me, "Don't go."

I tried maybe four months to make my mom satisfied. She say, "OK, you can go." But not with her heart just for saying that, "OK,

On vacation, Niagara Falls, 1999

you can go. Go ahead."

I told her, "You know, here I'm going to lose everything. I cannot improve myself. I cannot marry, because I cannot get a very good job that make good money for my life." I could marry, I could get a good job, but the money is not enough for a comfortable life. I'm not looking for really high life, but a normal life that I want in my values. I think I couldn't make it with that salary, with that money, so I explained for them. I tried to get their agree because I didn't want just leave them. I care about them a lot. Still, I'm caring about them. Still, if I can send money, I send money for them.

I remember exactly the date. 1995, 23rd of July. I just bring a big suitcase and some clothes and my documents. I translate everything that I have. I translate my experiences that was in English. I translate my bachelor's degree, the experience job over there, my birth certificate, anything that I think maybe help me.

I came B-1 visa, business visa, three months. Without anything. I like to challenge. This is always inside me. I knew that it was going to be very, very hard for me. And if I want to write a book about my situation the first year I was here, it's like something. When I came here, immediately I go to Itasca in Holiday Inn hotel. I brought like $5,000 with myself. I took a taxi to Itasca because before that, when I came here, I know that. I said, "OK, let's go over there." When I was over there I paid like $70 per night. For me, it was very expensive. Now I know for here it's also expensive, not just for me!

I didn't know anybody over here. I had a friend, his sister lived over here, and I called them if they can help me. They said, "OK, we will help you." But I know they are busy, they cannot help me.

And two weeks or three weeks I was in Itasca. I said, "OK, I should do something otherwise I finish up my money." And I try to change my place. And just I see three weeks passed and I didn't do anything. And I opened the newspaper the first time, I found a place like $70 per week. I said, "Oh, that's very good." And it was in Clark [Street] and Division [Street, Chicago]. Very bad place, very bad place. I went over there I said, "My God, look at here. I cannot live over here." I said, "But I have no choice."

When I go to get the hotel, they told me, "What is your social security number?"

I said, "I don't have social security number. What is that?"

They said, "No, we cannot give you room."

"Oh, my God. I need room. Please help me."

"No I can't."

I just come back again to Itasca. Again I stay there. My friends come over there once and they pick me up. They bring me in Lincoln [Avenue] in a motel like $25 per night. It was very good. And they told me this neighborhood, you can find Iranian people. Finally, I saw two guys that they were painting. They speak Persian. I told them, "Oh, are you from Iran?"

They say, "Yes."

I told them, "My situation is like this. I don't have anybody. Can you help me to get a job?"

They said, "Look at us. We are just painting."

I said, "I don't care about anything. I just care about work. I don't care what kind of work do you have."

They said, "OK, we will come over there to pick you up tomorrow to work." And I went over there and work for them three days. They pay me $100 for three days. That time my story is very bad. And when I was there I see another Iranian guy and ask about apartment and they introduce me here. And I came here. I didn't have anything. I sleep on the floor. I didn't have even this carpet. The first thing I get, I get my bed because I have backache. You know you live in the Holiday Inn

and then come over here, very hard. I got my bed, and little by little I get everything that I have. It's funny. See this microwave? This is very good microwave. I went to garage sale to buy something for my house, and they put this microwave by the garbage can. And I say, "How much is this one?"

They say, "You can take it." And I took it and I bring it here and just change the fuse. That's it. It's working perfect.

[My friends] told me, "You need here ID card. You need here social security. You need here this, this. You should try to get all of those."

I got my ID card. I got my social security, everything. Just a funny thing I remember. I went to get my driver's license. And usually in the back of the license they ask you if you agree to donate your organs. And I was new. I was here like one month. I tried to get my driver's license. And the guy ask me, "Do you want to give your organ?" Something like that.

And I didn't know organ means also tissue. I thought organ means, "Can you play organ?" [Laughs.]

I said, "What is relation between driving and playing organ? Why is he asking me?" I said, "I cannot play organ."

He told me, "Oh, we cannot give you driver's license then!" [Laughs.] He just teasing me. He said, "You cannot do any playing? Nothing? Guitar? Anything?"

I said, "No." [Laughs.]

I tried to find a work. Any place I go I ask for a job. And he [Iranian guy] told me to come over here work. They asked me about the transmission, "Can you fix the transmission."

I said, "What is transmission?" They told me transmission was the gearbox. "I know gearbox," I said.

"Transmission is just automatic, if you can fix it."

I said, "If you wanted to change it inside there, I can."

They said, "Oh, yeah. We want to save everything, just change it."

And they gave me very, very bad car. I mean the hardest one, BMW 735. It has very huge transmission. When I open it up, "Oh, my God. What I did mistake. I cannot fix this one." It's like maybe more than 100 pieces inside that. When I open it, I was very confused. What should I do? I just put them in arrange that I knew which one go in first, which one go in last. Then I changed that stuff. I put it back again. I put it in the car. And they try it. It worked. I got very happy. When they try the reverse, it didn't work. And I didn't have any idea what should I try to find the fault, because I didn't know what is this gear, what is that one, what is the clutch. I didn't know which one is for reverse. I just tried, tried.

They told me, "Open it up again." I opened it up again. I couldn't do anything. But I got idea. I read the book about transmission. I read about the converter. I read everything. Now I got idea after this.

He told me, "OK, you can work for yourself, fix transmission and divide it [the money] by two. I give you just the place." The place was full of the junk things. He told me, "Clean up here." And he didn't pay me for clean up. He said, "You working for yourself." Like two weeks, I was cleaning up everything. And he didn't pay me anything. And after I start transmission job, there I did like two transmission for Chevy 350. And after, he wants to give me money. He said, "OK, for Mercedes I give you $100. For that one I give you 50 bucks." He gave like $200 for me because two transmissions $50, and one $100.

I know that he charge him like $1,200, because Mercedes is very expensive car. And I said, "And you're giving me $100 for that?"

He said, "If you like you can work. If you don't like, go." Just that's it, after two months, $200 in my hand. And I knew that guy.

I said, "OK, forget him. If I work with him, I'm going to lose the money."

And I went with another guy working with him for electric construction, everything. And he didn't pay me, like $3,000. I trusted him. He said, "I don't have money right now. I just bought a house."

I said, "OK." But after it got to $5,000, I said, "I need my money. Give me my money."

He give me $2,000 and he said, "Is this OK?"

I said, "No, you owe me still $3,000."

"No, I don't owe you."

I said, "Yeah, this is the bill that I bought for you." I trust him a lot because the first time we start, he was like my friend. Really I feeling like as a friend. So even I spend my money for him sometime for his job, with my credit card, I pay for him. I didn't even think that he won't pay me. When he told me like that I said, "No." I explained for him. I bring the bills for him. He didn't give me and I said, "I don't want to work anymore for you." I didn't work.

I had very, very bad situation over here. The work that I had is like, the people, they want to abuse me. I did anything just for survive, just for pay my bills. Anything that they told me, "Can you do that?"

I said, "Yes, I can." Just for survive. Even I repaired the rug.

Like two years, at least two years, very, very bad situation. I didn't have money, I didn't have job, I didn't have anything. Any minute that I passed, it was very hard. I thought it just was me, but when I talk to people, all people say we have like this experience, other immigrants. Just being taken advantage. I thought it was just me.

I didn't used to work, like physical work. But when I came here, I should. I didn't have any choice. I didn't come here to work like that. I said, "I'll get my master's degree in computer and after that, I can work for a company. I show myself, OK, I have this quality, and I'm qualified for your job and they are going to ask for H-1 [work] visa for me and then I can get everything." This was my goal.

I had feeling that I should stay here. I'm kind of people that the hardness bothering me, but it doesn't break me or doesn't push me back from my goal, from my idea.

Meanwhile, I changed my B-1 [business] visa to F-1 [student] visa. I got the school in U.I.C. [University of Illinois-Chicago, just for English]. I went over there. Yeah, I paid like $2,300 because, you know, I had that money and I wanted to be legal here. I didn't want anything to happen, you know. I decided to go [to Truman College] because the people told me if you go, there is English classes free. I wanted to improve my English. It was always my goal to learn English. Still, I'm not satisfied my English. I know it's terrible, my speaking, but I try my best to improve myself in English. I can express my idea and I can make the people understand me, but I know I don't use proper word and proper sentence and proper English grammatic. I try to bring myself exact use in grammar. Now I'm stuck, you see! One of my problems is this. I speak English, but I know I have lots of trouble. I understand very good English, but I cannot speak. I don't know why. It's like something lock in my mouth. It doesn't let me express myself. It doesn't let me to be relaxed and to be fluent in English.

I don't feel like American. I don't think I am like American. They have their own values and I have my own values. They are different. I hope all American is not like what I watch in the shows, especially Jerry Springer or other shows. When I watch them—oh, my God. But I think they are minority of Americans. But when I saw them I thought, "Their society is like that, or just some of them is like that?" I'm still confused. But I think it's some of the minority of people are like that.

I have like five or six American friends. They are very good. Two of them are my teachers and two of them, I used to work for them.

At home, Chicago, 2000

When I'm talking about friends, I mean close friends. I always believe having friends is very good because we have an expression in my country that says, "A thousand of friends is not enough, but one enemy is more than enough." More enemies can cause lots of trouble for you, but a thousand of friends is not enough because friends always take care of you. I would like to have friends. But I don't feel lonely. I have many friends from all over the world. From Mexico, from America, from Germany, from Iran, from Africa. I would like to have more American friends because of my English. Right now I have friend when I talk with her, she immediately correct me and I improve a lot. And I ask them, "Don't hesitate. I don't mind if you correct me." I know I am new in this language. I want to improve myself. I am not such a people they don't like if they correct themselves.

Still I am learning something over here. I am studying microprocessor, computer hardware and software together. And I think I finish this one and next semester I can change my business completely to software for myself.

Right now I have some customers. They call me and I go their house. If they have any problem with electric, with air conditioner, with heating, I fix for them and they pay me. And in summer I have so many customers that I don't have time. Just word of mouth. I have some friend. I go by them, work for them, and they tell other people. They see my job, they like my job, and they introduce me to other people. When somebody ask for something they say, "Oh, I know somebody." They give him my pager number and they call me, page me.

I want to get to the master's degree program for computer. I tried many universities, but I didn't want to go to cheap university. Not cheap price, I mean cheap quality. So, I had some friend over in St. Louis. I applied for some university over there. I applied for U.I.C. over here. But all of them was very expensive, and those time I didn't have any money.

But the problem is now I cannot again renew my F-1 visa. It passed, expired already. Past time I didn't have money to go. Now I have money, I cannot go inside. I don't have F-1 visa. They won't give me.

I decided to leave it like that and I go to Canada. It is the best way that I can. When I was in Iran, I knew that their plan, they accept immigrants. And I applied over there, but everything happen I come here and I didn't continue. From here again I applied for them and they send me the document that I need. And I send my document over there in Association of Engineers in Canada. They accept my document.

When I see all doors are closed over here to me, I say, "The best thing is going to Canada." So there I can study, I can get good job. I can start my life, real life.

I have a friend. He used to work with me in same company, and he get his immigration stuff from Iran and he come with his family, his wife, and now he has a son. He told me, "If you come over there, you can get work, job in computer field." Right now he is software engineer for JAVA, Internet language, and I'm going to go by him. He helped a lot to me. He sent my document to the Association of Engineers in Canada.

I just sent a letter for them, and they sent for me all the documents that I need and the form that I should fill. I just went to Internet to Manitoba to get some information that I'm going over there. I say, "What opportunity for work do you have?"

They say, "We are very happy that you choose us. Expenses is not too much over here. And anytime your visa get ready, again contact us. We will be happy to help you to settle over here."

And then I applied for Canadian embassy. They give me interview for right now, after four months I think. They sent me the form for medical examination.

I would like to stay here, and I'd rather to stay here than go to Canada, but I have to see. I cannot get my immigrant [visa] in the United States. There is some ways to get my immigrant [visa], maybe H-1 visa, or marriage. I just wanted to be everything legal, and I have like confliction with myself. Should I pay taxes? What should I do?

You know, let me tell you something. I could stay here without any problem. I have a girlfriend, American girlfriend. She says, "Oh, I want to be with you. I love you." But I can't. Believe me. Many people did like that, and they get citizenship over here. But I can't. For me it's very hard. It's like playing with somebody. I think God never forgive me if I play with somebody for my aim, my goal. I'm not free.

Here is lots of things. More freedom. More opportunity to do everything you want. I think everything you want, just you have to try it, you will get it. It doesn't anything stop you to reach to your goals in my opinion. For example, in my country if you want to go to university, you have to pass very, very hard test because the university has limited space. Not all people can go even they want, they desire to go. They want, they like, but they cannot. Here you can do whatever you want. Just you have to pay money.

One thing is bothering me: the value here is money always here. They just talk about money. If you watch TV, any advertisement, just make money, save money. Money, only hear about money. Everything is money. Nobody think about anything else. This one for me is not very good. Money is not just the important thing in life. It is important, but not that much that you forget everything. But here I think they forget everything, other values.

Here, one thing for example, the kids, I watch in TV, they don't respect their parents. I even couldn't imagine my children doing this

After building a beauty salon, Chicago, 2000

to me. I couldn't imagine. I went to work for an Iranian guy. He has one boy and one daughter and the boy talking to the parents. He pick up the phone and say, "I'm busy. Mom, I'm busy I cannot talk to you. Bye-bye." I never can talk, I never ever. I just talk to them and then if they let me, if I'm busy, if they let me, I go. But here they don't respect at all. I don't know. This is the culture. They grow up like this.

When I was in my country, the main book of [Anthony Robbins] was "The Secret Of How To Be Successful." I read three books of him. I think he's right in most of things he wrote about in this book. But you cannot do or follow his instructions in anywhere in the world. Maybe in here, yeah. But when I wanted to use over there I said, "Oh, I cannot." There everything is not stable. If you see in economic, inflation is always changed. You cannot count on even your money. You cannot count on your situation or tomorrow what will happen. But when I came here—oh, here I can. I like it.

I think here really they say, "land of opportunity." It is. I think it is. You can do anything you want. When I see homeless in the street I wonder, "They have everything. They have permit to work. They are American. But they still asking for a quarter of me, that I don't have anything." When I was coming here, really I didn't have anything. They ask me for money. It was funny. The first time, I scared a lot. I wanted to come back my country. I was working downtown. And I see a guy. He get a sign like that, "Work for Food."

I said, "My God, which country I came? Here he wants even to work for food. Wow, what should I do?" I was thinking. I was scared a lot. When I saw him, I said, "My God, is it possible? He really cannot find work for money? He want just work for food?"

When I saw my friend I told them. He say, "They are homeless. Don't worry. They don't want to work, really. They want living like

214

that. You can do anything you want over here." And really I can do anything I want. If I didn't have this limitation over here, I would improve myself during these four years that I lived over here. But still I am happy. I have everything right now. I have my car. I have my computer. I am paying my rent, my bills.

I never been pessimistic in all my life, even [when] I know something happen is negative for me. I don't know why I'm like that. It's really bad because if you know something bad will happen, you can do something to prevent it. But I'm not like that. I always say, "Maybe, maybe for some reason it not happen." So, I'm optimistic for maybe something happen I don't know. Maybe something future happen, and I stay here.

JAVAD LIVES IN CHICAGO AND OWNS AN INTERNET CAFÉ. He also does computer repair, programming, and web design. In addition, he still works for himself as a handyman, electrician and contractor.

MY NAME IS MARDOCHÉE JEAN CHARLES

I came here on the **24TH MARCH, '99.** *I'm 28 years old right now and* **I'M FROM PORT-AU-PRINCE, HAITI. BIZOTON.** *It's a neighborhood around the city.*

IT'S A LITTLE MIDDLE CLASS, BUT IT'S NOT REALLY MIDDLE CLASS. There are just some houses, like the ghetto. We can use the word "ghetto" here. Some people, they don't have food and the house is just somewhere you can live just for the day. When it's rain, they have a big problem because the house can swamp by the water. Mardochée is from the Bible. In English they translate to Mordechai, but this is Mardochée in French. Jean Charles is just my family's name. We got the Jean from the Bible, John. And I don't know about the Charles. [Laughs.] There is no Charles in the Bible, but I know about John.

We used to live in only one big room. That was a big room. And we all slept together and do things together. If you wanna go to the bathroom, you have to go out and go to the bathroom and use it. Sometimes, I remember one day when I was eight, and that day, that was sad. And I remember my mom, she cried every day because we got only one room and slept together everybody, my mom, my father, me, my brother, and my oldest brother together in the same room. And my mom she was so… I can't find the word to explain it. She felt like something missing in the family. And she went somewhere and asked for a job and she got that job. And after two years, we built a little house. I share a room with my brother. And we live together.

This is the way life is in Haiti, the general life. In Haiti, most people they live just like this. Only one room sometime for eight, ten, twelve people. And sometime they have a group, they come to sleep at 8:00 or 10:00 P.M. to 12:00 or 1:00 A.M. and they have to just get up and go out and the other group come and sleep. This is the life in Haiti. And the food. This is the biggest problem in Haiti. People, every day they struggle for the food. They are starving. They don't have enough food. And if you go to Haiti right now, you can see those young boy and young girl on the street. They ask you for money. They need food. They need clothes. And sometimes their parents send them out to go and ask people for money and bring the money home, because if a grown person comes to you and asks you for money, you will probably say, "Go get a job." But if a little boy, little girl, you gonna say, "He really needs that money. She really needs that money. Let me give her the money," because I'm not gonna tell that little boy, little girl, "Go and find a job."

My father is in that transportation business in Haiti. Because you can buy your own minibus or van and you can make money. You can have one or two or three if you have money to buy two or three minibus. Those minivan you have 18 passengers, and you can make money. He owned one before, but now it's two: a minivan and a little pick-up. They call it *camionette,* or "top-top" in Haiti. A pick-up truck with seat and a cover when it's raining.

My father is a very strong man. He's like the kind of man that all his life he struggled to survive. He worked hard, and wake up early in the morning and come home very late, to have money for the family, for the house. He's that kind of man.

The culture is my country is only the husband needs to go to work. But my mother, she used to have a little shop to sell food.

Their education, I think, is just like elementary school. Because back then, parents they didn't like to send their kids to school. If you can sign your name, you can read a paper, that was it. And they didn't like to send you to school to learn more, to become someone very educated. And that was the reason my father and my mother, they just left school in elementary school. That's it. But they can read and write something and write their name and do things.

I learned from both and also from the Bible, because I read the Bible almost every day. And my mother, father, and brother, they all are Jehovah's Witnesses. And we read the Bible a lot. And my mother, she is a very humble person. I can say that. My father, also. But my mother she always tell me, "If you wanna help yourself, if you wanna become very helpful, you have to help people around you, not think people gonna come to you and help you. But you have to go to them and help them. And this is the only way you can do something." I think she is someone she can just share, share her food, or her money with people, even though she doesn't have enough for herself. She wanna share with people because this is the kind of person she is.

I remember one day. I didn't know that, in Haiti, sometime people put their money in the bank, but some of them, they just keep their money in their house. And my mom saved some money. And one day I remember I came to her. I say, "Mom, I need some money. I wanna go somewhere and buy something." And she told me she didn't have enough money.

And my uncle, my mom's brother, he came that day and asked my mom, because he had a problem, if my mom could lend him maybe

In front of his father's camionette, Haiti, 1994

$60. And after a while, I was watching my mom, and she walked around and she went somewhere and just opened something and she gave my uncle $60. And I think I understand that maybe she didn't have the money for me, but my uncle came that day and explained to her, "I have a problem. I need that money." She told me that day she didn't have the money to go buy food and cook for that day, and she found the money to give to my uncle. That's the kind of person. Maybe she's hungry or she needs something, she needs to buy something because she's sick and she saved money for others.

And sometimes I tell my mom, "You need your money. You need to go buy your medicine and this and that."

And she goes like, "OK. I understand I'm sick, but I'm not gonna change anything. He needs the money. I need, too, but he needs the money. I think he's in trouble. I have to come and help those people, because God gonna give me what I need. This is in the Bible when God say he's not gonna leave you alone. And God wants what you need." And she always tells me that about the Bible. "God's gonna provide, gonna give you what you need, gonna give you everything you gonna ask him when you pray." And she's the kind of gracious person.

When I was younger, maybe I can say much younger, eight years old, my personality was, I can say a little proud. I can use the word proud, but not really proud when you're a grown up person. I want to be the best in the family, and that caused me problem with my brother at that time. Because my brother, always when we go to school, I say, "OK, father, I'm gonna bring you my score. You're gonna see my record and I'm gonna be the best in the family." And we used to fight over that thing. But now I feel like that was a mistake, because I thought like this, "I can be the best." But now I think if you wanna be the best, you have to be very humble, a humble person. Help people and help yourself and help your family. And only way you can be the best, if you

218

can help your family to become just as you are. And this is the only way you can do that.

I went to the public school in Haiti. I became a good student because one day my father, he told me, "Right now I'm struggling to earn something, to have food for the family, and I don't want you to do the same thing as I'm doing right now." And he told me, "Only one thing I can give you. If you wanna learn and go to school, you gonna become someone after."

And I think that was something that, I don't know if we use the same word in English, stimulate me and push me to do that and say, "OK, this is the only thing he can give me. I'm gonna do my best and take it and to learn more and become a very great student."

Because he didn't receive a better education, that's the reason why he kept telling me that, "You have to go to school and learn, because right now I have to struggle, I have to fight to survive. I don't want you to." Because he told me, "Only one thing I can do. I can write my name and read something. But if I went to school and learned more, maybe I don't know, I would be a lawyer or something, accounting, and make more money. And that's the reason I want you to go to school and do your best to be a great student."

I remember when I was 20. I remember at that time I went to school. My father, he lost his job and his business went down. No money. And I had to go to school. No money to pay the bus, and no food sometime when I came back home. No food on the table and I have to study. And that was something that made me stronger that day. Because I say, "OK. If that happen today, I have to study more because I don't want that happen all my life and I have to come home, no food on the table." And that period of the time, I went to school and go to study right after school. Didn't go back home and just go somewhere and study.

Life in Haiti when you're in the lower middle class sometimes, maybe two or three years you can be OK. You have food. You have money OK for expenses. You're not rich. You're in the lower middle class. This year if your family got a job, you got food, you can go to school, no problem. And the year after, if something happen in the system, you're gonna be just like those poor people. No food, no clothes. But the clothes you can save them, but not food. That was the reason why I went to the public school. I say, "I don't want one day I have to stop because I don't have money to pay for the private school." I say, "Even though my father maybe one day, if he loses his job, I can be able to go to school and learn something."

I wanted to study diplomacy. It's when you work in the foreign ministry. You go somewhere, go to other countries and when they have a problem, you have to talk to them, find a fair solution and you don't need to fight for something. You have to talk. After college [high school] in Haiti, I wanted to go there, but the first year I went there to register we had a problem, the political crisis in Haiti that time in 1993. That was after they pushed Aristide out of power, and we have those military. Those militaries, they used to come and get you from the school and kill you sometime. I was scared. I decided to stay home because I was involved in politics before that, because I used to do some march for Aristide when they push him. And I was afraid and I was so scared and I just say, "OK. Just forget it." I gave up that day. And I say, "I wonder maybe one day Aristide gonna come back." And I stay home. I say, "If he comes back one day, I will go back to school." But that was my priority.

When Aristide was doing his campaign, most students were involved. They were involved in that campaign and that's the reason why the result after [the military] pushed him out, they come to the school, to the university and took the students out and killed them sometime, beat them up. I remember one day we did something and those militaries, they come and I don't know the word they use here, like when they circle the school and they keep you inside. They just keep all of us inside from 8:00 [A.M.] to 5:00 or 6:00 [P.M.], and I escaped from the back of the school. That day, they knew my name and they called the director of the school and they told him they gonna come to arrest me and two others. That was 1991. And the director called my father and say, "Don't let him come to school for one or two weeks." And I escaped to a province just to save my life.

I wasn't a leader. We were a group. We were doing things together. But I can say, sometimes I can say leader. Because I remember one day, they want to push me out of the school because I did something. The other students they came and say to the teacher, the director and the principal, they say, "You can't push him out because if you push him out, we gonna stop coming to school and come every day and have a march on the front yard."

We supported Aristide because he promised all the students he's gonna do something for us. We're gonna have a better education. We're gonna have better schools. We're gonna have a better university. We're gonna have all the things we need to learn to do things. That's the reason why we supported Aristide at that time. And maybe I don't know,

With high school friends, Haiti, 1992

after they pushed him, we still had that thing in our mind, "If he comes back, he's gonna do something for us, he's gonna bring us what he promised us to give us."

My father at that time, he had a van. I was a taxi driver that day. I drove the van for my father and make some money. I did that only for six months because Aristide came back on October 15, '94, and now I went to that Haitian National Police to register and I had my chance. The Haitian National Police is the force they used to replace the army we had before. [The army] killed a lot of people during 1991 to 1994. They killed over 5,000 people. And that's the reason why they decide to get rid of that force and come with the Haitian police. The purpose is different from the army. The army was something to defend the country, but the Haitian police [were supposed] to protect and serve people. When they formed that institution, that was a great thing. Everybody thought everything gonna be OK, everything gonna be all right with that force because most police officers, they are very educated. And they think everything gonna change because those former militaries before, some of them they didn't go to school, they just know how to use a weapon, that's it.

I went to register because I think this is a way to help my country. And I think this is the last chance my country can have. Because when you're police officer, the purpose is to serve and protect people. It's the

purpose. That's the reason why I went there and register, because I think we gonna serve and protect our people and our country.

I started working in March 4, '96 and that day I was just a patroller, just making patrol on the street, but that wasn't the city. I used to work in a province that was far from Port-au-Prince. And when I went to work I stayed there for 15 days or month. And I have sometime two or three days to go to Port-au-Prince. Maybe it's more than 120 miles from Port-au-Prince, because it's close to Dominican Republic. But we have a problem. It's not the distance, but it's just the road. The condition to travel from Port-au-Prince to there. Sometime it took us four, five hours or six and sometime a day, the whole day. Because if it rains one day, it would be very impossible to get there six or four hours.

And after maybe six or four months, I had a promotion. And I became not a patroller, but I became a clerk. When people come, I have to just write something and take their names, and if they have a testimony about something I have to write it down. And after, I was working in that station where we have the radio. We had to talk to the other police stations. I was responsible for that office from '98 to '99, when I left the police. But that was great. Sometime I went out to arrest people, to prevent something, and to talk. And sometime I went to some meeting and talk to students and tell them what they have to do, who is a police officer, their job, and we can work together. It's like, we can say, public relations.

In that job I carried a gun because you know, police always they have a gun anyway. They trained me to use a gun, but I didn't feel comfortable with that gun because sometimes I go to work without that gun. After the first year, I stopped going to work with that gun, because I think the gun not gonna change anything. And I remember my superior one day he told me, "You're a police officer. Where's your gun?"

I say, "I don't need the gun. Why do I have to come with the gun, because I'm not gonna use it anyway. I can talk to the person."

One day, I went to arrest a man and that man escaped. And when that man escaped, I just take out my gun and I was about to shoot that man. And I think for some reason, I just change my mind and say, "OK, let him go. Maybe he's gonna come."

And the day after, that man came to the office and say, "I'm sorry for yesterday because I escaped for one reason. I didn't wanna come and sleep in the cell, sleep in the prison. That's the reason why I escape."

And that man come to me and say, "I'm sorry, because I know it was raining and I'm one of the reasons you dirtied your clothes, because of me yesterday. I'm sorry for that."

And when that man said that, I say, "You know what? If yesterday I killed that man, how I'm gonna feel today because I killed someone for no reason?" And that was the reason why I stopped carrying that gun from '97 to '99.

I felt like I was doing something for my country. I was a little proud for the first year, but after that everything went a little wrong. After a while, something changed because they come with some former militaries. They bring them into the Haitian National Police. They say, "OK, we can use those guys." And that was the problem now. When they came into the Haitian police, they came with the same thing they used to do before when they were in the army. And some of them came with that corruption they used to involve. And some new police officers also, they involved in that. So that was the situation in the Haitian police.

That's the reason why I say, "OK. Then, let me do my job as they taught me to do my job, but I'm not gonna think about them, just do my job for the three years." Because that was a three-year term. I say, "After that three years, I'm gonna leave anyway."

When I came here [to the United States], I came just to visit my cousin. Just a vacation, two weeks. I didn't resign already. I didn't resign. I just wrote it down, but I didn't give it to my superior. I keep it because I wanted to come back and give it to him and try to do something else.

Because I believe in God, maybe I can say God gave me that visa because that was really difficult. That was December 18, '98, and I went to the American consulate to ask for that visa. And one of my friends, a police officer also, he told me, "Why do you wanna go there and waste your time because they're not gonna give you that visa." Because he knew it's really difficult to get one. Even though if you have everything you need, they ask for, it was difficult. It's still difficult.

And I went there. I said, "OK. I know I'm gonna get mine today because maybe someone else, God, gonna give me mine." Because I wanna go there and visit and come back and work. And I went there and I got it.

And after, one of my friends say, "Did you do something before you go there, because I can't believe that. You the only one that day!"

And December is one of the difficult months to get a visa. And I said, "OK. But God gave it to me and that's it."

I was really excited to come up here and see the difference. Because

Graduating from high school, Haiti, 1993

all those advertising on TV, you can see is a beautiful country, the biggest country in the world. Life is different. In the United States, you have a lot of opportunities to become the person who you wanna be. And I was so excited to come. And when I got here in March, in Miami first, I stayed there for 22 days with my aunt, my cousin's mother. And that was a little great. When I came up here [Chicago] in April 14, '99, I saw a lot of difference between here and Miami. I thought, "Oh, maybe this is the biggest city because it's so nice, beautiful, and I like it here better than Miami." And I was excited.

When I came here, my cousin told me to stay because she told me, "Maybe if you go back, you can get killed. The life in Haiti is difficult now and all those problems. And I know you had an accident, all those stuff."

And I say, "OK, then I can stay, but I have to call my mom first." And I called my mom. I asked her, "Do you want me to stay here or to come back, because I'm gonna miss you."

And she told me, "I know you're gonna miss me. I'm gonna miss you, too, but I would rather ask you to stay there than to come back, because I know if you come back, you're gonna come back to that Haitian police. I don't want you to involve in the police no more."

I called my mom three or four times because I wanted to go back. The second time she said, "No. I want you to stay there. Don't come back." And the third time she said, "No." And the fourth time when I called her she said, "No."

After that, four times "no," and I said, "OK. Now I have no chance. Just stay here and live with my cousin." And a month after that I decided to send the letter to them to let them know I resign. I decided to prepare my future to have a career here. And first I say, "But now I need a job." I didn't have papers, just a tourist visa.

I didn't have papers and my cousin say, "I'm gonna help to get a job." And I got a job, my first job.

And I remember my first job they paid me like, $5 an hour. But I didn't have any choices. I say, "OK, then. I need that job because I need some money to help my cousin and to help myself also."

I was driving a van. That was a medical van. I was driving a van and pick up some sick people, take them to the hospital and take them back to the nursing home. I enjoyed that job. I enjoyed. But only one thing: I had to wake up at 4:00 in the morning and go to work, and I got off work at 3:00, 3:30, sometimes 4:00 [P.M.]. And after work I had to go to school, go straight to school every day, Monday to Thursday. Got to work, go to school, go to work, go to school. And sometime I had only two or three hours to sleep, because I had to study at night and I had to do things. That was really difficult.

I remember one day. That day I was driving the truck, and I fell asleep. And when I woke up, that was right before the stop light. And after that I say, "If I can't find another job, I will quit anyway because this job maybe one day something gonna happen and I'm gonna be in trouble, and I don't have any papers yet." And I decided to quit.

I learned English in school in Haiti but just for the exam, grammar and things. But they didn't teach me how to speak. And when I came here I didn't know how to talk, how to speak English, how to express myself. If I want to ask someone for something, I didn't know how to ask, how to tell this, how to say that. And that was difficult, but anyway I say, "I have to do something." I remember that first job I had, one day the dispatcher, he told me one day, "You're very intelligent. You're very smart. I can't believe that you got here. You don't know how to speak English and you are doing the job very well."

And I said, "Thank you."

And when I decided to quit, one day the dispatcher, he came to me and said, "I'm gonna miss you. You're one of the best employees I had and I think I'm gonna miss you a lot. And if you wanna stay, that would be great. Don't quit."

I say, "But I have to quit because I need more money. You only pay me $5. I can't live with only $5. I have to go to school to prepare for my future."

The job I have now is in a warehouse. We ship books all over the state and all over the country. My position right now is shipper and receiver.

After a while I say, "I have to go out and meet people, meet Haitian people in my community." My cousin's friend, she introduced me to her friend, Lionel. He's a best friend of mine now.

And that man one day say, "You can help us at the radio. Can you come with me one day at the radio station? We can do something, and we can see if you can help us at the radio."

I say, "OK. No problem."

The radio is a radio for the Haitian community, but we have three segments. The first one is the English segment for the American people because we have some listeners, American people, they listen to the radio every Saturday. The second is the French segment for French people who live here. And we have the Creole segment for the Haitian community. The first two segments is for 30 minutes. And the Creole segment is for one hour. We discuss about Haiti. Not only news about Haiti, but we discuss about everything. News here and Haiti, somewhere else. And if it's something very important, the front page news, we discuss about that. It's just reporting news only and music, Haitian music. The radio station is 88.7 [FM]. The time is between 4:00 and 6:00 [P.M.] every Saturday. It's live.

And I went there one day with him. And the first day, he asked me to talk on the air. I say, "No, I'm not gonna talk because I just wanna watch."

And the following week, he came to me again and say, "Do you wanna come this weekend again?"

I say, "Yes!" because I have nothing else to do. [Laughs.]

And after three weeks, the third weekend, he came, he say, "Now you wanna talk?"

I say, "Yes, I'm gonna talk." And I talked about Haiti, my job, I was a police officer, what I used to do and that's it.

One day we had a broadcast. And after that broadcast, I met a man on the street. And that man say, "You are Mardochée?"

I say, "Yes, I am."

And he say, "I was listening to you today. The way you talk, I like it. You have something. You can help the community." That's one thing make me feel like I was doing something there, and I have to keep doing it because some people, they like the way I talk, the way I present the problem. I told him we can find a way to help our country, to solve the problem in Haiti. I can say I'm a little proud of that. It's not proud in a negative way, but it's proud because when you do something and people like it, that means you are doing something really good. And I'm very proud and very happy because I'm doing something for my community and for others.

Also I was thinking about going to college, or learn something, go to law school. Most of the time, when I talk to my friends, my family, my girlfriend also, and they always say, "You can be a lawyer, the way you talk, the way you act."

And I say, "OK, then." I remember when I was in Haiti, people always tell me that, and now here the same thing. OK, I want to go to law school and learn and become a lawyer. This is my goal, my aim right now. But I don't know if I'm gonna make it, but I'm gonna try.

For me to become a lawyer is not I want a better job to make money. I wanna learn the law in the U.S. and I can use that law to help people. The human rights is my goal. Because when you know the law, you can use it to help people and to help other countries, not only my country. Because think only about my country is a little selfish. You have to think for others, for people. That's the reason I wanna become a lawyer. Not become a lawyer, become someone very important, make money, and have a good job and so on and so forth. I wanna just do something to help people, and help myself, and help my country.

My legal status now, I applied for the asylum. My visa expired since 1999. And right now, I'm waiting for the immigration office. They gonna call me and let me know what happened and if everything is OK. If they say no, I'm not gonna be disappointed because Haiti is my

On the beach, Haiti, 1994

country anyway. And one day, I will have to go back to my country. But the problem now is not a question of disappointed. I have to go back and start over everything, restart everything. Because when I left Haiti, I didn't wanna come and live here. I had something. But now, if they decide, "OK. We deny your application. We can't give you the asylum here. You have to go home," one thing can happen. I have to go home and restart everything. This is the biggest problem now.

My father, he always tells me, "When you go somewhere, don't think about where you were before. Think about where you live." Now I'm in the U.S. I don't have to think about when I was in Haiti. I have to try to integrate myself in this community I live around now. And second, "When you live somewhere, you don't have to think about money. Because money, that's not gonna change anything." Most people, the problem they have, they think about they have to come here and make money and become rich and go back home and show off or something. That's the reason they always have some problem.

I'm not gonna say I'm not homesick, either. I am. But just because I miss my family. Here I'm struggling also, but I'm seeing like this is a family also. People around me the same as my country. That's why I feel so comfortable here. People can say, "You seem like you've been here for many years." But it's not a problem because United States, when I go out, it's just as I think it is my country. I walk on the street. I see people. Say, "Hi." I don't think about the money. I know I need money for my bills and my expenses. That's it. And if I have money for my food, bills, and I can save something to send to my mom and that's it, I'm not gonna be worried every day, "I need money. I need to go. I need two jobs. I need to do this." That's why only it seems for others I'm very comfortable, like I've been here for maybe three or maybe ten years. I'm gonna do my best to keep myself like I am right now. There is no way to avoid some things. And I think now, everything is OK for me and I have my goal. I know where I really wanna go and nothing gonna change my mind, nothing gonna keep me away. I can't find the right word, but nothing gonna distract me or push me out of my way. And I think I'm gonna just follow this way right now.

You have to struggle. You have to fight to get something. It's not gonna be easy to get something. I come from a poor country. I know I have to fight. It's the strongest part of my culture. I can say now, fighting for everything is the culture in my country right now because you have to fight for food, for clothes, for everything. And this is the best thing, the strongest thing that helps me to live here, to stay here. Because I know I have to fight. I have to face the problem. Don't try to escape from that problem, but try to face the problem and to solve the problem.

One thing I like the most is American people here. First, before coming here, I thought people in U.S., they were prejudiced or something. But now in the U.S. and in Chicago, I can say American people, they are friendly. They are very helpful. Sometime on the street when you have problem and someone come to you and say, "Can I help you? Can I give you a hand? Can I do this for you?" And this is one thing I like the most. People here, they are very friendly, but not all of them. Everywhere you got good things and bad things.

I remember one day, I met a girl at my first job and she helped me about my English. I said something and she said, "No. I know you are new. This is the way you need to say that." That made me feel like it's not a question about discrimination. Because before I thought in the U.S. there were a lot of difference between the white people and the black. But now here I can say it's not really. It's just like two different groups of people live at the same place and live together.

I don't think that way [that there is discrimination], because I don't wanna put myself down. Because when you think that way, you put yourself down. And sometime you're gonna develop the same discrimi-

In the military police training academy, Haiti, 1996

nation. The discrimination you're talking about, the white people they are prejudiced, you're gonna develop the same thing because you're gonna think they are a little superior. You think, "OK. I have to keep myself away from them." And that's the reason why I don't think they are prejudiced. Because when you think people are prejudiced, you are prejudiced! This is the way it goes. If they are prejudiced, you're prejudiced because you're gonna try to keep yourself away from them, and that's why you're gonna feel that discrimination you are thinking.

I feel very comfortable here. I can say it's my home. Because here now, I have friends. I have things I can do. I have a goal. I can say I have a family now. I can say Haiti is my country. It's a part of my life because of my family. I'm not gonna change to become American. But if my mom can be with me, and my brother, my father, if they can be with me, I think I'm gonna feel more comfortable. It's not a problem of the country, the culture. If I'm here, I'm an American as long I live here. And if I decide to move one day to go to Haiti, I'm gonna live as Haitian people. And when I'm here, I have to follow the rule, the law, the rights, and everything here.

I think being separated from your family is one of the, I can say, the saddest problem. Because when it comes to a holiday, you're alone. Like last year, January 1st is the Independence Day in Haiti. And we're always together. And January 2nd, always together. We make squash soup every January 1st and we're always together. And every January 1st I'm gonna feel the same problem every January I'm gonna be here. And I felt that way last year, and I'm gonna feel the same thing this year, this January again. But I think that's not gonna stay like that for the rest of my life. I think one day, maybe I will be able to go back home, or maybe to take them here and live with me. This is really, really sad when someone is separated from his family. When you live some place else and you're far from your family, it's a sad thing.

Now I think I changed a little, because now I think the best way to live your life peaceful is when you try to do things to help people, to solve people's problem. And this is the best way. In the Bible they say, "When you give to someone, you do the best thing. And when you pray for your enemy, you do the best thing." That's what I'm thinking right now. I changed because now the best thing I can do, is don't think for myself. Think for me and for others. And when someday I talk to someone and the person say, "I like the way you talk. I like the way you think," it's not me. All what I'm saying in the Bible. You read the Bible, you know. God for me, I can say, is not only part of my life. He is my life.

I'm not going to say I'm Haitian only. I'm Mardochée Jean Charles. I feel everywhere I go is my country, I can live. Even if someone wanna send me to Africa, I'm not gonna have any problems to go there, because I'm gonna live anyway. I'm a person and the world is for everybody. It's not Haiti for me and U.S. for you. I'm Haitian because my culture, my country, but I'm not gonna say, "I'm Haitian," like I wanna be just Haitian. I'm a man in the world.

MARDOCHÉE WORKS AS A TRUCK DRIVER and is still focused on becoming a lawyer.
He is working on a second radio program in Chicago.